A VIETNAM READER

A VIETNAM READER
SOURCES AND ESSAYS

Edited by
George Donelson Moss

With Original Essays Contributed by

Paul Conway

Stephen E. Ambrose

Jack Colldeweih

George Donelson Moss

Kevin O'Keefe

PRENTICE HALL, Englewood Cliffs, N.J. 07632

Library of Congress Cataloging-in-Publication Data

A Vietnam reader : sources and essays / George Donelson Moss, ed. with
    original essays contributed by Paul Conway . . . [et al.].
        p. cm.
    Includes bibliographical references.
    ISBN 0-13-946625-8
    1. Vietnamese Conflict. 1961–1975—Sources. 2. Vietnamese
Conflict, 1961–1975. 3. Indochina—History—1945—Sources.
4. United States—Foreign relations—Indochina—Sources.
5. Indochina—Foreign relations—United States—Sources. I. Moss,
George, 1935–   . II. Conway, Paul (Paul Alwyn)
DS557.4.V56 1991
959.704'3—dc20   90–39787
                                                        CIP

Editorial/production supervision: bookworks
Interior design: Sharen Levine
Cover design: Ray Lundgren Graphics, Ltd.
Manufacturing buyers: Debbie Kesar and Mary Ann Gloriande

 ©1991 by Prentice-Hall, Inc.
A Division of Simon & Schuster
Englewood Cliffs, New Jersey 07632

Printed in the United States of America
10 9 8 7 6 5 4

ISBN 0-13-946625-8

Prentice-Hall International (UK) Limited, *London*
Prentice-Hall of Australia Pty. Limited, *Sydney*
Prentice-Hall Canada Inc., *Toronto*
Prentice-Hall Hispanoamericana, S.A., *Mexico*
Prentice-Hall of India Private Limited, *New Delhi*
Prentice-Hall of Japan, Inc. *Tokyo*
Simon & Schuster Asia Pte. Ltd., *Singapore*
Editora Prentice-Hall do Brasil, Ltda., *Rio de Janeiro*

CONTENTS

PREFACE

This book represents an innovative approach to the study of the long American involvement in Indochina, an involvement that led to the U.S.–Vietnam war and eventual strategic and political disaster for both the United States and the people that America tried to help in that ill-starred region. The book provides, in one accessible and easy-to-use volume, both a sizable selection of important primary source documents used by all historians of the American Indochina intervention, and a collection of new, interpretive articles written by scholars who bring a variety of disciplines, methodologies, and analytic perspectives to the study of America's involvement in Vietnam. The U.S. presence in Indochina continues to attract the attention of many scholars, and the articles contained in the second half of this reader provide a sampling of the important work currently being done in this dynamic field.

  This text is designed primarily for use in courses examining America's Indochina experience that are being offered at the nation's colleges and universities. It can be used either in tandem with George Donelson Moss's general historical study of U.S. involvement, *Vietnam: An American Ordeal,* or it can be used independently as an important collection of sources and essays. It is also of use in courses concerned with modern U.S. foreign policy, courses that place a special emphasis on American intervention in Vietnam. In addition, the text can be read by those who want to understand and to come to terms with the most important American foreign-policy initiative since World War II.

  The story of America's long entanglement in the affairs of Vietnam and in Indochina itself is complex and controversial, and it is tinged with irony and tragedy. Controversies abound among scholars over many issues: over the reasons for U.S. involvement in an area where, at least initially, no vital American interests appeared to be at stake; over the reasons for the eventual American defeat; and over the legacies of Vietnam. The primary sources and interpretive essays made available in this reader can elucidate these controversies and others, if not resolve them. They are resources that you can call upon to help you confront and to examine thoughtfully the causes, the nature, and the consequences of the greatest foreign-policy disaster in American history.

A VIETNAM READER

Introduction

AN AMERICAN ENTANGLEMENT: U.S. INVOLVEMENT IN INDOCHINA, 1942–1975

George Donelson Moss

It is time we recognized that
ours, in truth, was a noble cause.

Ronald Reagan

We designed a war we were going to lose, and
we managed to lose it the way we designed it.

Newt Gingrich

History may judge that going into Vietnam
was one of our country's greatest mistakes.

William Westmoreland

I regard the war in Indochina as the greatest military, political,
economic, and moral blunder in our national history.

George McGovern

This is the real lesson of Vietnam—not that we should abandon power,
but that unless we learn to use it effectively to defend our interests,
the tables of history will be turned against us and all we believe in.

Richard Nixon

ORIGINS

Significant American interest in Indochina originated during World War II in Asia. At the outset of the war, the Japanese occupied Indochina, which had been a French colony for nearly 80 years. The Japanese exploited Indochina's rich resources; they also used it as a staging area for their continuing war against China and for their expansion in the South Pacific. Americans flying with the famed Flying Tigers of Claire Chennault bombed and strafed targets in northern Vietnam in 1942/1943. During the final phases of World War II in Asia, American naval aircraft from the Third Fleet bombed Japanese shipping in the port of Saigon. U.S. Army Air Corps planes flying from Clark Field in the Philippines bombed harbors and railroads in Vietnam in 1945. They severed Indochina's remaining links to China and the Japanese home islands.

Teams of American OSS operatives out of the U.S. China mission in Kungming parachuted into Vietnam during 1944/1945 to link up with Vietnamese guerrillas who called themselves the Vietminh. The Vietminh leader was a professional Communist organizer and Vietnamese patriot named Ho Chi Minh. Ho enjoyed a popular following in northern Vietnam and commanded a small army of perhaps 5,000 guerrillas who harassed the Japanese. Ho and his Vietminh compatriots were determined to end the Japanese presence in their homeland and to prevent the return of the French after the war. These wartime U.S. Indochinese experiences confirmed the region's importance: as a vital source of foodstuffs and raw materials, and its strategic location astride major shipping lanes linking India, the islands of the South Pacific, China, and Japan.

The Vietminh worked with the Americans in Vietnam to rescue downed U.S. flyers and to collect intelligence data on the Japanese. The Vietminh hoped that cooperation with the Americans would earn them U.S. support for their drive to reclaim Vietnam's independence following the defeat of the Japanese. On September 2, 1945, shortly after the Japanese surrender, the Vietminh formed a provisional government in Hanoi and Ho declared Vietnam's independence.

President Franklin Delano Roosevelt believed that European colonialism in Asia was moribund. He wanted to align U.S. postwar policy with emergent nationalist forces in the Far East. Roosevelt also disliked the imperious French leader Charles De Gaulle. Roosevelt initially opposed French intentions to return to Indochina; he hoped to find a formula that would lead eventually to independence for the nations that had formerly constituted French Indochina: Vietnam, Cambodia, and Laos. But as the end of the war approached, Roosevelt, concerned about maintaining good relations with important European allies, did not oppose the French goal of returning to Indochina. Roosevelt was also not happy with the prospect of a Communist leader coming to power in Vietnam.

Roosevelt's successor, Harry Truman, who took office in April 1945, did not share Roosevelt's concern for Asian nationalism. His top postwar foreign-policy priority was containing Soviet expansion in Europe. Truman was determined to strengthen western Europe, particularly France, to help those nations resist both Soviet pressures and the internal threats posed by domestic Communist parties. When the French began their effort to reclaim Vietnam, Truman permitted them a free hand in Indochina as part of the Euro-centered U.S. policy of backing France in the face of Communist threats. Officially, the United States took a neutral stance when war between the French and Vietminh began in 1946, but it was, in effect, a pro-French neutrality. The United States furnished covert economic and military assistance to the French. Whatever misgivings Washington may have had about either the morality or the efficacy of French colonialism in Indochina was offset by the American dread of political disorder in Southeast Asia and of a Communist leader holding sway in Vietnam. In any event, during the years between 1946 and 1949, the political future of Southeast Asia was a minor American concern; it was an appendage of America's Euro-centered foreign policy of containing Soviet Communism.

A major turning point in evolving American interests in Southeast Asia occurred during late 1949. Two crucial events were the Soviet explosion of an atomic device, which shattered the U.S. nuclear monopoly, and the successful Maoist revolution in China that overthrew the Nationalist government of Jiang Jieshi. In the aftermath of the Soviet nuclear weapon and revolution in China, American leaders redefined their vital interests in Asia. Containment of Communism, which had originated in Truman's response to Soviet pressures in southern Europe in 1947, was extended to Asia. Washington viewed Chinese Communism as part of an international expansionist conspiracy headquartered in Moscow and whose ultimate goal was world domination. The outbreak of the Korean war and subsequent Chinese intervention in that conflict confirmed American Cold War concerns.

Truman and Secretary of State Dean Acheson incorporated the French military effort to reimpose colonialism on the Vietnamese into the new U.S. foreign-policy objective of containing Chinese expansionism in Southeast Asia. What had been a peripheral U.S. concern became a vital American foreign-policy interest. The Truman administration viewed the French war in Indochina as preventing the fall of Vietnam, Laos, and Cambodia to Communism. American officials also concerned themselves with protecting the security of Japan, America's former enemy that had become the principal Asian ally of the United States following the Chinese revolution. Any remaining American scruples about endorsing French colonialism in Southeast Asia were overcome by the larger necessity of containing Communism in that strategic region.

By the time the United States embraced France's war in Vietnam, the Vietminh controlled about two-thirds of Vietnamese territory, and the Chinese Communists were furnishing weapons, training, and political support to Ho's forces, who now numbered in the hundreds of thousands. French control had been reduced to mostly urban areas, and French casualties were heavy. The rising costs of the war also drained the French treasury.

Unable to defeat the Vietminh forces militarily, France tried to undercut them politically. The French created "free governments" in Vietnam, Laos, and Cambodia nominally headed by local leaders who they hoped would rally the people in these countries to the French cause and wean them away from the insurgents. However, these regimes lacked most of the attributes of sovereignty. Bao Dai, a direct descendant of the last Vietnamese royal family, headed the puppet regime set up in Saigon. Bao Dai could not win the support of most Vietnamese; he achieved only the support of a few wealthy landowners and businessmen. Prominent patriots refused to back him, and the Vietnamese villagers proved either hostile or apathetic to his pseudo-government.

The United States shipped about $25 million worth of surplus World War II military equipment to the French in September 1950 and established programs to provide economic and military assistance to the Bao Dai government. Although he had no inkling of the chain of events that he had set in motion, President Truman began an American involvement in Vietnam that would last 25 years, an involvement that would eventually cost the lives of over 58,000 Americans, $150 billion, and much pride and self-respect.

Before Truman's presidency ended, American support of the French war in Indochina had grown significantly from its small beginnings in the summer of 1950. In 1952, Truman's final year in office, the United States spent more than $150 million on military assistance to the fading French effort in Indochina. But Truman made it clear to the French that he opposed any direct commitment of U.S. forces to Indochina. America would provide the French and loyalist Vietnamese with extensive economic and military aid, but it was up to the French and their Vietnamese auxiliaries to do the fighting and dying for a good cause.

TO THE BRINK OF WAR

President Dwight Eisenhower and his energetic secretary of state, John Foster Dulles, inherited and continued the Truman-Acheson policies in Southeast Asia. The new administration applied the Cold War ideology to the struggle between Asian nationalists and European imperialists. Washington viewed the Indochina war as part of the global conflict between "free world" forces and Communism. Eisenhower and Dulles saw Ho Chi Minh as an agent of international Communism; they rejected the notion that he could also be the embodiment of Asian anticolonial nationalism. American officials also believed that the defeat of the French in Indochina would be a Free World catastrophe. It would open the way for the fall of Southeast Asia to the Communists and would have major adverse consequences for the United States. Washington's failure to understand the force of Third World Nationalism, coupled to its persistent habit of defining anticolonial insurgencies as Communist aggression fomented from Beijing and Moscow, seriously flawed American diplomacy in Southeast Asia.

Eisenhower expanded U.S. economic and military aid to the French. By 1954 the United States was paying 80 percent of the cost of the French war. But Eisenhower, as did Truman before him, insisted that no American troops would be sent to fight in Indochina. The French and their Vietnamese supporters would continue to bear the full burden of the fighting.

Despite significant American aid, the French were losing the Franco-Vietminh war. By 1954 Vietminh forces controlled most of Vietnam. Urged on by the Americans, the French tried to regain the military initiative. To challenge the rebels, the French put 11,000 of their best troops in Dien Bien Phu, a remote site in northwestern Vietnam near the Laotian border located deep within guerrilla-held territory. French leaders believed that Asians could not defeat European forces in a large-scale conventional battle. General Vo Nguyen Giap, the Vietminh military commander, accepted the challenge posed by the French at Dien Bien Phu. Giap's forces besieged the garrison. Within weeks the French position grew desperate. With war weariness strong in France after eight years of costly and futile fighting, the fall of Dien Bien Phu would mean victory for the Vietminh revolutionaries and the end of French efforts to return to Indochina.

Facing imminent ruin in Southeast Asia, France made an eleventh-hour appeal to the Americans to intervene and save them. Eisenhower considered U.S. air strikes to break the siege around Dien Bien Phu. However, the president insisted that American allies join the effort and that Congress support it. The British rebuffed Dulles's efforts to enlist them in the campaign. Senate leaders informed Eisenhower that without allied participation the Senate would not approve a resolution sanctioning American military intervention in Southeast Asia. Lacking allied and congressional support, Eisenhower rejected the French request. Dien Bien Phu fell to the Communists on May 7, 1954.

The next day an international conference meeting at Geneva began discussions to find a political solution to the Franco-Vietminh war. By July the conferees had worked out a settlement. According to its terms, the French and Vietminh agreed to a cease-fire and to a temporary partition of Vietnam at the 17th parallel of north latitude. French and Vietnamese loyalist forces were to regroup south of that line, and Vietminh forces north of it. The Geneva agreements also called for free elections to be held within two years to unify the country. During the interim, the French were to help the Vietnamese in the south prepare for independence and then depart. Any Vietnamese who wanted to leave or felt compelled to leave Vietnam would depart with the French.

The United States opposed the Geneva accords but could not prevent them. The American delegate, Walter Bedell Smith, refused to sign the accords, but he agreed to accept them and pledged that the United States would never use force to upset the arrangements. However, President Eisenhower announced that the United States government did not sign the accords, nor did America consider itself bound by them. Ho Chi Minh, whose army verged on taking all of Vietnam, was willing to settle for just the northern half of the country at Geneva because he was confident that he could defeat Bao Dai politically were elections to take place. Ho would then emerge as the leader of a united and independent Vietnam.

After Geneva, Dulles salvaged what he could from what Washington regarded as a disastrous defeat for the Free World—a major Communist victory that gave the Communists half of Vietnam and potentially threatened all of Southeast Asia. In September 1954, Dulles arranged for Great Britain, France, Australia, New Zealand, Thailand, Pakistan, and the Philippines to forge the Southeast Asia Treaty Organization (SEATO). Signatories agreed to "meet and confer" should one of them be attacked. A separate protocol to the SEATO treaty extended protection to Laos, Cambodia, and the part of Vietnam that lay south of the 17th parallel. SEATO provided a legal basis for the projection of American power into Southeast Asia in the aftermath of the French defeat and the Geneva conference, which had tried to neutralize Indochina.

The United States also backed a new government headed by Ngo Dinh Diem that emerged in southern Vietnam in 1954/1955. Americans trained and equipped Diem's army and security forces and established a variety of other aid programs designed to modernize and stabilize Diem's fledgling regime. Washington promoted the diplomatic fiction that the 17th parallel had become a national boundary separating two sovereign states, "South Vietnam" and "North Vietnam." The United States also backed Diem in 1955 and 1956 when he refused to negotiate with the North Vietnamese or permit elections to unify Vietnam to take place. As French military and civilian officials left South Vietnam, Americans replaced them.

Eisenhower believed that if South Vietnam fell to the Communists, the other nations of Southeast Asia would follow. He compared their falling to knocking over a row of standing dominoes: you knock one over and the rest fall quickly. After Geneva, America committed itself to creating a new nation in southern Vietnam that would serve as a proving ground for democracy and would block the further expansion of Communism in Southeast Asia. In effect, the American effort to help create a new nation called South Vietnam sabotaged the Geneva accords, which had envisaged a unified, independent, and Communist-controlled Vietnam emerging in the aftermath of the Vietminh military victory over the French.

Between 1955 and 1957, Diem, with American backing, tried to eliminate all opposition to his regime. His repressive actions provoked violent opposition. Local Diemist officials were assassinated by Communist and non-Communist opponents, all of whom Diem called "Vietcong," meaning Vietnamese who are Communists. The Communist leaders in Hanoi infiltrated men and supplies south of the 17th parallel to take control of the anti-Diemist insurgency. Small-scale war had begun in South Vietnam. In 1960, the National Liberation Front (NLF) was formed. By then, Hanoi's leaders had also committed themselves to supporting the southern insurgency. They viewed the anti-Diemist rebellion in South Vietnam as a continuation of their revolution to reclaim Vietnam's independence that had begun in 1945. Few Americans noticed at the time, but the second Indochina war had begun. The United States had committed itself to defending South Vietnam; North Vietnam was determined to control the entire country. Washington and Hanoi had launched themselves on collision courses.

RAISING THE STAKES

During John F. Kennedy's presidency, the United States increased significantly its involvement in Indochina. Kennedy first turned his attention to the small, landlocked country of Laos, which had been the scene of conflict for years. Neutral under the terms of the 1954 Geneva agreements, Laos was engulfed in a low-intensity, three-way civil war involving pro-Western, pro-Communist, and neutralist forces. Kennedy, inheriting the Laotian conflict from Eisenhower, rejected the outgoing president's suggestions for a military solution. Instead, Kennedy opted for a political solution that guaranteed a neutral and independent Laos. Another Geneva conference worked out a political settlement for Laos; on June 12, 1961, the leaders of the three Laotian factions formed a neutralist coalition government.

Although he chose a political settlement in Laos, Kennedy significantly escalated U.S. military involvement in South Vietnam in response to Hanoi's stepped-up efforts to subvert Diem's government. President Kennedy viewed the war in southern Vietnam as a crucial part of the Cold War struggle between the United States and the Soviet-Chinese axis. Ironically, Kennedy, when he had been a senator, had criticized President Eisenhower's foreign policy for its failure to understand the powerful appeal of nationalism in countries that were emerging from long periods of colonial domination by Western imperial powers. Specifically, Senator Kennedy had criticized America's backing of French efforts to re-impose colonialism in Indochina by trying to suppress a popular nationalist insurgency. But as president, Kennedy apparently could not understand that Ho Chi Minh's Communist ideology served as a vehicle for expressing Vietnamese aspirations to be rid of all foreign domination. Kennedy also failed to understand that many Vietnamese, Communist and non-Communist alike, viewed American support of the Diem government as a continuation of Western imperialism in their country. Kennedy also applied the domino theory to Vietnam. He stated that Vietnam represented the cornerstone of the Free World in Southeast Asia. If South Vietnam fell to the Communists, then Laos, Cambodia, Burma, Thailand, India, Japan, and the Philippines would be threatened.

Kennedy, Secretary of Defense Robert McNamara, Secretary of State Dean Rusk, National Security Adviser McGeorge Bundy, and other high officials in the new administration shared the ideological fundaments of the Cold War with their predecessors in the Eisenhower and Truman administrations. They believed that it was imperative for the United States to contain Communist expansion in Southeast Asia. The legacy of McCarthyism also stalked the Democrats in power. Ever since the early 1950s, they had been vulnerable to charges that they were "soft on Communism" both at home and abroad. Kennedy was convinced that he could not appear irresolute in Vietnam lest his administration suffer domestic political reprisals at the hands of Republican critics.

The Kennedy team also shared a faith in American wealth, military power, technical expertise, and good intentions. They believed that the United States would succeed in Vietnam where the French had failed. For the "New Frontiersmen," Vietnam offered an opportunity for nation building in the Third World. A potent combination of economic aid, military support, CIA covert operations, and counterinsurgency tactics would show the world that wars of national liberation backed by Moscow and Beijing could not succeed in Indochina.

Kennedy was eager to deploy the U.S. Army Special Forces, the "Green

Berets," in Southeast Asia. The Special Forces brought a new dimension, a key component of the flexible response capability recently added to the American Cold War arsenal. Kennedy expected Green Beret operations to counter Communist insurgencies in peripheral regions without provoking confrontations with the Soviets or Chinese that could lead to nuclear war. Kennedy, who had read Mao Zedong's writings on peasant revolution, believed that the Green Berets, specially trained and equipped for counterinsurgency warfare, would help Diem win the hearts and minds of his people.

In May 1961, Kennedy sent Vice-President Lyndon Johnson to Vietnam to emphasize the American commitment to Diem's government and to assess Diem's military needs. In Saigon, Johnson hailed Diem as the "Winston Churchill of Southeast Asia." Upon his return to Washington, Johnson advised Kennedy to increase American aid to South Vietnam. During the next 18 months, Kennedy sent 16,000 military advisers to Vietnam. They joined the 600 American advisers already there at the time of Eisenhower's departure. In 1962 and 1963 some of these military advisers increasingly found themselves involved in combat situations. Some 60 Americans were killed in Vietnam in 1963.

Despite the large increase in American support in 1962 and 1963, forces loyal to Diem continued to lose the war to the Vietcong insurgents and their North Vietnamese patrons. Worried U.S. officials tried to persuade Diem to implement social reforms and to curb his repressive police forces. He refused to do either. Diem and his brother, Nhu, both believed that they knew how to govern South Vietnam better than the Americans who were trying to tell them what to do. The Diem government failed to win the support of the villagers, who constituted 85 percent of the South Vietnamese population in the early 1960s. At the "rice-roots" level Diem was not winning many hearts and minds. His failure to establish a broad base of support in the countryside for his government helped bring about his downfall.

Even though Diem's power was declining and the insurgents controlled most of the South Vietnamese territory and people outside the cities, the American military-assistance command in Saigon reported only favorable news about the war. They ignored negative field reports filed by American advisers who accompanied South Vietnamese forces into battle and who realized that Diem's troops were losing the war. David Halberstam, a New York *Times* reporter who interviewed some of the U.S. advisers such as Colonal John Paul Vann, filed news stories contradicting the official optimism. Kennedy, who read Halberstam's columns, tried to get the *Times* to recall him for reporting unfavorably about the war. The publishers of the *Times* refused the president's request and Halberstam stayed in Vietnam. But most Americans did not read Halberstam or the few other reporters who filed similar stories, and they probably held unrealistically optimistic views of the situation prevailing in Vietnam because of official dishonesty and news manipulation.

A crisis suddenly erupted in South Vietnam in June 1963 that within a few months brought an end to the Diem regime. The mayor of Hue refused to allow Buddhists to fly banners celebrating the Buddha's birthday. When the

Buddhists took to the streets in protest, their rebellion was brutally crushed. In response to this repression, a Buddhist monk set himself on fire at a busy downtown Saigon intersection. Photographs of the gruesome spectacle made the front pages of newspapers around the world and provoked a storm of protest against the Diem government. Other monks immolated themselves in similar fashion as popular opposition to the government mounted in the major cities of South Vietnam.

Knowing that Diem's political base had been reduced to family members and a few loyal army generals, and fearing that the war against the Vietcong was being lost, senior officials in the Kennedy administration concluded that Diem and his brother would have to be removed from office. On November 1, 1963, an Army coup, acting with the foreknowledge and support of American officials, including President Kennedy, overthrew the Diem government. Coup leaders also murdered Diem and his brother, Nhu. American officials then backed a junta of generals who formed a new government and tried to continue the war. Three weeks after the coup that brought Diem down, Kennedy himself was murdered in Dallas.

At the time of Kennedy's death, America's Vietnam policy was in disarray. Although he had significantly raised the American stake in Vietnam, Kennedy had hinted at times that he might reappraise his commitment to South Vietnam in light of Diem's continuing political failures. But in September 1963, Kennedy publicly reaffirmed the American commitment in Southeast Asia, and there is no firm evidence that he was prepared to abandon Vietnam. Kennedy had inherited a difficult situation in Indochina from Eisenhower; his actions during his abbreviated presidency greatly raised America's commitment to Vietnam and ensured that the United States would remain there for a long time. Had Kennedy lived and had he been reelected president in 1964, he would probably have reacted as Lyndon Johnson did in 1965 and committed the United States to war in Vietnam rather than accept a Communist victory.

AMERICA GOES TO WAR

During his first year in office, President Lyndon Baines Johnson focused his energies on establishing his leadership, persuading Congress to enact Kennedy's stalled civil rights and social-reform measures, and developing his own Great Society program. In Indochina, the new president continued Kennedy's policy of supplying economic and military assistance to the government in Saigon, but the political situation in South Vietnam continued to deteriorate. Diem was followed by a succession of military regimes that could neither govern nor fight effectively. Supported and directed by Hanoi, the National Liberation Front (NLF) forces, which Americans called the Vietcong, extended their control over the countryside.

Johnson, as had Kennedy previously, dismissed any possibility of America withdrawing from Vietnam or of accepting any political solution that did not guarantee the survival of an independent non-Communist government in South Vietnam. Johnson vowed that he would not be the first American president to lose a war; he would not allow Southeast Asia to go the way of China. He retained most of Kennedy's senior advisers, and he relied on their expertise and shared their commitment to contain Chinese expansion in Southeast Asia.

Johnson increased the number of American advisers from 16,500 to 24,000 and raised the level of economic assistance to South Vietnam during his first year in office. He also authorized a series of covert operations against North Vietnam that included dropping propaganda leaflets, intelligence overflights, commando raids along the coast, and the infiltration of Special Forces and CIA operatives. Johnson also warned Hanoi's leaders that if they continued to support the Vietcong rebels in South Vietnam they would face devastation. Johnson's subtle shift toward the north opened the door through which he walked into a wider war.

In early August 1964, as the U.S. presidential election was beginning, there began a series of incidents in the developing Vietnam war that had major consequences. On August 1, while engaged in electronic surveillance off the North Vietnamese coast, the U.S. destroyer *Maddox* was attacked by North Vietnamese torpedo boats. *Maddox*, aided by naval aircraft, returned the fire and repulsed the attackers. *Maddox* resumed its spy operations and was joined by another destroyer, *Turner Joy*. On the night of August 4, as the two ships operated in heavy seas about 50 miles from the North Vietnamese coast, both ships reported that they were under attack. No one on either ship sighted any attackers; the initial reports were based on radar and sonar contacts. Captain John Herrick, commander of the destroyer operation who was onboard the *Maddox*, later reported that weather effects and a misreading of sonar data may have been responsible for the reported attacks. Although evidence of a second attack was dubious, Johnson ordered retaliatory air strikes against North Vietnamese naval bases. U.S. aircraft from the carrier *Ticonderoga* carried out the raids and wrought extensive damage to North Vietnamese ships, docks, and oil-storage facilities.

Johnson also asked Congress to approve a resolution authorizing him to take "all necessary measures to repel any armed attack against the forces of the United States and to prevent further aggression." Johnson requested the resolution because he wanted to send a message to Hanoi that Americans were united in their resolve to stand firm in Vietnam. Johnson's use of force coupled to his appeal for public support silenced Barry Goldwater, his hawkish Republican challenger.

In presenting the administration's case for enacting what has come to be called the Gulf of Tonkin resolution, Secretary of Defense Robert McNamara misled Congress. He did not inform the legislators that the *Maddox* was on a spy mission when it was attacked, nor did he tell them that the evidence for a second attack was cloudy. McNamara characterized both attacks as mindless acts of aggression against American ships on routine patrols in international waters. After perfunctory debate, the Senate approved the Tonkin Gulf resolution by a vote of 88–2, and the House of Representatives passed it unanimously. Public-opinion polls showed that a large majority of Americans supported Johnson's actions and his popularity rating zoomed upward.

The Vietnam war was not a major issue in the 1964 presidential campaign. Neither Goldwater nor Johnson talked much about it. At the time, most Americans were uninformed and unconcerned about a dirty little war going on in a faraway place. But Johnson did tell campaign audiences that he did not want to get involved in a war in Southeast Asia and that Americans would not be sent to fight there. On September 25, 1964, he told an audience in Eufaula, Oklahoma, "We don't want to get involved . . . in a land war in Asia." At Akron, Ohio, on October 21, Johnson stated that he was not about "to send American boys nine or ten thousand miles away from home to do what Asian boys ought to be doing for themselves."

At the time that he made these remarks, Johnson had not yet committed himself to further bombing of North Vietnam nor had he decided to send American combat troops to South Vietnam. But Johnson was committed to not losing South Vietnam and he had ruled nothing out. He knew that both the military and political situation in South Vietnam was deteriorating and that the insurgents were growing in strength. He also knew that his advisers had developed contingency plans, which included bombing North Vietnam and sending U.S. troops to South Vietnam—plans that he might have to implement in the future. Johnson misled the American people during the presidential campaign of 1964. He conveyed the impression that he would limit American efforts in Vietnam to offering assistance to one side in the conflict. Johnson offered himself as the peace candidate in contrast to his opponent, Barry Goldwater, who might take America to war if elected. Voters who thought they were voting for Johnson and peace in November 1964 soon got war.

In January 1965 the South Vietnamese government verged on defeat, in part because U.S. advisers had trained its army to fight conventional wars and it could not cope with the NLF's guerrilla tactics. The Army of the Republic of South Vietnam (ARVN) also faced more fundamental problems. Its officers were chosen for their political loyalty to Diem, not for their fighting abilities. Many were Catholic northerners who had come south with the French after the defeat at Dien Bien Phu. Many were corrupt and used their high military offices to enrich themselves and their families. The enlisted men, nearly all draftees, were mainly southern Buddhist peasants. They found nothing to fight for in the ARVN—no leader, no ideal. They were serving time in the army, not a cause. Draft avoidance and desertion rates were chronically high. American advisers observed that their NLF foes usually fought harder and more courageously than most ARVN soldiers. No amount of American aid could compensate for the ARVN's ineptitude, corruption, and lack of fighting spirit.

Johnson confronted a dilemma in Vietnam in early 1965 that was largely of his own making. Since he had ruled out a U.S. withdrawal from Indochina, there remained only the options of negotiation or escalation. Given the military realities prevailing in South Vietnam at that time, negotiations with Hanoi meant having to accept a coalition government for South Vietnam with NLF participation. Johnson feared, rightly, that such a government would soon be dominated by the NLF, would declare itself neutral, would ask the Americans to leave, and would eventually seek reunion with the north. Equating neutrality with defeat, Johnson ruled out negotiations until the military situation grew more favorable, that is, until the South Vietnamese were winning the war. Consequently, Johnson made his decision to escalate the war. He authorized a sustained, gradually expanding bombing campaign against North Vietnam starting February 13, 1965, and he expanded the much larger air war in South Vietnam.

Within two weeks, General William Westmoreland, the American commander in Vietnam, requested Marine combat units to defend a large U.S. Air Force base at Danang because he could not rely on ARVN security forces. On March 8, two Marine battalions in full battle gear splashed ashore on the beaches just south of Danang. They were greeted by the mayor of Danang and a cluster of pretty Vietnamese women who placed leis of gladioli and dahlias around the necks of the Marines. On this festive note the American war in Vietnam began.

During the final week of July 1965, President Johnson, in consultation with his senior civilian and military advisers, made a series of fateful decisions that set the United States on a course in Vietnam from which it did not deviate for nearly three years, and which began more than seven years of war. Johnson and his advisers approved Westmoreland's requests for expanded bombing in South Vietnam and for expanding the air war against North Vietnam. Also approved was the sending of 50,000 combat troops to Vietnam, with more to follow as needed. In addition, Johnson made an open-ended commitment to use American forces in South Vietnam as the situation demanded, in effect giving Westmoreland a free hand to assume the major burden of the fighting. These July decisions plunged the United States into a major war in Southeast Asia.

At the time he was making these critical decisions, President Johnson never informed the American people of what he was doing and refused to submit his policies to Congress for review. He did not want to arouse public passions, and he feared congressional debate might undermine support for this Great Society program. He refused to seek a formal declaration of war against North Vietnam. He insisted that the Gulf of Tonkin resolution granted him authority to wage war in Vietnam.

However, at the time that Johnson had requested the Tonkin Gulf resolution, he was not seeking a declaration of war, and Congress never intended that it be one. Senator William J. Fulbright, chairman of the Senate Foreign Relations Committee, who had guided the resolution through the Senate, was one of the first senators to turn against the Vietnam war. Fulbright believed that he and other senators had been tricked into supporting a war that they had never intended be fought. In later years, when the war became controversial, many Americans believed that Johnson had stealthily committed the nation to an undeclared war in Southeast Asia. The president had gambled that he could persuade most members of Congress and most of the American people to support both his war and his domestic policies.

The Johnson administration's war decisions were based on two major errors in judgment. The first was that the administration significantly underestimated the abilities of the NLF and North Vietnamese forces, aided by the Soviets and Chinese, to resist—for years—large-scale applications of U.S. military power. At the outset of the war, McNamara had assumed that a point would be reached within a year or two when North Vietnam would break from the ever-increasing punishment inflicted by U.S. bombers, abandon its support of the southern insurgency, and accept American terms for a settlement. America's leaders could not bring themselves to believe that a poor Asian country about the size of New Mexico could stand up militarily to the wealthiest and mightiest nation in the world.

The Johnson administration's second major error flowed from its first. Having underestimated the enemy, the administration also drastically underestimated the costs of the war in lives and dollars and overestimated the willingness of the American people to go on passively paying for those escalating costs year after year. Johnson, in that fateful summer of 1965, had launched the nation on what would become its longest, most frustrating, and divisive war, with only the dimmest glimmer of what lay ahead and without a clear mandate from Congress or the American people.

THE AMERICAN WAY OF WAR

The United States relied heavily on air power to win the war in Vietnam. Air Force and Navy pilots had two primary missions: The first was to stem the flow of men, supplies, and weapons coming south from North Vietnam along the Ho Chi Minh trail. The second was to destroy military targets, transportation systems, and industrial targets in North Vietnam until Hanoi abandoned its support of the insurgency in South Vietnam and came to the bargaining table prepared to accept American terms. Massive use of air power in the form of extensive bombings failed to achieve either goal.

Although air power did not achieve its strategic objectives, the heavy bombings did inflict severe damage on North Vietnam and it slowed the rate of infiltration down the Ho Chi Minh trail. Bombing disrupted North Vietnam's agricultural economy, destroyed much of its industrial base, and leveled some of its cities. Thousands of civilians were killed or wounded. But the bombing never appreciably reduced North Vietnam's war-making abilities. The Soviets and Chinese quickly replaced Hanoi's lost war materiel. The bombing never came close to breaking North Vietnam's will or causing the enemy to consider abandoning their support of the insurgents in the south.

Although it failed to achieve its goals, the air war proved extremely costly for the United States. Between 1965 and 1968, America lost nearly 1,000 fixed-wing aircraft worth more than $6 billion. Hundreds of pilots and crew members were killed or captured by the enemy. The bombing also handed the Communists a potent propaganda weapon. Domestic and foreign critics of America's role in Vietnam often denounced the air war against North Vietnam. To these critics, America's continuous pounding of a small, poor Asian country appeared excessively costly, futile, and immoral. "Stop the bombing!" became a rallying cry for antiwar activists.

American ground combat operations escalated dramatically between July 1965 and the end of 1967 when nearly 500,000 troops were deployed in South Vietnam. General Westmoreland used a strategy of attrition against the main-force units of the NLF and the North Vietnamese Army (NVA) units fighting in the south. Westmoreland attempted to employ superior American mobility and firepower in "search and destroy" operations to eradicate enemy soldiers and force their leaders to the bargaining table. Westmoreland believed that America's technological superiority would defeat the enemy's guerrilla-warfare tactics. Herbicides were used extensively to deprive the Vietcong of forest cover and food crops. Aerial spray units poured more than 100 million gallons of defoliants, which eventually destroyed about 40 percent of South Vietnamese forests. The air war in South Vietnam, much larger than the aerial war waged against North Vietnam, was an integral part of the war of attrition. The most frequent air operations of the southern air war included bombing attacks on enemy positions, often done by high-flying B–52 strategic bombers, the most fearsome weapon in the American arsenal, and close air support missions carried out by tactical bombers and helicopter gunships.

Because all of South Vietnam became a combat zone, Americans fought a war without fronts or territorial objectives. The only measure of progress toward victory in a formless war of attrition came to be statistics: numbers of enemy weapons and stores captured, numbers of villages pacified, numbers of defectors, and most important, numbers of enemy soldiers killed, wounded or captured. Attrition warfare represented war by the numbers, which never added up to an American victory, before popular support for the war collapsed and time ran out. As 1967 ended, official U.S. estimates of enemy soldiers killed-in-action (KIAs) had reached 220,000. American battle deaths for the same period came to 15,747. Assuming the numbers of enemy KIA to be considerably inflated, it is evident that American forces had inflicted severe losses on the NLF/NVA forces during three years of attrition warfare.

Johnson's decision to Americanize the war in 1965 prevented a certain South Vietnamese defeat. But the United States could only achieve a military stalemate, not victory, in South Vietnam. General Westmoreland based his attrition strategy on the assumption that U.S. forces could use their superior mobility and firepower to inflict irreplaceable losses on the enemy while keeping their own casualties low. Even though the Americans did inflict heavy casualties on the enemy, both the NLF and NVA forces were able to replace their losses. They matched each American escalation with one of their own. The Vietcong also used their foot mobility, their knowledge of the local terrain, and they exploited limits that Washington placed on U.S. military operations to retain the strategic initiative and to control the tempo of their losses. The NLF political infrastructure remained intact and continued to organize and administer many of the villages of South Vietnam that were under their control.

American artillery and bombing campaigns below the 17th parallel disrupted the South Vietnamese economy. Rice production declined. Thousands of villagers were killed and millions were driven into the arms of the Vietcong or became refugees. Angry and bewildered victims of the war, these refugees often ended up in squalid internment camps or else in the slums and back-alley labyrinths of Saigon, Danang, and other cities. The violent U.S. assault undermined the social fabric of a fragmented nation and alienated much of the rural populace from a fragile regime that had never enjoyed the trust, affection, or loyalty of millions of its subjects. A Marine Corps medic, walking through a village destroyed by U.S. artillery fire and seeing its wailing inhabitants, observed: "If anyone thinks this is the way to win their hearts and minds, he's out of his mind." The American take-over of the war also further weakened the fighting resolve of the ARVN forces. The South Vietnamese army was more than willing to let Americans do the fighting and dying for them. The Republic of South Vietnam (RVN, or GVN) became more dependent than ever on its American connection.

In 1966, a South Vietnamese military government headed by Air Marshal Nguyen Cao Ky and General Nguyen Van Thieu nearly fell to a Buddhist uprising that had clear anti-American overtones. An angry mob burned the U.S. consulate in Hue. There were other protests and anti-American demonstrations in Danang. With strong American backing, Ky and Thieu finally crushed the Buddhist revolt.

In the aftermath of the Buddhist uprising, responding to firm prodding from Washington, Ky and Thieu attempted to build popular support for their government among the rural population with pacification and rural development programs. ARVN forces provided a security screen and government teams moved into villages to furnish medical care and social services. They also trained villagers in self-government and self-defense techniques. Their goal was to insulate the villagers from the appeals and reprisals of the Vietcong. By providing both security and services to the villagers, they would promote a national rebirth while the American forces defeated the Communists militarily.

Pacification efforts sometimes succeeded, but more often they failed in 1966 and 1967. American forces occasionally shelled or bombed friendly villages by mistake. Vietcong terrorists assassinated thousands of South Vietnamese rural development workers. Often the government workers were inept or corrupt, or both, and often the ARVN troops that were supposedly providing security for the villagers harassed and brutalized them. Soldiers stole their pigs and chickens, their tools, and much of their rice. Westmoreland and most other senior American officials in Vietnam regarded nation building as secondary to the war effort. The inability of a succession of South Vietnamese governments either to win the loyalty of the rural population or to solve their country's massive social problems proved to be a major cause of the eventual failure of the U.S. intervention in Vietnam.

The Ky-Thieu government survived not because it was intrinsically strong or because it was popular with most South Vietnamese, but because it received strong U.S. political, economic, and military backing. Relations between American officials and their Vietnamese clients were often strained and ambivalent. The Vietnamese resented American arrogance and the inability of Americans to understand Vietnamese culture or psychology. Americans were frustrated by Vietnamese corruption, dishonesty, and inefficiency. Vietnamese officials often did not understand what Americans wanted. Concepts such as "reform" and "democracy" do not travel well across vast cultural chasms dividing Westerners and Asians. Many South Vietnamese viewed the Americans as replacements for the departed French and the U.S. presence in their country as an imperialistic scourge. American soldiers—fighting in steamy jungles and swamps in an alien land, not always able to tell friendly Vietnamese from a deadly enemy—often distrusted and despised the very people they were trying to save from Communism.

The steady escalation of the Vietnam war between 1965 and 1967 generated both international and domestic pressures for a cease-fire to be followed by a negotiated settlement. But the continuing stalemate on the battlefield ensured that neither side would make the concessions necessary to get negotiations started. For political reasons, both sides strove to appear responsive to peace initiatives and both depicted their opponent as the criminal aggressor and chief obstacle to peace. Hanoi's strategy was to get maximum propaganda value out of the peace initiatives while inflicting casualties on the allies and matching each U.S. escalation until the Americans wearied of the war and pulled out. Ho Chi Minh believed that time was on his side and that his cause would ultimately prevail. Johnson believed that the steadily expanding U.S. military effort would eventually break Hanoi and contain the southern insurgency.

Hanoi maintained that the American presence in South Vietnam violated the 1954 Geneva accords and that the bombing of North Vietnam was unprovoked aggression. The North Vietnamese refused to negotiate until the United States ceased all acts of war against the country, in both the north and the south, and withdrew its troops. Hanoi also insisted that what they called the puppet regime in Saigon, the Ky-Thieu government, would have to be replaced by a coalition government.

While insisting that it favored unconditional negotiations, the Johnson administration refused to withdraw its forces from South Vietnam until a government that excluded the National Liberation Front was securely in place. Washington also refused to halt the bombing of North Vietnam, which it maintained was necessary to keep the Communists from overrunning South Vietnam. The war dragged on, and numerous third-party peace initiatives came to nought in 1966 and 1967.

While the expanding war in Vietnam remained stalemated and efforts to start negotiations failed, within the United States supporters and opponents of the war engaged in debates of rising intensity. On one side were the hawks; the most prominent hawks were conservative civilian and military leaders who urged an expanded war effort to ensure military victory. On the other side were the doves, who challenged both the effectiveness and morality of the war. Doves represented a more diverse group, old-line pacifists, student radicals, civil rights leaders, some college professors, and liberal politicians. The most prominent dove was Senator William J. Fulbright. Initially a supporter of the war, Fulbright had joined the ranks of the doves by 1966.

Opposition to the war escalated in 1966 and 1967 and took many forms. Senator Fulbright held televised hearings on the conduct of the war before the Senate Foreign Relations Committee, which he chaired. He and his dovish colleagues on the committee grilled administration spokesmen such as Secretary of State Dean Rusk for hours about all aspects of the war. They also provided critics of the war, such as George Kennan and General James Gavin, a national forum for airing their dovish views. Americans opposed to the war marched around the White House chanting "Hey, Hey, LBJ, how many kids did you kill today?" On October 21, 1967, an estimated 100,000 antiwar protesters gathered in front of the Pentagon, the nerve center of the war effort. Thousands of young men resisted or evaded the draft. Heavyweight boxing champion Muhammad Ali refused induction into the Army on religious grounds although the government rejected his bid for conscientious-objector status.

Most Americans in 1966 and 1967 were neither hawks nor doves. Most citizens had supported the initial escalations, which had "Americanized" the war. Expecting a relatively quick and easy victory, they had rallied around the flag in support of military intervention. But after two years of rising costs and mounting casualties, with military victory still eluding the United States, popular frustration with the conflict mounted. Public opinion polls taken in August 1967 showed, for the first time, that a majority of Americans believed that sending U.S. combat troops to Vietnam had been a mistake.

Despite Johnson's assurances that there were "no deep divisions" within the country over his conduct of the war, *Time* magazine writers found "a clashing disharmony ringing loud and clear the length of the land." Newspapers, which had previously supported the war, turned against it and called for a negotiated settlement. The "credibility gap," the contrast between what the government said and what it did, widened as the public became increasingly distrustful of the public statements made about the war by the president and other administration officials. Urban riots, spiraling crime rates, and militant antiwar demonstrations indicated rising levels of domestic violence that paralleled the violence of war abroad.

Americans who opposed the war in 1967 formed no consensus. They divided over whether to escalate the war drastically and win it or to negotiate an American withdrawal. The growing divisiveness strained the social fabric. An Iowa housewife summed up the dilemma facing the average American: "I want to get out, but I don't want to give up." Meanwhile, the war dragged on, draft calls increased, and the numbers of American dead and wounded rose.

Johnson, trying to dampen growing criticism of his war policy within the media and in Congress, brought General Westmoreland to Washington in November 1967. Speaking before the National Press Club on November 21, Westmoreland gave an optimistic appraisal of the war. He said the enemy, although not yet licked, was hurting badly. Pacification was going so well that the enemy could no longer mount a major offensive anywhere in the country. "We have reached a point where the end begins to come into view," Westmoreland stated. The president held a press conference in which he vigorously defended his war policy, exuded confidence that victory would be achieved in the near future, and criticized his detractors. These public-relations gambits proved effective. Popular support for the war rose as the year ended.

TET AND ITS CONSEQUENCES

Choosing Tet, the Vietnamese New Year and Vietnam's most important holiday, to attack, some 84,000 Vietcong and NVA soldiers suddenly staged surprise assaults on district towns, provincial capitals, and major cities all over South Vietnam in early 1968. Catching the allies by surprise, the enemy brought the war to the urban population of the country, those who had hitherto been spared the ravages of war. A VC suicide squad even broke into the U.S. embassy compound in downtown Saigon and held a courtyard for a few hours. At most of the attack sites, enemy troops were beaten back within a few hours or a few days and they sustained heavy losses. Within a month they had lost all the cities that they had originally occupied.

Hanoi had planned its Tet-68 offensive carefully. It was designed to give the Communists smashing military victories over the South Vietnamese forces. The Communists expected that these victories would prove to the South Vietnamese urban populations that neither the government in the south nor the Americans could protect them. They also believed that it could result in a mass popular uprising that would bring down the South Vietnamese government, force the Americans to leave, and end the war. But Tet-68 failed to achieve any of Hanoi's military or political objectives.

Within the United States, the Tet-68 offensive had a tremendous psychological impact that had not been anticipated by its North Vietnamese planners. Tet proved to be a major psychological and political victory for the Communists. At a press conference held on February 2, 1968, President Johnson insisted that both American and ARVN leaders had known of the coming attacks and had reacted quickly to contain them. The fact was that the administration was shocked by the scale and intensity of the Tet-68 assaults, by the ability of an enemy that was thought to be incapable of carrying out large-scale, coordinated attacks against supposedly secure sites over the length and breadth of South Vietnam. After Tet, the Chairman of the Joint Chiefs, General Earle Wheeler, told President Johnson that Tet had been a very close call and that Westmoreland would need an additional 206,000 troops to accomplish American strategic goals in Vietnam.

The president, angered and confused by events, asked his new secretary of defense, Clark Clifford, to conduct a thorough study of the proposed troop increase. Clifford headed a committee that not only examined the proposed troop increase but, at his urging, also conducted a full review of the American war effort. The Clifford task force sought precise answers to basic questions that Johnson had never asked: Would the additional 206,000 troops win the war? What would the impact of such a troop increase be on the American economy? Can the bombing win the war? How much longer must the United States continue to carry the main burden of combat in Vietnam?

The answers Clifford got to these and other questions dismayed him. Furnishing 206,000 additional troops for Vietnam would require calling up reserves, increasing draft calls, reducing domestic spending, and raising taxes. American casualties would rise and so would domestic opposition to the war. The divisions within American society would widen and intensify. Civilian analysts in the Pentagon told Clifford that Johnson's strategy of graduated escalation was bankrupt. It could not bring victory, even with the proposed 206,000 troop increase, because Hanoi had both the will and the capability to match the proposed U.S. escalation just as it had matched all previous ones. The Pentagon analysts recommended putting a cap on the number of troops deployed to Vietnam, turning over more responsibility for the war to the South Vietnamese, and making greater efforts to achieve a negotiated settlement.

Tet also had a major effect on elite public opinion within the United States, on members of Congress, and on the media. Television news coverage of the war changed dramatically. Previously, television had presented a well-ordered version of the war: on-the-scene reports of large-scale operations that usually resulted in U.S. victories, analytical reports of the war's progress, and stories about successful pacification programs. With Tet-68, viewers saw for the first time the dramatic consequences of Communist attacks all over South Vietnam. Viewers recoiled from a flood of violent and confusing images: dead Vietcong sappers lying inside the American embassy compound, deadly fighting in the streets of Saigon and Hue, and the summary execution of a Vietcong terrorist on a Saigon street by the head of the South Vietnamese police. The chaos in Vietnam that Americans viewed on television appeared to contradict all the official reports and media coverage of the previous three years, which had conveyed the idea of steady progress toward inevitable military victory. Tet-68 exploded that notion in a few dramatic days. The years of bombing, of search-and-destroy operations, of rural development, of defoliation, of body counts, and of computer printouts that supposedly told Americans that they were winning the war—all these had not meant a thing. Instead, Tet-68 suggested something else. If the enemy could stage surprise attacks all over South Vietnam whenever it chose, all that America had achieved in Vietnam by 1968 was an unending stalemate.

Public opinion polls taken after Tet revealed sharp rises in popular disillusionment with the war. One poll showed 78 percent of Americans believed that the United States was not winning the war. Only 26 percent approved of Johnson's war policy. On February 23, 1968, the *Wall Street Journal,* long a hawkish supporter of the Vietnam war, editorialized that Americans had better prepare themselves to face the fact "that the whole Vietnam effort may be doomed." Four days later, the nation's most influential television journalist, CBS's Walter Cronkite, told his viewers that the war was a stalemate and that the only rational way for Americans to extricate themselves from Vietnam was to negotiate a settlement and take the best deal that they could get.

Congressional opposition to the war also escalated after Tet. Antiwar sentiments on Capitol Hill boosted the presidential candidacy of an obscure Minnesota senator, Eugene McCarthy, who had announced in December 1967 that he would challenge Lyndon Johnson and run as an antiwar candidate for the Democratic nomination. Initially, McCarthy's efforts against the powerful and politically astute incumbent were dismissed as the quixotic gestures of a political lightweight. But after Tet, McCarthy's campaign gained momentum. In the New Hampshire primary held March 12, 1968, McCarthy, aided by hundreds of student volunteers, got 42 percent of the vote, almost as much as Lyndon Johnson. New Hampshire came as a political revelation. The president was evidently far more unpopular and vulnerable than anyone had realized. Four days later, Senator Robert Kennedy, a far more formidable antiwar candidate, heartened by McCarthy's strong showing in New Hampshire, announced that he too would seek the Democratic presidential nomination in 1968.

At the White House, President Johnson struggled with his failed Vietnam policy. At times he talked as if he wanted to escalate the war, to strike back hard at his treacherous foes. At Clark Clifford's behest he convened a panel of distinguished civilian and military advisers who had previously endorsed his war policy. But Tet and its consequences had changed many of their minds. Most of these "wise men," as Johnson called them, led by former Secretary of State Dean Acheson, told the president that his policy of graduated escalation had failed. Acheson stated that neither the time nor the assets needed to win the war were available. Acheson also stated that the war could not be won save at unacceptable risk to national interests at home and abroad. Anguished and bitter, Johnson, after taking a few days to reflect upon the "wise men's" counsel, accepted Clifford's recommendations to scale down the war.

On March 31, 1968, President Johnson told the American people he would not meet the Army's request for 206,000 additional troops and he would reduce the bombing of North Vietnam to try to get negotiations underway. He also stated that South Vietnam would be required to assume a greater burden of the fighting. As he neared the end of his nationally televised speech, he stunned the nation by announcing that he would not seek nor accept the nomination of his party for another presidential term. To restore unity in America, Johnson would remove himself from politics and try to achieve peace in Vietnam. To end the war at home that was tearing the nation apart, he would try to end the war that he had begun three years earlier. Thus, Lyndon Johnson announced not only the end of his military policy of graduated escalation but also the end of his presidency.

The Tet offensive, although it left the Communists with devastating defeats and casualties, also brought them a tremendous psychological and military victory over the United States that forced the president to abandon the strategy of graduated escalation. Johnson's change of tactics was brought about by domestic political pressures, economic considerations, and, most of all, by the advice of Clark Clifford and the "wise men." He replaced this strategy with an early version of what would be called "Vietnamization" by his successor, Richard Nixon.

Tet proved to be the major turning point of the Vietnam war. The president's decisions of March 1968 set in motion a process that eventually unravelled America's involvement in Southeast Asia. After Tet, a U.S. military victory in

Vietnam was unattainable primarily because the American people no longer had the patience or political will to continue providing the vast resources required to achieve it. Tet was the great watershed of the Vietnam war. The partial bombing halt began a diplomatic process that would one day bring an end to the war and open the door to a Communist triumph. In the short run, Tet was a major American tactical victory; in the long run Tet proved to be a critical Communist strategic victory and a fatal American political defeat.

A WAR TO END A WAR

Richard Nixon sought the presidency in 1968, promising to end the divisions at home and to bring peace with honor to Vietnam. The American public responded and elected Nixon president. Upon assuming office in January 1969, he and his principal foreign-policy adviser, Henry Kissinger, implemented a more flexible and realistic Vietnam policy than did his predecessor. But Nixon's approach suffered from the same basic flaw as did Johnson's. The new president sought to achieve an independent non-Communist government in South Vietnam, which the North Vietnamese absolutely refused to accept. Hence the American adventure in Vietnam was fated to continue another four years, to the immense disappointment of most Americans.

Nixon understood that his top foreign-policy priority must be ending the war. It had become a divisive force threatening to tear the nation apart. He also believed that his political future depended on his ability to extract the United States from its entanglement in Southeast Asia. But, as Johnson had done previously, Nixon also vowed that he would not be the first American president to lose a war. He also believed that the United States could not pull out of Vietnam abruptly and leave the South Vietnamese government at the mercy of its powerful foes. If the South Vietnamese government collapsed shortly after a sudden American pullout, Nixon feared that the American people would be demoralized. He also feared the international consequences of such an act. It would dishearten America's allies and embolden the Communists, and it would jeopardize his new foreign policy based on détente with the Soviet Union and China. Kissinger believed that an American unilateral withdrawal from Indochina would unleash anarchic forces in the world that would undermine international order and render diplomacy impossible.

Although Hanoi had consistently rejected any settlement that left a non-Communist government in South Vietnam, Nixon and Kissinger believed that they could compel the North Vietnamese to accept one. They planned to use the Soviets by linking arms control agreements and increased trade with the USSR to Soviet willingness to pressure Hanoi into accepting U.S. terms in Vietnam. Nixon also planned to escalate the war by removing limits that Johnson had placed on American military operations in Indochina. Nixon, acting through Soviet intermediaries, also offered the North Vietnamese more realistic peace terms. At the same time, to placate American public opinion, Nixon announced a phased withdrawal of American combat troops from Vietnam. Lest Hanoi read the wrong message into the troop withdrawals, Nixon expanded the bombing in Laos and began a secret bombing operation against Communist bases in Cambodia. Initially, Nixon and Kissinger confidently believed that their complex plan would end the war soon and save the South Vietnamese government.

They were mistaken. Hanoi was neither intimidated by threats nor lured by concessions into abandoning its diplomatic position. Peace negotiations, which had begun in Paris in May 1968, remained deadlocked. Hanoi continued to demand the unilateral withdrawal of all U.S. forces from South Vietnam and the creation of a coalition government in Saigon that would exclude General Thieu, who had emerged as the leader of the government of South Vietnam (GVN) in the fall of 1967. The Soviets also refused to cooperate with the United States; linkage proved a failure in 1969.

With his plan for ending the war shelved, Nixon faced a dilemma. Unable to extract the slightest concession from Hanoi, he had to choose between a major escalation of the war or a humiliating withdrawal. Nixon's instinct was to mount an all-out military assault, but his advisers persuaded him not to by convincing him that it would be futile and it would provoke a domestic backlash. Unwilling to make concessions, unable to use greater force, Nixon fell back on "Vietnamization," essentially policies inherited from Lyndon Johnson and Clark Clifford. America would continue to withdraw its troops while furnishing large-scale economic and military assistance to the GVN. Nixon claimed that South Vietnam would be strong enough to defend itself within two years.

In a major speech to the American people on November 3, 1969, the president stated that Vietnamization represented the road to "peace with honor." It would preserve the South Vietnamese government and it would permit American extrication from the war. Nixon also attacked the antiwar movement. He called its members an irrational minority that was undermining U.S. foreign policy. He also appealed for support from the mass of Americans whom he called the "great silent majority." It was a shrewd and successful speech. Polls taken soon after the speech showed that a large majority of Americans supported Vietnamization. Doves were put on the defensive.

At the time Nixon announced his "new" Vietnamization policy, it had already been in place for a year; he had merely provided it with a new label. While American troops battled the Communists, U.S. advisers hastened to build up the ARVN forces. Pacification and rural development programs accelerated. Thieu implemented a new land reform program. In March 1970, Nixon announced Vietnamization was on schedule and that 150,000 troops would be withdrawn during the year. Both General Creighton Abrams, who had replaced Westmoreland as the U.S. commander in Vietnam, and General Thieu protested the proposed troop withdrawals. Abrams feared for the security of the remaining U.S. forces in Vietnam, and Thieu knew that his army was unready to take over the fighting.

In March 1970, in neighboring Cambodia, the neutralist leader, Prince Norodom Sihanouk, was overthrown by his pro-American prime minister, Lon

Nol. The new leader promptly ordered the Vietcong and NVA forces, which had been using the eastern provinces of his country bordering South Vietnam as sanctuaries and staging areas, to get out of Cambodia. Determined to stay in these areas, which were crucial to their conduct of the war in South Vietnam, Hanoi sent the NVA forces in Cambodia driving west in the direction of the capital, Phnom Penh, to overthrow the Lon Nol government.

Nixon, fearing that the North Vietnamese might take over Cambodia and responding to a long-standing request from the military to flush out the Communist sanctuaries in that country, ordered U.S. troops to attack an area of Cambodia 55 miles northwest of Saigon. He also believed that the Cambodian invasion would pressure Hanoi into making concessions at the bargaining table.

Militarily, the Cambodian incursion generated mixed results. It relieved pressure on Saigon and bought more time for Vietnamization. It destroyed the Communist basing areas in Cambodia and closed the port of Sihanoukville, which had been a major source of supply for the insurgents. But it also widened the war and provoked Hanoi into full-scale support of the Khmer Rouge, an indigenous Cambodian insurgency fighting Lon Nol's forces. The United States now had two fragile client states in Southeast Asia to defend against insurgents backed by North Vietnam.

There was a furious domestic reaction to the Cambodian incursion. College campuses across the nation exploded at the news of an unexpected widening of the war that the president had promised to phase out. Tragedy struck at Kent State University in Ohio when National Guard troops fired into a crowd of students. Four were killed and nine were wounded. Following the shootings, hundreds of student strikes forced many colleges and universities to shut down. More than 100,000 demonstrators gathered in Washington to protest the Cambodian invasion and campus killings.

The Cambodian invasion triggered the most serious congressional challenge to presidential authority to conduct the Indochina war. The Senate repealed the Gulf of Tonkin resolution and voted to cut off all funds for military operations in Cambodia. The fund cut-off failed to clear the House and never became law. Nixon's hope that the Cambodian incursion would make Hanoi more amenable to U.S. proposals at the Paris peace talks proved to be erroneous. North Vietnam broke off the negotiations in protest, confident that domestic pressures would eventually force an American withdrawal from Cambodia and South Vietnam.

During the 1970 midterm elections, Nixon toured the country seeking support for his Indochina policy. He denounced opponents of the war and campaigned for candidates favoring his policy. Election results disappointed him. A few doves lost, but others were elected. Congress remained solidly in control of the Democrats. Nixon failed to get an endorsement or mandate for Vietnamization.

After two years of fighting, diplomacy, and political maneuver, the American position in Vietnam was worse than when Nixon took office. Both the war and peace talks were stalemated. The antiwar movement and congressional opposition were stronger than ever. The war had been widened to include Cambodia. North Vietnam had also infiltrated additional forces into Laos. Even though it had been a manifest failure, Nixon, perhaps for want of an alternative, continued to adhere to Vietnamization.

To appease dovish critics in Congress and the media, Nixon accelerated the timetable of troop withdrawals in 1971. He also expanded the air wars in Laos and Cambodia. He escalated the war further when he authorized an ARVN raid into Laos to disrupt enemy supply routes and destroy their stores. The expedition failed. South Vietnamese politics and tactical incompetence impaired the operation. North Vietnamese regular forces attacked the invaders and drove them back into South Vietnam with heavy casualties. The Laotian fiasco also signalled that Vietnamization was not working.

During the spring and summer of 1971, two events shocked an increasingly war-weary nation. The first of these involved the conviction of Lt. William Calley of mass murder; the second involved the publication of the so-called Pentagon Papers. In March 1968, Lt. Calley had ordered his Army infantry platoon to kill more than a hundred unarmed Vietnamese civilians in the hamlet of My Lai. At his court martial, Calley claimed that he was only following orders. Army attorneys argued that Calley had misunderstood his orders. No one else was convicted. Many Americans felt sympathy for Calley and his men. Both hawks and doves denounced the verdict, hawks because they did not believe a soldier should ever be convicted for doing his duty in wartime, doves because they feared a junior officer was being sacrificed while others escaped punishment.

At the time that the massacre at My Lai became public knowledge (in November of 1969), many Americans worried that there might be many such atrocities that had gone undetected. Scores of veterans testified in various forums that they had participated in, observed, or heard of similar atrocities against civilians. Other Americans found cold comfort in the fact that both the Vietcong and North Vietnamese soldiers engaged in systematic atrocities against South Vietnamese civilians and GVN officials. There was also a troubling inconsistency about convicting one junior officer of mass murder when aerial bombing and artillery fire had killed thousands of civilians since the American takeover of the war in 1965. What the My Lai massacre revealed above all was that the hellish circumstances of combat, which could generate intense confusion, rage, fear, and hate, sometimes brought out the worst in men. There is no evidence that the military ever had a policy of deliberately killing civilians or that other My Lai-type massacres occurred and went unreported. Most American soldiers serving in Vietnam did not commit atrocities against unarmed civilians.

No sooner did the uproar over Lt. Calley's conviction subside than the New York *Times* began publishing excerpts from the *Pentagon Papers,* secret government documents stolen by Daniel Ellsberg and Anthony Russo. These papers, which amounted to an official history of the U.S. involvement in Indochina to 1968, revealed that American leaders had deliberately escalated the war, had ignored peace offers, and had often lied to the public about their actions. The *Pentagon Papers* further undermined the credibility of government officials and reduced public support for the war.

Increasingly frustrated by his inability to end the war, Nixon fought back against the growing opposition to his war policy. He ordered illegal surveillance of antiwar groups by both the FBI and CIA. He ordered illegal wiretaps placed on the phones of government employees and journalists suspected of leaking information about secret operations to the public. He accused congressional doves of encouraging the enemy and prolonging the war. Nixon even tried to prevent the *Times* from publishing the *Pentagon Papers*. Attorney General John Mitchell secured a court injunction against their publication on the grounds that publishing them constituted a clear and present danger to national security. A federal judge, Gerhardt Gesell, quashed the injunction and the Supreme Court sustained him. A majority of the Supreme Court justices found only the public reputations of some former government officials endangered by publication of the papers.

Blocked by the Supreme Court, Nixon approved the creation of the notorious "plumbers," a special White House undercover unit, to prevent leaks from within the government and to discredit Daniel Ellsberg. Under pressure, Nixon had developed a siege mentality. He felt beset by enemies in Congress, in the media, in the federal bureaucracy, the universities, and the streets, all of whom he believed were working to undermine his policies and to weaken his ability to govern. It was a logical progression from the plumbers to the "dirty tricks" of the 1972 presidential campaign that culminated in the Watergate burglary and its attempted coverup. The seeds of the Watergate scandal, which would one day destroy his presidency, can be found in Nixon's inability to end the Vietnam war.

By the summer of 1971, polls showed that support for Vietnamization had dropped to 31 percent. Another poll revealed that two-thirds of Americans approved withdrawing all U.S. troops by the end of the year even if that meant a Communist takeover in South Vietnam. The Senate twice passed resolutions setting a deadline for withdrawal of all troops as soon as Hanoi released the American prisoners of war. Nixon responded to these indicators of war weariness by having Henry Kissinger, then Nixon's national security adviser, make new proposals to Hanoi: In exchange for release of the American prisoners, the United States would withdraw all its troops within six months. For the first time, Kissinger did not insist that Hanoi withdraw its troops that were fighting in South Vietnam. These concessions inaugurated the first serious negotiations since negotiations had begun. But the deadlock continued because Kissinger insisted that General Thieu remain in power, while Hanoi's delegate insisted that Thieu's removal was a precondition of any settlement. After a promising start, the talks eventually broke off and the war went on.

The American role in Vietnam entered its final phase in 1972. Knowing that most American combat troops had been withdrawn from South Vietnam, Hanoi launched its largest offensive of the war in late March. Some 120,000 NVA soldiers struck directly at ARVN forces along three fronts. At the same time, Vietcong guerrillas resumed their assaults in rural areas to disrupt GVN pacification programs, rural development, and land reform projects.

The United States retaliated with B-52 bombing raids in the vicinity of Hanoi and Haiphong. The NVA and VC forces continued to press their attacks against the beleaguered ARVN forces. Nixon then approved the most drastic escalation of the war. He ordered a naval blockade of North Vietnam, the mining of Haiphong harbor, and the largest bombing raids yet in both North and South Vietnam. The war in Southeast Asia reached new levels of destructiveness in the spring of 1972. In addition to his military response, Nixon had Kissinger approach the Soviets again about persuading Hanoi to accept a diplomatic settlement of the war.

Nixon's decisive response to the North Vietnamese offensive got strong support from the American public. Congress also backed the president. The bombing and blockade disrupted North Vietnamese supply lines sufficiently that the hard-pressed ARVN forces were able to stabilize their lines around major cities. The NVA offensive had stalled by summer. South Vietnam, with heavy air and naval support from the United States, had managed to survive. Both the Soviets and the Chinese, while publicly condemning the U.S. military action, privately pressured Hanoi to end its war with the United States. Linkage at last bore fruit and helped Nixon end the American involvement in Vietnam.

With the onset of the summer rains, the war once again stalemated. Hanoi had expected its spring offensive to force the United States to accept its terms and remove Thieu. But Nixon's bold response had neutralized the North Vietnamese assault and inflicted severe losses of men, weapons, and materiel. Soviet pressures pushed Hanoi toward a diplomatic settlement. Nixon's response had also strengthened him at home during a presidential election year. His Democratic challenger in 1972 was Senator George McGovern of South Dakota, an ineffective dove who posed no threat to Nixon or his war policy. A combination of military losses, economic strains, and diplomatic isolation finally convinced Hanoi that it could not drive the Americans out of Vietnam. North Vietnam would have to seek a settlement with the United States, provided that settlement did not conflict with Hanoi's long-sought goal of achieving a unified Vietnam under Communist control.

Secret negotiations resumed in Paris. Hanoi dropped its demand that Thieu must go before any settlement could be reached. Kissinger and the main North Vietnamese emissary, Le Duc Tho, bargained intensively. By October 11, 1972, they had forged the essentials of an agreement: Within 60 days after a cease-fire, the United States would remove all its remaining troops from South Vietnam and North Vietnam would release the American POWs. The Thieu government would remain in power pending a political settlement in South Vietnam. North Vietnamese troops in the South would remain in place. The Provisional Revolution Government (PRG), previously formed by the NLF, would be accorded political status.

But Thieu, who had the most to fear from these arrangements, refused to accept them. Nixon, rejecting Kissinger's advice to ignore Thieu and sign the agreement without him, supported Thieu. The North Vietnamese, believing themselves betrayed, refused to accept any changes in the October agreement. Nixon, perceiving a settlement unlikely, then broke off negotiations.

Reelected by a landslide in November 1972, Nixon decided to use military force in one final effort to get a peace agreement with Hanoi before his new term began. He ordered another air assault on North Vietnam. Nixon told the chairman of the Joint Chiefs, Admiral Thomas Moorer, that he wanted to inflict maximum damage on the North. The response was the most massive attack in the history of aerial warfare. This bombing campaign, quickly dubbed the "Christmas bombing" by the media, occurred between December 18 and 29, 1972. While the bombing—designed to force Hanoi to return to the bargaining table—raged, the president also increased drastically the amount of military aid going to South Vietnam and bluntly told General Thieu to accept the peace terms or else the United States would sign without him.

For the Christmas bombing campaign, U.S. planners targeted only military sites, but some civilian structures were inadvertently destroyed and there were civilian casualties. The bombing provoked worldwide criticism and a storm of protest at home. Nixon's standing in the polls dropped sharply. Congressional leaders indicated that as soon as the new Congress convened, they would take steps to cut off all funding for the war. North Vietnamese air defenders, equipped with Soviet surface-to-air missiles (SAMs) shot down about 15 B-52s, the first time any of the big planes had been brought down by enemy fire. With time running out on his options, Nixon informed the North Vietnamese that if they agreed to resume negotiations, he would halt the bombing. Hanoi accepted the offer and talks resumed in Paris on January 8, 1973.

Kissinger and Le Duc Tho, the chief North Vietnamese negotiator, reached an agreement signed by all parties on January 27. The same day the treaty was signed, Nixon ended the draft at home. The January agreement was the same in all its major provisions as the suspended October agreement. This time Nixon imposed the settlement on Thieu, who signed reluctantly. In order to make the treaty more palatable to Thieu, Nixon pledged in writing that America would respond in full force if North Vietnam violated the agreement. Nixon, subsequently, was unable to honor this commitment.

The January 27, 1973, accords produced neither peace nor honor despite the president's claim that it did both. It was an agreement that permitted the Americans to withdraw from a war they no longer believed in and to retrieve their POWs. It permitted Hanoi to keep an estimated 150,000 troops in South Vietnam and it granted the PRG political legitimacy. The South Vietnamese government received nothing from the agreements, except the opportunity to maintain a precarious existence for a few years. The major question for which the war had been fought for a decade, who would govern in the south, was deferred. According to the agreement, it would be resolved by political means. But the political provisions of the treaty proved unworkable and the question was ultimately resolved by force of arms.

THE END OF THE TUNNEL

There never was an effective cease-fire. The war continued even as Henry Kissinger and Le Duc Tho signed the Paris accords. The Nixon administration continued to support the South Vietnamese government after the U.S. withdrawal, but American efforts were limited by the terms of the agreement, by a lack of public and congressional support, and by Nixon's own deepening involvement in the Watergate scandal that was gradually consuming his presidency. Between 1973 and 1975, Congress further restricted the president's power to reinvolve U.S. forces in the war and reduced the amount of economic and military aid going to the GVN.

When North Vietnam mounted another spring offensive in 1975, South Vietnam suddenly collapsed. This time there was no U.S. military intervention to save the GVN. With South Vietnam's government and people demoralized, its armies lost the will to fight, and the invaders quickly overran its territory. With the end of South Vietnam fast approaching, President Gerald Ford, who had replaced Nixon after he resigned the presidency in August 1974, requested $722 million in emergency aid from Congress for that imperiled nation. Congress refused Ford's request and the president then pronounced the war "finished as far as America is concerned," making American abandonment of South Vietnam official. General Thieu, convinced that the United States had betrayed his country in its hour of desperate need, denounced America and resigned his post. The last Americans and eligible Vietnamese were evacuated from the U.S. embassy in Saigon during the early morning hours of April 30, 1975. Hours later, a phalanx of North Vietnamese tanks pulled up in front of the South Vietnamese capitol building. NVA troops went inside the building and placed the GVN officials they found there under arrest. Announcements over Saigon radio declared the revolution a success. Saigon was renamed Ho Chi Minh City. South Vietnam was swept into the dustbin of history.

The long U.S. effort to prevent a Communist takeover in South Vietnam had finally run its course. It ended in disaster for America and for the people that the United States had tried so hard to help. It was the longest, least popular war in American history. It divided Americans more deeply than any conflict since the Civil War, and it was the first major war that the United States ever lost.

Its aftermath refuted the Cold War assumptions upon which American intervention was based and suggested that the containment ideology itself was dubious. American security was not threatened. American alliances elsewhere were not weakened nor were U.S. allies disheartened by the outcome in Southeast Asia. There was also no unified Communist takeover of Indochina itself. This was because the various states quickly fell to warring among themselves. A vicious Marxist regime, which overthrew Lon Nol's rickety government in Cambodia two weeks before the fall of Saigon, proceeded to slaughter at least a million of its own people. Vietnam, pursuing an imperialistic agenda of its own, invaded Cambodia, then renamed Kampuchea, overthrew the Khmer Rouge, and installed a pro-Vietnamese puppet backed by 180,000 Vietnamese troops. China, allied with Kampuchea and angry at Vietnamese aggression, invaded northern Vietnam. In Laos, the neutralist government was taken over by the Communist Pathet Lao. In these intramural Communist conflicts, the Soviet Union backed the Vietnamese against the Chinese and Khmer Rouge. The United States found itself quietly backing the Chinese in their efforts to contain Vietnamese expansionism. The

Communist leaders' conception of their national interests turned out to be far stronger guides to action than Marxist ideologies. Military victory in Indochina accentuated the internal divisions within the Communist world.

There was no bitter "who lost Vietnam?" debate within the United States. There was no resurgence of McCarthyism or red-baiting. Instead, amnesia set in. For years, few Americans wanted to think about Vietnam or talk about it, much less argue about it or indulge in recriminations.

While the fallacies of the American Cold War ideology may have been exposed by the aftermath of the Vietnam war, and the complex of important American alliances and interests in the Far East remained intact, the harm done to the United States by its long, losing war was nevertheless severe and lasting. George Kennan, the principal theorist of containment, called the Vietnam intervention "the most disastrous of all America's undertakings over the whole two hundred years of its history." The war killed over a million Vietnamese and turned a fourth of the population into refugees. It left 58,000 Americans dead and another 300,000 wounded. There were few parades for returning Vietnam veterans. Most were not welcomed home. A people who had sent them off to fight for a cause in which most no longer believed were embarrassed by their presence. They wanted to ignore the veterans, or worse, condemn them.

The war experience for many veterans had been an ordeal. In addition to facing the usual risks and ravages of combat, many soldiers returned disillusioned by their war experience. The wholesale rejection of the war by the civilian population and eventual U.S. defeat made it difficult for many veterans to derive any meaning from their military service. Thousands of veterans returned maimed, addicted to drugs, or with serious emotional disorders that made it impossible or very difficult for them to adapt successfully to civilian life.

In addition to its human toll, the economic toll of the Vietnam adventure was staggering. Its cost, about $150 billion, was more than any other war in American history except World War II. President Johnson's efforts to finance both a major war and expensive domestic social programs ignited inflation. His refusal to trim domestic spending, raise taxes, or implement economic controls—because he was trying to hide the true costs of war—brought economic decline and lowered living standards for millions of American families.

There were other costs as well. Vietnam undermined public faith in the competence and integrity of government officials. Military service was discredited for years. The war shattered the bipartisan ideological consensus that had guided American foreign policy since the late 1940s. Losing the war proved that American technology and wealth could not defeat a poor Third World nation determined to prevail, nor could the United States support forever an ineffective regime. Americans discovered that there were limits to U.S. power and there were limits to the burdens Americans were willing to bear in pursuit of foreign-policy objectives. For the first time since the Cold War began, many Americans questioned the validity of their global mission to contain Communism. The specter of Vietnam lurked in the background of every foreign-policy debate of the 1970s and 1980s. An arrogance about the use of U.S. military power that existed before the war had been supplanted by a diffident neo-isolationist post-Vietnam yearning to avoid all military involvement in the world. The ultimate domino was America's mythic conception of itself. America's vision of itself as a powerful and benevolent nation perished in the jungles, swamps, and rice paddies of Vietnam.

BOOK I   *Sources*

1

THE ORIGINS
OF AMERICAN
INVOLVEMENT:
1944–1954

Serious American interest in Indochina originated during World War II in Southeast Asia when American armed forces fought in that area to defeat the Japanese, who had occupied the region since 1941. As the war against Japan neared its end, President Franklin Delano Roosevelt concerned himself with Indochina's postwar political status. Disliking and distrusting the French, who had been colonial rulers in Indochina for nearly 80 years preceding the war, Roosevelt initially opposed French efforts to return to Indochina after the Japanese defeat. He searched for a political formula that would lead eventually to independence for the nations that had formerly constituted French Indochina: Vietnam, Cambodia, and Laos. He proposed that Indochina be administered by some sort of international trusteeship for an unspecified number of years. But as the end of the war approached, Roosevelt, concerned about retaining good relations with important European allies, did not oppose French plans to return to Indochina.

**DOCUMENT 1. Roosevelt's Memo to Secretary of State Cordell Hull,
January 24, 1944.**

I saw Halifax [Lord Halifax, the British ambassador to the United States] last week and told him quite frankly that it was perfectly true that I had, for over a year, expressed the opinion that Indo-China should not go back to France, but that it should be administered by an international trusteeship. . . .

    As a matter of interest, I am wholeheartedly supported in this view by Generalissimo Chiang Kai-Shek and by Marshall Stalin. . . . The only reason they [the British] seem to oppose it is that they fear the effect it would have on their possessions and those of the Dutch. They have never liked the idea of trusteeship because it is, in some instances, aimed at future independence. This is true in the case of Indochina.

   Each case must, of course, stand on its own feet, but the case of Indo-China is perfectly clear. France has milked it for one hundred years. The people of Indo-China are entitled to something better than that.

SOURCE: Samuel I. Rosenman, *Public Papers ... of Franklin D. Roosevelt, 1944–1945*, p. 556.

During August 1945, Ho Chi Minh and the Vietminh, taking advantage of the defeat of the Japanese and the temporary absence of French forces, staged a revolution that brought independence to Vietnam for the first time in nearly 80 years. Ho and the Vietminh enjoyed the support of American military and intelligence officers serving in Vietnam. These Americans had previously cooperated with the Vietnamese revolutionaries to defeat the Japanese. On September 2, Ho made a public declaration of Vietnamese independence before an estimated 500,000 people assembled in Hanoi's Ba Dinh Square. Ho, who admired the United States because of its revolutionary tradition, because it had defeated Japan, and because of its official commitment to self-determination for Asian peoples following the war, quoted liberally in his speech from America's Declaration of Independence.

DOCUMENT 2. The Vietnamese Declaration of Independence, September 2, 1945.

"All men are created equal. They are endowed by their Creator with certain inalienable rights; among these are Life, Liberty, and the pursuit of Happiness."

   This immortal statement was made in the Declaration of Independence of the United States of America in 1776. In a broader sense, this means: All the peoples on the earth are equal from birth, all the peoples have a right to live, to be happy and free.

   The Declaration of the French Revolution made in 1791 on the Rights of Man and the Citizen also states: "All men are born free and with equal rights, and must always remain free and have equal rights."

   Those are undeniable truths.

   Nevertheless, for more than eighty years, the French imperialists, abusing the standard of Liberty, Equality, and Fraternity, have violated our Fatherland and oppressed our fellow-citizens. They have acted contrary to the ideals of humanity and justice.

   In the field of politics, they have deprived our people of every democratic liberty.

   They have enforced inhuman laws; they have set up three distinct political regimes in the North, the Center and the South of Vietnam in order to wreck our national unity and prevent our people from being united.

They have built more prisons than schools. They have mercilessly slain our patriots; they have drowned our uprisings in rivers of blood.

They have fettered public opinion; they have practised obscurantism against our people.

To weaken our race they have forced us to use opium and alcohol.

In the field of economics, they have fleeced us to the backbone, impoverished our people, and devastated our land.

They have robbed us of our rice fields, our mines, our forests, and our raw materials. They have monopolized the issuing of bank-notes and the export trade.

They have invented numerous unjustifiable taxes and reduced our people, especially our peasantry, to a state of extreme poverty.

They have hampered the prospering of our national bourgeoisie; they have mercilessly exploited our workers.

In the autumn of 1940, when the Japanese Fascists violated Indochina's territory to establish new bases in their fight against the Allies, the French imperialists went down on their bended knees and handed over our country to them.

Thus, from that date, our people were subjected to the double yoke of the French and the Japanese. Their sufferings and miseries increased. The result was that from the end of last year to the beginning of this year, from Quang Tri province to the North of Vietnam, more than two million of our fellow-citizens died from starvation. On March 9, the French troops were disarmed by the Japanese. The French colonialists either fled or surrendered showing that not only were they incapable of "protecting" us, but that, in the span of five years, they had twice sold our country to the Japanese. . . .

For these reasons, we, members of the Provisional Government, representing the whole Vietnamese people, declare that from now on we break off all relations of a colonial character with France; we repeal all the international obligation that France has so far subscribed to on behalf of Vietnam and we abolish all the special rights the French have unlawfully acquired in our Fatherland.

The whole Vietnamese people, animated by a common purpose, are determined to fight to the bitter end against any attempt by the French colonialists to reconquer their country.

We are convinced that the Allied nations, which at Tehran and San Francisco have acknowledged the principles of self-determination and equality of nations, will not refuse to acknowledge the independence of Vietnam.

A people who have courageously opposed French domination for more than eight years, a people who have fought side by side with the Allies against the Fascists during these last years, such a people must be free and independent.

For these reasons, we, members of the Provisional Government of the Democratic Republic of Vietnam, solemnly declare to the world that Vietnam has the right to be a free and independent country—and in fact is so already. The entire Vietnamese people are determined to mobilize all their physical and mental strength, to sacrifice their lives and property in order to safeguard their independence and liberty.

SOURCE: Ho Chi Minh, *Selected Works*, Vol. 3, pp. 17–21.

Roosevelt's successor, Harry Truman, who took office following FDR's death in April 1945, did not share Roosevelt's commitment to postwar Asian nationalism. His foreign policy was grounded on containing Soviet expansion in Europe. He was determined to strengthen western European nations, particularly France, to help them resist both Soviet pressures and the internal threats posed by domestic Communist parties. When the French began their efforts to reclaim Vietnam, Truman permitted them a free hand in Indochina as a supporting part of America's Euro-centered policy of backing France in the face of Communist threats.

DOCUMENT 3. United States Statement of Policy, October 1945.

US has no thought of opposing the reestablishment of French control in Indo-china and no official statement by US GOVT has questioned even by implication French sovereignty over Indochina. However, it is not the policy of this GOVT to assist the French to reestablish their control over Indochina by force and the willingness of the US to see the French control reestablished assumes that French claim to have the support of the population of Indochina is borne out by future events.

SOURCE: Mike Gravel (ed.), *The Pentagon Papers*, Vol. 1, pp. 16–17.

Amidst a complex political environment in Vietnam in the fall of 1945, Ho Chi Minh maneuvered desperately to save his fledgling government. In accordance with secret agreements worked out at the Potsdam conference among the victorious Allied powers, the French, with British and American assistance, had returned to southern Vietnam. At the same time, Chinese Nationalist forces occupied northern Vietnam. The Soviet Union had no interest in Vietnam at this juncture and was not involved despite Ho's Marxist commitments and his previous residency in the USSR. Isolated and without allies, Ho and the Vietminh had to face their powerful enemies alone. Ho tried to persuade American leaders to support United Nations' intervention in support of Vietnamese independence. Altogether, Ho wrote seven letters to President Truman and to Secretary of State James F. Byrnes. Because Washington did not recognize Ho's government nor regard him as a true head of state, his missives were ignored. None, including the following letter, were ever answered.

DOCUMENT 4. Ho Chi Minh's Letter to Secretary of State James F. Byrnes, October 22, 1945.

Excellency: The situation in South Vietnam has reached its critical stage, and calls for immediate interference on the part of the United Nations. I wish by the present letter to bring your excellency some more light on the case of Vietnam which has come for the last three weeks into the international limelight. . . .

After 80 years of French oppression and unsuccessful though obstinate Vietnamese resistance, we at last saw France defeated in Europe, then her betrayal of the Allies successively on behalf of Germany and of Japan. Though the odds were at that time against the Allies, the Vietnamese, leaving aside all differences in political opinion, united in the Vietminh League and started on a ruthless fight against the Japanese. Meanwhile, the Atlantic Charter was concluded, defining the war aims of the Allies and laying the foundation of peace-work. The noble principles of international justice and equality of status laid down in that charter strongly appealed to the Vietnamese and contributed in making of the Vietminh resistance in the war zone a nation-wide anti-Japanese movement which found a powerful echo in the democratic aspirations of the people. The Atlantic Charter was looked upon as the foundation of future Vietnam. A nation-building program was drafted which was later found in keeping with San Francisco Charter and which has been fully carried out these last years: continuous fight against the Japanese bringing about the recovery of national independence on August 19th, voluntary abdication of Ex-Emperor Baodai, establishment of the Democratic Republic of Vietnam, assistance given to the Allies Nations in the disarmament of the Japanese, appointment of a provisional Government whose mission was to carry out the Atlantic and San Francisco Charters and have them carried out by other nations.

As a matter of fact, the carrying out of the Atlantic and San Francisco Charters implies the eradication of imperialism and all forms of colonial oppression. This was unfortunately contrary to the interest of some Frenchmen, and France, to whom the colonists have long concealed the truth on Indochina, instead of entering into peaceable negotiations, resorted to an aggressive invasion, with all the means at the command of a modern nation. Moreover, having persuaded the British that the Vietnamese are wishing for a return of the French rule, they obtained, first from the British command in Southeast Asia, then from London, a tacit recognition of their sovereignty and administrative responsibility as far as South Vietnam is concerned. The British gave to understand that they had agreed to this on the ground that the reestablishment of French administration and, consequently, of Franco-Vietnamese collaboration would help them to speed up the demobilization and the disarmament of the Japanese. But subsequent events will prove the fallacy of the argument. The whole Vietnamese nation rose up as one man against French aggression. The first hours of September 23rd soon developed into real and organized warfare in which losses are heavy on both sides. The bringing in of French important reinforcements on board of the most powerful of their remaining warships will extend the war zone further. As murderous fighting is still going on in Indonesia, and as savage acts on the part of Frenchmen are reported every day, we may expect the flaring up of a general conflagration in the Far-East.

As it is, the situation in South Vietnam calls for immediate interference. The establishment of the Consultative Commission for the Far-East has been enthusiastically welcomed here as the first effective step toward an equitable settlement of the pending problems. The people of Vietnam, which only asks for full independence and for the respect of truth and justice....

SOURCE: Gareth Porter (ed.), *Vietnam: The Definitive Documentation of Human Decisions*, Vol. 1, pp. 84–85.

While Ho Chi Minh was trying to persuade the United States to support the cause of Vietnamese independence, he also entered into negotiations with the French. While conducting these negotiations with Ho in early 1946, the French also simultaneously negotiated an agreement with the Chinese Nationalists. The French, in exchange for renouncing all their remaining concessions in China, persuaded the Chinese to withdraw their forces from Tonkin (northern Vietnam). The British had meanwhile withdrawn from Cochinchina (southern Vietnam), leaving the French forces in control of Saigon. Still trying to maneuver for space in which to preserve his revolutionary government, Ho reached an accord with the French on March 6, 1946. It provided for temporarily stationing French troops in Tonkin to replace the departing Chinese in exchange for France's apparent recognition of the Vietminh government, The Democratic Republic of Vietnam (DRV), as a "free state" forming part of the "French Union."

DOCUMENT 5. The Franco-Vietminh Accord, March 6, 1946.

1. The French Government recognizes the Vietnamese Republic as a Free State having its own Government, its own Parliament, its own Army, and its own Finances, forming part of the Indochinese Federation and of the French Union....

2. The Vietnamese Government declares itself ready to welcome amicably the French Army when, conforming to international agreements, it relieves the Chinese Troops....

SOURCE: Gravel (ed.), *Pentagon Papers*, Vol. 1, pp. 18–19.

In subsequent negotiations with the French, the Vietnamese discovered that Paris had no intention of recognizing the Democratic Republic of Vietnam or conceding it sovereignty. The French appeared determined to reimpose colonialism on the

Vietnamese, who were absolutely determined to prevent it even if it meant fighting a war against their former imperial masters. The Franco-Vietminh war began in late November 1946.

Washington adopted a neutral stance toward the Franco-Vietminh war, but it was, in effect, a pro-French neutrality. The United States furnished covert economic and military assistance to the French war. Whatever misgivings Washington may have felt about either the efficacy or morality of French colonialism in Indochina was offset by the American dread of political disorder in that region and of a Communist leader coming to power in Vietnam.

The French were unable to defeat the Vietminh forces and the war dragged on inconclusively for years. A major turning point in evolving U.S. interests in Indochina occurred in 1949. In the aftermath of the Soviets achieving a nuclear capability and of the Maoist revolution in China, American leaders redefined American vital interests in Southeast Asia. Containment of Communism, originating in Washington's response to Soviet pressures in southern Europe in 1947, was extended to Southeast Asia. The Truman administration viewed Chinese Communism as a component of an international expansionist conspiracy headquartered in Moscow whose ultimate goal was world domination. President Truman and Secretary of State Dean Acheson incorporated the French effort to recolonize the Vietnamese into a new U.S. foreign policy objective: containing Communist China. An area, formerly of merely peripheral concern, had become a vital American foreign policy interest. Washington expanded the purposes of the French imperialist effort in Indochina to include preventing the fall of Vietnam, Cambodia, and Laos to Communism. During the summer of 1950, the United States began sending military and economic aid to a Vietnamese regime that the French had installed in Saigon under former emperor Bao Dai.

DOCUMENT 6. Secretary of State Dean Acheson's Statement of U.S. Indochina Policy, May 22, 1950.

... We have noted the fact that the problem of meeting the threat to the security of Vietnam, Cambodia, and Laos which now enjoy independence within the French Union is primarily the responsibility of France and the Governments and peoples of Indochina. The United States recognizes that the solution of the Indochina problem depends both upon the restoration of security and upon the development of genuine nationalism and that United States assistance can and should contribute to these major objectives.

The United States Government, convinced that neither national independence nor democratic evolution exists in any area dominated by Soviet imperialism, considers the situation to be such as to warrant its according economic aid and military equipment to the Associated States of Indochina and to France in order to assist them in restoring stability and permitting these states to pursue their peaceful and democratic development.

SOURCE: *Department of State Bulletin*, No. 22, May 22, 1950, p. 821.

The first U.S. military aid to the French colonial war in Vietnam arrived in September 1950. Each year for the remainder of the war, the amount of American aid increased. By 1954, the United States was paying nearly 80 percent of the cost of France's Indochina war. Yet, despite extensive American aid, the French and their Vietnamese supporters were losing the war. The war turned in favor of the Vietminh in 1951, and by 1954 the French position in Indochina had badly deteriorated. President Eisenhower, who had succeeded Truman in January 1953, promptly embraced the policy of backing the French war. In a famous press conference held April 7, 1954, Eisenhower commented on the strategic importance of Indochina for America and the free world. In defending U.S. Indochina policy, the president set forth the domino theory, which, in various formulations, would serve as the prime ideological justification for later American intervention in Vietnam.

DOCUMENT 7. Eisenhower Counts the Dominoes, April 7, 1954.

Q. ROBERT RICHARDS, COPLEY PRESS: Mr. President, would you mind commenting on the strategic importance of Indochina to the free world? I think there has been, across the country, some lack of understanding on just what it means to us.

THE PRESIDENT: You have, of course, both the specific and the general when you talk about such things.

First of all, you have the specific value of a locality in its production of materials that the world needs.

Then you have the possibility that many human beings pass under a dictatorship that is inimical to the free world.

Finally, you have broader considerations that might follow what you would call the "falling domino" principle. You have a row of dominoes set up, you knock over the first one, and what will happen to the last one is the certainty that it will go over very quickly. So you could have a beginning of a disintegration that would have the most profound influences.

Now, with respect to the first one, two of the items from this particular area that the world uses are tin and tungsten. They are very important. There are others, of course, the rubber plantations and so on.

Then with respect to more people passing under this domination, Asia, after all, has already lost some 450 million of its peoples to the Communist dictatorship, and we simply can't afford greater losses.

But when we come to the possible sequence of events, the loss of Indochina, of Burma, of Thailand, of the Peninsula, and Indonesia following, now you begin to talk about areas that not only multiply the disadvantages that you would suffer through loss of materials, sources of materials, but now you are talking really about millions and millions and millions of people.

Finally, the geographical position achieved thereby does many things. It turns the so-called island defensive chain of Japan, Formosa, of the Philippines and to the southward; it moves in to threaten Australia and New Zealand.

It takes away, in its economic aspects, that region that Japan must have as a trading area or Japan, in turn, will have only one place in the world to go—that is, toward the Communist areas in order to live.

So, the possible consequences of the loss are just incalculable to the free world.

SOURCE: *Public Papers of the Presidents of the United States: Dwight D. Eisenhower, 1954*, pp. 381–390.

By 1954 the Vietminh forces controlled most of Vietnam. Pressured by the Americans, the French tried to regain the military initiative. They put thousands of their best troops in Dien Bien Phu, a remote site in northwestern Vietnam near the Laotian border, deep within enemy-controlled territory. French leaders did not believe that Asian guerrillas could defeat European forces in a large-scale conventional battle. But General Vo Nguyen Giap, the Vietminh commander, quickly crafted a strategy to defeat the French. After weeks of siege warfare, the French position grew desperate. The Vietminh verged on victory. With war weariness strong in France after eight years of costly and futile fighting, the fall of Dien Bien Phu would mean victory for the Vietminh revolutionaries and the expulsion of France from Indochina.

Facing imminent ruin, the French appealed to Washington to intervene and save them. Eisenhower considered U.S. air strikes to break the siege around Dien Bien Phu, but he insisted that America's allies join the effort and that Congress support it. When he was rebuffed by the British and told by Senate leaders that they could not approve intervention without allied support, Eisenhower refused the French request. Dien Bien Phu fell on May 7, 1954.

The next day an international conference meeting in Geneva began to seek a political solution to the Franco-Vietminh war. By late July, a settlement had been reached. Both sides agreed to a cease-fire and to a temporary partition of Vietnam at the 17th parallel. French and Vietnamese loyalist forces were to regroup south of that line and Vietminh forces and their supporters north of it. The Geneva agreements also called for free elections to be held within two years to unify the country. During the interim, the French forces were to help the Vietnamese prepare for independence and the forthcoming elections and then depart.

DOCUMENT 8. The Final Declarations of the Geneva Conference, July 21, 1954.

1. The Conference takes note of the Agreements ending hostilities in Cambodia, Laos, and Viet-nam and organizing international control and the supervision of the execution of the provisions of these agreements.

2. The Conference expresses satisfaction at the ending of hostilities in Cambodia, Laos, and Viet-nam; the Conference expresses its conviction that the execution of the provisions set out in the present Declaration and in the Agreements on the cessation of hostilities will permit Cambodia, Laos and Viet-nam henceforth to play their part, in full independence and sovereignty, in the peaceful community of nations.

3. The Conference takes note of the declarations made by the Governments of Cambodia and of Laos of their intention to adopt measures permitting all citizens to take their place in the national community, in particular by participating in the next general elections, which, in conformity with the constitution of each of these countries, shall take place in the course of the year 1955, by secret ballot and in conditions of respect for fundamental freedoms.

4. The Conference takes note of the clauses in the Agreement on the cessation of hostilities in Viet-nam prohibiting the introduction into Vietnam of foreign troops and military personnel as well as all kinds of arms and munitions. The Conference also takes note of the declarations made by the Governments of Cambodia and Laos of their resolution not to request foreign aid, whether in war material, in personnel or in instructors except for the purpose of the effective defence of their territory and, in the case of Laos, to the extent defined by the Agreements on the cessation of hostilities in Laos.

5. The Conference takes note of the clauses in the Agreement on the cessation of hostilities in Viet-nam to the effect that no military base under the control of a foreign State may be established in the regrouping zones of the two parties, the latter having the obligation to see that the zones allotted to them shall not constitute part of any military alliance and shall not be utilized for the resumption of hostilities or in the service of an aggressive policy. The Conference also takes note of the declarations of the Governments of Cambodia and Laos to the effect that they will not join in any agreement with other States if this agreement includes the obligation to participate in a military alliance not in conformity with the principles of the Charter of the United Nations or, in the case of Laos, with the principles of the Agreement on the cessation of hostilities in Laos or, so long as their security is not threatened, the obligation to establish bases on Cambodian or Laotian territory for the military forces of foreign powers.

6. The Conference recognizes that the essential purpose of the Agreement relating to Viet-nam is to settle military questions with a view to ending hostilities and that the military demarcation line is provisional and should not in any way be interpreted as constituting a political or territorial boundary. The Conference expresses its conviction that the execution of the provisions set out in the present Declaration and in the Agreement on the cessation of hostilities creates the necessary basis for the achievement in the near future of a political settlement in Viet-nam.

7. The Conference declares that, so far as Viet-nam is concerned, the settlement of political problems, effected on the basis of respect for principles of independence, unity and territorial integrity, shall permit the Vietnamese people to enjoy the fundamental freedoms, guaranteed by democratic institutions established as a result of free general elections by secret ballot. In order to ensure that sufficient progress in the restoration of peace has been made and that all the necessary conditions obtain for free expression of the national will, general elections shall be held in July 1956, under the supervision of an international commission composed of representatives of the Member States of the International Supervisory Commission, referred to in the Agreement on the cessation of hostilities. Consultations will be held on this subject between the competent representative authorities of the two zones from 20 July, 1955 onwards.

8. The provisions of the Agreements on the cessation of hostilities intended to ensure the protection of individuals and of property must be most strictly applied and must, in particular, allow everyone in Viet-nam to decide freely in which zone he wishes to live.

9. The competent representative authorites of the Northern and Southern zones of Viet-nam, as well as the authorities of Laos and Cambodia, must not permit any individual or collective reprisals against persons who have collaborated in any way with one of the parties during the war, or against members of such persons' families.

10. The Conference takes note of the declaration of the Government of the French Republic to the effect that it is ready to withdraw its troops from the territory of Cambodia, Laos and Viet-nam, at the request of the governments concerned and within periods which shall be fixed by agreement between the parties except in the cases where, by agreement between the two parties, a certain number of French troops shall remain at specified points and for a specified time.

11. The Conference takes note of the declaration of the French Government to the effect that for the settlement of all the problems connected with the re-establishment and consolidation of peace in Cambodia, Laos and Viet-nam, the French Government will proceed from the principle of respect for the independence and sovereignty, unity and territorial integrity of Cambodia, Laos and Viet-nam.

12. In their relations with Cambodia, Laos and Viet-nam, each member of the Geneva Conference undertakes to respect the sovereignty, the independence, the unity and the territorial integrity of the above-mentioned States, and to refrain from any interference in their internal affairs.

13. The members of the Conference agree to consult one another on any question which may be referred to them by the International Supervisory Commission, in order to study such measures as may prove necessary to ensure that the Agreements on the cessation of hostilities in Cambodia, Laos and Vietnam are respected.

SOURCE: Gravel (ed.), *Pentagon Papers*, Vol. 1, pp. 279–282.

The American position at the Geneva conference was an awkward one. Washington would have much preferred for the French to continue their war in Indochina with American backing rather than negotiate with the Vietminh. The Eisenhower administration feared that any political settlement coming out of the conference would be tantamount to a Communist victory. The United States opposed the accords, but was powerless to prevent them. Undersecretary of State Walter Bedell Smith delivered the American response to the Geneva declarations. The United States pledged to refrain from the use of force to "disturb" the agreements and also promised to do nothing to prevent the reunification of Vietnam by free elections.

DOCUMENT 9. The American Response to the Geneva Declarations, July 21, 1954.

Declaration

The Government of the United States being resolved to devote its efforts to the strengthening of peace in accordance with the principles and purposes of the United Nations takes note of the agreements concluded at Geneva on July 20 and 21, 1954 between (a) the Franco-Laotian Command and the Command of the Peoples Army of Viet-Nam; (b) the Royal Khmer Army Command and the Command of the Peoples Army of Viet-Nam; (c) Franco-Vietnamese Command and the Command of the Peoples Army of Viet-Nam and of paragraphs 1 to 12 inclusive of the declaration presented to the Geneva Conference on July 21, 1954 declares with regard to the aforesaid agreements and paragraphs that (i) it will refrain from the threat or the use of force to disturb them, in accordance with Article 2(4) of the Charter of the United Nations dealing with the obligation of members to refrain in their international relations from the threat or use of force; and (ii) it would view any renewal of the aggression in violation of the aforesaid agreements with grave concern and as seriously threatening international peace and security.

In connection with the statement in the declaration concerning free elections in Viet-Nam my Government wishes to make clear its position which it has expressed in a declaration made in Washington on June 29, 1954, as follows:

> In the case of nations now divided against their will, we shall continue to seek to achieve unity through free elections supervised by the United Nations to insure that they are conducted fairly.

With respect to the statement made by the representative of the State of Viet-Nam, the United States reiterates its traditional position that peoples are entitled to determine their own future and that it will not join in an arrangement which would hinder this. Nothing in its declaration just made is intended to or does indicate any departure from this traditional position.

We share the hope that the agreements will permit Cambodia, Laos and Viet-Nam to play their part, in full independence and sovereignty, in the peaceful community of nations, and will enable the peoples of that area to determine their own future.

SOURCE: Neil Sheehan and others (eds.), *The Pentagon Papers*, pp. 52–53.

After the Geneva Conference, the Eisenhower administration salvaged what it could from what it regarded as a disastrous defeat for the free world, namely a major Communist victory that gave the Communists half of Vietnam and threatened all Southeast Asia. In September 1954, Secretary of State John Foster Dulles arranged with several Southeast Asian and European nations to create the Southeast Asia Treaty Organization (SEATO). A separate protocol to the SEATO treaty extended protection to Laos, Cambodia, and that part of Vietnam lying south of the 17th parallel. SEATO provided a legal basis for the projection of American power into Indochina in the aftermath of the French disaster in Vietnam and the Geneva accords.

DOCUMENT 10. Protocol to the SEATO Treaty, September 8, 1954.

Designation of States and Territory as to Which Provisions of Article IV and Article III are to be Applicable.

The Parties to the Southeast Asia Collective Defense Treaty unanimously designate for the purposes of Article IV of the Treaty the States of Cambodia and Laos and the free territory under the jurisdiction of the State of Vietnam.

The Parties further agree that the above mentioned states and territory shall be eligible in respect of the economic measures contemplated by Article III.

This Protocol shall enter into force simultaneously with the coming into force of the Treaty.

IN WITNESS WHEREOF, the undersigned Plenipotentiaries have signed this Protocol to the Southeast Asia Collective Defense Treaty.

Done at Manila, this eighth day of September, 1954.

SOURCE: U.S. Department of State, *American Foreign Policy, 1950–1955*, pp. 912–913.

In the aftermath of the Geneva settlement, along with the formation of the SEATO alliance, the United States made a fateful decision to intervene directly in southern Vietnam. Washington extended military and economic support to a new government emerging in South Vietnam headed by Premier Ngo Dinh Diem, a staunch anti-Communist nationalist. American advisers trained and equipped Diem's army and security forces, and U.S. technical experts established a variety of aid programs designed to modernize and stabilize the government and economy of South Vietnam.

DOCUMENT 11. Eisenhower's Letter of Support to Ngo Dinh Diem, October 23, 1954.

Dear Mr. President: I have been following with great interest the course of developments in Viet-Nam, particularly since the conclusion of the conference at Geneva. The implications of the agreement concerning Viet-Nam have caused grave concern regarding the future of a country temporarily divided by an artificial military grouping, weakened by a long and exhausting war and faced with enemies without and by their subversive collaborators within.

Your recent requests for aid to assist in the formidable project of the movement of several hundred thousand loyal Vietnamese citizens away from areas which are passing under a *de facto* rule and political ideology which they abhor, are being fulfilled. I am glad that the United States is able to assist in this humanitarian effort.

We have been exploring ways and means to permit our aid to Viet-Nam to be more effective and to make a greater contribution to the welfare and stability of the government of Viet-Nam. I am, accordingly, instrucing the American Ambassador to Viet-Nam to examine with you in your capacity as Chief of Government, how an intelligent program of American aid given directly to your Government can serve to assist Viet-Nam in its present hour of trial, provided that your Government is prepared to give assurances as to the standards of performance it would be able to maintain in the event such aid were supplied.

The purpose of this offer is to assist the Government of Viet-Nam in developing and maintaining a strong, viable state, capable of resisting attempted subversion or aggression through military means. The Government of the United States expects that this aid will be met by performance on the part of the Government of Viet-Nam in undertaking needed reforms. It hopes that such aid, combined with your own continuing efforts, will contribute effectively toward an independent Viet-Nam endowed with a strong government. Such a government would, I hope, be so responsive to the nationalist aspirations of its people, so enlightened in purpose and effective in performance, that it will be respected both at home and abroad and discourage any who might wish to impose a foreign ideology on your free people.

Sincerely,

Dwight D. Eisenhower

SOURCE: *Department of State Bulletin*, November 15, 1954, pp. 735–736.

In addition to sending military advisers and various technical personnel to help strengthen the emergent South Vietnamese government and economy, Washington assigned a team of CIA operatives, led by Air Force Colonel Edward G. Landsdale, to South Vietnam. Operating under the auspices of the Saigon Military Mission, they undertook various covert and paramilitary operations to strengthen Diem's control, to organize resistance against Vietminh forces in southern Vietnam, and to carry out paramilitary, espionage, and sabotage activities against the North Vietnamese.

DOCUMENT 12. Excerpts from the *Report of the Saigon Military Mission,* 1954–1955.

d. October 1954

Hanoi was evacuated on 9 October. The northern SMM team left with the last French troops, disturbed by what they had seen of the grim efficiency of the Vietminh in their takeover, the contrast between the silent march of the victorious Vietminh troops in their tennis shoes and the clanking armor of the well-equipped French whose Western tactics and equipment had failed against the Communist military-political-economic campaign.

The northern team had spent the last days of Hanoi in contaminating the oil supply of the bus company for a gradual wreckage of engines in the buses, in taking the first actions for delayed sabotage of the railroad (which required teamwork with a CIA special technical team in Japan who performed their part brilliantly), and in writing detailed notes of potential targets for future paramilitary operations (U.S. adherence to the Geneva Agreement prevented SMM from carrying out the active sabotage it desired to do against the power plant, water facilities, harbor, and bridge). The team had a bad moment when contaminating the oil. They had to work quickly at night, in an enclosed storage room. Fumes from the contaminant came close to knocking them out. Dizzy and weak-kneed, they masked their faces with handkerchiefs and completed the job.

Meanwhile, Polish and Russian ships had arrived in the south to transport southern Vietminh to Tonkin under the Geneva Agreement. This offered the opportunity for another black psywar strike. A leaflet was developed by Binh with the help of Capt Arundel, attributed to the Vietminh Resistance Committee.

Among other items, it reassured the Vietminh they would be kept safe below decks from imperialist air and submarine attacks, and requested that warm clothing be brought; the warm clothing item would be coupled with a verbal rumor campaign that Vietminh were being sent into China as railroad laborers.

SMM had been busily developing G-5 of the Vietnamese Army for such psywar efforts. Under Arundel's direction, the First Armed Propaganda Company printed the leaflets and distributed them, by soldiers in civilian clothes who penetrated into southern Vietminh zones on foot. (Distribution in Camau was made while columnist Joseph Alsop was on his visit there which led to his sensational, gloomy articles later; our soldier "Vietminh" failed in an attempt to get the leaflet into Alsop's hands in Canau; Alsop was never told this story.) Intelligence reports and other later reports revealed that village and delegation committees complained about "deportation" to the north, after distribution of the leaflet. . . .

Contention between Diem and Hinh had become murderous. . . . Finally, we learned that Hinh was close to action; he had selected 26 October as the morning for an attack on the Presidential Palace. Hinh was counting heavily on Lt-Col Lan's special forces and on Captain Giai who was running Hinh's secret headquarters at Hinh's home. We invited these two officers to visit the Philippines, on the pretext that we were making an official trip, could take them along and open the way for them to see some inner workings of the fight against Filipino Communists which they probably would never see otherwise. Hinh reluctantly turned down his own invitation; he had had a memorable time of it on his last visit to Manila in 1952. Lt-Col Lan was a French agent and the temptation to see behind-the-scenes was too much. He and Giai accompanied SMM officers on the MAAG C–47 which General O'Daniel instantly made available for the operation. 26 October was spent in the Philippines. The attack on the palace didn't come off.

e. November 1954

General Lawton Collins arrived as Ambassador on 8 November. . . .

Collins, in his first press conference, made it plain that the U.S. was supporting President Diem. The new Ambassador applied pressure on General Hinh and on 29 November Hinh left for Paris. His other key conspirators followed.

Part of the SMM team became involved in staff work to back up the energetic campaign to save Vietnam which Collins pushed forward. Some SMM members were scattered around the Pacific, accompanying Vietnamese for secret training, obtaining and shipping supplies to be smuggled into north Vietnam and hidden there. In the Philippines, more support was being constructed to help SMM, in expediting the flow of supplies, and in creating Freedom Company, a non-profit Philippines corporation backed by President Magsaysay, which would supply Filipinos experienced in fighting the Communist Huks to help in Vietnam (or elsewhere). . . .

On 23 November, twenty-one selected Vietnamese agents and two cooks of our Hao paramilitary group were put aboard a Navy ship in the Saigon River, in daylight. They appeared as coolies, joined the coolie and refugee throng moving on and off ship, and disappeared one by one. It was brilliantly planned and executed, agents being picked up from unobtrusive assembly points throughout the metropolis. Lt Andrews made the plans and carried out the movement under the supervision of Major Allen. The ship took the Hao agents, in compartmented groups, to an overseas point, the first stage in a movement to a secret training area.

f. December 1954

. . . discussions between the U.S., Vietnamese and French had reached a point where it appeared that a military training mission using U.S. officers was in the immediate offing. General O'Daniel had a U.S.-French planning group working on the problem, under Col. Rosson. One paper they were developing was a plan for pacification of Vietminh and dissident areas; this paper was passed to SMM for its assistance with the drafting. SMM wrote much of the paper, changing the concept from the old rigid police controls of all areas to some of our concepts of winning over the population and instituting a classification of areas by the amount of trouble in each, the amount of control required, and fixing responsibilities between civil and military authorities. With a few changes, this was issued by President Diem on 31 December as the National Security Action (Pacification) Directive. . . .

There was still much disquite in Vietnam, particularly among anti-Communist political groups who were not included in the government. SMM officers were contacted by a number of such groups who felt that they "would have to commit suicide in 1956" (the 1956 plebiscite promised in the 1954 Geneva agreement), when the Vietminh would surely take over against so weak a government. One group of farmers and militia in the south was talked out of migrating to Madagascar by SMM and staying on their farms. A number of these groups asked SMM for help in training personnel for eventual guerrilla warfare if the Vietminh won. Persons such as the then Minister of Defense and Trinh Minh The were among those loyal to the government who also requested such help. It was decided that a more basic guerrilla training program might be undertaken for such groups than was available at the secret training site to which we had sent the Binh and Hao groups. Plans were made with Major Bohanan and Mr. John C. Wachtel in the Philippines for a solution of this problem; the United States backed the development, through them, of a small Freedom Company training camp in a hidden valley on the Clark AFB reservation.

Till and Peg Durdin of the N. Y. Times, Hank Lieberman of the N. Y. Times, Homer Bigart of the N. Y. Herald-Tribune, John Mecklin of Life-Time, and John Roderick of Associated Press, have been warm friends of SMM and worked hard to penetrate the fabric of French propaganda and give the U.S. an objective account of events in Vietnam. The group met with us at times to analyze objectives and motives of propaganda known to them, meeting at their own request as U.S. citizens. These mature and responsible news correspondents performed a valuable service for their country. . . .

SOURCE: Sheehan and others (eds.), *Pentagon Papers*, pp. 60–63.

2
GETTING IN DEEPER: 1955–1963

Diem's government nearly fell in the spring of 1955 when he challenged two powerful religious sects, the Cao Dai and the Hoa/Hao, and also confronted the Binh Xuyen, the crime lords of Saigon and Cholon. Open war raged in the streets of Saigon. It looked as if Diem were going to be defeated and Washington about to abandon him. But Diem, with crucial assistance from Col. Landsdale, who headed the CIA operatives, vanquished his foes and survived. The French, who had backed Diem's opponents, abandoned whatever remained of their hopes to retain influence in South Vietnam and prepared to depart. Diem also moved to eliminate Bao Dai, who was still the nominal head of the emerging South Vietnamese nation. Diem conducted a rigged election on October 23, 1955, to determine whether he or Bao Dai would be head of state. Diem's officials, who counted the votes, announced that their man had won with 98.2 percent of the votes! A constitutional convention met and drafted an outline for a republican form of government modeled on the U.S. Constitution. The Eisenhower administration re-embraced Diem, and Secretary of State John Foster Dulles praised Diem for the progress that he had made.

DOCUMENT 13. Secretary of State John Foster Dulles Praises Ngo Dinh Diem, 1956.

Diem has done a wonderful job, of course with our help, in cleaning up his sect armies. There were three independent groups: the Binh Xuyen, who had charge of the police in Saigon, and who dispensed the prostitution and the gambling privileges; and then there were the Hoa/Hao and the Cao Dai.

All of them now have been liquidated, at least as far as their independent army or police was concerned, and there are small mopping-up operations still to be done. But the back of the problem has been broken, and Diem's authority throughout the area is now generally accepted.

That, as I say, has been done with the great help from the United States in training and equipping his national forces. They have performed loyally and efficiently, and have brought central authority into the country to a degree which is really quite amazing. . . .

They have had there the general elections, and the day I left, they were holding their first constituent assembly convention meeting, and the foundation has just been laid for a representative form of government.

Bao Dai has been eliminated, and there is a chance for really building a strong and effective anti-Communist regime in an area where for a time it looked as though it would be swept away as a result of the French defeat in the Hanoi area, notably, at Dienbienphu, and by the unfavorable armistice terms.

SOURCE: United States Senate, *Senate Foreign Relations Committee Hearings*, Vol. 8, pp. 159–161.

During 1956, as the deadline approached for holding nationwide elections in Vietnam to unify the country as called for in the Geneva accords, Diem refused to permit them in his half of Vietnam. The United States supported Diem's actions even though it was inconsistent with America's calls for free elections in other divided countries such as Germany and Korea, and it contradicted the U.S. statement issued at the time of the accords by Undersecretary of State Walter Bedell Smith pledging support of the elections (see Document 9).

Diem justified his refusal to hold elections on the grounds that his government did not consider itself bound by protocols that it did not sign. He also claimed that North Vietnam had violated the terms of the agreements, which was true, and that Hanoi would never permit free elections. Diem failed to mention another reason for not holding the elections: President Eisenhower acknowledged that had the elections been held during the summer of 1956 to reunite Vietnam in accordance with the provisions of the Geneva accords, Ho Chi Minh would have gotten 80 percent of the vote. Diem's government had also committed more violations of the Geneva agreements than had Hanoi.

DOCUMENT 14. *Report of the International Commission for Supervision and Control in Vietnam, 1956–1957, pp. 26–31.*

Co-operation of the Parties to the Agreement

Difficulties in South Vietnam
Cases where the Commission's Activities are being hindered

71. Another major difficulty is the time notice restrictions placed by the authorities in South Vietnam on the Commission's Fixed Teams. . . .

The Commission had made it clear that the existence of such time notices makes it impossible for its teams to carry out all their duties effectively....

72. The provisions of Articles 16 and 17 ... have not been fully implemented by the French High Command. The notifications which the parties have undertaken to give under the provisions of these Articles were not received regularly by the Commission. Thirty-six cases have been recorded where no notifications have been received by the Commission's team in Saigon and on fourteen occasions the team actually saw military personnel deplaning at Saigon airfield. The Commission has repeatedly taken serious objection to the failure of the French High Command to give the required notifications under Articles 16 and 17. On April 25, 1956, the French High Command informed the Commission that the Government of the Republic of Vietnam had indicated its consent to give the required notifications.

73. The Commission has been unable to conduct reconnaissance and control of ... airfields in South Vietnam ... The Commission had asked that immediate arrangements should be made for the reconnaissance and control of the airfields as the case may be. Because of this lack of co-operation, the Commission has not been able to supervise all airfields in the discharge of its statutory duties under Article 36(*d*)....

76. Apart from the hindrances in South Vietnam mentioned above, there are cases where specific recommendations of the Commission have not been implemented by the French High Command or where implementation has been delayed. The majority of cases concern recommendations made by the Commission regarding release of civilian internees from prisons in South Vietnam....

In spite of repeated requests, twenty-one recommendations regarding release of civilian internees have not been implemented. In nineteen cases, the authorities of the Republic of Vietnam have rejected the Commission's recommendations on the ground that the persons concerned were former members of the [Vietminh] armed forces.... [T]he Commission gave very careful consideration to the legal aspect of the matter and confirmed its recommendations. In spite of this, the recommendations have not been implemented....

77. The Commission conveyed on February 24, 1956, its recommendations that notifications of import of war material and introduction of military personnel should be given in writing to the Central Joint Commission as laid down in Articles 16 and 17 and for this purpose a Central Secretariat should be set up. The French High Command has not accepted these recommendations.

Difficulties in North Vietnam
Cases where the Commission's Activities are being hindered

79. There also exist cases in North Vietnam where the Commission's activities are being hindered. The case of Mobile Team F-44 ... [in which] the Commission has been experiencing a major difficulty, has been pending with the Commission since April 1955, and the Commission's repeated efforts to complete the investigation have not been successful so far. Various reasons have been given by the P.A.V. High Command for not arranging for the interview of the seminarists, including the reason of the reluctance of the religious authorities to allow the team to interview the seminarists inside the seminary.... [W]ith a view to expediting the matter, the Commission has decided to interview the persons concerned at Vinh and has made a recommendation to that effect. This recommendation has not been implemented....

83. One difficulty of a serious nature where the Commission's recommendation has not been implemented has been the withdrawal of the Commission's mobile team from Phuc Hoa....

84. Under the Cease-Fire Agreement the parties have, apart from the obligation to implement all the Articles fully, accepted the obligation to afford full protection and all possible assistance and co-operation to the International Commission and its inspection teams in the performance of functions and tasks assigned to them by the Agreement. Neither party has fulfilled in their entirety these obligations. As has been revealed in the preceding paragraphs, the degree of co-operation given to the Commission by the two parties has not been the same. While the Commission has experienced difficulties in North Vietnam, the major part of its difficulties has arisen in South Vietnam.

SOURCE: Marvin E. Gettleman (ed.), *Vietnam: History, Documents, and Opinions on a Major World Crisis*, pp. 170–172.

American economic, technical, and military aid enabled Diem's government to take hold in Saigon. By 1957, the U.S. experiment in nation building in South Vietnam appeared to be a stunning success. Diem led a stable government sustained by a flourishing consumer economy and protected by a modern army. South Vietnam and its leader enjoyed a positive image in the American press. To celebrate his achievements, America's mandarin made a triumphal visit to the United States in May 1957. Washington rolled out the red carpet and President Eisenhower welcomed the visiting head of state at the airport:

DOCUMENT 15. President Eisenhower Welcomes Ngo Dinh Diem, May 1957.

You have exemplified in your corner of the world patriotism of the highest order. You have brought to your great task of organizing your country the greatest courage, the greatest of statemanship....

SOURCE: Transcript of video documentary, "America's Mandarin," part three of the television documentary series *Vietnam: A Television History.*

The Diem regime tried to eliminate or suppress all opposition in South Vietnam. The major targets were Vietminh supporters who had remained in South Vietnam following the Geneva agreements. These "stay-behinds" controlled or had political influence in many southern villages. Diem issued ordinances in 1956 and 1959 that gave government officials virtually a free hand to root out any opposition to his regime. Diemist repression provoked a rebellion in the South that was soon supported and taken over by the North Vietnamese. This rebellion became a civil war and in time involved the United States militarily.

DOCUMENT 16. Excerpts from Law 10/59, May 6, 1959.

Article 1

Sentence of death, and confiscation of the whole or part of his property, ... will be imposed on whoever commits or attempts to commit one of the following crimes with the aim of sabotage, or upon infringing upon the security of the State, or injuring the lives or property of the people:

1. Deliberate murder, food poisoning, or kidnapping.
2. Destruction, or total or partial damaging, of one of the following categories of objects by means of explosives, fire, or other means:
   (a) Dwelling-houses, whether inhabited or not, churches, pagodas, temples, warehouses, workshops, farms and all outbuildings belonging to private persons;
   (b) Public buildings, residences, offices, workshops, depots, and, in a more general way, all constructions of any kind belonging to the State, and any other property, movable or unmovable, belonging to, or controlled by the State, or which is under the system of concession, or of public management;
   (c) All ... means of transport, all kinds of vehicles;
   (d) Mines, with machines and equipment;
   (e) Weapons, military material and equipment, posts, buildings, offices, depots, workshops, and constructions of any kind relating to defense or police work;
   (f) crops, draft animals and farm equipment ... ;
   (g) Installations for telecommunications, postal service, broadcasting, the production and distribution of electricity and water ... ;
   (h) Dikes, dams, roads, railways, airfields, seaports, bridges, channels, or works relating to them;
   (i) Waterways, large or small, and canals....

Article 3

Whoever belongs to an organization designed to help to prepare or to perpetuate crimes enumerated in Article 1 ... , or takes pledges to do so, will be subject to the sentences provided for....

Article 6

Three special military courts are set up and based in Saigon, Ban Me Thuot, and Hue.... As the need arises, other special military courts may be set up, by decree, ...

Article 16

The decisions of the special military court are not subject to appeal....

Article 20

All legal provisions which are contrary to the present law are hereby repealed....

Ngo Dinh Diem
Saigon, May 6, 1959

SOURCE: Gettleman (ed.), *Vietnam: History, Documents, and Opinions,* pp. 256–260.

As the 1950s were ending, the civil war in southern Vietnam was expanding. The Communist leaders in Hanoi had authorized the use of limited guerrilla warfare against Diemist forces, and scattered fighting occurred in various locales in South Vietnam. Hanoi's leaders also ordered the North Vietnamese army to develop a capability for moving people, weapons, and supplies along an infiltration route from North Vietnam via Laos to South Vietnam. This infiltration route became the famed Ho Chi Minh trail. The North Vietnamese also began sending southern cadres who had regrouped in North Vietnam following the 1954 armistice down the Ho Chi Minh trail to join the insurgents in the South.

DOCUMENT 17. Hanoi's View of the Southern Insurgency, February 1960.

... In order to fulfill the task before them, what path must the Vietnamese people in general and people of the Southern zone in particular, take to defeat the U.S.-Diem government and establish a People's Democratic coalition government in the South?

The path of Vietnamese revolution in the South at present is the path of general uprising to seize political power. General uprising to seize political power is the fundamental path of development of the Vietnamese revolution in the South. General uprising to overthrow the My Diem government, seize political power and return it to the hands of the people is the objective and line of the struggle of the whole Party and people at present. Therefore all facets of activities must be actively carried out, and prepared in all respects in accord with that objective and line. If we are separated from that in objective and line in daily activities, we will make big mistakes in regard to the general line.

The line of the Vietnamese revolution in the South of general uprising to seize political power is the only correct line, is precise and very appropriate to the present situation.

At present, the socialist camp, headed by the Soviet Union, has become stronger than the forces of the imperialist camp, headed by the United States, and the peace forces have become stronger than the forces provoking war. But imperialism still remains and the threat of war still remains. In the country the North is still building socialism, the Northern people are about to complete the three-year state plan and to enter into the five year plan. In the South, the struggle front against U.S.–Diem is being consolidated and developed. Our party and people have been forged in six years of political struggle, and the Southern people have a definite level of political consciousness, so that at present the majority of the masses feel they cannot live under the U.S.–Diem regime. Thus the desire to overthrow the U.S.–Diem regime grows stronger everyday.

The American imperialists and the Ngo Dinh Diem government, though cruel and ferocious, are contrary to the rights of the people, and therefore their people—selling and country—selling face is being revealed and has been heavily defeated politically; indicating their weak, stagnant and hopeless position. They are on the path of destruction and are about to be destroyed.

The above situation puts before the entire Party and people the task of actively preparing in all spheres for the general uprising to seize political power. That is the only correct way; apart from it there is no other way. But the general uprising to seize political power is a path which must be prepared for a long time, for which we must accumulate our forces, preserve them, consolidate and develop them, create the opportune moment and seize it well to act, determined not to be either premature or passive waiting for something to happen....

How must we conceive of the armed struggle?

The concept of armed struggle at present is armed struggle according to the line of general uprising to seize political power and not armed struggle as during the period of resistance war in which we took the countryside to surround the cities and finally liberated cities. Armed struggle at the present time is not guerrilla war, nor is it protracted interzonal warfare, fighting to liberate area and establish a government as during the resistance period.

Armed struggle at the present time means the whole people armed for self-defense and propaganda. If we wish to achieve the whole people armed and propagandizing, we must rely on the political forces of the masses, rely on the organized masses and on that basis arm the masses with the main factor being arms for the people. The people must get their own arms, in order to defend themselves, oppose and annihilate puppet personnel, militia, security agents, spies, and cruel and stubborn landlords in order to protect their rights and their homes, preserve the country and keep their own land. They must not passively sit and wait but must stand up and liberate themselves. But on the other hand, the people must also have armed self-defense units in order to join with the people and help the people destroy the stubborn and cruel group within the government and army of U.S.–Diem and with the forces of the entire people, make the U.S.–Diem army disintegrate in terms of morale and organization.

The task and requirement of the armed self-defense activity is to serve the interests of the political struggle. But on the other hand, the political struggle also has the significance and objective of guarding and pushing forward the armed struggle. But the main task and requirement of the armed struggle is serve the political struggle, build, assemble, organize and develop the political forces of workers, peasants, and other classes. On the other hand, the armed struggle must also aim at destroying security agents, spies, militia, puppet officials, cruel and stubborn landlords, at reducing the influence of the enemy, causing the enemy to shrink, clearing out and destroying concentration centers of the enemy, raising high the political influence of the Party and masses, and maintaining the long-term legal position of the masses.

To a certain degree and in a certain number of localities, our armed forces must also oppose the mop-up and terror operations of the enemy and when necessary thrust deep to fight battles and carry out armed propaganda to affect the morale of the enemy in order to push the political struggle of the masses in the rural area and the cities, creating favorable conditions to promote more strongly the building, assembly and organizing of the political forces of the masses.

The line of operation of the armed forces is that they must assemble and disperse quickly, be lively, secret, concise, hide and not show off, not make the enemy vigilant, take precautions against commandoes, avoid attrition, know how to consolidate and develop the armed forces in accordance with the possibilities of each locality, and avoid negligence and carelessness.

Speaking generally, only when we have built the political forces and led the political struggle movement of the working class and urban poor and the political struggle movement of the peasants in the rural area with the vast majority of the population can we protect, strengthen and develop the armed forces and push the armed struggle movement forward. On the contrary, only by pushing arms and combining it correctly can we conduct the political struggle movement forward.

SOURCE: Gareth Porter (ed.), *Vietnam: The Definitive Documentation of Human Decisions*, 2 Vols., "Article in *A Lao Dong*, Party Internal Journal in the South" (February 1960), pp. 54, 56.

As the southern insurgency escalated, Communist party leaders meeting in Hanoi formally endorsed the rebellion. They adopted a resolution stating that the Vietnamese revolution now had two primary goals: completing the socialist revolution in North Vietnam and liberating South Vietnam in order to complete the reunification of the country. Following the Hanoi meeting, the insurgent military cadres met in southern Vietnam to form a united military command, thereby creating the People's Liberation Armed Force (PLAF). It is the PLAF forces that American soldiers called the "Vietcong." While the PLAF was forming, the southern political cadres also met to form the National Liberation Front. The NLF was a reincarnation of the Vietminh adapted to southern political conditions. At their founding conference, the NLF organizers adopted a 10-point program that stressed nationalistic rather than revolutionary goals.

DOCUMENT 18. National Liberation Front Program, December 22, 1960.

I. *Overthrow the camouflaged colonial regime of the American imperialists and the dictatorial power of Ngo Dinh Diem, servant of the Americans, and institute a government of national democratic union.*

The present South Vietnamese regime is a camouflaged colonial regime dominated by the Yankees, and the South Vietnamese Government is a servile government, implementing faithfully all the policies of the American imperialists. Therefore, this regime must be overthrown and a government of national and democratic union put in its place composed of representatives of all social classes, of all nationalities, of the various political parties, of all religions; patriotic, eminent citizens must take over for the people the control of economic, political, social, and cultural interests and thus bring about independence, democracy, well-being, peace, neutrality, and efforts toward the peaceful unification of the country.

II. *Institute a largely liberal and democratic regime.*

1. Abolish the present constitution of the dictatorial powers of Ngo Dinh Diem, servant of the Americans. Elect a new National Assembly through universal suffrage. 2. Implement essential democratic liberties: freedom of opinion, of press, of assembly, of movement, of trade-unionism; freedom of religion without any discrimination; and the right of all patriotic organizations of whatever political tendency to carry on normal activities. 3. Proclaim a general amnesty for all political prisoners and the dissolution of concentration camps of all sorts; abolish fascist law 10/59 and all the other antidemocratic laws; authorize the return to the country of all persons persecuted by the American-Diem regime who are now refugees abroad. 4. Interdict all illegal arrests and detentions; prohibit torture; and punish all the Diem bullies who have not repented and who have committed crimes against the people.

III. *Establish an independent and sovereign economy, and improve the living conditions of the people.*

1. Suppress the monopolies imposed by American imperialists and their servants; establish an independent and sovereign economy and finances in accordance with the national interests; confiscate to the profit of the nation the properties of the American imperialists and their servants. 2. Support the national bourgeoisie in the reconstruction and development of crafts and industry;

provide active protection for national products through the suppression of production taxes and the limitation or prohibition of imports that the national economy is capable of producing; reduce customs fees on raw materials and machines. 3. Revitalize agriculture; modernize production, fishing, and cattle raising; help the farmers in putting to the plow unused land and in developing production; protect the crops and guarantee their disposal. 4. Encourage and reinforce economic relations between the city and country, the plain and the mountain regions; develop commercial exchanges with foreign countries, regardless of their political regime, on the basis of equality and mutual interests. 5. Institute a just and rational system of taxation; eliminate harassing penalties. 6. Implement the labor code; prohibition of discharges of penalties, of ill-treatment of wage earners; improvement of the living conditions of workers and civil servants; imposition of wage scales and protective measures for young apprentices. 7. Organize social welfare: find work for jobless persons; assume the support and protection of orphans, old people, invalids; come to the help of the victims of the Americans and Diemists; organize help for areas hit by bad crops, fires, or natural calamities. 8. Come to help of displaced persons desiring to return to their native areas and to those who wish to remain permanently in the South; improve their working and living conditions. 9. Prohibit expulsions, spoliation, and compulsory concentration of the population; guarantee job security for the urban and rural working populations.

    IV. *Reduce land rent; implement agrarian reform with the aim of providing land to the tillers.*

    1. Reduce land rent; guarantee to the farmers the right to till the soil; guarantee the property right of accession to fallow lands to those who have cultivated them; guarantee property rights to those farmers who have already received land. 2. Dissolve "prosperity zones," and put an end to recruitment for the camps that are called "agricultural development centers." Allow those compatriots who already have been forced into "prosperity zones" and "agricultural development centers" to return freely to their own lands. 3. Confiscate the land owned by American imperialists and their servants, and distribute it to poor peasants without any land or with insufficient land; redistribute the communal lands on a just and rational basis. 4. By negotiation and on the basis of fair prices, repurchase for distribution to landless peasants or peasants with insufficient land those surplus lands that the owners of large estates will be made to relinquish if their domain exceeds a certain limit, to be determined in accordance with regional particularities. The farmers who benefit from such land distribution will not be compelled to make any payment or to submit to any other conditions.

    V. *Develop a national and democratic culture and education.*

    1. Combat all forms of culture and education enslaved to Yankee fashions; develop a culture and education that is national, progressive, and at the service of the Fatherland and people. 2. Liquidate illiteracy; increase the number of schools in the fields of general education as well as in those of technical and

professional education, in advanced study as well as in other fields; adopt Vietnamese as the vernacular language; reduce the expenses of education and exempt from payment students who are without means; resume the examination system. 3. Promote science and technology and the national letters and arts; encourage and support the intellectuals and artists so as to permit them to develop their talents in the service of national reconstruction. 4. Watch over public health; develop sports and physical education.

VI. *Create a national army devoted to the defense of the Fatherland and the people.*

1. Establish a national army devoted to the defense of the Fatherland and the people; abolish the system of American military advisers. 2. Abolish the draft system; improve the living conditions of the simple soldiers and guarantee their political rights; put an end to ill-treatment of the military; pay particular attention to the dependents of soldiers without means. 3. Reward officers and soldiers having participated in the struggle against the domination by the Americans and their servants; adopt a policy of clemency toward the former collaborators of the Americans and Diemists guilty of crimes against the people but who have finally repented and are ready to serve the people. 4. Abolish all foreign military bases established on the territory of Vietnam.

VII. *Guarantee equality between the various minorities and between the two sexes; protect the legitimate interests of foreign citizens established in Vietnam and of Vietnamese citizens residing abroad.*

1. Implement the right to autonomy of the national minorities: found autonomous zones in the areas with minority population, those zones to be an integral part of the Vietnamese nation. Guarantee equality between the various nationalities: each nationality has the right to use and develop its language and writing system, to maintain or to modify freely its *mores* and customs; abolish the policy of the Americans and Diemists of racial discrimination and forced assimilation. Create conditions permitting the national minorities to reach the general level of progress of the population: development of their economy and culture; formation of cadres of minority nationalities. 2. Establish equality between the two sexes; women shall have equal rights with men from all viewpoints (political, economic, cultural, social, etc.). 3. Protect the legitimate interests of foreign citizens established in Vietnam. 4. Defend and take care of the interests of Vietnamese citizens residing abroad.

VIII. *Promote a foreign policy of peace and neutrality.*

1. Cancel all unequal treaties that infringe upon the sovereignty of the people and that were concluded with other countries by the servants of the Americans. 2. Establish diplomatic relations with all countries, regardless of their political regime, in accordance with the principles of peaceful coexistence adopted at the Bandung Conference. 3. Develop close solidarity with peace-loving nations and neutral countries; develop free relations with the nations of Southeast Asia, in particular with Cambodia and Laos. 4. Stay out of any military bloc; refuse any military alliance with another country. 5. Accept economic aid from any country willing to help us without attaching any conditions to such help.

IX. *Re-establish normal relations between the two zones, and prepare for the peaceful reunification of the country.*

The peaceful reunification of the country constitutes the dearest desire of all our compatriots throughout the country. The National Liberation Front of South Vietnam advocates the peaceful reunification by stages on the basis of negotiations and through the seeking of ways and means in conformity with the interests of the Vietnamese nation. While awaiting this reunification, the governments of the two zones will, on the basis of negotiations, promise to banish all separatist and war-mongering propaganda and not to use force to settle differences between the zones. Commercial and cultural exchanges between the two zones will be implemented; the inhabitants of the two zones will be free to move about throughout the country as their family and business interests indicate. The freedom of postal exchanges will be guaranteed.

X. *Struggle against all aggressive war; actively defend universal peace.*

1. Struggle against all aggressive war and against all forms of imperialist domination; support the national emancipation movements of the various peoples. 2. Banish all war-mongering propaganda; demand general disarmament and the prohibition of nuclear weapons; and advocate the utilization of atomic energy for peaceful purposes. 3. Support all movements of struggle for peace, democracy, and social progress throughout the world; contribute actively to the defense of peace in South-east Asia and in the world.

SOURCE: Marvin E. Gettleman and others (eds.), *Vietnam and America: A Documentary History*, pp. 188–191.

On January 20, 1961, John F. Kennedy succeeded Dwight Eisenhower as president of the United States. Kennedy's first Southeast Asian foreign-policy challenge came in Laos rather than Vietnam. In a final briefing between the outgoing and incoming presidents held at the White House on January 19, 1961, Eisenhower had warned Kennedy that Laos was the most acute Cold War crisis of the moment. In Laos, the United States had been backing a right-wing government engaged in small-scale, low-intensity civil war with neutralist and Communist forces that were backed by North Vietnam and the Soviet Union. Eisenhower recommended to Kennedy the need for American military intervention in Laos if necessary to save that country from a Communist takeover.

**DOCUMENT 19. Eisenhower Briefs Kennedy on the Crisis in Laos,
January 19, 1961.**

President Eisenhower opened the session on Laos by stating that the United States was determined to preserve the independence of Laos. It was his opinion that if Laos should fall to the Communists, then it would be just a question of time until South Vietnam, Cambodia, Thailand, and Burma would collapse. He felt that the Communists had designs on all of Southeast Asia, and that it would be a tragedy to permit Laos to fall.

President Eisenhower gave a brief review of the various moves and coups that had taken place in Laos involving the Pathet Lao, Souvanna Phouma, Boun Oum, and Kong Le. He said that the evidence was clear that Communist China and North Vietnam were determined to destroy the independence of Laos. He also added that the Russians were sending in substantial supplies in support of the Pathet Lao in an effort to overturn the government. . . .

President Eisenhower said with considerable emotion that Laos was the key to the entire area of Southeast Asia. He said that if we permitted Laos to fall, then we would have to write off all the area. He stated that we must not permit a Communist take-over. He reiterated that we should make every effort to persuade member nations of SEATO or the ICC to accept the burden with us to defend the freedom of Laos.

As he concluded these remarks, President Eisenhower stated it was imperative that Laos be defended. He said that the United States should accept this task with our allies, if we could persuade them, and alone if we could not. He added that "our unilateral intervention would be our last desperate hope" in the event we were unable to prevail upon the other signatories to join us. . . .

Commenting upon President Eisenhower's statement that we would have to go to the support of Laos alone if we could not persuade others to proceed with us, President-elect Kennedy asked the question as to how long it would take to put an American division into Laos. Secretary Gates replied that it would take from twelve to seventeen days but that some of that time could be saved if American forces, then in the Pacific, could be utilized. Secretary Gates added that the American forces were in excellent shape and that modernization of the Army was making good progress.

President-elect Kennedy commented upon the seriousness of the situation in Laos and in Southeast Asia and asked if the situation seemed to be approaching a climax. General Eisenhower stated that the entire proceeding was extremely confused but that it was clear that this country was obligated to support the existing government in Laos. . . .

SOURCE: Gravel (ed.), *Pentagon Papers*, Vol. 2, pp. 635–637.

President Kennedy, during the spring of 1961, took several courses of action in Southeast Asia. He considered, then rejected, military intervention in Laos and opted, instead, for a political solution, namely a neutral Laos under a coalition government. Kennedy also authorized increases in U.S. military assistance for the Diem government, which was continuing to lose ground in its struggle with the Vietcong. He also dispatched Vice-President Lyndon Johnson on a fact-finding mission to Saigon. Johnson returned in late May 1961 and reported his findings and recommendations to the president.

DOCUMENT 20. Excerpts from Lyndon Johnson's Report to President Kennedy, May 23, 1961.

... I took to Southeast Asia some basic convictions about the problems faced there. I have come away from the mission there—and to India and Pakistan—with many of those convictions sharpened and deepened by what I saw and learned. I have also reached certain other conclusions which I believe may be of value as guidance for those responsible in formulating policies.

These conclusions are as follows:

1. The battle against Communism must be joined in Southeast Asia with strength and determination to achieve success there—or the United States, inevitably, must surrender the Pacific and take up our defenses on our own shores. Asian Communism is compromised and contained by the maintenance of free nations on the subcontinent. Without this inhibitory influence, the island outposts—Philippines, Japan, Taiwan—have no security and the vast Pacific becomes a Red Sea.

2. The struggle is far from lost in Southeast Asia and it is by no means inevitable that it must be lost. In each country it is possible to build a sound structure capable of withstanding and turning the Communist surge. The will to resist—while now the target of subversive attack—is there. The key to what is done by Asians in defense of Southeast Asia freedom is confidence in the United States.

3. There is no alternative to United States leadership in Southeast Asia. Leadership in individual countries—or the regional leadership and cooperation so appealing to Asians—rests on the knowledge and faith in United States power, will and understanding. . . .

6. Any help—economic as well as military—we give less developed nations to secure and maintain their freedom must be a part of a mutual effort. These nations cannot be saved by United States help alone. To the extent the Southeast Asian nations are prepared to take the necessary measures to make our aid effective, we can be—and must be—unstinting in our assistance. It would be useful to enunciate more clearly than we have—for the guidance of these young and unsophisticated nations—what we expect or require of them.

7. In large measure, the greatest danger Southeast Asia offers to nations like the United States is not the momentary threat of Communism itself, rather that danger stems from hunger, ignorance, poverty and disease. We must—whatever strategies we evolve—keep these enemies the point of our attack, and make imaginative use of our scientific and technological capability in such enterprises.

8. Vietnam and Thailand are the immediate—and most important—trouble spots, critical to the U.S. These areas require the attention of our very best talents—under the very closest Washington direction—on matters economic, military and political.

The basic decision in Southeast Asia is here. We must decide whether to help these countries to the best of our ability or throw in the towel in the area and pull back our defenses to San Francisco and a "Fortress America" concept. More important, we would say to the world in this case that we don't live up to treaties and don't stand by our friends. This is not my concept. I recommend that we move forward promptly with a major effort to help these countries defend themselves. I consider the key here is to get our best MAAG people to control, plan, direct and exact results from our military aid program. In Vietnam and Thailand, we must move forward together.

a. In Vietnam, Diem is a complex figure beset by many problems. He has admirable qualities, but he is remote from the people, is surrounded by persons less admirable and capable than he. The country can be saved—if we move quickly and wisely. We must decide whether to support Diem—or let Vietnam fall. We must have coordination of purpose in our country team, diplomatic and military. The Saigon Embassy, USIS, MAAG and related operations leave much to be desired. They should be brought up to maximum efficiency. The most important thing is imaginative, creative, American management of our military aid program. The Vietnamese and our MAAG estimate that $50 million of U.S. military and economic assistance will be needed if we decide to support Vietnam.

The fundamental decision required of the United States—and time is of the greatest importance—is whether we are to attempt to meet the challenge of Communist expansion now in Southeast Asia by a major effort in support of the forces of freedom in the area or throw in the towel. This decision must be made in a full realization of the very heavy and continuing costs involved in terms of money, of effort and of United States prestige. It must be made with the knowledge that at some point we may be faced with the further decision of whether we commit major United States forces to the area or cut our losses and withdraw should our other efforts fail. We must remain master in this decision. What we do in Southeast Asia should be part of a rational program to meet the threat we face in the region as a whole. It should include a clear-cut pattern of specific contributions to be expected by each partner according to his ability and resources. I recommend we proceed with a clear-cut and strong program of action. . . .

SOURCE: Sheehan and others (eds.), *Pentagon Papers*, pp. 127–130.

In the fall of 1961, the Diem government continued to decline. Its popular base of support shrank even more and the NLF forces continued to gain in strength. President Kennedy, influenced by reports and recommendations from General Maxwell Taylor, Secretary of State Dean Rusk, and Secretary of Defense Robert S. McNamara, approved significant increases in the level of U.S. support to the Republic of Vietnam (RVN) to try to arrest its political and strategic deterioration. Kennedy also approved large increases in the number of American military advisers assigned to

South Vietnam, increases that violated the 1954 Geneva accords. Kennedy's decisions made in mid-November 1961 to escalate the American effort in South Vietnam formed the basis of America's Vietnam policy for the duration of his presidency.

DOCUMENT 21. Excerpts from Rusk-McNamara Report to Kennedy, November 11, 1961.

1. United States National Interests in South Viet-Nam.

The deteriorating situation in South Viet-Nam requires attention to the nature and scope of United States national interests in that country. The loss of South Viet-Nam to Communism would involve the transfer of a nation of 20 million people from the free world to the Communism bloc. The loss of South Viet-Nam would make pointless any further discussion about the importance of Southeast Asia to the free world; we would have to face the near certainty that the remainder of Southeast Asia and Indonesia would move to a complete accommodation with Communism, if not formal incorporation with the Communist bloc. The United States, as a member of SEATO, has commitments with respect to South Viet-Nam under the Protocol to the SEATO Treaty. Additionally, in a formal statement at the conclusion session of the 1954 Geneva Conference, the United States representative stated that the United States "would view any renewal of the aggression . . . with grave concern and seriously threatening international peace and security."

The loss of South Viet-Nam to Communism would not only destroy SEATO but would undermine the credibility of American commitments elsewhere. Further, loss of South Viet-Nam would stimulate bitter domestic controversies in the United States and would be seized upon by extreme elements to divide the country and harass the Administration. . . .

3. The United States' Objective in South Viet-Nam.

The United States should commit itself to the clear objective of preventing the fall of South Viet-Nam to Communist [sic]. The basic means for accomplishing this objective must be to put the Government of South Viet-Nam into a position to win its own war against the Guerillas. We must insist that that Government itself take the measures necessary for that purpose in exchange for large-scale United States assistance in the military, economic and political fields. At the same time we must recognize that it will probably not be possible for the GVN to win this war as long as the flow of men and supplies from North Viet-Nam continues unchecked and the guerrillas enjoy a safe sanctuary in neighboring territory.

We should be prepared to introduce United States combat forces if that should become necessary for success. Dependent upon the circumstances, it may also be necessary for United States forces to strike at the source of the aggression in North Viet-Nam.

4. The Use of United States Forces in South Viet-Nam.

The commitment of United States forces to South Viet-Nam involves two different catgories: (A) Units of modest size required for the direct support of South Viet-Namese military effort, such as communications, helicopter and other forms of airlift, reconnaissance aircraft, naval patrols, intelligence units, etc., and (B) larger organized units with actual or potential direct military mission. *Category (A) should be introduced as speedily as possible.* Category (B) units pose a more serious problem in that they are much more significant from the point of view of domestic and international political factors and greatly increase the probabilities of Communist block escalation. Further, the employment of United States combat forces (in the absence of Communist bloc escalation) involves a certain dilemma: if there is a strong South-Vietnamese effort, they may not be needed; if there is not such an effort, United States forces could not accomplish their mission in the midst of an apathetic or hostile population. Under present circumstances, therefore, the question of injecting United States and SEATO combat forces should in large part be considered as a contribution to the morale of the South Vietnamese in their own effort to do the principal job themselves. . . .

In the light of the foregoing, the Secretary of State and the Secretary of Defense recommend that:

1. We now take the decision to commit ourselves to the objective of preventing the fall of South Viet-Nam to Communism and that, in doing so, we recognize that the introduction of United States and other SEATO forces may be necessary to achieve this objective. (However, if it is necessary to commit outside forces to achieve the foregoing objective our decision to introduce United States forces should not be contingent upon unanimous SEATO agreement thereto.)

2. The Department of Defense be prepared with plans for the use of United States forces in South Viet-Nam under one or more of the following purposes:

(a) Use of a significant number of United States forces to signify United States determination to defend Viet-Nam and to boost South Viet-Nam morale.

(b) Use of substantial United States forces to assist in suppressing Viet Cong insurgency short of engaging in detailed counter-guerrilla operations but including relevant operations in North Viet-Nam.

(c) Use of United States forces to deal with the situation if there is organized Communist military intervention.

3. We immediately undertake the following actions in support of the GVN:

. . . **(c)** Provide the GVN with small craft, including such United States uniformed advisers and operating personnel as may be necessary for quick and effective operations in effecting surveillance and control over coastal waters and inland waterways. . . .

(e) Provide such personnel and equipment as may be necessary to improve the military-political intelligence system beginning at the provincial level and extending upward through the Government and the armed forces to the Central Intelligence Organization.

(f) Provide such new terms of reference, reorganization and additional personnel for United States military forces as are required for increased United States participation in the direction and control of GVN military operations and to carry out the other increased responsibilities which accrue to MAAG under these recommendations. . . .

(i) Provide individual administrators and advisers for insertion into the Governmental machinery of South Viet-Nam in types and numbers to be agreed upon by the two Governments. . . .

SOURCE: Sheehan and others (eds.), *Pentagon Papers*, pp. 150–153.

In May 1963, a crisis suddenly exploded in South Vietnam that proved to be the beginning of the end of the Diem government. In Hue, Diem's soldiers fired into a crowd protesting orders forbidding the flying of flags celebrating Buddha's birthday. The Buddhist revolt heightened when an elderly monk set fire to himself on a downtown Saigon street. Soon, photographs and accounts of the burning monk made the front pages and television news in America and around the world. American advisers brought intense pressure on Diem to conciliate the Buddhists, but he refused. In August 1963, Diem, encouraged by his brother and most influential adviser, Ngo Dinh Nhu, raided pagodas in several cities. Temples were desecrated, 1,420 monks were arrested, and dozens more were killed or injured. Because of the political turmoil provoked by Diem's war against the Buddhists, the campaign against the Vietcong in the countryside ground to a halt and Diem's popular base was reduced to family members and a few loyal military retainers.

As South Vietnam rapidly descended into chaos, alarmed ARVN generals began to plot the overthrow of the Ngo family rule before disaster befell everyone. The new U.S. ambassador to South Vietnam, Henry Cabot Lodge, supported the coup plotters. President Kennedy himself vacillated, adhering to a policy of not overtly supporting a coup, but not discouraging one either. Kennedy relied on Lodge's judgment, and he appears mainly to have been worried that either the coup might fail or that the United States would be implicated. The *coup d'etat* that destroyed the Diem regime and resulted in the deaths of Diem and Nhu began at 1:30 P.M. local time on November 1, 1963. While the coup was in progress, Diem made a telephone call to Lodge. The following conversation ensued.

DOCUMENT 22. Phone Conversation Between Ngo Dinh Diem and Henry Cabot Lodge, November 1, 1963.

DIEM: Some units have made a rebellion and I want to know, what is the attitude of the U.S.?

LODGE: I do not feel well enough informed to be able to tell you. I have heard the shooting, but am not acquainted with all the facts. Also, it is 4:30 A.M. in Washington and the U.S. Government cannot possibly have a view.

DIEM: But you must have some general ideas. After all, I am Chief of State. I have tried to do my duty. I want to do now what duty and good sense require. I believe in duty above all.

LODGE: You have certainly done your duty. As I told you only this morning, I admire your courage and your great contribution to your country. No one can take away from you the credit for all you have done. Now I am worried about your physical safety. I have a report that those in charge of the current activity offer you and your brother safe conduct out of the country if you resign. Had you heard this?

DIEM: No. (pause) You have my phone number.

LODGE: Yes. If I can do anything for your physical safety, please call me.

DIEM: I am trying to re-establish order (hangs up).

SOURCE: Sheehan and others (eds.), *Pentagon Papers*, p. 232.

Three weeks after the coup, Kennedy's assassination in Dallas, Texas, overshadowed the murders in Saigon. At the time of his death, Kennedy's Vietnam policy was in disarray. The president's apologists are on record suggesting that had he lived he was planning to extricate the United States from South Vietnam and that there would have been no American war in that region. The historical record suggests otherwise. Kennedy retained a strong commitment to America's Vietnam effort to the end, a commitment that he often publicly reaffirmed during his final months in office. Here is an example taken from a televised interview broadcast September 2, 1963.

DOCUMENT 23. Excerpt from Kennedy's Televised Interview with Walter Cronkite, September 2, 1963.

... Those people who say that we ought to withdraw from Vietnam are wholly wrong, because if we withdraw from Vietnam, the Communists would control Vietnam. Pretty soon Thailand, Cambodia, Laos, Malaya would go and all of Southeast Asia would be under the control of the Communists and under the domination of the Chinese.

SOURCE: Transcript of videotape, "Lyndon Johnson Goes to War, 1964–1965," from the television series *Vietnam: A Television History.*

3
GOING TO WAR:
1964–1965

Lyndon Johnson embraced the U.S. commitment in Vietnam as he assumed the presidency following John F. Kennedy's assassination. Johnson inherited a deteriorating situation in southern Vietnam. Despite the continuing deterioration of the GVN, the new president initially opted for a continuation of Kennedy's policy of sending U.S. military advisers to South Vietnam along with substantial amounts of economic and military aid. Johnson also approved the conduct of covert operations in Laos and North Vietnam. Secretary of Defense Robert McNamara, who like most of Johnson's senior advisers was a Kennedy holdover, filed the following pessimistic report on the deteriorating Vietnam situation early in Johnson's presidency.

DOCUMENT 24. Excerpts from McNamara's Report to Johnson, December 21, 1963.

In accordance with your request this morning, this is a summary of my conclusions after my visit to Vietnam on December 19–20.

   1. Summary. The situation is very disturbing. Current trends, unless reversed in the next 2–3 months, will lead to neutralization at best and more likely to a Communist-controlled state.

   2. The new government is the greatest source of concern. It is indecisive and drifting. Although Minh states that he, rather than the Committee of Generals, is making decisions, it is not clear that this is actually so. In any event, neither he nor the Committee are experienced in political administration and so far they show little talent for it. There is no clear concept on how to re-shape or conduct the strategic hamlet program; the Province Chiefs, most of whom are new and inexperienced, are receiving little or no direction because the generals are so preoccupied with essentially political affairs. A specific example of the present situation is that General [name illegible] is spending little or no time commanding III Corps, which is in the vital zone around Saigon and needs full-time direction. I made these points as strongly as possible to Minh, Don, Kim, and Tho.

3. The Country Team is the second major weakness. It lacks leadership, has been poorly informed, and is not working to a common plan. A recent example of confusion has been conflicting USOM and military recommendations both to the Government of Vietnam and to Washington on the size of the military budget. Above all, Lodge has virtually no official contact with Harkins. Lodge sends in reports with major military implications without showing them to Harkins, and does not show Harkins important incoming traffic. My impression is that Lodge simply does not know how to conduct a coordinated administration. This has of course been stressed to him both by Dean Rusk and myself (and also by John McCone), and I do not think he is consciously rejecting our advice; he has just operated as a loner all his life and cannot readily change now. . . .

4. Viet Cong progress has been great during the period since the coup, with my best guess being that the situation has in fact been deteriorating in the countryside since July to a far greater extent than we realized because of our undue dependence on distorted Vietnamese reporting. The Viet Cong now control very high proportions of the people in certain key provinces, particularly those directly south and west of Saigon. The Strategic Hamlet Program was seriously over-extended in those provinces, and the Viet Cong has been able to destroy many hamlets, while others have been abandoned or in some cases betrayed or pillaged by the government's own Self-Defense Corps. In these key provinces, the Viet Cong have destroyed almost all major roads, and are collecting taxes at will.

As remedial measures, we must get the government to reallocate its military forces so that its effective strength in these provinces is essentially doubled. We also need to have major increases in both military and USOM staffs, to sizes that will give us a reliable, independent U.S. appraisal of the status of operations. Thirdly, realistic pacification plans must be prepared, allocating adequate time to secure the remaining government-controlled areas and work out from there.

This gloomy picture prevails predominantly in the provinces around the capital and in the Delta. Action to accomplish each of these objectives was started while we were in Saigon. The situation in the northern and central areas is considerably better, and does not seem to have deteriorated substantially in recent months. General Harkins still hopes these areas may be made reasonably secure by the latter half of next year. . . .

5. Infiltration of men and equipment from North Vietnam continues using (a) land corridors through Laos and Cambodia; (b) the Mekong River waterways from Cambodia; (c) some possible entry from the sea and the tip of the Delta. The best guess is that 1000–1500 Viet Cong cadres entered South Vietnam from Laos in the first nine months of 1963. The Mekong route (and also the possible sea entry) is apparently used for heavier weapons and ammunition and raw materials which have been turning up in increasing numbers in the south and of which we have captured a few shipments. . . .

6. Plans for Covert Action into North Vietnam were prepared as we had requested and were an excellent job. They present a wide variety of sabotage and psychological operations against North Vietnam from which I believe we should aim to select those that provide maximum pressure with minimum risk. In accordance with your direction at the meeting. General Krulak of the JCS is chairing a group that will lay out a program in the next ten days for your consideration. . . .

SOURCE: Sheehan and others (eds.), *Pentagon Papers*, pp. 271–274.

Early in Johnson's presidency, the Joint Chiefs of Staff, aware of the continuing deterioration of South Vietnam, proposed that the United States begin preparing for various types of military actions to be taken against Laos and North Vietnam. Long before the Gulf of Tonkin incidents, there was a growing tendency among U.S. officials, especially the senior military advisers, to look to North Vietnam for a solution that continued to elude them in the South.

DOCUMENT 25. Joint Chiefs of Staff Memo to Secretary of Defense McNamara, January 22, 1964.

. . . 2. The Joint Chiefs of Staff are increasingly mindful that our fortunes in South Vietnam are an accurate barometer of our fortunes in all of Southeast Asia. It is our view that if the U.S. program succeeds in South Vietnam it will go far toward stabilizing the total Southeast Asia situation. Conversely, a loss of South Vietnam to the communists will presage an early erosion of the remainder of our position in that subcontinent.

3. Laos, existing on a most fragile foundation now, would not be able to endure the establishment of a communist—or pseudo neutralist—state on its eastern flank. Thailand, less strong today than a month ago by virtue of the loss of Prime Minister Sarit, would probably be unable to withstand the pressures of infiltration from the north should Laos collapse to the communists in its turn. Cambodia apparently has estimated that our prospects in South Vietnam are not promising and, encouraged by the actions of the French, appears already to be seeking an accommodation with the communists. Should we actually suffer defeat in South Vietnam, there is little reason to believe that Cambodia would maintain even a pretense of neutrality.

4. In a broader sense, the failure of our programs in South Vietnam would have heavy influence on the judgments of Burma, India, Indonesia, Malaysia, Japan, Taiwan, the Republic of Korea, and the Republic of the Philippines with respect to U.S. durability, resolution, and trustworthiness. Finally, this being the first real test of our determination to defeat the communist wars of national liberation formula, it is not unreasonable to conclude that there would be a corresponding unfavorable effect upon our image in Africa and in Latin America.

5. All of this underscores the pivotal position now occupied by South Vietnam in our world-wide confrontation with the communists and the essentiality that the conflict there would be brought to a favorable end as soon as possible. However, it would be unrealistic to believe that a complete suppression of the insurgency can take place in one or even two years. The British effort in Malaya is a recent example of a counterinsurgency effort which required approximately ten years before the bulk of the rural population was brought completely under control of the government, the police were able to maintain order, and the armed forces were able to eliminate the guerrilla strongholds.

6. The Joint Chiefs of Staff are convinced that . . . the United States must make plain to the enemy our determination to see the Vietnam campaign through to a favorable conclusion. To do this, we must prepare for whatever level of activity may be required and, being prepared, must then proceed to take actions as necessary to achieve our purposes surely and promptly.

7. Our considerations, furthermore, cannot be confined entirely to South Vietnam. Our experience in the war thus far leads us to conclude that, in this respect, we are not now giving sufficient attention to the broader area problems of Southeast Asia. The Joint Chiefs of Staff believe that our position in Cambodia, our attitude toward Laos, our actions in Thailand, and our great effort in South Vietnam do not comprise a compatible and integrated U.S. policy for Southeast Asia. U.S. objectives in Southeast Asia cannot be achieved by either economic, political, or military measures alone. All three fields must be integrated into a single, broad U.S. program for Southeast Asia. The measures recommended in this memorandum are a partial contribution to such a program.

8. Currently we and the South Vietnamese are fighting the war on the enemy's terms. He has determined the locale, the timing, and the tactics of the battle while our actions are essentially reactive. One reason for this is the fact that we have obliged ourselves to labor under self-imposed restrictions with respect to impeding external aid to the Viet Cong. These restrictions include keeping the war within the boundaries of South Vietnam, avoiding the direct use of U.S. combat forces, and limiting U.S. direction of the campaign to rendering advice to the Government of Vietnam. These restrictions, while they may make our international position more readily defensible, all tend to make the task in Vietnam more complex, time-consuming, and in the end, more costly. In addition to complicating our own problem, these self-imposed restrictions may well now be conveying signals of irresolution to our enemies—encouraging them to higher levels of vigor and greater risks. A reversal of attitude and the adoption of a more aggressive program would enhance greatly our ability to control the degree to which escalation will occur. It appears probable that the economic and agricultural disappointments suffered by Communist China, plus the current rift with the Soviets, could cause the communists to think twice about undertaking a large-scale military adventure in Southeast Asia.

9. In adverting to actions outside of South Vietnam, the Joint Chiefs of Staff are aware that the focus of the counter-insurgency battle lies in South Vietnam itself, and that the war must certainly be fought and won primarily in the minds of the Vietnamese people. At the same time, the aid now coming to the Viet Cong from outside the country in men, resources, advice, and direction is sufficiently great in the aggregate to be significant—both as help and as encouragement to the Viet Cong. It is our conviction that if support of the insurgency from outside south Vietnam in terms of operational direction, personnel, and material were stopped completely, the character of the war in South Vietnam would be substantially and favorably altered. Because of this conviction, we are wholly in favor of executing the covert actions against North Vietnam which you have recently proposed to the President. We believe, however, that it would be idle to conclude that these efforts will have a decisive effect on the communist determination to support the insurgency; and it is our view that we must therefore be prepared fully to undertake a much higher level of activity, not only for its beneficial tactical effect, but to make plain our resolution, both to our friends and to our enemies.

10. Accordingly, the Joint Chiefs of Staff consider that the United States must make ready to conduct increasingly bolder actions in Southeast Asia; specifically as to Vietnam to:

(a) Assign to the U.S. military commander responsibilities for the total U.S. program in Vietnam.

(b) Induce the Government of Vietnam to turn over to the United States military commander, temporarily, the actual tactical direction of the war.

(c) Charge the United States military commander with complete responsibility for conduct of the program against North Vietnam.

(d) Overfly Laos and Cambodia to whatever extent is necessary for acquisition of operational intelligence.

(e) Induce the Government of Vietnam to conduct overt ground operations in Laos of sufficient scope to impede the flow of personnel and material southward.

(f) Arm, equip, advise, and support the Government of Vietnam in its conduct of aerial bombing of critical targets in North Vietnam and in mining the sea approaches to that country.

(g) Advise and support the Government of Vietnam in its conduct of large-scale commando raids against critical targets in North Vietnam.

(**h**) Conduct aerial bombing of key North Vietnam targets, using U.S. resources under Vietnamese cover, and with the Vietnamese openly assuming responsibility for the actions.

(**i**) Commit additional U.S. forces, as necessary, in support of the combat action within South Vietnam.

(**j**) Commit U.S. forces as necessary in direct actions against North Vietnam.

11. It is our conviction that any or all of the foregoing actions may be required to enhance our position in Southeast Asia. The past few months have disclosed that considerably higher levels of effort are demanded of us if U.S. objectives are to be attained. . . .

SOURCE: Sheehan and others (eds.), *Pentagon Papers*, pp. 274–277.

During the first few days of August 1964, a number of incidents occurred in the Gulf of Tonkin involving U.S. and North Vietnamese naval forces. These incidents brought about the implementation of many of the proposed military actions against North Vietnam including the first U.S. bombings of North Vietnamese military targets. Following alleged attacks on two U.S. destroyers on the night of August 4 in the Gulf of Tonkin, President Johnson ordered U.S. naval aircraft to carry out a series of retaliatory attacks on North Vietnamese patrol boat bases and oil supply depots. At the same time that he ordered the retaliatory raids, the president decided that the time had come to ask Congress to approve a resolution authorizing military action against North Vietnam. Johnson had been planning to submit the resolution for months, ever since the military had begun its contingency planning for taking the war to North Vietnam. On August 6, the Senate began debate on the resolution.

Later there was considerable controversy over whether or not U.S. ships were ever attacked the night of August 4 in the Gulf of Tonkin. Congress also discovered that administration officials had misled them when presenting their case for the resolution. The debate in both the Senate and the House had been perfunctory. The Senate passed the measure by a vote of 88–2 and the House by a vote of 416–0. Ironically, Senator Fulbright, who had steered the resolution through the Senate, became the most prominent senatorial opponent of the Vietnam war.

DOCUMENT 26. The Senate Debates the Tonkin Gulf Resolution,
August 6–7, 1964.

To Promote the Maintenance of International Peace and Security in Southeast Asia

Whereas naval units of the Communist regime in Vietnam, in violation of the principles of the Charter of the United Nations and of international law, have deliberately and repeatedly attacked United States naval vessels lawfully present in international waters, and have thereby created a serious threat to international peace; and

Whereas these attacks are part of a deliberate and systematic campaign of aggression that the Communist regime in North Vietnam has been waging against its neighbors and the nations joined with them in the collective defense of their freedom; and

Whereas the United States is assisting the peoples of southeast Asia to protect their freedom and has no territorial, military or political ambitions in that area, but desires only that these peoples should be left in peace to work out their own destinies in their own way: Now, therefore, be it

Resolved by the Senate and House of Representatives of the United States of America in Congress assembled.

That the Congress approves and supports the determination of the President as Commander in Chief, to take all necessary measures to repel any armed attack against the forces of the United States and to prevent further aggression.

SEC. 2. The United States regards as vital to its national interest and to world peace the maintenance of international peace and security in southeast Asia. Consonant with the Constitution of the United States and the Charter of the United Nations and in accordance with its obligations under the Southeast Asia Collective Defense Treaty, the United States is, therefore, prepared, as the President determines, to take all necessary steps, including the use of armed force, to assist any member or protocol state of the Southeast Asia Collective Defense Treaty requesting assistance in defense of its freedom.

SEC. 3. This resolution shall expire when the President shall determine that the peace and security of the area is reasonably assured by international conditions created by action of the United Nations or otherwise, except that it may be terminated earlier by concurrent resolution of the Congress.

MR. NELSON: [Gaylord Nelson, Dem.-Wis.] . . . Am I to understand that it is the sense of Congress that we are saying to the executive branch: "If it becomes necessary to prevent further aggression, we agree now, in advance, that you may land as many divisions as deemed necessary, and engage in a direct military assault on North Vietnam if it becomes the judgment of the Executive, the Commander in Chief, that this is the only way to prevent further aggression"?

MR. FULBRIGHT: [J. William Fulbright, Dem.-Ark.]. As I stated, section 1 is intended to deal primarily with aggression against our forces. . . .

I do not know what the limits are. I do not think this resolution can be determinative of that fact. I think it would indicate that he [the President] would take reasonable means first to prevent any further aggression, or repel further aggression against our own forces. . . . I do not

know how to answer the Senator's question and give him
an absolute assurance that large numbers of troops would
not be put ashore. I would deplore it. . . .

MR. NELSON: . . . my concern is that we in Congress could give the impression to the public that we are prepared at this time to
change our mission and substantially expand our commitment. If that is what the sense of Congress is, I am opposed
to the resolution. I therefore ask the distinguished Senator
from Arkansas if he would consent to accept an amendment [that explicitly says Congress wants no extension of
the present military conflict and no U.S. direct military
involvement].

MR. FULBRIGHT: . . . The Senator has put into his amendment a statement
of policy that is unobjectionable. However, I cannot accept
the amendment under the circumstances. I do not believe
it is contrary to the joint resolution, but it is an enlarge-
ment. I am informed that the House is now voting on this
resolution. The House joint resolution is about to be presented to us. I cannot accept the amendment and go to
conference with it, and thus take responsibility for delay-
ing matters. . . .

MR. GRUENING: [Ernest Gruening, Dem.-Alaska] . . . Regrettably, I find myself in disagreement with the President's southeast Asian
policy. . . . The serious events of the past few days, the attack by North Vietnamese vessels on American warships
and our reprisal, strikes me as the inevitable and foreseeable concomitant and consequence of U.S. unilateral military aggressive policy in southeast Asia. . . .

We now are about to authorize the President if he sees
fit to move our Armed Forces . . . not only into South Vietnam, but also into North Vietnam, Laos, Cambodia, Thailand, and of course the authorization includes all the rest
of the SEATO nations. That means sending our American
boys into combat in a war in which we have no business,
which is not our war, into which we have been misguidedly
drawn, which is steadily being escalated. This resolution
is a further authorization for escalation unlimited. I am
opposed to sacrificing a single American boy in this ven-
ture. We have lost far too many already. . . .

MR. MORSE: [Wayne Morse, Demo.-Ore.] . . . I believe that history will
record that we have made a great mistake in subverting
and circumventing the Constitution of the United
States. . . . I believe this resolution to be a historic mistake.
I believe that within the next century, future generations
will look with dismay and great disappointment upon a

Congress which is now about to make such a historic mistake.

SOURCE: *Congressional Record*, August 6–7, 1964, pp. 18132–33, 18406–7, 18458–59, and 18470–71.

During the fall 1964 presidential campaign, neither Johnson nor his Republican challenger, Barry Goldwater, devoted much time to the developing situation in Vietnam. Public interest in Vietnam was not yet very strong. When Johnson did address the subject, he sought to assure the American people that he did not intend to Americanize the war in South Vietnam. His stance was misleading, because he was actively involved in contingency planning for possible air attacks against North Vietnam and for sending U.S. combat troops to South Vietnam. Although he may have still hoped to avoid a war in Vietnam, he knew that the situation was continuing to deteriorate and that he might have to intervene militarily to prevent the defeat of the South Vietnamese forces.

DOCUMENT 27. Notes of Meeting Between Johnson and Advisers, September 14, 1964.

The meeting began with the President's review of a memorandum, "Courses of Action for South Vietnam," dated September 8, 1964. Initial attention was concentrated on the four specific recommendations in this paper. The Secretary of Defense reported that these recommendations, with minor adjustments, had the approval of the Joint Chiefs, but he reported also that there was an important division among the Chiefs, in that the Chief of Staff of the Air Force and the Commandant of the Marine Corps believed that it was now necessary in addition to execute extensive U.S. air strikes against North Vietnam. General Wheeler explained that these two officers now felt that the situation would continue to deteriorate unless such drastic action was taken now. He said that he and the other two colleagues were persuaded by the argument of Ambassador Taylor—the man on the spot—that it was important not to overstrain the currently weakened GVN by drastic action in the immediate future. General Taylor repeated that this was indeed his view, but he emphasized that he also believed that in the long run the current in-country program would not be sufficient. He had held this view for many months, but it had been reinforced by recent events in the field. . . .

The President asked Director McCone for his opinion and the Director replied that in the judgment of his Agency the four recommended actions were appropriate, and that a sustained air attack at present would be dangerous because of the weakness of the GVN. Such an attack might also trigger major increases in Chinese Communist participation. The Agency remained very gravely concerned by the internal situation in South Vietnam, which the Director estimated a shade more pessimistically than Ambassador Taylor. . . .

The President said that in his judgment the proper answer to those advocating immediate and extensive action against the North was that we should not do this until our side could defend itself in the streets of Saigon. We obviously wanted to strengthen the GVN. We believed it could be strengthened. But what specifically were we going to do in this direction?

Ambassador Taylor replied that we needed to move on in meshing our team with the GVN. This had been well started before the unrest of August. The problem was not in planning but in execution, and in the quality of the individuals in the GVN. Nevertheless we should continue to seek better individuals and continue to strengthen our cooperative effort with them.

The President accepted this as a first purpose and then asked whether we needed additional equipment as well. Ambassador Taylor said that while the additional U.S. advisers would be helpful, there was currently no equipment need beyond that which was being supplied.

Secretary McNamara emphasized the importance of politico-economic action in the urban areas . . . to lower the level of student and Buddhist pressure and increase the political base of support for the GVN. Mr. McCone endorsed this judgment. He further expressed his opinion that Hanoi and Peking now believed that they were doing very well and that they were not having second thoughts about their basic policy (an implied disagreement with the Secretary of State). The Agency was also disturbed by the prospect that internal movement toward negotiations might be increasing, and that there was some sign also of anti-American feeling in South Vietnam. It could happen that the President would find that the purposes originally set forth in Eisenhower's 1954 letter were no longer supported by the people of Vietnam themselves. . . .

The President asked whether the situation was better or worse than when Ambassador Taylor went out. Ambassador Taylor said he thought it was somewhat worse, but made it clear in response to a further question that this weakening was political, not military. Ambassador Taylor also emphasized his belief that sooner or later we would indeed have to act more forcefully against the North. He simply did not think now was the best time. . . .

SOURCE: William Appleman Williams and others (eds.), *America in Vietnam: A Documentary History*, pp. 239–241.

DOCUMENT 28. Excerpts from Johnson's Campaign Speeches, Fall, 1964.

At Eufaula, Oklahoma, on September 25, 1964, Johnson said:

> We don't want our American boys to do the fighting for Asian boys. We don't want to get involved in a nation with 700 million people and get tied down in a land war in Asia.

At Akron, Ohio, on October 21, 1964, Johnson stated:

> But we are not about to send American boys nine or ten thousands miles away from home to do what Asian boys ought to be doing for themselves.

SOURCE: Eric Goldman, *The Tragedy of Lyndon Johnson*, p. 279, 281.

Following Johnson's landslide victory over Barry Goldwater, the Vietcong escalated their war in South Vietnam. As the fighting intensified, political instability reigned in Saigon as factions of South Vietnamese leaders maneuvered for power. As the year ended, the Communists were close to victory. Johnson's advisers concluded that only the bombing of North Vietnam could save the South. Johnson delayed implementing the bombing for a time because of the political instability in the South. He wanted the South Vietnamese leaders to put their political house in order and to demonstrate that they could carry on the war against the rebels. As the Vietcong continued their assaults and began targeting American installations and personnel, Johnson changed his mind. Early on the morning of February 7, 1965, Vietcong forces attacked a U.S. airfield at Pleiku. Soon thereafter, Johnson ordered U.S. bombing raids against North Vietnamese targets. National Security Adviser McGeorge Bundy, who was visiting Vietnam at the time of the Pleiku attack, wrote Johnson a long memo calling for the implementation of sustained bombing.

DOCUMENT 29. Excerpts from McGeorge Bundy's Memo to President Johnson, February 7, 1965.

I. Introductory

We believe that the best available way of increasing our chance of success in Vietnam is the development and execution of a policy of *sustained reprisal* against North Vietnam—a policy in which air and naval action against the North is justified by and related to the whole Viet Cong campaign of violence and terror in the South.

While we believe that the risks of such a policy are acceptable, we emphasize that its costs are real. It implies significant U.S. air losses even if no full air war is joined, and it seems likely that it would eventually require an extensive and costly effort against the whole air defense system of North Vietnam. U.S. casualties would be higher—and more visible to American feelings—than those sustained in the struggle of South Vietnam.... And even if it fails to turn the tide—as it may—the value of the effort seems to us to exceed its costs....

3. Once a program of reprisals is clearly underway, it should not be necessary to connect each specific act against North Vietnam to a particular outrage in the South. It should be possible, for example, to publish weekly lists of outrages in the South and to have it clearly understood that these outrages are the cause of such action against the North as may be occurring in the current period. Such a more generalized pattern of reprisal would remove much of the difficulty involved in finding precisely matching targets in response to specific atrocities. Even in such a more general pattern, however, it would be important to insure that the general level of reprisal action remained in close correspondence with the level of outrages in the South. We must keep it clear at every stage both to Hanoi and to the world, that our reprisals will be reduced or stopped when outrages in the South are reduced or stopped—and that we are *not* attempting to destroy or conquer North Vietnam.

4. In the early stages of such a course, we should take the appropriate occasion to make clear our firm intent to undertake reprisals on any further acts, major or minor, that appear to us and the GVN as indicating Hanoi's support. We would announce that our two governments have been patient and forebearing in the hope that Hanoi would come to its senses without the necessity of our having to take further action; but the outrages continue and now we must react against those who are responsible; we will not provoke; we will not use our force indiscriminately; but we can no longer sit by in the face of repeated acts of terror and violence for which the DRV is responsible. . . .

9. We are convinced that the political values of reprisal require a *continuous* operation. Episodic responses geared on a one-for-one basis to "spectacular" outrages would lack the persuasive force of sustained pressure. More important still, they would leave it open to the Communists to avoid reprisals entirely by giving up only a small element of their own program. The Gulf of Tonkin affair produced a sharp upturn in morale in South Vietnam. When it remained an isolated episode, however, there was a severe relapse. It is the great merit of the proposed scheme that to stop it the Communists would have to stop enough of their activity in the South to permit the probable success of a determined pacification effort. . . .

We emphasize that our primary target in advocating a reprisal policy is the improvement of the situation in *South* Vietnam. Action against the North is usually urged as a means of affecting the will of Hanoi to direct and support the VC. We consider this an important but longer-range purpose. The immediate and critical targets are in the South—in the minds of the South Vietnamese and in the minds of the Viet Cong cadres. . . .

The Vietnamese increase in hope could well increase the readiness of Vietnamese factions themselves to join together in forming a more effective government.

We think it plausible that effective and sustained reprisals, even in a low key, would have a substantial depressing effect upon the morale of Viet Cong cadres in South Vietnam. This is the strong opinion of CIA Saigon. It is based upon reliable reports of the initial Viet Cong reaction to the Gulf of Tonkin episode, and also upon the solid general assessment that the determination of

Hanoi and the apparent timidity of the mighty United States are both major items in Viet Cong confidence. . . .

While emphasizing the importance of reprisals in the South, we do not exclude the impact on Hanoi. We believe, indeed, that it is of great importance that the level of reprisal be adjusted rapidly and visibly to both upward and downward shifts in the level of Viet Cong offenses. We want to keep before Hanoi the carrot of our desisting as well as the stick of continued pressure. We also need to conduct the application of force so that there is always a prospect of worse to come.

We cannot assert that a policy of sustained reprisal will succeed in changing the course of the contest in Vietnam. It may fail, and we cannot estimate the odds of success with any accuracy—they may be somewhere between 25% and 75%. What we can say is that even if it fails, the policy will be worth it. At a minimum it will damp down the charge that we did not do all that we could have done, and this charge will be important in many countries, including our own. Beyond that, a reprisal policy—to the extent that it demonstrates U.S. willingness to employ this new norm in counter-insurgency—will set a higher price for the future upon all adventures of guerrilla warfare, and it should therefore somewhat increase our ability to deter such adventures. We must recognize, however, that that ability will be gravely weakened if there is failure for any reason in Vietnam. . . .

SOURCE: Sheehan and others (eds.), *Pentagon Papers*, pp. 423–427.

On February 13, 1965, President Johnson ordered "Rolling Thunder," a systematic, gradually expanding bombing campaign, using both American and South Vietnamese aircraft to strike at North Vietnamese targets. This gradualist air strategy soon proved i effective. Morale in the South did not rise, the Vietcong were not deterred, and Hanoi continued its strong backing of the southern insurgency. Administration officials now had to consider the possibility of sending U.S. combat troops or else watch South Vietnam fall to the Communists.

DOCUMENT 30. Assistant Secretary of Defense John T. McNaughton's Memo to McNamara, March 24, 1965.

First Draft of "Annex—Plan for Action for South Vietnam," appended to memorandum from John T. McNaughton, Assistant Secretary of Defense for International Security Affairs, for Secretary of Defense Robert S. McNamara, March 24, 1965.

1. U.S. Aims:

70%—To avoid a humiliating U.S. defeat (to our reputation as a guarantor).

20%—To keep SVN (and the adjacent) territory from Chinese hands.

10%—To permit the people of SVN to enjoy a better, freer way of life.

ALSO—To emerge from crisis without unacceptable taint from methods used.

NOT—to "help a friend," although it would be hard to stay in if asked out.

2. The Situation:

The situation in general is bad and deteriorating. The VC have the initiative. Defeatism is gaining among the rural population, somewhat in the cities, and even among the soldiers—especially those with relatives in rural areas. The Hop Tac area around Saigon is making little progress; the Delta stays bad; the country has been severed in the north. GVN control is shrinking to the enclaves, some burdened with refugees. In Saigon we have a remission: Quat is giving hope on the civilian side, the Buddhists have calmed, and the split generals are in uneasy equilibrium.

3. The Preliminary question:

Can the situation inside SVN be bottomed out (a) without extreme measures against the DRV and/or (b) without deployment of large numbers of U.S. (and other) combat troops inside SVN? The answer is perhaps, but probably no.

4. Ways GVN Might Collapse:

(a) VC successes reduce GVN control to enclaves, causing:
  (1) insurrection in the enclaved population,
  (2) massive defections of ARVN soldiers and even units,
  (3) aggravated dissension and impotence in Saigon,
  (4) defeatism and reorientation by key GVN officials,
  (5) entrance of left-wing elements into the government,
  (6) emergence of a popular-front regime,
  (7) request that U.S. leave,
  (8) concessions to the VC, and
  (9) accommodations to the DRV.
(b) VC with DRV volunteers concentrate on I and II Corps,
  (1) conquering principal GVN-held enclaves there,
  (2) declaring Liberation Government
  (3) joining the I & II Corps areas to the DRV, and
  (4) pressing the course in (a) above for rest of SVN.
(c) While in a temporary funk, GVN might throw in sponge:
  (1) dealing under the table with VC,
  (2) asking the U.S. to cease at least military aid,
  (3) bringing left-wing elements into the government,

(4) leading to a popular-front regime, and

(5) ending in accommodations to the VC and DRV.

(d) In a surge of anti-Americanism, GVN could ask the U.S. out and pursue course otherwise similar to (c) above.

5. The "Trilemma":

US policy appears to be drifting. This is because, while there is consensus that efforts inside SVN (para 6) will probably fail to prevent collapse, all three of the possible remedial courses of action have so far been rejected:

(a) Will-breaking strikes on the North (para 7) are balked (1) by flash-point limits, (2) by doubts that the DRV will cave and (3) by doubts that the VC will obey a caving DRV. (Leaving strikes only a political and anti-infiltration nuisance.)

(b) Large U.S. troop deployments are blocked by "French-defeat" and "Korea" syndromes, and Quat is queasy. (Troops could be net negatives, and be besieged.)

(c) Exit by negotiations is tainted by the humiliation likely to follow.

Effort Inside South Vietnam:

Progress inside SVN is our main aim. Great, imaginative efforts on the civilian political as well as military side must be made, bearing in mind that progress depends as much on GVN efforts and luck as on added U.S. efforts. While only a few of such efforts can pay off quickly enough to affect the present ominous deterioration, some may, and we are dealing here in small critical margins. Furthermore, such investment is essential to provide a foundation for the longer run.

(a) Improve spirit and effectiveness. (fill out further, drawing from State memo to the President)

(1) Achieve governmental stability.

(2) Augment the psy-war program.

(3) Build a stronger pro-government infrastructure.

(b) Improve physical security. (fill out)

(c) Reduce infiltration. (fill out). . . .

SOURCE: Sheehan and others (eds.), *Pentagon Papers*, pp. 432–435.

The first American combat troops arrived in South Vietnam on March 8, 1965. They consisted of Marine amphibious forces assigned to provide security for a U.S. Air Force base in Da Nang. The U.S. commander in Vietnam, General William C. Westmoreland, soon requested additional combat forces. On April 1, 1965, President

Johnson made a series of decisions that moved America closer to war. He authorized sending an additional 20,000 combat troops and he also expanded the mission of the Marines at Da Nang to include offensive operations against the Vietcong out to a radius of 50 miles from the base. On April 6, McGeorge Bundy issued National Security Action Memorandum 328 (NSAM 328) implementing Johnson's decisions. Johnson chose not inform the American people of these important moves, and Bundy's memorandum reflected the president's wishes.

DOCUMENT 31. **National Security Action Memorandum**
Number 328 April 6, 1965, signed by McGeorge Bundy
and addressed to the Secretary of State, Secretary
of Defense, and the Director of the Central
Intelligence Agency.

On Thursday, April 1, The President made the following decisions with respect to Vietnam: . . . .

The President approved an 18–20,000 man increase in U.S. military support forces to fill out existing units and supply needed logistic personnel.

The President approved the deployment of two additional Marine Battalions and one Marine Air Squadron and associated headquarters and support elements.

The President approved a change of mission for all Marine Battalions deployed to Vietnam to permit their more active use under conditions to be established and approved by the Secretary of Defense in consultations with the Secretary of State.

The President approved the urgent exploration, with the Korean, Australian, and New Zealand governments, of the possibility of rapid deployment of significant combat elements from their armed forces. . . .

The President approved the following . . . continuing action against North Vietnam and Laos:

We should continue roughly the present slowly ascending tempo of ROLLING THUNDER operations, being prepared to add strikes in response to a higher rate of VC operations, or conceivably to slow the pace in the unlikely event the VC slacked off sharply. . . .

Blockade or aerial mining of North Vietnamese ports needs further study and should be considered for future operations. It could have major political complications, especially in relation to the Soviets. . . .

Air operations in Laos, particularly route blocking operations in the Panhandle area, should be stepped up. . . .

The President desires that the . . . actions themselves should be taken as rapidly as practicable, but in ways that should minimize any appearance of sudden changes in policy, . . . The President's desire is that these movements and changes should be understood as being gradual and wholly consistent with existing policy.

SOURCE: Sheehan and others (eds.), *Pentagon Papers*, pp. 442–443.

On April 7, 1965, President Johnson, aware of growing hawkish and dovish criticisms of his Vietnam policy, delivered a major speech at Johns Hopkins University. In the speech, he reaffirmed the American commitment to Vietnam. He tried to appear tough enough to satisfy the hawks, but soft enough to give the doves hope. While asserting that he would use whatever force was necessary to deter aggression, he also stated the readiness of American officials to begin "unconditional discussions" if they would lead to a peaceful settlement. Johnson also added a billion-dollar developmental project for the Mekong river valley once the war was over. The project would even include North Vietnam.

DOCUMENT 32. Excerpts from Speech Given by President Johnson at Johns Hopkins University, April 7, 1965.

Viet-Nam is far away from this quiet campus. We have no territory there, nor do we seek any. The war is dirty and brutal and difficult. And some 400 young men, born into an America that is bursting with opportunity and promise, have ended their lives on Viet-Nam's steaming soil.

Why must we take this painful road?

Why must this Nation hazard its ease, and its interest, and its power for the sake of a people so far away?

We fight because we must fight if we are to live in a world where every country can shape its own destiny. And only in such a world will our own freedom be finally secure. . . .

The first reality is that North Viet-Nam has attacked the independent nation of South Viet-Nam. Its object is total conquest.

Of course, some of the people of South Viet-Nam are participating in attack on their own government. But trained men and supplies, orders and arms, flow in a constant stream from north to south. . . .

Over this war—and all Asia—is another reality: the deepening shadow of Communist China. The rulers in Hanoi are urged on by Peking. This is a regime which has destroyed freedom in Tibet, which has attacked India, and has been condemned by the United Nations for aggression in Korea. . . .

Why are these realities our concern? Why are we in South Viet-Nam?

We are there because we have a promise to keep. Since 1954 every American President has offered support to the people of South Viet-Nam. We have helped to build, and we have helped to defend. Thus, over many years, we have made a national pledge to help South Viet-Nam defend its independence.

And I intend to keep that promise. . . .

We are also there to strengthen world order. Around the globe, from Berlin to Thailand, are people whose well-being rests, in part, on the belief that they can count on us if they are attacked. To leave Viet-Nam to its fate would shake the confidence of all these people in the value of an American commitment and in the value of America's word. The result would be increased unrest and instability, and even wider war.

We are also there because there are great stakes in the balance. Let no one think for a moment that retreat from Viet-Nam would bring an end to conflict. The battle would be renewed in one country and then another. The central lesson of our time is that the appetite of aggression is never satisfied. To withdraw from one battlefield means only to prepare for the next. We must say in southeast Asia—as we did in Europe—in the words of the Bible: "Hitherto shalt thou come, but no further." . . .

Our objective is the independence of South Viet-Nam, and its freedom from attack. We want nothing for ourselves—only that the people of South Viet-Nam be allowed to guide their own country in their own way.

We will do everything necessary to reach that objective. And we will do only what is absolutely necessary.

In recent months attacks on South Viet-Nam were stepped up. Thus, it became necessary for us to increase our response and to make attacks by air. This is not a change of purpose. It is a change in which we believe that purpose requires. . . .

These countries of southeast Asia are homes for millions of impoverished people. Each day these people rise at dawn and struggle through until the night to wrestle existence from the soil. They are often wracked by disease, plagued by hunger, and death comes at the early age of 40. . . .

For our part I will ask the Congress to join in a billion dollar American investment in this effort as soon as it is underway. . . .

The task is nothing less than to enrich the hopes and the existence of more than a hundred million people. And there is much to be done.

The vast Mekong River can provide food and water and power on a scale to dwarf even our own TVA. . . .

SOURCE: *Public Papers of the Presidents of the United States: Lyndon B. Johnson, 1965*, pp. 394–397.

Hanoi responded quickly to Johnson's speech and offer of "unconditional negotiations." North Vietnam's premier, Pham Van Dong, stated his government's basis for negotiations. It consisted of four major points: (1) The United States would have to stop its bombing and withdraw from Vietnam; (2) the 1954 Geneva agreements must be reinstituted; (3) the internal affairs of South Vietnam must be settled in accordance with the program of the National Liberation Front; and (4) Vietnam was to be reunified. Neither side appeared to be serious about negotiating a settlement in the spring of 1965.

DOCUMENT 33. The North Vietnamese Diplomatic Position, April 8, 1965.

. . . . 1. Recognition of the basic national rights of the Vietnamese people—peace, independence, sovereignty, unity and territorial integrity. According to the Geneva Agreements, the United States government must withdraw from South Viet-Nam United States troops, military personnel, and weapons of all kinds, dismantle all United States military bases there, cancel its "military alli-ance" with South Viet-Nam. It must end its policy of intervention and aggression in South Viet-Nam. According to the Geneva Agreements, the United States gov-ernment must stop its acts of war against North Viet-Nam, completely cease all encroachments on the territory and sovereignty of the D.R.V.

2. Pending the peaceful reunification of Viet-Nam, while Viet-Nam is still temporarily divided into two zones, the military provisions of the 1954 Ge-neva Agreements on Viet-Nam must be strictly respected. The two zones must refrain from joining any military alliance with foreign countries. There must be no foreign military bases, troops, or military personnel in their respective terri-tory.

3. The internal affairs of South Viet-Nam must be settled by the South Vietnamese people themselves, in accordance with the program of the NFLSV [the Viet-Cong] without any foreign interference.

4. The peaceful reunification of Viet-Nam is to be settled by the Viet-namese people in both zones, without any foreign interference....

If this basis is recognized, favorable conditions will be created for the peaceful settlement of the Viet-Nam problem, and it will be possible to consider the reconvening of an international conference along the pattern of the 1954 Geneva Conference on Viet-Nam.

The government of the D.R.V. declares that any approach contrary to the above-mentioned stand is inappropriate. Any approach tending to secure a United Nations intervention in the Viet-Nam situation is also inappropriate be-cause such approaches are basically at variance with the 1954 Geneva Agree-ments on Viet-Nam.

SOURCE: Williams and others (eds.), *America in Vietnam*, pp. 244–245.

In June 1965, pressures mounted on Johnson to make a large-scale commitment of U.S. ground combat forces to stave off defeat of the South Vietnamese forces. Among Johnson's senior advisers, only one man, Undersecretary of State George Ball, counseled against sending large numbers of American troops to fight in Viet-nam. He warned that the United States could be humiliated in Vietnam even after making a major commitment of its manpower and prestige. Ball advised Johnson to opt for a negotiated settlement. Johnson read Ball's memo carefully, but then disregarded Ball's advice and committed America to a major war in South Vietnam.

Document 34. Undersecretary of State George Ball's Memo to President Johnson, July 1, 1965.

(1) A Losing War: The South Vietnamese are losing the war to the Viet Cong. No one can assure you that we can beat the Viet Cong or even force them

to the conference table on our terms, no matter how many hundred thousand *white foreign* (U.S.) troops we deploy.

No one has demonstrated that a white ground force of whatever size can win a guerrilla war—which is at the same time a civil war between Asians—in jungle terrain in the midst of a population that refuses cooperation in the white forces (and the South Vietnamese) and thus provides a great intelligence advantage to the other side. Three recent incidents vividly illustrate this point:

(a) the sneak attack on the Da Nang Air Base which involved penetration of a defense perimeter guarded by 9,000 Marines. This raid was possible only because of the cooperation of the local inhabitants;

(b) the B52 raid that failed to hit the Viet Cong who had obviously been tipped off;

(c) the search and destroy mission of the 173rd Air Borne Brigade which spent three days looking for the Viet Cong, suffered 23 casualties, and never made contact with the enemy who had obviously gotten advance word of their assignment.

(2) The Question to Decide: Should we limit our liabilities in South Vietnam and try to find a way out with minimal long-term costs?

The alternative—no matter what we may wish it to be—is almost certainly a protracted war involving an open-ended commitment of U.S. forces, mounting U.S. casualties, no assurance of a satisfactory solution, and a serious danger of escalation at the end of the road.

(3) Need for a Decision Now: So long as our forces are restricted to advising and assisting the South Vietnamese, the struggle will remain a civil war between Asian peoples. Once we deploy substantial numbers of troops in combat it will become a war between the U.S. and a large part of the population of South Vietnam, organized and directed from North Vietnam and backed by the resources of both Moscow and Peiping.

The decision you face now, therefore, is crucial. Once large numbers of U.S. troops are committed to direct combat, they will begin to take heavy casualties in a war they are ill-equipped to fight in a non-cooperative if not downright hostile countryside.

Once we suffer large casualties, we will have started a well-nigh irreversible process. Our involvement will be so great that we cannot—without national humiliation—stop short of achieving our complete objectives. *Of the two possibilities I think humiliation would be more likely than the achievement of our objectives—even after we have paid terrible costs....*

(4) Compromise Solution: Should we commit U.S. manpower and prestige to a terrain so unfavorable as to give a very large advantage to the enemy—or should we seek a compromise settlement which achieves less than our stated objectives and thus cut our losses while we still have the freedom of maneuver to do so.

(5) Costs of a Compromise Solution: The answer involves a judgment as to the cost to the U.S. of such a compromise settlement in terms of our relations with the countries in the area of South Vietnam, the credibility of our commitments, and our prestige around the world. In my judgment, if we act before we commit substantial U.S. troops to combat in South Vietnam we can, by accepting some short-term costs, avoid what may well be a long-term catastrophe. I believe we tended grossly to exaggerate the costs involved in a compromise settlement. . . .

Now is the time to start some serious diplomatic feelers looking towards a solution based on some application of a self-determination principle.

I would recommend approaching Hanoi rather than any of the other probable parties, the NLF—or Peiping. Hanoi is the only one that has given any signs of interest in discussion. Peiping has been rigidly opposed. Moscow has recommended that we negotiate with Hanoi. The NLF has been silent.

There are several channels to the North Vietnamese but I think the best one is through their representative in Paris, Mai Van Bo. Initial feelers of Bo should be directed toward a discussion both of the four points we have put forward and the four points put forward by Hanoi as a basis for negotiation. We can accept all but one of Hanoi's four points, and hopefully we should be able to agree on some ground rules for serious negotiation—including no preconditions.

If the initial feelers lead to further secret, exploratory talks, we can inject the concept of self-determination that would permit the Viet Cong some hope of achieving some of their political objectives through local elections or some other device.

The contact on our side should be handled through a non-governmental cut-out (possibly a reliable newspaper man who can be repudiated).

If progress can be made at this level a basis can be laid for a multinational conference. At some point, obviously, the government of South Vietnam will have to be brought on board, but I would postpone this step until after a substantial feeling out of Hanoi. . . .

(7) Before moving to any formal conference we should be prepared to agree once the conference is started:

(a) The U.S. will stand down its bombing of the North.

(b) The South Vietnamese will initiate no offensive operations in the South, and

(c) the DRV will stop terrorism and other aggressive action against the South.

(8) The negotiations at the conference should aim at incorporating our understanding with Hanoi in the form of a multinational agreement guaranteed by the U.S., the Soviet Union and possibly other parties, and providing for an international mechanism to supervise its execution. . . .

. . . On balance, I believe we would more seriously undermine the effectiveness of our world leadership by continuing the war and deepening our involvement than by pursuing a carefully plotted course toward a compromise solution. In spite of the number of powers that have—in response to our pleading—given verbal support from feeling of loyalty and dependence, we cannot ignore the fact that the war is vastly unpopular and that our role in it is perceptively eroding the respect and confidence with which other nations regard us. We have not persuaded either our friends or allies that our further involvement is essential to the defense of freedom in the cold war. Moreover, the men we deploy in the jungles of South Vietnam, the more we contribute to a growing world anxiety and mistrust.

[Words illegible] the short run, of course, we could expect some catcalls from the sidelines and some vindictive pleasure on the part of Europeans jealous of American power. But that would, in my view, be a transient phenomenon with which we could live without sustained anguish. Elsewhere around the world I would see few unhappy implications for the credibility of our commitments. No doubt the Communists will to gain propaganda value in Africa, but I cannot seriously believe that the Africans care too much about what happens in Southeast Asia. Australia and New Zealand are, of course, special cases since they feel lonely in the far reaches of the Pacific. Yet even their concern is far greater with Malaysia than with South Vietnam, and the degree of their anxiety would be conditioned largely by expressions of our support for Malaysia.

SOURCE: Sheehan and others (eds.), *Pentagon Papers*, pp. 449–454.

In mid-July of 1965, Secretary of Defense McNamara returned to Washington after another of his many trips to South Vietnam. In a report to the president, he warned Johnson that failure to send more U.S. combat troops to Vietnam would spell defeat for the GVN within a few months. He recommended that Johnson meet General Westmoreland's requests for additional forces, which would bring the total number of U.S. troops in South Vietnam to about 175,000 by the end of the year. McNamara's recommendations set off a week of intensive discussions among Johnson and his senior advisers, stretching from July 21 to July 28, during which the president made his fateful decisions that put America on a course from which it did not deviate for nearly three years and which opened the way for seven years of bloody combat in Vietnam. McNamara's memo triggered the decision-making process that brought about the Vietnam war.

DOCUMENT 35. Summary of Secretary of Defense Robert S. McNamara's Memo to President Johnson, July 20, 1965.

McNamara's Recommendations

Secretary McNamara's 20 July 1965 Memorandum for the President [Doc. 261] spelled out the troop requirements for Vietnam as follows: The forces for 1965 should be brought up to about 175,000, and "It should be understood that the deployment of more men (perhaps 100,000) may be necessary in early 1966, and that the deployment of additional forces thereafter is possible but will depend on developments."

This 100,000-man possible addition was broken down in a cable from COMUSMACV to CINCPAC as providing 27 maneuver battalions with associated combat and service support elements, bringing the total number of maneuver battalions to 61 sometime in 1966. The question arises as to how this 100,000-man 27-battalion figure was reached. In the absence of documentary evidence, it seems simplest to assume that Westmoreland was given pretty much what he asked for. However, the 61 battalion figure comes very close to the number of battalions the Secretary of Defense was thinking about earlier in July, when a memorandum for the record dated 12 July shows a proposal to strengthen U.S. forces by 63 battalions through a combination of calling up reserves, extending tours of duty, and increasing the draft. In fact, the 63 battalion figure appears again in the Secretary's 20 July memorandum to the President, allowing one to speculate that the size of the build-up had already been fixed in early July prior to the trip.

In either case, the result was that Phase II was recommended to the President at a level of roughly 100,000 which when added to the then current estimates for Phase I of 175,000 gave a total estimate of 275,000 by the end of 1966.

Secretary McNamara envisioned that the employment of U.S. forces would be as follows:

> . . . *Use of forces.* The forces will be used however they can be brought to bear most effectively. The US third-country ground forces will operate in coordination with South Vietnamese forces. They will defend their own bases; they will assist in providing security in neighboring areas; they will augment Vietnamese forces, assuring retention of key logistic areas and population centers. Also, in the initial phase they will maintain a small reserve-reaction force, conducting nuisance raids and spoiling attacks, and opening and securing selected lines of communication; as in-country ground strength increases to a level permitting extended US and third-country offensive action, the forces will be available for more active combat missions when the Vietnamese Government and General Westmoreland agree that such active missions are needed. The strategy for winning this stage of the war will be to take the offensive—to take and hold the initiative. The concept of tactical operations will be to exploit the offensive, with the objects of putting the VC/DRV battalion forces out of operation and of destroying their morale. The South Vietnamese, US and third-country forces, by aggressive exploitation of superior military forces, are to gain and hold the initiative—keeping the enemy at a disadvantage, maintaining a tempo such as to deny them time to recuperate or regain their balance, and pressing the fight against VC/DRV main force units in South Vietnam to run them to ground and to destroy them. The operations should combine to compel the VC/DRV to fight at a higher and more sustained intensity with resulting higher logistical consumption and, at the same time, to limit his capability to resupply forces in combat at that scale by attacking his LOC. The concept assumes vigorous prosecution of the air and sea anti-infiltration campaign and includes increased use of air in-country, including B-52s, night and day to harass VC in their havens. Following destruction of the VC main force units, the South Vietnamese must reinstitute the Program of Rural Reconstruction as an antidote to the continuing VC campaign of terror and subversion.

... *Evaluation.* ARVN overall is not capable of successfully resisting the VC initiatives without more active assistance from more US/third-country ground forces than those thus far committed. Without further outside help, the ARVN is faced with successive tactical reverses, loss of key communication and population centers particularly in the highlands, piece-meal destruction of ARVN units, attrition of RVNAF will to fight, and loss of civilian confidence. Early commitment of additional US/third-country forces in sufficient quantity, in general reserve and offensive roles, should stave off GVN defeat.

The success of the program from the military point of view turns on whether the Vietnamese hold their own in terms of numbers and fighting spirit, and on whether the US forces can be effective in a quick-reaction reserve role, a role in which they are only now being tested. The number of US troops is too small to make a significant difference in the tradition 10–1 government-guerrilla formula, but it is not too small to make a significant difference in the kind of war which seems to be evolving in Vietnam—a "Third Stage" or conventional war in which it is easier to identify, locate and attack the enemy.

The plan is such that the risk of escalation into war with China or the Soviet Union can be kept small. US and South Vietnamese casualties will increase—just how much cannot be predicted with confidence, but the US killed-in-action might be in the vicinity of 500 a month by the end of the year. The South Vietnamese under one government or another will probably see the thing through and the United States public will support the course of action because it is a sensible and courageous military-political program designed and likely to bring about a success in Vietnam.

It should be recognized, however, that success against the larger, more conventional, VC/PAVN forces could merely drive the VC back into the trees and back to their 1960–64 pattern—a pattern against which US troops and aircraft would be of limited value but with which the GVN, with our help, could cope. The questions here would be whether the VC could maintain morale after such a setback, and whether the South Vietnamese would have the will to hang on through another cycle.

SOURCE: Gravel (ed.), *Pentagon Papers*, Vol. 4, pp. 297–299.

4
AMERICA AT WAR: 1966–1968

By the summer of 1965 America's combat role in the Vietnam war was underway. The number of U.S. combat forces in South Vietnam increased rapidly until there were 184,300 troops in the country by year's end. American troops fought in several major battles during that first year of combat involvement. The air war against North Vietnam also escalated. Polls demonstrated that American public opinion was generally supportive of the war during its first year. *Time* magazine named General Westmoreland its "Man of the Year." Even so, opposition to the war quickly surfaced. "Teach-ins" were held on several college campuses and the first antiwar demonstration took place in the nation's capital in April 1965. Members of Congress also began to voice misgivings about the escalating war in Vietnam. Senator J. William Fulbright, chairman of the Senate Foreign Relations Committee and the nation's most prominent dove, staged televised hearings on the war in February 1966. Fulbright and some of his dovish colleagues subjected Secretary of State Dean Rusk, the principal administration defender of the U.S. role in Vietnam, to a sustained grilling on all facets of war policy.

DOCUMENT 36. Excerpts of Testimony During Senate Foreign Relations Committee Hearings on the Vietnam War, February 4–17, 1966.

SECRETARY RUSK: To put it in its simplest terms, Mr. Chairman, we believe that the South Vietnamese are entitled to a chance to make their own decisions about their own affairs and their own future course of policy: that they are entitled to make these decisions without having them imposed on them by force from North Vietnam or elsewhere from the outside. We are perfectly prepared to rely upon the South Vietnamese themselves to make that judgment by elections, through their own Government, by whatever way is suitable for them to make that decision.

Now, we have indicated a good many points which have a bearing on this matter. We are not, for example, trying to acquire a new ally. If South Vietnam and the South Vietnamese people wish to pursue a nonaligned course by their own option, that is an option which is open to them.

If they wish to join in the regional activities in the area, such as Mekong River development and projects of that sort, that is open to them. But we do believe they are entitled not to have these answers decided for them on the basis of military force organized from Hanoi through an aggression initiated from Hanoi, in the leadership of a front which was organized in Hanoi in 1960 for the purpose of taking over South Vietnam by force.

THE CHAIRMAN: Do you think they can be a completely free agent with our occupation of the land with 200,000 or 400,000 men?

SECRETARY RUSK: If the infiltration of men and arms from the north were not in the picture, these troops of ours could come home. We have said that repeatedly. They went in there, the combat troops went in there, because of infiltration of men and arms from the north. That is the simple and elementary basis for the presence of American combat forces.

THE CHAIRMAN: May I ask what is the explanation of why in 1956, contrary to the terms of the Geneva accords, elections were not held? You have stated several times that the aggression started in 1960. But the events between 1954 when the agreement was signed and 1960 were not without significance.

We backed Diem, did we not? Didn't we have much to do with putting him in power?

SECRETARY RUSK: Well, we supported him.

THE CHAIRMAN: That is what I mean.

SECRETARY RUSK: That is correct.

THE CHAIRMAN: And he was, to an extent had, a certain dependence upon us, did he not?

SECRETARY RUSK: We were giving him very considerable aid, Mr. Chairman.

THE CHAIRMAN: I am informed that in 1955, in accordance with the treaty provisions, he was requested by the north to consult about elections, and that he refused to do so. Is that correct?

SECRETARY RUSK: Well, neither his government nor the Government of the United States signed that agreement....

THE CHAIRMAN: Not having signed it, what business was it of ours for intervening and encouraging one of the participants not to follow it, specifically Diem?

SECRETARY RUSK: Well, the prospect of free elections in North and South Vietnam was very poor at that time.

THE CHAIRMAN: Now, they have always been poor, and will be for a hundred years, won't they? That was not news to you. I mean, this was a device to get around the settlement, was it not?

SECRETARY RUSK: No, no, Mr. Chairman. I do not believe the prospects of free elections, in South Vietnam anyhow, are all that dim.

THE CHAIRMAN: Have they ever had them in 2,000 years of history?

SECRETARY RUSK: They have had some free elections in the provinces and municipalities in May of last year....

THE CHAIRMAN: But all I am really trying to say is I do not think that this dispute is worthy of an escalation that would result in a confrontation with China in a world war. I do not believe that there is much evidence that this is the kind of a test in which it would follow that, if we should make a compromise, then all the world will collapse because we have been defeated.

This country is much too strong, in my opinion, that it would suffer any great setback. We are much stronger than the Russians were when they withdrew from Cuba. For a week maybe people said they had had a rebuff and within a month everyone was complimenting them for having contributed to the maintenance of peace....

SECRETARY RUSK: Yes. I do not understand though, Mr. Chairman, just what the substance of the compromise would be.

THE CHAIRMAN: Well, it strikes me that the essence—

SECRETARY RUSK: I mean some of the things you said suggested that we should abandon the effort in South Vietnam.

THE CHAIRMAN: No. I am not suggesting that we should abandon it, but that we should have a conference. I do not think you will get it until you propose reasonable terms that would allow the Vietnamese, even the liberation front, to have an opportunity to participate in an election.

After all, Vietnam is their country. It is not our country. We do not even have the right that the French did. We have no historical right. We are obviously intruders from their point of view. We represent the old Western imperialism in their eyes. I am not questioning our motives. I think our motives are very good, as has been testified on numerous occasions.

But I still think from their point of view it is their country, however bad the people have acted. Other countries have had civil wars; we had one. In my part of the country we resented it for a long time. So did yours. You can remember the feelings that were there. . . .

SENATOR MCCARTHY: Mr. Secretary, I have one question. I think we accepted for 5 or 6 years the ideas expressed by General [Douglas] MacArthur, General Eisenhower, General [James] Gavin, General [Matthew] Ridgway, and others that a land war in Asia was unthinkable.

Is that theoretical position still held or do we have among the military figures in America today a changed point of view?

SECRETARY RUSK: Senator, the nature of a struggle of this sort, where the initiative is not ours, where we did not start it, and where we didn't want it to begin with, and where the aggression comes from the other side is, of course, substantially determined by the other side.

At the present time the situation in South Vietnam does not take the form of armies, land armies, locked in combat with each other. It continues to be basically a guerrilla operation. The overwhelming part of the problem is terror and sabotage. The fixed units that the other side has—battalions or regiments—occasionally engage in combat. . . .

SENATOR MCCARTHY: I know that to be the case.

SECRETARY RUSK: The fire power that is available to the government and allied forces out there is very large indeed, and the other side has found it very difficult to sustain battalions or regiments in action for any protracted period. . . .

SENATOR CHURCH: It seems to me that there is a difference between guerrilla war or revolution and the kind of aggression that we faced in Korea and in Europe, and, further, that the underdeveloped world is going to be beset with guerrilla wars, regardless of the outcome in Vietnam, and that we will have to live in a world afflicted with such revolutions for a long time to come.

That is why it is so important to try to determine what our basic foreign policy attitude is going to be in dealing with these revolutionary wars in many parts of the underdeveloped world in the future; and, as I have listened to your explanations this morning, I gather that wherever a revolution occurs against an established government, and that revolution, as most will doubtlessly be, is infiltrated by Communists, that the United States will intervene, if necessary, to prevent a Communist success.

This, at least, has been the policy we followed in the Dominican Republic and in Vietnam. I wonder whether this is going to continue to be the policy as we face new guerrilla wars in the future?

SECRETARY RUSK: Senator, I think it is very important that the different kinds of revolutions be distinguished. We are in no sense committed against change. As a matter of fact, we are stimulating, ourselves, very sweeping revolutions in a good many places. The whole weight and effort of the Alliance for Progress is to bring about far-reaching social, economic changes.

SENATOR CHURCH: That is change sought, Mr. Secretary, without violence. History shows that the most significant change has been accompanied by violence.

Do you think that with our foreign aid program we are going to be able, with our money, to avert serious uprisings in all of these destitute countries in future years?

SECRETARY RUSK: Not necessarily avert all of them, but I do believe there is a fundamental difference between the kind of revolution which the Communists call their wars of national liberation, and the kind of revolution which is congenial to our own experience, and fits into the aspirations of ordinary men and women right around the world.

There is nothing liberal about that revolution that they are trying to push from Peiping. This is a harsh, totalitarian regime. It has nothing in common with the great American revolutionary tradition, nothing in common with it.

SENATOR CHURCH: The objectives of Communist revolution are clearly very different indeed from the earlier objectives of our own. But objectives of revolutions have varied through the centuries.

The question that I think faces this country is how we can best cope with the likelihood of revolt in the underdeveloped world in the years ahead, and I have very serious doubts that American military intervention will often be the proper decision. I think too much intervention on our part may well spread communism throughout the ex-colonial world rather than thwart it.

Now, the distinction you draw between the Communist

type of guerrilla war and other kinds of revolution, if I have understood it correctly, has been based upon the premise that in Vietnam the North Vietnamese have been meddling in the revolution in the south and, therefore, it is a form of aggression on the part of the north against the south.

But I cannot remember many revolutions that have been fought in splendid isolation. There were as many Frenchmen at Yorktown when Cornwallis surrendered as there were American Continentals.

Senator Pell tells me more. I accept the correction.

In any case, it seems to me that the Communists have not changed the rules of revolution by meddling in them, regardless of how much we disapprove of their goals.

When we were an infant nation we stood up for the right of revolution, . . .

SOURCE: United States Senate, Committee on Foreign Relations, *Hearings*, February 4–17, 1966.

During 1966 the U.S. air war against North Vietnam gradually escalated. In June of that year, U.S. aircraft bombed North Vietnam's POL (petroleum products, i.e., gasoline, oil, and lubricants) storage facilities near Hanoi and Haiphong. Even though these and other air strikes knocked out a high percentage of North Vietnam's oil-storage capacity, they destroyed only a small amount of the POL stores that had been decentralized. They had been stored in small camouflaged sites that were hard to locate and to attack from the air. POL imports via rail from China quickly replaced the losses. Hanoi retained the capability of supporting the expanding insurgency in South Vietnam. While American pilots attacked various targets in North Vietnam, Secretary of Defense McNamara commissioned a study of the bombing, which was undertaken by the Institute for Defense Analysis (IDA), an independent agency made up of U.S. scientists who worked on Department of Defense matters. The IDA report bluntly announced the failure of the air war and the reasons why it failed.

DOCUMENT 37: Excerpts from the Institute for Defense Analysis Bombing Evaluation, August 29, 1966.

1. As of July 1966 the U.S. bombing of North Vietnam (NVN) had had no measurable direct effect on Hanoi's ability to mount and support military operations in the South at current levels.

Although the political constraints seem clearly to have reduced the effectiveness of the bombing program, its limited effect on Hanoi's ability to provide such support cannot be explained solely on that basis. The countermeasures introduced by Hanoi effectively reduced the impact of U.S. bombing. More fundamentally, however, North Vietnam has basically a subsistence agricultural economy that presents a difficult and unrewarding target system for air attack.

The economy supports operations in the South mainly by functioning as a logistics funnel and by providing a source of manpower. The industrial sector produces little of military value. Most of the essential military supplies that the VC/NVN forces in the South require from external sources are provided by the USSR and Communist China. Furthermore, the volume of such supplies is so low that only a small fraction of the capacity of North Vietnam's rather flexible transportation network is required to maintain the flow. The economy's relatively underemployed labor force also appears to provide an ample manpower reserve for internal military and economic needs including repair and reconstruction and for continued support of military operations in the South.

2. Since the initiation of the ROLLING THUNDER program the damage to facilities and equipment in North Vietnam has been more than offset by the increased flow of military and economic aid, largely from the USSR and Communist China. . . .

3. The aspects of the basic situation that have enabled Hanoi to continue its support of military operations in the South and to neutralize the impact of U.S. bombing by passing the economic costs to other Communist countries are not likely to be altered by reducing the present geographic constraints, mining Haiphong and the principal harbors in North Vietnam, increasing the number of armed reconnaissance sorties and otherwise expanding the U.S. air offensive along the lines now contemplated in military recommendations and planning studies.

An expansion of the bombing program along such lines would make it more difficult and costly for Hanoi to move essential military supplies through North Vietnam to the VC/NVN forces in the South. The low volume of supplies required, the demonstrated effectiveness of the countermeasures already undertaken by Hanoi, the alternative options that the NVN transportation network provides and the level of aid the USSR and China seem prepared to provide, however, make it quite unlikely that Hanoi's capability to function as a logistic funnel would be seriously impaired. Our past experience also indicates that an intensified air campaign in NVN probably would not prevent Hanoi from infiltrating men into the South at the present or a higher rate, if it chooses. Furthermore there would appear to be no basis for assuming that the damage that could be inflicted by an intensified air offensive would impose such demands on the North Vietnamese labor force that Hanoi would be unable to continue and expand its recruitment and training of military forces for the insurgency in the South. . . .

5. The indirect effects of the bombing on the will of the North Vietnamese to continue fighting and on their leaders' appraisal of the prospective gains and costs of maintaining the present policy have not shown themselves in any tangible way. Furthermore, we have not discovered any basis for concluding that the indirect punitive effects of bombing will prove decisive in these respects. . . .

The major effect of the attack on North Vietnam was to force Hanoi to cope with disruption to normal activity, particularly in transportation and distribution. . . .

Much of the damage was to installations the North Vietnamese did not need to sustain the military effort. . . .

Evidence regarding the effect of the bombing on the morale of the North Vietnamese people suggests that the results were mixed. The bombing clearly strengthened popular support of the regime by engendering patriotic and nationalistic enthusiasm to resist the attacks. On the other hand, those more directly involved in the bombing underwent personal hardships and anxieties caused by the raids. . . .

Initial plans and assessments for the ROLLING THUNDER program clearly tended to overestimate the persuasive and disruptive effects of the U.S. air strikes and, correspondingly, to underestimate the tenacity and recuperative capabilities of the North Vietnamese. This tendency, in turn, appears to reflect a general failure to appreciate the fact, well-documented in the historical and social scientific literature, that a direct, frontal attack on a society tends to strengthen the social fabric of the nation, to improve the determination of both the leadership and the populace to fight back. . . .

In general, current official thought about U.S. objectives in bombing NVN implicitly assumes two sets of causal relationships:

1. That by increasing the damage and destruction of resources in NVN, the U.S. is exerting pressure to cause the DRV to stop their support of the military operations in SVN and Laos; and our bombing of North Vietnam was designed to serve three purposes:

—**(1)** To retaliate and to lift the morals [*sic*] of the people in the South who were being attacked by agents of the North.

—**(2)** To add to the pressure on Hanoi to end the war.

—**(3)** To reduce the flow and/or to increase the cost of infiltrating men and material from North to South.

We cannot ignore that a limitation on bombing will cause serious psychological problems among the men, officers and commanders, who will not be able to understand why we should withhold punishment from the enemy. General Westmoreland said that he is "frankly dismayed at even the thought of stopping the bombing program." But this reason for attacking North Vietnam must be scrutinized carefully. We should not bomb for punitive reasons if it serves no other purpose—especially if analysis shows that the actions may be counterproductive. It costs American lives; it creates a backfire of revulsion and opposition by killing civilians; it creates serious risks; it may harden the enemy.

With respect to added pressure on the North, it is becoming apparent that Hanoi may already have "written off" all assets and lives that might be destroyed by U.S. military actions short of occupation of annihilation [sic]. They can and will hold out at least so long as a prospect of winning the "war of attrition" in the South exists. And our best judgment is that a Hanoi prerequisite to negotiations is significant retrenchment (if not complete stoppage of U.S. military actions against them—at the least, a cessation of bombing. In this connection, Con-sul–General Rice (Hong Kong 7581, 5/1/67) said that, in his opinion, we cannot by bombing reach the critical level of pain in North Vietnam and that, "below that level, pain only increases the will to fight." Sir Robert Thompson said to Mr. Vance on April 28 that our bombing, particularly in the Red River Delta, "is unifying North Vietnam."

With respect to interdiction of men and material, it now appears that no combination of actions against the North short of destruction of the regime or occupation of North Vietnamese territory will physically reduce the flow of men and materiel below the relatively small amount needed by enemy forces to con-tinue the war in the South. Our effort can and does have severe disruptive effects, which Hanoi can and does plan on and prestock against. Our efforts physically to cut the flow meaningfully by actions in North Vietnam therefore largely fail and, in failing, transmute attempted interdiction into pain, or pressure on the North (the factor discussed in the paragraph next above.) The lowest "ceiling" on infiltration can probably be achieved by concentration on the North Vietnamese "funnel" south of 20° and on the Trail in Laos.

But what if the above analyses are wrong? Why not escalate the bombing and mine the harbors (and perhaps occupy southern North Vietnam)—on the gamble that it would constrict the flow, meaningfully limiting enemy action in the South, and that it would bend Hanoi? The answer is that the costs and risks of the actions must be considered.

2. That the combined effect of the total military effort against NVN—including U.S. air strikes in NVN and Laos, and the land, sea, and air operations in SVN—will ultimately cause the DRV (the government of North Vietnam) to perceive that its probable losses accruing from the war have become greater than its possible gains and, on the basis on this net evaluation, the regime will stop its support of the war in the South.

These two sets of interrelationships are assumed in military planning, but it is not clear that they are systematically addressed in current intelligence estimates and assessments. . . .

It must be concluded, therefore, that there is currently no adequate basis for predicting the levels of U.S. military effort that would be required to achieve the stated objectives—indeed, there is no firm basis for determining if there is *any* feasible level of effort that would achieve these objectives. . . .

SOURCE: Sheehan and others (eds.), *Pentagon Papers*, pp. 502–507.

The failure of the POL raids disillusioned Robert McNamara, who had been one of the principal architects of the air war against North Vietnam. He began to identify with the small but growing number of Washington officials who were becoming disenchanted with U.S. involvement in Vietnam. By the spring of 1967, McNamara was resisting the demands of the Joint Chiefs for an expanded bombing campaign and for the sending of large numbers of additional U.S. combat troops to South Vietnam.

DOCUMENT 38. Excerpts from McNamara Memo to President Johnson, May 19, 1967.

... There continues to be no sign that the bombing has reduced Hanoi's will to resist or her ability to ship the necessary supplies south. Hanoi shows no signs of ending the large war and advising the VC to melt into the jungles. The North Vietnamese believe they are right; they consider the Ky regime to be puppets; they believe the world is with them and that the American public will not have staying power against them. Thus, although they may have factions in the regime favoring different approaches, they believe that, in the long run, they are stronger than we are for the purpose. They probably do not want to make significant concessions, and could not do so without serious loss of face....

The primary costs of course are U.S. lives: the air campaign against heavily defended areas costs us one pilot in every 40 sorties. In addition, an important but hard–to–measure cost is domestic and world opinion: There may be a limit beyond which many Americans and much of the world will not permit the United States to go. The picture of the world's greatest superpower killing or seriously injuring 1,000 noncombatants a week, while trying to pound a tiny backward nation into submission on an issue whose merits are hotly disputed, is not a pretty one. It could conceivably produce a costly distortion in the American national consciousness and in the world image of the United States—especially if the damage to North Vietnam is complete enough to be "successful."

The most important risk, however, is the likely Soviet, Chinese and North Vietnamese reaction to intensified U.S. air attacks, harbor-mining, and ground actions against North Vietnam.

At the present time, no actions—except air strikes and artillery fire necessary to quiet hostile batteries across the border—are allowed against *Cambodian* territory. In Laos, we average 5,000 attack sorties a month against the infiltration routes and base areas, we fire artillery from South Vietnam against targets in Laos, and we will be providing 3-man leadership for each of 20 12-man U.S.-Vietnamese Special Forces teams that operate to a depth of 20 kilometers into Laos. Against North Vietnam, we average 8,000 or more attack sorties a month against all worthwhile fixed and LOC targets; we use artillery against ground targets across the DMZ; we fire from naval vessels at targets ashore and afloat up to 19°; and we mine their inland waterways, estuaries ... up to 20°.

Intensified air attacks against the same types of targets, we would anticipate, would lead to no great change in the policies and reactions of the Communist powers beyond the furnishing of some new equipment and manpower. China, for example, has not reacted to our striking MIG fields in North Vietnam, and we do not expect them to, although there are some signs of greater Chinese participation in North Vietnamese air defense....

To U.S. ground actions in North Vietnam, we would expect China to respond by entering the war with both ground and air forces. The Soviet Union could be expected in these circumstances to take all actions listed above under the lesser provocations and to generate a serious confrontation with the United States at one or more places of her own choosing. . . .

Yet we believe that, short of threatening and perhaps toppling the Hanoi regime itself, pressure against the North will, if anything, harden Hanoi's unwillingness to talk and her settlement terms if she does. China, we believe, will oppose settlement throughout. We believe that there is a chance that the Soviets, at the brink, will exert efforts to bring about peace; but we believe also that intensified bombing and harbor-mining, even if coupled with political pressure from Moscow, will neither bring Hanoi to negotiate nor affect North Vietnam's terms. . . .

The time has come for us to eliminate the ambiguities from our minimum objectives—our commitments—in Vietnam. Specifically, two principles must be articulated, and policies and actions brought in line with them: (1) Our commitment is only to see that the people of South Vietnam are permitted to determine their own future. (2) This commitment ceases if the country ceases to help itself.

It follows that no matter how much we might *hope* for some things, our *commitment* is *not:*

—to expel from South Vietnam regroupees, who are South Vietnamese (though we do not like them),

—to ensure that a particular person or group remains in power, nor that the power runs to every corner of the land (though we prefer certain types and we hope their writ will run throughout South Vietnam),

—to guarantee that the self-chosen government is non-Communist (though we believe and strongly hope it will be), and

—to insist that the independent South Vietnam remain separate from North Vietnam (though in the short-run, we would prefer it that way).

(Nor do we have an obligation to pour in effort out of proportion to the effort contributed by the people of South Vietnam or in the face of coups, corruption, apathy or other indications of Saigon failure to cooperate effectively with us.)

We *are* committed to stopping or offsetting the effect of North Vietnam's application of force in the South, which denies the people of the South the ability to determine their own future. Even here, however, the line is hard to draw. Propaganda and political advice by Hanoi (or by Washington) is presumably not barred; nor is economic aid or economic advisors. . . .

SOURCE: Sheehan and others (eds.), *Pentagon Papers*, pp. 577–584.

By 1967 the Vietnam war had expanded far beyond what Americans had anticipated when U.S. officials had made a series of decisions that Americanized the conflict nearly two years earlier. Instead of a relatively quick victory over Communist aggressors, the United States found itself locked into an escalating stalemate of rising casualties and costs. At home, the war was increasingly dividing Americans. Neither Washington nor Hanoi appeared ready to make the kinds of concessions that might get serious negotiations underway. The Americans insisted that South Vietnam be permitted to live in peace as an independent state under a non-Communist government. The Communists insisted that the Americans get out and that Vietnam be unified under their control.

An exchange of letters between President Lyndon Johnson and President Ho Chi Minh highlighted the chasm separating the negotiating stances of the two nations and also the vastly different perspectives they brought to the conflict.

DOCUMENT 39. Letter from President Lyndon B. Johnson to President Ho Chi Minh, February 1967.

His Excellency Ho Chi Minh
President, Democratic Republic of Vietnam

Dear Mr. President,

I am writing to you in the hope that the conflict in Vietnam can be brought to an end. The conflict has already taken a heavy toll—in lives lost, in wounds inflicted, in property destroyed, and in simple human misery. If we fail to find a just and peaceful solution, history will judge us harshly.

Therefore, I believe that we both have a heavy obligation to seek earnestly the path to peace. It is in response to that obligation that I am writing directly to you. We have tried over the past several years, in a variety of ways and through a number of channels, to convey to you and your colleagues our desire to achieve a peaceful settlement. For whatever reasons, these efforts have not achieved any results.

It may be that our thoughts and yours, our attitudes and yours, have been distorted or misinterpreted as they passed through these various channels. Certainly that is always a danger in indirect communication.

There is one good way to overcome this problem and to move forward in the search for a peaceful settlement. That is for us to arrange for direct talks between trusted representatives in a secure setting and away from the glare of publicity. Such talks should not be used as a propaganda exercise but should be a serious effort to find a workable and mutually acceptable solution.

In the past two weeks, I have noted public statements by representatives of your government suggesting that you would be prepared to enter into direct bilateral talks with representatives of the U.S. Government, provided that we ceased "unconditionally" and permanently our bombing operations against your country and all military actions against it. In the last days, serious and responsible parties have assured us indirectly that this is in fact your proposal.

Let me frankly state that I see two great difficulties with this proposal. In view of your public position, such action on our part would inevitably produce worldwide speculation that discussions were under way and would impair the privacy and secrecy of those discussions. Secondly, there would inevitably be grave concern on our part whether your government would make use of such action by us to improve its military position.

With these problems in mind, I am prepared to move even further toward an ending of the hostilities than your government has proposed in either public statements or through private diplomatic channels. I am prepared to order a cessation of bombing against your country and the stopping of further augmentation of U.S. forces in South Vietnam as soon as I am assured that infiltration into South Vietnam by land and by sea has stopped. These acts of restraint on both sides would, I believe, make it possible for us to conduct serious and private discussions leading toward an early peace.

I make this proposal to you now with a specific sense of urgency arising from the imminent New Year holidays in Vietnam. If you are able to accept this proposal I see no reason why it could not take effect at the end of the New Year, or Têt, holidays. The proposal I have made would be greatly strengthened if your military authorities and those of the government of South Vietnam could promptly negotiate an extension of the Têt truce.

As to the site of the bilateral discussions I propose, there are several possibilities. We could, for example, have our representatives meet in Moscow where contacts have already occurred. They could meet in some other country such as Burma. You may have other arrangements or sites in mind, and I would try to meet your suggestions. . . .

Sincerely,

LYNDON B. JOHNSON

Ho Chi Minh responded promptly:

DOCUMENT 40. President Ho Chi Minh's response to President Johnson's letter, February 1967.

To His Excellency Mr Lyndon B. Johnson,
President
United States of America

Your Excellency,

On February 10, 1967, I received your message. This is my reply.

Vietnam is thousands of miles away from the United States. The Vietnamese people have never done any harm to the United States. But contrary to the pledges made by its representative at the 1954 Geneva Conference, the U.S. Government has ceaselessly intervened in Vietnam, it has unleashed and intensified the war of aggression in South Vietnam with a view to prolonging the partition of Vietnam and turning South Vietnam into a neo-colony and a military base of the United States. For over two years now, the U.S. Government has, with its air and naval forces, carried the war to the Democratic Republic of Vietnam, an independent and sovereign country.

The U.S. Government has committed war crimes, crimes against peace and against mankind. In South Vietnam, half a million U.S. and satellite troops have resorted to the most inhuman weapons and the most barbarous methods of warfare, such as napalm, toxic chemicals and gases, to massacre our compatriots, destroy crops, and raze villages to the ground. In North Vietnam, thousands of U.S. aircraft have dropped hundreds of thousands of tons of bombs, destroying towns, villages, factories, roads, bridges, dykes, dams, and even churches, pagodas, hospitals, schools. In your message, you apparently deplored the sufferings and destructions in Vietnam. May I ask you: Who has perpetrated these monstrous crimes? It is the U.S. and satellite troops. The U.S. Government is entirely responsible for the extremely serious situation in Vietnam.

The U.S. war of aggression against the Vietnamese people constitutes a challenge to the countries of the socialist camp, a threat to the national independence movement, and a serious danger to peace in Asia and the world.

The Vietnamese people deeply love independence, freedom and peace. But in the face of the U.S. aggression, they have risen up, united as one man, fearless of sacrifices and hardships; they are determined to carry on their Resistance until they have won genuine independence and freedom and true peace. Our just cause enjoys strong sympathy and support from the peoples of the whole world including broad sections of the American people.

The U.S. Government has unleashed the war of aggression in Vietnam. It must cease this aggression. This is the only way to the restoration of peace. The U.S. Government must stop definitively and unconditionally its bombing raids and all other acts of war against the Democratic Republic of Vietnam, withdraw from South Vietnam all U.S. and satellite troops, recognize the South Vietnam National Front for Liberation, and let the Vietnamese people settle themselves their own affairs. Such is the basic content of the four-point stand of the Government of the Democratic Republic of Vietnam, which embodies the essential principles and provisions of the 1954 Geneva Agreements on Vietnam. It is the basis of a correct political solution to the Vietnam problem.

In your message, you suggested direct talks between the Democratic Republic of Vietnam and the United States. If the U.S. Government really wants these talks, it must first of all stop unconditionally its bombing raids and all other acts of war against the Democratic Republic of Vietnam. It is only after the unconditional cessation of the U.S. bombing raids and all other acts of war against the Democratic Republic of Vietnam that the Democratic Republic of Vietnam and the United States could enter into talks and discuss questions concerning the two sides.

The Vietnamese people will never submit to force; they will never accept talks under the threat of bombs.

Our cause is absolutely just. It is to be hoped that the U.S. Government will act in accordance with reason.

Sincerely,

HO CHI MINH

SOURCE: Copies of both letters found in Williams and others (eds.), *America in Vietnam*, pp. 259–262.

Despite growing divisions within the country and rising opposition to the controversial war in Vietnam, the Johnson administration continued its policy of graduated escalation, confident that it would eventually force Hanoi to abandon its support of the Vietcong and to seek a negotiated settlement on American terms. American military leaders continued to make optimistic pronouncements and their official reports showed steady progress toward an inevitable victory. General Westmoreland, speaking in Washington in November 1967, said that allied forces had reached a stage when "the end begins to come into view." Admiral U.S. Grant Sharp, Commander-in-Chief, Pacific Forces, filed an encouraging report at the end of the year showing steady progress in the air war, which he commanded.

DOCUMENT 41. Excerpts from Admiral U.S. Grant Sharp's Report to the Joint Chiefs of Staff, January 1, 1968.

The overall effect of our effort to reduce external assistance has resulted not only in destruction and damage to the transportation systems and goods being transported thereon but has created additional management, distribution and manpower problems. In addition, the attacks have created a bottleneck at Haiphong where inability effectively to move goods inland from the port has resulted in congestion on the docks and a slowdown in offloading ships as they arrive. By October, road and rail interdictions had reduced the transportation clearance capacity at Haiphong to about 2700 short tons per day. An average of 4400 short tons per day had arrived in Haiphong during the year. . . .

Although men and material needed for the level of combat now prevailing in South Vietnam continue to flow despite our attacks on LOCs, we have made it very costly to the enemy in terms of material, manpower, management, and distribution. From 1 January through 15 December 1967, 122,960 attack sorties were flown in Rolling Thunder route packages I through V and in Laos, SEA Dragon offensive operations involved 1,384 ship-days on station and contributed materially in reducing enemy seaborne infiltration in southern NVN and in the vicinity of the DMZ. Attacks against the NVN transport system during the past 12 months resulted in destruction of carriers, cargo carried, and personnel casualties. Air attacks, throughout North Vietnam and Laos destroyed or damaged 5,261 motor vehicles, 2,475 railroad rolling stock, and 11,425 watercraft from 1 January through 20 December 1967. SEA DRAGON accounted for another 1,473 WBLC destroyed or damaged from 1 January–30 November. There were destroyed rail-lines, bridges, ferries, railroad yards and shops, storage areas, and truck parks. Some 3,685 land targets were struck by Sea Dragon forces, including the destruction or damage of 303 coastal defense and radar sites. Through external assistance, the enemy has been able to replace or rehabilitate many of the items damaged or destroyed, and transport inventories are roughly at the same level they were at the beginning of the year. Nevertheless, construction problems have caused interruptions in the flow of men and supplies, caused a great loss of work-hours, and restricted movement particularly during daylight hours. . . .

A primary effect of our efforts to impede movement of the enemy has been to force Hanoi to engage from 500,000 to 600,000 civilians in full-time and part-time war-related activities, in particular for air defense and repair of the LOCs. This diversion of manpower from other pursuits, particularly from the agricultural sector, has caused a drawdown on manpower. The estimated lower food production yields, coupled with an increase in food imports in 1967 (some six times that of 1966), indicate that agriculture is having great difficulty in adjusting to this changed composition of the work force. The cost and difficulties of the war to Hanoi have sharply increased, and only through the willingness of other communist countries to provide maximum replacement of goods and material has NVN managed to sustain its war effort.

Air attacks were authorized and executed by target systems for the first time in 1967, although the attacks were limited to specific targets within each system. A total of 9,740 sorties was flown against targets on the ROLLING THUNDER target list from 1 January–15 December 1967. The campaign against the power system resulted in reduction of power generating capability to approximately 15 percent of original capacity. Successful strikes against the Thau Nguyen iron and steel plant and the Haiphong cement plant resulted in practically total destruction of these two installations. NVN adjustments to these losses have had to be made by relying on additional imports from China, the USSR or the Eastern European countries. The requirement for additional imports reduces available shipping space for war supporting supplies and adds to the congestion at the ports. Interruptions in raw material supplies and the requirement to turn to less efficient means of power and distribution has degraded overall production.

Economic losses to North Vietnam amounted to more than $130 million dollars in 1967, representing over one-half of the total economic losses since the war began. . . .

SOURCE: Sheehan and others (eds.), *Pentagon Papers*, pp. 613–615.

Just as the Lunar New Year celebrations were beginning in Vietnam, January 31, 1968, the VC/NVA forces attacked big cities, provincial capitals, and district centers all over South Vietnam. The Tet-68 Offensive, the largest military campaign of the war, caught the American and South Vietnamese forces by surprise. It also surprised and stunned Americans back home, both the leaders in Washington and ordinary citizens, who had been led to believe that the Allied forces were on the verge of winning the war. For the first time, television news reports included graphic scenes of fighting in the streets of Saigon and Hue. Even though caught by surprise, U.S. and South Vietnamese troops fought hard and effectively. Most of the Communist attacks were beaten back within a few hours or a few days. Tactically, Tet-68 amounted to a major allied victory. Psychologically and politically, the Communists scored a great victory at Tet-68. In its aftermath, the Johnson administration went through an agonizing reappraisal of its policy of graduated escalation, which had not produced victory so much as a seemingly interminable stalemate. The reappraisal process began when the Chairman of the Joint Chiefs, Army General Earle Wheeler, submitted a pessimistic assessment of the Tet-68 Offensive and called for sending General Westmoreland an additional 206,000 troops.

DOCUMENT 42. Excerpts from Chairman, Joint Chiefs of Staff, General Earle G. Wheeler's Report to President Johnson, February 27, 1968.

- The current situation in Vietnam is still developing and fraught with opportunities as well as dangers.
- There is no question in the mind of MACV that the enemy went all out for a general offensive and general uprising and apparently believed that he would succeed in bringing the war to an early successful conclusion.
- The enemy failed to achieve his initial objective but is continuing his effort. Although many of his units were badly hurt, the judgment is that he has the will and the capability to continue.
- Enemy losses have been heavy; he has failed to achieve his prime objectives of mass uprisings and capture of a large number of the capital cities and towns. Morale in enemy units which were badly mauled or where the men were oversold the idea of a decisive victory at TET probably has suffered severely. However, with replacements, his indoctrination system would seem capable of maintaining morale at a generally adequate level. His determination appears to be unshaken.
- The enemy is operating with relative freedom in the countryside, probably recruiting heavily and no doubt infiltrating NVA units and personnel. His recovery is likely to be rapid; his supplies are adequate; and he is trying to maintain the momentum of his winter-spring offensive.
- The structure of the GVN held up but its effectiveness has suffered.
- The RVNAF held up against the initial assault with gratifying, and in a way, surprising strength and fortitude. However, RVNAF is now in a defensive posture around towns and cities and there is concern about how well they will bear up under sustained pressure.
- The initial attack nearly succeeded in a dozen places, and defeat in those places was only averted by the timely reaction of U.S. forces. In short, it was a very near thing.

- There is no doubt that the RD Program has suffered a severe set back.
- RVNAF was not badly hurt physically—they should recover strength and equipment rather quickly (equipment in 2–3 months—strength in 3–6 months). Their problems are more psychological than physical.
- U.S. forces have lost none of their pre-TET capability. . . .

a. Enemy Capabilities.

(1) The enemy has been hurt badly in the populated lowlands, is practically intact elsewhere. He committed over 67,000 combat maneuver forces plus perhaps 25% or 17,000 more impressed men and boys, for a total of about 84,000. He lost 40,000 killed, at least 3,000 captured, and perhaps 5,000 disabled or died of wounds. He had peaked his force total to about 240,000 just before TET, by hard recruiting, infiltration, civilian impressment, and drawdowns on service and guerrilla personnel. So he has lost about one fifth of his total strength. About two-thirds of his trained, organized unit strength can continue offensive action. He is probably infiltrating and recruiting heavily in the countryside while allied forces are securing the urban areas. (Discussions of strengths and recruiting are in paragraphs 1, 2 and 3 of Enclosure (1)). The enemy has adequate munitions, stockpiled in-country and available through the DMZ, Laos, and Cambodia, to support major attacks and countrywide pressure; food procurement may be a problem. . . .

b. RVNAF Capabilities:

(1) Current Status of RVNAF: (South Vietnamese Forces)
    (a) Strength . . .
    —As of 31 Dec RVNAF strength was 643,116 (Regular Forces—342,951; RF—151,376; and PF—148,789)

Date	Auth	PFD	% of Strength
31 Dec.	112,435	96,667	86
10 Feb.	112,435	77,000	68.5
15 Feb.	112,435	83,935	74.7

. . . (d) The redeployment of forces has caused major relocations of support forces, logistical activities and supplies.
    (e) The short range solutions to the four major areas listed above were: (a) Emergency replacement of major equipment items and ammunition from the CONUS and (b) day-to-day emergency actions and relocation of resources within the theater. In summary, the logistics system in Vietnam has provided adequate support throughout the TET offensive.

d. GVY Strength and Effectiveness:

(1) Psychological—the people in South Vietnam were handed a psychological blow, particularly in the urban areas where the feeling of security had been strong. There is a fear of further attacks.

(2) The structure of the Government was not shattered and continues to function but at greatly reduced effectiveness.

(3) In many places, the RD program has been set back badly. In other places the program was untouched in the initial stage of the offensive. MACV reports that of the 555 RD cadre groups, 78 remain in hamlets, 245 are in district and province towns on security duty, while 32 are unaccounted for. It is not clear as to when, or even whether, it will be possible to return to the RD program in its earlier form. As long as the VC prowl the countryside it will be impossible, in many places, even to tell exactly what has happened to the program.

(4) Refugees—An additional 470,000 refugees were generated during the offensive. A breakdown of refugees is at Enclosure (7). The problem of caring for refugees is part of the larger problem of reconstruction in the cities and towns. It is anticipated that the care and reestablishment of the 250,000 persons or 50,000 family units who have lost their homes will require from GVN sources the expenditure of 500 million piasters for their temporary care and resettlement plus an estimated 30,000 metric tons of rice. Form U.S. sources, there is a requirement to supply aluminum and cement for 40,000 refugee families being reestablished under the Ministry of Social Welfare and Refugee self-help program. Additionally, the GVN/Public Works City Rebuilding Plan will require the provision of 400,000 double sheets of aluminum, plus 20,000 tons [words illegible]. . . .

a. *Probable Enemy Strategy.* (Reference paragraph 7b, Enclosure (1). We see the enemy pursuing a reinforced offensive to enlarge his control throughout the country and keep pressures on the government and allies. We expect him to maintain strong threats in the DMZ area, at Khe Sanh, in the highlands, and at Saigon, and to attack in force when conditions seem favorable. He is likely to try to gain control of the country's northern provinces. He will continue efforts to encircle cities and province capitals to isolate and disrupt normal activities, and infiltrate them to create chaos. He will seek maximum attrition of RVNAF elements. Against U.S. forces, he will emphasize attacks by fire on airfields and installations, using assaults and ambushes selectively. His central objective continues to be the destruction of the Government of SVN and its armed forces. As a minimum he hopes to seize sufficient territory and gain control of enough people to support establishment of the groups and committees he proposes for participation in an NLF dominated government.

b. *MACV Strategy:*

(1) MACV believes that the central thrust of our strategy now must be to defeat the enemy offensive and that if this is done well, the situation overall will be greatly improved over the pre-TET condition.

(2) MACV accepts the fact that its first priority must be the security of Government of Vietnam in Saigon and provincial capitals. MACV describes its objectives as:

- First, to counter the enemy offensive and to destroy or eject the NVA invasion force in the north.
- Second, to restore security in the cities and towns.
- Third, to restore security in the heavily populated areas of the country-side.
- Fourth, to regain the initiative through offensive operations . . .

A. Forces currently assigned to MACV, plus the residual Program Fives forces yet to be delivered, are inadequate in numbers to carry out the strategy and to accomplish the tasks described above in the proper priority. To contend with, and defeat, the new enemy threat, MACV has stated requirements for forces over the 525,000 ceiling imposed by Program Five. The add-on requested totals 206,756 spaces for a new proposed ceiling of 731,756, with all forces being deployed into country by the end of CY 68. Principal forces included in the add-on are three division equivalents, 15 tactical fighter squadrons and augmentation for current Navy programs. . . .

SOURCE: Sheehan and others (eds.), *Pentagon Papers*, pp. 615–620.

Alarmed by General Wheeler's pessimistic report, coupled to the general's request for more than 200,000 additional U.S. combat troops for Vietnam, President Johnson directed his new Secretary of Defense, Clark Clifford, to study the general's troop request. Clifford, a long-time friend of the president, had previously been supportive of the U.S. war effort, and Johnson thought that he had appointed a hawkish successor to McNamara. But Clifford, unbeknownst to Johnson, came to office with misgivings about the stalemated war. Clifford used his authority to conduct a review of the troop request to range far beyond the question of force size and to conduct a thorough review of the entire American war policy in Vietnam. During the course of his studies, Clifford concluded that the policy of graduated escalation was strategically and politically bankrupt. Then he set out to persuade the president to abandon it.

DOCUMENT 43. Excerpts from Clark M. Clifford, "A Vietnam Reappraisal: The Personal History of One Man's View and How It Evolved," an article published in *Foreign Affairs* (July 1969).

. . . Here are some of the principal issues and some of the answers as I understood them:

"Will 200,000 more men do the job?" I found no assurance that they would.

"If not, how many more might be needed—and when?" There was no way of knowing.

"What would be involved in committing 200,000 more men to Viet Nam?" A reserve call-up of approximately 280,000, an increased draft call and an extension of tours of duty of most men then in service.

"Can the enemy respond with a build-up of his own?" He could and he probably would.

"What are the estimated costs of the latest requests?" First calculations were on the order of $2 billion for the remaining four months of that fiscal year, and an increase of $10 to $12 billion for the year beginning July 1, 1968.

"What will be the impact on the economy?" So great that we would face the possibility of credit restrictions, a tax increase and even wage and price controls. The balance of payments would be worsened by at least half a billion dollars a year.

"Can bombing stop the war?" Never by itself. It was inflicting heavy personnel and materiel losses, but bombing by itself would not stop the war.

"Will stepping up the bombing decrease American casualties?" Very little, if at all. Our casualties were due to the intensity of the ground fighting in the South. We had already dropped a heavier tonnage of bombs than in all the theaters of World War II. During 1967, an estimated 90,000 North Vietnamese had infiltrated into South Viet Nam. In the opening weeks of 1968, infiltrators were coming in at three to four times the rate of a year earlier, despite the ferocity and the intensity of our campaign of aerial interdiction.

"How long must we keep on sending our men and carrying the main burden of combat?" The South Vietnamese were doing better, but they were not ready yet to replace our troops and we did not know when they would be.

When I asked for a presentation of the military plan for attaining victory in Viet Nam, I was told that there was no plan for victory in the historic American sense. Why not? Because our forces were operating under three major political restrictions. The President had forbidden the invasion of North Viet Nam because this could trigger the mutual assistance pact between North Viet Nam and China; the President and forbidden the mining of the harbor at Haiphong, the principal port through which the North received military supplies; the President had forbidden our forces to pursue the enemy into Laos and Cambodia, for to do so would spread the war, politically and geographically, with no discernible advantage. These and other restrictions which precluded an all-out, no-holds-barred military effort were wisely designed to prevent our being drawn into a larger war. We had no inclination to recommend to the President their cancellation.

"Given these circumstances, how can we win?" We would, I was told, continue to evidence our superiority over the enemy; we would continue to attack in the belief that he would reach the stage where he would find it inadvisable to go on with the war. He could not afford the attrition we were inflicting on him. And we were improving our posture all the time.

I then asked, "What is the best estimate as to how long this course of action will take? Six months? One Year? Two Years?" There was no agreement on an answer. Not only was there no agreement, I could find no one willing to assert that he could see "light at the end of the tunnel" or that American troops would be coming home by the end of the year.

After days of this type of analysis, my concern had greatly deepened. I could not find out when the war was going to end; I could not find out the manner in which it was going to end; I could not find out whether the new requests for men and equipment were going to be enough, or whether it would take more and, if more, when and how much; I could not find out how soon the South Vietnamese forces would be ready to take over. All I had was the statement, given with too little self-assurance to be comforting, that if we persisted for an indeterminate length of time, the enemy would choose not to go on.

And so I asked, "Does anyone see any diminution in the will of the enemy after four years of our having been there, after enormous casualties and after massive destruction from our bombing?"

The answer was that there appeared to be no diminution in the will of the enemy. This reply was doubly impressive, because I was more conscious each day of domestic unrest in our country. Draft card burnings, marches in the streets, problems on school campuses, bitterness and divisiveness were rampant. Just as disturbing to me were the economic implications of a struggle to be indefinitely continued at an ever-increasing cost. The dollar was already in trouble, prices were escalating far too fast and emergency controls on foreign investment imposed on New Year's Day would be only a prelude to more stringent controls, if we were to add another $12 billion to Viet Nam spending—with perhaps still more to come.

I was also conscious of our obligations and involvements elsewhere in the world. There were certain hopeful signs in our relations with the Soviet Union, but both nations were hampered in moving toward vitally important talks on the limitation of strategic weapons so long as the United States was committed to a military solution in Viet Nam. We could not afford to disregard our interests in the Middle East, South Asia, Africa, Western Europe, and elsewhere. Even accepting the validity of our objective in Viet Nam, that objective had to be viewed in the context of our overall national interest, and could not sensibly be pursued at a price so high as to impair our ability to achieve other, and perhaps even more important, foreign policy objectives. . . .

I could see no reason at this time for us to continue to add to our commitment. Finally, there was no assurance that a 40 percent increase in American troops would place us within the next few weeks, months or even years in any substantially better military position than we were in then. All that could be predicted accurately was that more troops would raise the level of combat and automatically raise the level of casualties on both sides.

And so, after these exhausting days, I was convinced that the military course we were pursuing was not only endless, but hopeless. A further substantial increase in American forces could only increase the devastation and the Americanization of the war, and thus leave us even further from our goal of a peace that would permit the people of South Viet Nam to fashion their own political and economic institutions. Henceforth, I was also convinced, our primary goal should be to level off our involvement, and to work toward gradual disengagement. . . .

It now became my purpose to emphasize to my colleagues and to the President, that the United States had entered Viet Nam with a limited aim—to prevent its subjugation by the North and to enable the people of South Viet Nam to determine their own future. . . .

SOURCE: Clark Clifford, "A Viet Nam Reappraisal: The Personal History of One Man's View and How It Evolved," *Foreign Affairs*, 47:4 (July 1969), pp. 610–613.

As part of his campaign to convince Johnson that he must abandon his bankrupt strategy of graduated escalation, Clifford arranged for the president to meet with a group of distinguished former senior advisers and office-holders, who were nick-named the "wise men." These men had met with Johnson previously and had generally supported his war policy. But at this meeting, held March 26, 1968, most of them told the president that his policy was not working and must be changed. Tet-68 had changed their minds. Although he was surprised and angered by the "wise men's" counsel, Johnson, who respected their expertise and judgment in foreign-policy matters, was persuaded to change his war policy. A major turning point in the war had been reached.

DOCUMENT 44. Notes of the Meeting of President Johnson and the "Wise Men," March 26, 1968.

MCGEORGE BUNDY: There is a very significant shift in our position. When we last met we saw reasons for hope.

    We hoped then there would be slow but steady progress. Last night and today the picture is not so hopeful particularly in the countryside.

    Dean Acheson summed up the majority feeling when he said that we can no longer do the job we set out to do in the time we have left and we must begin to take steps to disengage.

    That view was shared by:

      George Ball
      Arthur Dean
      Cy Vance
      Douglas Dillon
      and myself (McGeorge Bundy)

    We do think we should do everything possible to strengthen in a real and visible way the performance of the Government of South Vietnam.

    There were three of us who took a different position:

> General Bradley
> General Taylor
> Bob Murphy

They all feel that we should not act to weaken our position and we should do what our military commanders suggest.

General Ridgway has a special point of view. He wanted to so strengthen the Army of South Vietnam that we could complete the job in two years.

On negotiations, Ball, Goldberg and Vance strongly urged a cessation of the bombing now. Others wanted a halt at some point but not now while the situation is still unresolved in the I Corps area.

On troop reenforcements the dominant sentiment was that the burden of proof rests with those who are urging the increase. Most of us think there should be a substantial escalation. We all felt there should not be an extension of the conflict. This would be against our national interest.

The use of atomic weapons is unthinkable.

HENRY CABOT LODGE: We should shift from search-and-destroy strategy to a strategy of using our military power as a shield to permit the South Vietnamese society to develop as well as North Vietnamese society has been able to do. We need to organize South Vietnam on a block-by-block, precinct-by-precinct basis.

DOUGLAS DILLON: We should change the emphasis. I agree with Acheson. The briefing last night led me to conclude we cannot achieve a military victory. I would agree with Lodge that we should cease search-and-destroy tactics and head toward an eventual disengagement. I would send only the troops necessary to support those there now.

GEORGE BALL: I share Acheson's view. I have felt that way since 1961— that our objectives are not attainable. In the U.S. there is a sharp division of opinion. In the world, we look very badly because of the bombing. That is the central defect in our position. The disadvantages of bombing outweigh the advantages. We need to stop the bombing in the next six weeks to test the will of the North Vietnamese. As long as we continue to bomb, we alienate ourselves from the civilized world. I would have the Pope or U Thant [Secretary-General of the United Nations] suggest the bombing halt. It cannot come from the President.

A bombing halt would quieten [*sic*] the situation here at home.

CY VANCE: McGeorge Bundy stated my views. I agree with George Ball.

Unless we do something quick, the mood in this country may lead us to withdrawal. On troops, we should send no more than the 13,000 support troops....

ACHESON: The issue is can we do what we are trying to do in Vietnam. I do not think we can. Fortas said we are not trying to win a military victory. The issue is can we by military means keep the North Vietnamese off the South Vietnamese. I do not think we can. They can slip around and end-run them and crack them up.... Neither the effort of the Government of Vietnam or the effort of the U.S. government can succeed in the time we have left. Time is limited by reactions in this country. We cannot build an independent South Vietnam; therefore, we should do something by no later than late summer to establish something different.

SOURCE: Williams and others (eds.), *America in Vietnam*, pp. 270–272.

Two months after the Tet-68 offensive had shattered American confidence and optimism about the war, President Johnson, the period of indecision behind him, went before the American people to give his longest and most important speech on the Vietnam War. He announced what amounted to the abandonment of his policy of graduated escalation in pursuit of military victory, which had been followed for nearly three years, ever since the war was Americanized in the summer of 1965. Johnson announced a partial bombing halt as a gesture toward starting negotiations with Hanoi. He announced that General Westmoreland's request for a 206,000-man troop increase would not be met and indicated that a cap on the number of American troops to be sent to Vietnam had been reached. Johnson also announced that henceforth the South Vietnamese government would assume a greater role in defending itself. Johnson thus began the policy that his successor, Richard Nixon, would one day adopt and label Vietnamization. As he neared the end of his speech, Johnson stunned the nation by announcing that he would not seek reelection as president, in effect, resigning. The war had claimed its most famous victim.

DOCUMENT 45. Excerpts from President Johnson's Speech Announcing the Changes in His War Policy and His Impending Retirement, March 31, 1968.

Good evening, my fellow Americans:

Tonight I want to speak to you of peace in Vietnam and Southeast Asia.

No other question so preoccupies our people. No other dream so absorbs the 250 million human beings who live in that part of the world. No other goal motivates American policy in Southeast Asia....

We are prepared to move immediately toward peace through negotiations.

So, tonight, in the hope that this action will lead to early talks, I am taking the first step to deescalate the conflict. We are reducing—substantially reducing—the present level of hostilities.

And we are doing so unilaterally, and at once.

Tonight, I have ordered our aircraft and our naval vessels to make no attacks on North Vietnam, except in the area north of the demilitarized zone where the continuing enemy buildup directly threatens allied forward positions and where the movements of their troops and supplies are clearly related to that threat.

The area in which we are stopping our attacks includes almost 90 percent of North Vietnam's population, and most of its territory. Thus there will be no attacks around the principal populated areas or in the food-producing areas of North Vietnam.

Even this very limited bombing of the North could come to an early end—if our restraint is matched by restraint in Hanoi. But I cannot in good conscience stop all bombing so long as to do so would immediately and directly endanger the lives of our men and our allies. Whether a complete bombing halt becomes possible in the future will be determined by events.

Our purpose in this action is to bring about a reduction in the level of violence that now exists.

It is to save the lives of brave men—and to save the lives of innocent women and children. It is to permit the contending forces to move closer to a political settlement.

And tonight, I call upon the United Kingdom and I call upon the Soviet Union—as cochairmen of the Geneva Conferences, and as permanent members of the United Nations Security Council—to do all they can to move from the unilateral act of deescalation that I have just announced toward genuine peace in Southeast Asia.

Now, as in the past, the United States is ready to send its representatives to any forum, at any time, to discuss the means of bringing this ugly war to an end.

I am designating one of our most distinguished Americans, Ambassador Averell Harriman, as my personal representative for such talks. In addition, I have asked Ambassador Llewellyn Thompson, who returned from Moscow for consultation, to be available to join Ambassador Harriman at Geneva or any other suitable place—just as soon as Hanoi agrees to a conference. . . .

I pay tribute once again tonight to the great courage and endurance of its people. South Vietnam supports armed forces tonight of almost 700,000 men—I call your attention to the fact that this is the equivalent of more than 10 million in our own population. Its people maintain their firm determination to be free of domination by the North.

There has been substantial progress, I think, in building a durable government during these last 3 years. The South Vietnam of 1965 could not have survived the enemy's Tet offensive of 1968. The elected government of South

Vietnam survived that attack—and is rapidly repairing the devastation that it wrought.

The South Vietnamese know that further efforts are going to be required:

—to expand their own armed forces,

—to move back into the countryside as quickly as possible,

—to increase their taxes,

—to select the very best men that they have for civil and military responsibility,

—to achieve a new unity within their constitutional government, and

—to include in the national effort all those groups who wish to preserve South Vietnam's control over its own destiny.

Last week President Thieu ordered the mobilization of 135,000 additional South Vietnamese. He plans to reach—as soon as possible—a total military strength of more than 800,000 men.

To achieve this, the Government of South Vietnam started the drafting of 19-year-olds on March 1st. On May 1st, the Government will begin the drafting of 18-year-olds. . . .

We shall accelerate the reequipment of South Vietnam's armed forces—in order to meet the enemy's increased firepower. This will enable them progressively to undertake a larger share of combat operations against the Communist invaders.

On many occasions I have told the American people that we would send to Vietnam those forces that are required to accomplish our mission there. So, with that as our guide, we have previously authorized a force level of approximately 525,000.

Some weeks ago—to help meet the enemy's new offensive—we sent to Vietnam about 11,000 additional Marine and airborne troops. They were deployed by air in 48 hours, on an emergency basis. But the artillery, tank, aircraft, medical, and other units that were needed to work with and to support these infantry troops in combat could not then accompany them by air on that short notice.

In order that these forces may reach maximum combat effectiveness, the Joint Chiefs of Staff have recommended to me that we should prepare to send—during the next 5 months—support troops totaling approximately 13,500 men.

A portion of these men will be made available from our active forces. The balance will come from reserve component units which will be called up for service. . . .

There is division in the American house now. There is divisiveness among us all tonight. And holding the trust that is mine, as President of all the people, I cannot disregard the peril to the progress of the American people and the hope and the prospect of peace for all peoples.

So, I would ask all Americans, whatever their personal interests or concern, to guard against divisiveness and all its ugly consequences.

Fifty-two months and 10 days ago, in a moment of tragedy and trauma, the duties of this office fell upon me. I asked then for your help and God's, that we might continue America on its course, binding up our wounds, healing our history, moving forward in new unity, to clear the American agenda and to keep the American commitment for all of our people.

United we have kept that commitment. United we have enlarged that commitment.

Through all time to come, I think America will be a stronger nation, a more just society, and a land of greater opportunity and fulfillment because of what we have all done together in these years of unparalleled achievement.

Our reward will come in the life of freedom, peace, and hope that our children will enjoy through ages ahead.

What we won when all of our people united just must not now be lost in suspicion, distrust, selfishness, and politics among any of our people.

Believing this as I do, I have concluded that I should not permit the Presidency to become involved in the partisan divisions that are developing in this political year.

With America's sons in the fields far away, with America's future under challenge right here at home, with our hopes and the world's hopes for peace in the balance every day. I do not believe that I should devote an hour or a day of my time to any personal partisan causes or to any duties other than the awesome duties of this office—the Presidency of your country.

Accordingly, I shall not seek, and I will not accept, the nomination of my party for another term as your President.

But let men everywhere know, however, that a strong, a confident, and a vigilant America stands ready tonight to seek an honorable peace—and stands ready tonight to defend an honored cause—whatever the price, whatever the burden, whatever the sacrifice that duty may require.

Thank you for listening.

Good night and God bless all of you.

SOURCE: *Public Papers of the Presidents of the United States, 1968–1969*, pp. 468–476.

Although the American public would not learn about it until November of 1969, the most notorious actrocities committed by U.S. troops during the Vietnam war occurred about the time President Johnson was making his momentous decisions to change American war policy. On the morning of March 16, 1968, soldiers belonging to the 1st and 2nd Platoons of Charlie Company, 1st Battalion, 11th Brigade, attached to the Americal Division, massacred an estimated 300 to 400 civilians at two hamlets, My Lai and My Khe, located near the coast in the Son Tinh district of Quang Ngai province in northern South Vietnam. The victims were mostly old men, women, and children. For a year and a half, the Americal Division succeeded in covering up the war crimes that had been committed and suppressed all news of what had happened that dread morning at My Lai. In time the veil of secrecy was penetrated and the dramatic story came out, thanks in large part to the efforts of a young independent journalist, Seymour M. Hersh. The following account is taken from a book Hersh wrote about the My Lai massacre.

DOCUMENT 46. Excerpts from Seymour M. Hersh, *My Lai 4: Report on the Massacre and Its Aftermath*, 1970.

... The My Lai 4 assault was the biggest thing going in the Americal Division that day. To get enough airlift, Task Force Barker had to borrow helicopters from other units throughout the division. The air lanes above the action were carefully allotted to high-ranking officers for observation. Barker monitored the battle from the 1,000-foot level. Major General Samuel Koster, commanding general of the division, was allotted the air space at 2,000 feet. His helicopter was permanently stationed outside his door at division headquarters twenty-one miles to the north, waiting to fly him to the scene of any action within minutes. Oran K. Henderson, commander of the 11th Brigade, was given the top spot—at 2,500 feet. All of the helicopters were to circle counterclockwise over the battle area. Flying low, beneath the 1,000-foot level, would be the gunships, heavily armed helicopters whose mission was to shoot down any Viet Cong soldiers attempting to escape.

Brigade headquarters, sure that there would be a major battle, sent along two men from the Army's 31st Public Information Detachment to record the event for history. Jay Roberts of Arlington, Virginia, a reporter, and photographer Ronald L. Haeberle of Cleveland, Ohio, arrived with the second wave of helicopters and immediately attached themselves to the third platoon, which was bringing up the rear.

The hamlet itself had a population of about 700 people, living either in flimsy thatch-covered huts—"hootches," as the GIs called them—or in solidly made red-brick homes, many with small porches in front. There was an east-west footpath just south of the main cluster of homes; a few yards further south was a loose surface road that marked a hamlet boundary. A deep drainage ditch and then a rice paddy marked the eastern boundary. To the south of My Lai 4 was a large center, or plaza area—clearly the main spot for mass meetings. The foliage was dense: there were high bamboo trees, hedges and plant life everywhere. Medina couldn't see thirty feet into the hamlet from the landing zone.

The first and second platoons lined up carefully to begin the hundred-meter advance into My Lai 4. Walking in line is an important military concept; if one group of men gets too far in front, it could be hit by bullets from behind—those fired by colleagues. Yet even this went wrong. Ron Grzesik was in charge of a small first-platoon fire team of riflemen and a machine gunner; he took his job seriously. His unit was supposed to be on the right flank, protecting Calley and his men. But Grzesik's group ended up on Calley's left.

As Brooks' second platoon cautiously approached the hamlet, a few Vietnamese began running across a field several hundred meters on the left. They may have been Viet Cong, or they may have been civilians fleeing the artillery shelling or the bombardment from the helicopter gunships. Vernado Simpson,

Jr., of Jackson, Mississippi, saw a man he identified as a Viet Cong soldier running with what seemed to be a weapon. A woman and a small child were running with him. Simpson fired . . . again and again. He killed the woman and the baby. The man got away. Reporter Roberts saw a squad of GIs jump off a helicopter and begin firing at a group of people running on a nearby road. One was a woman with her children. Then he saw them "shoot two guys who popped up from a rice field. They looked like military-age men . . . when certain guys pop up from rice fields, you shoot them." This was the young reporter's most dangerous assignment. He had never been in combat before. "You're scared to death out there. We just wanted to go home."

The first two platoons of Charlie Company, still unfired upon, entered the hamlet. Behind them, still in the rice paddy, were the third platoon and Captain Medina's command post. Calley and some of his men walked into the plaza area in the southern part of the hamlet. None of the people was running away; they knew that U.S. soldiers would assume that anyone running was a Viet Cong and would shoot to kill. There was no immediate sense of panic. The time was about 8 A.M. Grzesik and his fire team were a few meters north of Calley; they couldn't see each other because of the dense vegetation. Grzesik and his men began their usual job of pulling people from their homes, interrogating them, and searching for Viet Cong. The villagers were gathered up, and Grzesik sent Meadlo, who was in his unit, to take them to Calley for further questioning. Grzesik didn't see Meadlo again for more than an hour.

Some of Calley's men thought it was breakfast time as they walked in; a few families were gathered in front of their homes cooking rice over a small fire. Without a direct order, the first platoon also began rounding up the villagers. There still was no sniper fire, no sign of a large enemy unit. Sledge remembered thinking that "if there were VC around, they had plenty of time to leave before we came in. We didn't tiptoe in there."

The killings began without warning. Harry Stanley told the C.I.D. that one young member of Calley's platoon took a civilian into custody and then "pushed the man up to where we were standing and then stabbed the man in the back with his bayonet . . . The man fell to the ground and was gasping for breath." The GI then "killed him with another bayonet thrust or by shooting him with a rifle . . . There was so many people killed that day it is hard for me to recall exactly how some of the people died." The youth next "turned to where some soldiers were holding another forty- or fifty-year old man in custody." He "picked this man up and threw him down a well. Then [he] pulled the pin from a M26 grenade and threw it in after the man." Moments later Stanley saw "some old women and some little children—fifteen or twenty of them—in a group around a temple where some incense was burning. They were kneeling and crying and praying, and various soldiers . . . walked by and executed these women and children by shooting them in the head with their rifles. The soldiers killed all fifteen or twenty of them . . ."

There were few physical protests from the people; about eighty of them were taken quietly from their homes and herded together in the plaza area. A few hollered out, "No VC. No VC." But that was hardly unexpected. Calley left Meadlo, Boyce and a few others with the responsibility of guarding the group. "You know what I want you to do with them," he told Meadlo. Ten minutes later—about 8:15 A.M.—he returned and asked, "Haven't you got rid of them yet? I want them dead." Radioman Sledge, who was trailing Calley, heard the officer tell Meadlo to "waste them." Meadlo followed orders: "We stood about ten to fifteen feet away from them and then he [Calley] started shooting them. Then he told me to start shooting them. I started to shoot them. So we went ahead and killed them. I used more than a whole clip—used four or five clips." There are seventeen M16 bullets in each clip. Boyce slipped away, to the northern side of the hamlet, glad he hadn't been asked to shoot. Women were huddled against their children, vainly trying to save them. Some continued to chant, "No VC." Others simply said, "No.No.No."

Do Chuc is a gnarled forty-eight-year-old Vietnamese peasant whose two daughters and an aunt were killed by the GIs in My Lai 4 that day. He and his family were eating breakfast when the GIs entered the hamlet and ordered them out of their homes. Together with other villagers, they were marched a few hundred meters into the plaza, where they were told to squat. "Still we had no reason to be afraid," Chuc recalled. "Everyone was calm." He watched as the GIs set up a machine gun. The calm ended. The people began crying and begging. One monk showed his identification papers to a soldier, but the American simply said, "Sorry." Then the shooting started. Chuc was wounded in the leg, but he was covered by dead bodies and thus spared. After waiting an hour, he fled the hamlet.

Nguyen Bat, a Viet Cong hamlet chief who later defected, said that many of the villagers who were eating breakfast outdoors when the GIs marched in greeted them without fear. They were gathered together and shot. Other villagers who were breakfasting indoors were killed inside their homes.

The few Viet Cong who had stayed near the hamlet were safely hidden. Nguyen Ngo, a former deputy commander of a Viet Cong guerrilla platoon operating in the My Lai area, ran to his hiding place 300 meters away when the GIs came in shooting, but he could see that "they shot everything in sight." His mother and sister hid in ditches and survived because bodies fell on top of them. Pham Lai, a former hamlet security guard, climbed into a bunker with a bamboo top and heard but did not see the shootings. His wife, hidden under a body, survived the massacre.

By this time, there was shooting everywhere. Dennis I. Conti, a GI from Providence, Rhode Island, later explained to C.I.D. investigators what he thought had happened: "We were all psyched up, and as a result, when we got there the shooting started, almost as a chain reaction. The majority of us had expected to meet VC combat troops, but this did not turn out to be so. First we saw a few men running . . . and the next thing I knew we were shooting at everything. Everybody was just firing. After they got in the village, I guess you could say that the men were out of control." . . .

. . . Harry Stanley was standing a few feet away from Calley near some huts at the drainage ditch when the call came from Medina. He had a different recollection: "Medina called Calley and said, 'What the fuck is going on?' Calley said he got some VC, or some people that needed to be checked out." At this point Medina cautioned Calley to tell his men to save their ammunition because the operation still had a few more days to run.

It is not clear how soon or to whom Medina's order was given, but Stanley told the C.I.D. what Calley did next: "There was an old lady in a bed and I believe there was a priest in white praying over her . . . Calley told me to ask about the VC and NVA and where the weapons were. The priest denied being a VC or NVA." Charles Sledge watched with horror as Calley pulled the old man outside: "He said a few more words to the monk. It looked like the monk was pleading for his life. Lieutenant Calley then took his rifle and pushed the monk into a rice paddy and shot him point-blank."

Calley then turned his attention back to the crowd of Vietnamese and issued an order: "Push all those people in the ditch." Three or four GIs complied. Calley struck a woman with a rifle as he pushed her down. Stanley remembered that some of the civilians "kept trying to get out. Some made it to the top . . ." Calley began the shooting and ordered Meadlo to join in. Meadlo told about it later: "So we pushed our seven to eight people in with the big bunch of them. And so I began shooting them all. So did Mitchell, Calley . . . I guess I shot maybe twenty-five or twenty people in the ditch . . . men, women and children. And babies." Some of the GIs switched from automatic fire to single-shot to conserve ammunition. Herbert Carter watched the mothers "grabbing their kids and the kids grabbing their mothers. I didn't know what to do."

Calley then turned again to Meadlo and said, "Meadlo, we've got another job to do." Meadlo didn't want any more jobs. He began to argue with Calley. Sledge watched Meadlo once more start to sob. Calley turned next to Robert Maples and said, "Maples, load your machine gun and shoot these people." Maples replied, as he told the C.I.D., "I'm not going to do that." He remembered that "the people firing into the ditch kept reloading magazines into their rifles and kept firing into the ditch and then killed or at least shot everyone in the ditch." William C. Lloyd of Tampa, Florida, told the C.I.D. that some grenades were also thrown into the ditch. Dennis Conti noticed that "a lot of women had thrown themselves on top of the children to protect them, and the children were alive at first. Then the children who were old enough to walk got up and Calley began to shoot the children."

One further incident stood out in many GIs' minds: seconds after the shooting stopped, a bloodied but unhurt two-year-old boy miraculously crawled out of the ditch, crying. He began running toward the hamlet. Someone hollered, "There's a kid." There was a long pause. Then Calley ran back, grabbed the kid, threw him back in the ditch and shot him. . . .

. . . There were some small acts of mercy. A GI placed a blanket over the body of a mutilated child. An elderly woman was spared when some GIs hollered at a soldier just as he was about to shoot her. Grzesik remembered watching a GI seem to wrestle with his conscience while holding a bayonet over a wounded old man. "He wants to stab somebody with a bayonet," Grzesik thought. The GI hesitated . . . and finally passed on, leaving the old man to die.

Some GIs, however, didn't hesitate to use their bayonets. Nineteen-year-old Nguyen Thi Ngoc Tuyet watched a baby trying to open her slain mother's blouse to nurse. A soldier shot the infant while it was struggling with the blouse, and then slashed at it was his bayonet. Tuyet also said she saw another baby hacked to death by GIs wielding their bayonets.

Le Tong, a twenty-eight-year-old rice farmer, reported seeing one woman raped after GIs killed her children. Nguyen Khoa, a thirty-seven-year-old peasant, told of a thirteen-year-old girl who was raped before being killed. GIs then attacked Khoa's wife, tearing off her clothes. Before they could rape her, however, Khoa said, their six-year-old son, riddled with bullets, fell and saturated her with blood. The GIs left her alone.

There were "degrees" of murder that day. Some were conducted out of sympathy. Michael Terry, the Mormon who was a squad leader in the third platoon, had ordered his men to take their lunch break by the bloody ditch in the rear of the hamlet. He noticed that there were no men in the ditch, only women and children. He had watched Calley and the others shoot into that ditch. Calley seemed just like a kid, Terry thought. He also remembered thinking it was "just like a Nazi-type thing." When one solder couldn't fire any more and threw down his weapon, "Calley picked it up." Later, during lunch, Terry and his men saw that some of the victims were still breathing. "They were pretty badly shot up. They weren't going to get any medical help, and so we shot them. Shot maybe five of them."

James Bergthold saw an old man who had been shot in both legs: "He was going to die anyway, so I figured I might as well kill him." He took his .45-caliber pistol (as a machine-gun ammunition carrier, he was entitled to one), carefully placed the barrel against the upper part of the old man's forehead and blew off the top of his head. Carter had watched the scene and remembered thinking that Bergthold had done the old man a favor. "If me and you were together and you got wounded bad," Carter later told an interviewer, "and I couldn't get you to a doctor, I'd shoot you, too."

Most of the shooting was over by the time Medina called a break for lunch, shortly after eleven o'clock. By then Roberts and Haeberle had grabbed a helicopter and cleared out of the area, their story for the day far bigger than they wanted. Calley, Mitchell, Sledge, Grzesik and a few others were back to the command post west of My Lai 4 to take lunch with Captain Medina and the rest of his headquarter's crew. Grzesik recalled that at that point he'd thought there couldn't be a survivor left in the hamlet. But two little girls showed up, about ten and eleven years old. John Paul said they came in from one of the paddies, where they apparently had waited out the siege. "We sat them down with us [at the command post]," Paul recounted, "and gave them some cookies and crackers to eat." When a C.I.D. interrogator later asked Charles Sledge how many civilians he thought had survived, he answered, "Only two small children who had lunch with us."

In the early afternoon the men of Charlie Company mopped up to make sure all the houses and goods in My Lai 4 were destroyed. Medina ordered the underground tunnels in the hamlet blown up; most of them already had been blocked. Within another hour My Lai 4 was no more: its red-brick buildings demolished by explosives, its huts burned to the ground, its people dead or dying.

Michael Bernhardt later summarized the day: "We met no resistance and I only saw three captured weapons. We had no casualties. It was just like any other Vietnamese village—old papa-sans, women and kids. As a matter of fact, I don't remember seeing one military-age male in the entire place, dead or alive. The only prisoner I saw was in his fifties."

The platoons pulled out shortly after noon, rendezvousing in the rice paddies east of My Lai 4. Lieutenant Brooks' platoon had about eighty-five villagers in tow; it kept those of military age with them and told the rest to begin moving south. Following orders, Medina then marched the GIs northeast through the nearly deserted hamlets of My Lai 5 and My Lai 6, ransacking and burning as they went. In one of the hamlets, Medina ordered the residents gathered, and then told Sergeant Phu, the regular company interpreter, to tell them, as Phu later recalled, that "they were to go away or something will happen to them— just like what happened at My Lai 4."

By nightfall the Viet Cong were back in My Lai 4, helping the survivors bury the dead. It took five days. Most of the funeral speeches were made by the Communist guerrillas. Nguyen Bat was not a Communist at the time of the massacre, but the incident changed his mind. "After the shooting," he said, "all the villagers became Communists."

When Army investigators reached the barren area in November, 1969, in connection with the My Lai probe in the United States, they found mass graves at three sites, as well as a ditch full of bodies. It was estimated that between 450 and 500 people—most of them women, children and old men—had been slain and buried there. . . .

SOURCE: Hersh, Seymour M., *My Lai 4: A Report on the Massacre and Its Aftermath* (New York: Random House, 1970), pp. 46–51, 62–64, 72–75.

Violence in America during the late 1960s paralleled the violence taking place in Vietnam. During the summer of 1967, rioters burned and looted large areas of Newark and Detriot. In 1968, Martin Luther King, Jr., and Robert Kennedy were assassinated. Violence also engulfed the antiwar movement as militant protesters across the country fought with police and National Guard units. But the worst outbreak of violence occurred in Chicago in late August during the Democratic National Convention. Militant elements of the antiwar movement had vowed to disrupt the gathering. Mayor Richard Daley, official host for the Democratic convention, had vowed that there would be no disruptions. He mobilized his police force. Thousands of National Guardsmen and federal troops were also mobilized. The stage was set for a violent confrontation between protesters and police. The worst violence occurred the evening of August 28, 1968, at about 8:00 P.M., when police began attacking demonstrators who had refused orders to disperse and had sat down in the streets.

DOCUMENT 47. Excerpt from *Rights in Conflict: The Official Report*
to the National Commission on the Causes
and Prevention of Violence, 1968.

The Clash

Thus, at 7:57 P.M., with two groups of club-wielding police converging simultaneously and independently, the battle was joined. The portions of the throng out of the immediate area of conflict largely stayed put and took up the chant, "The whole world is watching," but the intersection fragmented into a collage of violence.

Re-creating the precise chronology of the next few moments is impossible. But there is no question that a violent street battle ensued.

People ran for cover and were struck by police as they passed. Clubs were swung indiscriminately.

Two Assistant U.S. Attorneys who were on the scene characterized the police as "hostile and aggressive." Some witnesses cited particularly dramatic personal stories.

"I saw squadrols of policemen coming from everywhere," a secretary quoted earlier said. "The crowd around me suddenly began to run. Some of us, including myself, were pushed back onto the sidewalk and then all the way up against . . . the Blackston Hotel along Michigan Avenue. I thought the crowd had panicked."

"Fearing that I would be crushed against the wall of the building . . . I somehow managed to work my way . . . to the edge of the street . . . and saw police everywhere. Demonstrators [nearest the police] tried to move, but couldn't because of the press of the crowd. There was no place for them to go."

The deputy superintendent of police recalls that he ordered his men to "hold your line there" . . . "stand fast" . . . "Lieutenant, hold your men steady there!" These orders, he said, were not obeyed by all.

"Two or three policemen broke formation and began swinging at everyone in sight," the McGovern worker says. The deputy superintendent states that police disregarded his order to return to the police lines—the beginning of what he says was the only instance in which he personally saw police discipline collapse. He estimates that ten to 15 officers moved off on individual forays against demonstrators. But the McGovern worker says "This became sort of spontaneous. Every few seconds more policemen would break formation and began swinging until . . . all the policemen from the original line at Balbo were just swinging through the crowd."

"I turned toward the north and was immediately struck on the back of the head from behind," says the UPI reporter. "I fell to the ground. . . ."

"As I looked up I was hit for the first time on the head from behind by what must have been a billy club. I was then knocked down and while on my hands and knees, I was hit around the shoulders. I got up again, stumbling and was hit again. As I was falling, I heard words to the effect of 'move, move' and the horrible sound of cracking billy clubs.

"After my second fall, I remember being kicked in the back, and I looked up and noticed that many policemen around me had no badges on. The police kept hitting me on the head."

Eventually she made her way to an alley behind the Blackstone and finally, "bleeding badly from my head wound," was driven by a friend to a hospital emergency room. Her treatment included the placing of 12 stitches.

Another young woman, who had been among those who sat down in the intersection, ran south on Michigan, a "Yippie flag" in her hand, when she saw the police. "I fell in the center of the intersection," she says. "Two policemen ran up on me, stopped and hit me on the shoulder, arm and leg about five or six times, severely. They were swearing and one of them broke my flag over his knee." By fleeing into Grant Park, she managed eventually to escape.

Another witness said: "To my left, the police caught a man, beat him to the ground and smashed their clubs on the back of his unprotected head. I stopped to help him. He was elderly, somewhere in his mid-50s. He was kneeling and holding his bleeding head. As I stopped to help him, the police turned on me. "Get that cock sucker out of here!" This command was accompanied by four blows from clubs—one on the middle of my back, one on the bottom of my back, one on my left buttock, and one on the back of my leg. No attempt was made to arrest me or anybody else in the vicinity. All the blows that I saw inflicted by the police were on the backs of heads, arms, legs, etc. It was the most slow and confused, and the least experienced people who got caught and beaten.

"The police were angry. Their anger was neither disinterested nor instrumental. It was deep, expressive and personal. 'Get out of here you cock suckers' seemed to be their most common cry.

"To my right, four policemen beat a young man as he lay on the ground. They beat him and at the same time told him to 'get up and get the hell out of here.' Meanwhile, I struggled with the injured man whom I had stopped to help. . . ."

One demonstrator said that several policemen were coming toward a group in which he was standing when one of the officers yelled, "Hey, there's a nigger over there we can get." They then are said to have veered off and grabbed a middle-aged Negro man, whom they beat.

A lawyer says that he was in a group of demonstrators in the park just south of Balbo when he heard a police officer shout, "Let's get 'em!" Three policemen ran up, "singled out one girl and as she was running away from them, beat her on the back of the head. As she fell to the ground, she was struck by the nightsticks of these officers." A male friend of hers then came up yelling at the police. The witness said, "He was arrested. The girl was left in the area lying on the ground."

The beating of two other girls was witnessed from a hotel window. The witness says, he saw one girl "trying to shield a demonstrator who had been beaten to the ground," whereupon a policeman came up "hitting her with a billy club." The officer also kicked the girl in the shoulder, the witness said.

A *Milwaukee Journal* reporter says in his statement, "when the police managed to break up groups of protesters they pursued individuals and beat them with clubs. Some police pursued individual demonstrators as far as a block . . . and beat them. . . . In many cases it appeared to me that when police had finished beating the protesters they were pursuing, they then attacked, indiscriminately, any civilian who happened to be standing nearby. Many of these were not involved in the demonstrations."

In balance, there is no doubt that police discipline broke during the melee. The deputy superintendent of police states that—although this was the only time he saw discipline collapse—when he ordered his men to stand fast, some did not respond and began to sally through the crowd, clubbing people they came upon. An inspector-observer from the Los Angeles Police Department, stated that during this week, "The restraint of the police both as individual members and as an organization, was beyond reason." However, he said that on this occasion:

> There is no question but that many officers acted without restraint and exerted force beyond that necessary under the circumstances. The leadership at the point of conflict did little to prevent such conduct and the direct control of officers by first-line supervisors was virtually non-existent.

The deputy superintendent of police has been described by several observers as being very upset by individual policemen who beat demonstrators. He pulled his men off the demonstrators, shouting "Stop, damn it, stop. For Christ's sake, stop it."

"It seemed to me," an observer says, "that only a saint could have swallowed the vile remarks to the officers. However, they went to extremes in clubbing the Yippies. I saw them move into the park, swatting away with clubs at girls and boys lying in the grass. More than once I witnessed two officers pulling at the arms of a Yippie until the arms almost left their sockets, then, as the officers put the Yippie in a police van, a third jabbed a riot stick into the groin of the youth being arrested. It was evident that the Yippie was not resisting arrest."

A witness adds: "I witnessed four or five instances of several officers beating demonstrators when it appeared the demonstrators could have been easily transported and confined to police vans waiting nearby."

"Anyone who was in the way of some of the policemen was struck," a UPI correspondent concludes in his statement, "Police continued to hit people in the back who were running away as fast as possible. I saw one man knocked to the street. . . . A policeman continued to poke his stick at the man's groin and kidney area. Several newsmen were struck. Individual incidents of violence were going on over the entire area at once, in any direction you might look.

"In one incident, a young man, who apparently had been maced, staggered across Michigan . . . helped by a companion. The man collapsed . . . Medical people from the volunteer medical organization rushed out to help him. A police officer (a sergeant, I think) came rushing forward, followed by the two other nightstick-brandishing policemen and yelled, 'Get him out of here; this ain't a hospital.' The medical people fled, half dragging and half carrying the young man with them. . . .

"Another incident I vividly recall is two policemen dragging one protester by one leg, with his shoulders and possibly his head dragging on the pavement as they ran toward a paddy wagon. So much violence was going on at one time. . . ."

A university student who was watching the melee from a hotel window says she saw one young man attempting to flee the police. "Two or three grabbed him and beat him until he fell to the ground." Then, she says, "Two or three more policemen were attracted to him and continued to beat him until he was dragged into a paddy wagon."

At another moment, the girl says, she saw another youth "felled by two or three policemen." A medic "dressed all in white and wearing a white helmet" came to aid him. When police saw him giving aid to the downed boy, "they came upon the medic and began to beat him."

"I saw a well-dressed man carrying a well-dressed woman screaming in his arms," said a *Chicago Daily News* reporter. "He tried to carry her to the Hilton Hotel front door and get in. It was secured, so it certainly would have been safe to permit them in. But the police stopped him, and he then carried her back into the crowd. She was hysterical, and I can see no reason for the police treatment of this injured woman." Also during the melee, the reporter says, he saw policeman using sawhorses as "battering rams" against the crowd.

The history professor quoted earlier says, "A number of motorcycle police drove up over the curb on the east side of Michigan and into the crowd." Police also charged demonstrators and onlookers gathered around the old car with the antidraft rally sign which earlier had been taken up to the police line in front of the Hilton.

A series of arrests were made around the antidraft car, some peaceful and some with considerable force. During the course of these arrests, one girl in this group lost her skirt. Although there have been unverified reports of police ripping the clothes from female demonstrators, this is the only incident on news film of any woman being disrobed in the course of arrest.

While violence was exploding in the street, the crowd wedged, behind the police sawhorses along the northeast edge of the Hilton, was experiencing a terror all its own. Early in the evening, this group had consisted in large part of curious bystanders. But following the police surges into the demonstrators clogging the intersection, protesters had crowded the ranks behind the horses in their flight from the police.

From force of numbers, this sidewalk crowd of 150 to 200 persons was pushing down toward the Hilton's front entrance. Policemen whose orders were to keep the entrance clear were pushing with sawhorses. Other police and fleeing demonstrators were pushing from the north in the effort to clear the intersection. Thus, the crowd was wedged against the hotel, with the hotel itself on the west, sawhorses on the southeast and police on the northeast.

Films show that one policeman elbowed his way to where he could rescue a girl of about ten years of age from the vise-like press of the crowd. He cradled her in his arms and carried her to a point of relative safety 20 feet away. The crowd itself "passed up" an elderly woman to a low ledge. But many who remained were subjected to what they and witnesses considered deliberate brutality by the police.

"I was crowded in with the group of screaming, frightened people," an onlooker states, "We jammed against each other, trying to press into the brick wall of the hotel. As we stood there breathing hard . . . a policeman calmly walked the length of the barricade with a can of chemical spray [evidently mace] in his hand. Unbelievably, he was spraying at us." Photos reveal several policeman using mace against the crowd.

Another witness, a graduate student, said she was on the periphery of the crowd and could see that "police sprayed mace randomly along the first line of people along the curb." A reporter who was present said a woman cried, "Oh no, not mace!" He said a youth moaned, "Stop it!" "We're not doing anything!" "Others," recalls another witness, "pleaded with the police to tell them where they should move and allow them to move there."

"Some of the police then turned and attacked the crowd," a Chicago reporter says. The student says she could see police clubbing persons pinned at the edge of the crowd and that there was "a great deal of screaming and pushing within the group." A reporter for a Cleveland paper said, "The police indiscriminately beat those on the periphery of the crowd." An Assistant U.S. attorney put it, "The group on the sidewalk was charged by police using nightsticks." A young cook caught in the crowd relates that:

> The police began picking people off. They would pull individuals to the ground and begin beating them. A medic wearing a white coat and an armband with a red cross was grabbed, beaten and knocked to the ground. His whole face was covered with blood.

"The cops just waded into the crowd," says a law student. "There was a great deal of clubbing. People were screaming, 'Help.'"

As a result, a part of the crowd was trapped in front of the Conrad Hilton and pressed hard against a big plate glass window of the Haymarket Lounge. A reporter who was sitting inside said, "Frightened men and women banged . . . against the window. A captain of the fire department inside told us to get back from the window, that it might get knocked in. As I backed away a few feet I could see a smudge of blood on the glass outside."

With a sickening crack, the window shattered, and screaming men and women tumbled through, some cut badly by jagged glass. The police came after them.

"I was pushed through by the force of large numbers of people," one victim said. "I got a deep cut on my right leg, diagnosed later by Eugene McCarthy's doctor as a severed artery.... I fell to the floor of the bar. There were ten to 20 people who had come through.... I could not stand on the leg. It was bleeding profusely.

"A squad of policemen burst into the bar, clubbing all those who looked to them like demonstrators, at the same time screaming over and over, 'We've got to clear this area.' The police acted literally like mad dogs looking for objects to attack.

"A patrolman ran up to where I was sitting. I protested that I was injured and could not walk, attempting to show him my leg. He screamed that he would show me I could walk. He grabbed me by the shoulder and literally hurled me through the door of the bar into the lobby....

"I stumbled out into what seemed to be a main lobby. The young lady I was with and I were both immediately set upon by what I can only presume were plainclothes police.... We were cursed by these individuals and thrown through another door into an outer lobby." Eventually a McCarthy aide took him to the 15th floor.

In the heat of all this, probably few were aware of the Haymarket's advertising slogan: "A place where good guys take good girls to dine in the lusty, rollicking atmosphere of fabulous Old Chicago...."

During the evening, at least one other window at the Hilton was also broken by crushing crowds.

There is little doubt that during this whole period, beginning at 7:57 P.M. and lasting for nearly 20 minutes, the preponderance of violence came from the police. It was not entirely a one-way battle, however.

Firecrackers were thrown at police. Trash baskets were set on fire and rolled and thrown at them. In one case, a gun was taken from a policeman by a demonstrator.

"Some hippies," said a patrolman in his statement, "were hit by other hippies who were throwing rocks at the police." Films reveal that when police were chasing demonstrators into Grant Park, one young man upended a sawhorse and heaved it at advancing officers. At one point the deputy superintendent of police was knocked down by a thrown sawhorse. At least one police three-wheeler was tipped over. One of the demonstrators says that "people in the park were prying up cobblestones and breaking them. One person piled up cobblestones in his arms and headed toward the police." Witnesses reported that people were throwing "anything they could lay their hands on. From the windows of the Hilton and Blackstone hotels, toilet paper, wet towels, even ash trays came raining down."

A police lieutenant stated that he saw policemen bombarded with "rocks, cherry bombs, jars of vaseline, jars of mayonnaise and pieces of wood torn from the yellow barricades falling in the street." He, too, noticed debris falling from the hotel windows.

A patrolman on duty during the melee states that among the objects he saw thrown at police officers were "rocks, bottles, shoes, a telephone and a garbage can cover. Rolls of toilet paper were thrown from hotel windows. I saw a number of plastic practice gold balls, studded with nails, on the street as well as plastic bags filled with what appeared to be human excrement." He said he saw two policemen, one of them wearing a soft hat, get hit with bricks.

A sergeant states that during the fracas, two men under his command had their plastic faceguards (which they pay for themselves) shattered by bricks or rocks.

A number of police officers were injured, either by flying missiles or in personal attacks. One, for example, was helping a fellow officer "pick up a hippie when another hippie gave [me] a heavy kick, aiming for my groin." The blow struck the officer partly on the leg and partly in the testicles. He went down, and the "hippie" who kicked him escaped.

An attorney who was present also told of seeing demonstrators kick policemen in the groin.

In another instance, a Chicago police reporter said in his statement, "a police officer reached down and grabbed a person who dove forward and bit the officer on the leg. . . . Three or four fellow policemen came to his aid. They had to club the demonstrator to make him break his clamp on the officer's leg." In another case, the witness saw a demonstrator "with a big mop of hair hit a police officer with an old British Army type metal helmet." The reporter said he also heard "hissing sounds from the demonstrators as if they were spraying the police." Later he found empty lacquer spray and hair spray cans on the street. Also he heard police cry out, "They're kicking us with knives in their shoes." Later, he said, he found that demonstrators "had actually inserted razor blades in their shoes."

Another type of police difficulty was described by a police captain and mentioned by several other officers in their statements. The captain said that when news cameramen equipped with portable flood lights turn them toward the police, this "caused temporary blindness" and reduced the police effectiveness.

Against the demonstrators' missile throwing and otherwise, police tended to move in groups of eight or ten, regrouping now and then in the street.

Squadrols continually drove into the intersection. "The police kept pulling as many people as they were able to get and taking them into the paddy wagons," says the ACLU representative quoted earlier. The manner in which this was done ranged from restraint to deliberate brutality. In one case, for example, a heavy woman in a muu-muu insisted on using the step at the back of the squadrol as a platform from which to address the crowd. The police repeatedly attempted to move her, but she continued to speak. Finally, a large policeman grabbed her under both arms and lifted her up and into the squadrol.

By contrast, police dragged some persons up the squadrol step, throwing them bodily inside and then hitting them. In one arrest, captured on film, a male demonstrator used his hand to trip one of two policemen carrying him to a paddy wagon. After picking himself up from the pavement, the officer severely beat the demonstrator on the head and chest with his baton. Another policeman joined in, repeatedly jabbing the youth in the groin with his baton.

A man who served as a medical liaison to the demonstration marshals states that he saw the police beat a boy incessantly before putting him into a paddy wagon. He said the boy looked as if he were already unconscious, but the police continued beating him. According to the university student, quoted earlier about her view from the hotel window. "When an individual was brought to the paddy wagon, two or three policemen stationed at the door would grab the person and continue to beat him."

An assistant U.S. Attorney who was at the battle reported later: "The arresting officers frequently used their clubs to hit the arrested person in the stomach and kidneys, even though the arrested persons were not in any way resisting arrest or struggling with the police officers." On the other hand, both police officers and a city observer who watched the loading of the paddy wagons state that no excessive force was used in placing nonresisting prisoners in the vans.

Meanwhile, more CTA buses with police reinforcements were pouring into the area. Blue police buses by now were bringing reinforcements into the area. A Chicago attorney who was near the Hilton watched one contingent unload. He says they "gave the finger" to subdued demonstrators in the vicinity and also made obscene remarks, like "Hippies eat shit." Moving quickly through the Balbo–Michigan intersection, they hurried to join their fellow officers pushing north on Michigan.

Says an ACLU representative: "The buses would discharge at the corner of Wabash and Balbo and then the men would form into a line and march down Balbo with their night sticks, chanting, "Kill, kill."

With each new police attack and flurry of arrests, the crowd dispersed farther into the park and east on Balbo.

Peck wound up on the east side of Michigan Avenue. From that vantage point, he said, he thought he saw the deputy superintendent of police and a person in civilian clothes, who he thought was a city official, coming across the avenue in his direction. In a similar situation during the Pentagon confrontation when federal marshals moved in against demonstrators, Peck says, he had been able to obtain a loudspeaker, address himself to commanding authority, calm the crowd and prevent further assaults. With this in mind, he said he went out to "resume negotiations" with the deputy superintendent and the other man. Peck admits he was "probably pretty emotional" at this point, but says he had his senses about him.

Using his hand to emphasize his words, he addressed the deputy: "Why did you have your police move against us when I said we were not violent? Isn't there any way we can get our people to safety?"

At this, Peck insists, they both lunged at him. Peck said he tightened up in "a defensive posture" to break their hold and then ran. Other police came after him. He again assumed the defensive posture and, he claims, was beaten brutally by the officers. Then, Peck says, he was dragged some 200 feet to a police van. Later, several stitches were taken on his head, his back and sides were bruised and his genitals were swollen.

A witness to this incident, the Chicago police reporter quoted earlier, says that Peck initiated the trouble by shouting at the deputy: "You're the cause of all this." Then, the witness states, Peck slugged the deputy in the right eye with his fist, knocking his glasses to the street. A police sergeant went after Peck, but was "grabbed by a group of demonstrators who beat the daylights out of him." Finally, another officer made a flying tackle of Peck as he was "trying to escape through the crowd." As Peck was arrested, "the demonstrators broke up a yellow wooden [saw] horse approximately ten or 12 feet long . . . and began throwing [the pieces] at the police." The deputy superintendent, the reporter said, was hit again. The sergeant was rescued from the mob only after several policemen used their batons against the demonstrators. The deputy's version of the incident agrees essentially with this account.

SOURCE: *Rights in Conflict: The Official Report to the National Commission on the Causes and Prevention of Violence* (New York: Signet, 1968), pp. 226–235.

5

THE WAR TO END A WAR AND ITS AFTERMATH: 1969–1975

Richard M. Nixon assumed the office of the presidency on January 20, 1969, committed to bringing the Vietnam war to an end. He had been elected by the narrowest of margins over Vice-President Hubert H. Humphrey, the Democratic candidate, and George C. Wallace, the American Independence Party standard bearer. Nixon knew that both his prospects for reelection and his ambitious plans for restructuring American foreign policy, based on détente with the major Communist powers, depended on closing down America's role in the Vietnam war.

Both Nixon and his principal foreign-policy adviser, Henry Kissinger, were convinced that they could succeed where Lyndon Johnson had failed. They would offer more realistic peace terms to the Communists and also make it clear to Hanoi that the United States was prepared to widen the war if North Vietnam was not responsive to their new initiatives. Nixon's announced goal was to achieve "peace with honor" in Vietnam. This vague rhetorical phrase meant at least that the U.S. withdrawal from Vietnam could not be, or ever appear to be, a defeat for the United States and that the peace terms would have to include the survival of a non-Communist government in southern Vietnam. Nixon and Kissinger soon learned what all their predecessors had learned from painful experience: that both their freedom of maneuver and their ability to influence events were limited; they also found that the North Vietnamese could neither be cowed by threats nor lured by more flexible terms into changing the basic negotiating stance that they had assumed when talks had first begun in Paris in May 1968.

On September 3, 1969, Ho Chi Minh, the great Vietnamese revolutionary leader, died. His final testament was read by Le Duan, the head of the Indochinese

Communist Party, on September 9, during a funeral service in Ho's honor. Ho's last words included an exhortation to his people not to compromise with the Americans and to fight on until total victory, that is, until the Americans had all departed, the South Vietnamese government overthrown, and Vietnam unified under Communist control.

DOCUMENT 48. Final Statement of Ho Chi Minh, September 9, 1969.

Our people's struggle against U.S. aggression, for national salvation, may have to go through even more difficulties and sacrifices, but we are bound to win total victory.

This is a certainty.

I intend, when that comes, to tour both North and South to congratulate our heroic compatriots, cadres and combatants, and visit old people and our beloved youth and children.

Then, on behalf of our people, I will go to the fraternal countries of the socialist camp and friendly countries in the world, and thank them for their wholehearted support and assistance to our people's patriotic struggle against U.S. aggression.

Tu Fu, the well-known Chinese poet of the T'ang period, wrote: "Few have ever reached the age of seventy."

This year, being seventy-nine, I count among those "few"; still, my mind has remained very lucid, though my health has somewhat declined in comparison with previous years. When one is on the wrong side of seventy, health deteriorates with age. This is no wonder.

But who can say how much longer I shall be able to serve the revolution, the Fatherland and the people?

I therefore leave these few lines in anticipation of the day when I shall go and join Karl Marx, V. I. Lenin and other elder revolutionaries; this way, our people throughout the country, our comrades in the Party, and our friends in the world will not be taken by surprise.

First about the Party: Thanks to its close unity and total dedication to the working class, the people and the Fatherland, our Party has been able, since its founding, to unite, organize and lead our people from success to success in a resolute struggle.

Unity is an extremely precious tradition of our Party and people. All comrades, from the Central Committee down to the cell, must preserve the unity and oneness of mind in the Party as the apple of their eye.

Within the Party, to achieve broad democracy and to practice self-criticism and criticism regularly and seriously is the best way to consolidate and further solidarity and unity. Comradely affection should prevail.

Ours is a Party in power. Each Party member, each cadre, must be deeply imbued with revolutionary morality, and show industry, thrift, integrity, uprightness, total dedication to public interests and complete selflessness. Our Party should preserve absolute purity and prove worthy of its role as leader and very loyal servant of the people.

About the working youth and union members and our young people: On the whole they are excellent; they are always ready to come forward, fearless of difficulties and eager for progress. The Party must foster their revolutionary virtues and train them as our successors, both "red" and "expert," in the building of socialism.

Training and educating future revolutionary generations is of great importance and necessity.

About our laboring peoples: In the plains as in the mountain areas, they have for ages endured hardships, feudal and colonial oppression and exploitation; they have moreover experienced many years of war.

Yet, our people have shown great heroism, courage, enthusiasm and industriousness. They have always followed the Party since it came into being, with unqualified loyalty.

The Party must work out a very effective plan for economic and cultural development constantly to raise the living standard of the people.

About the resistance war against U.S. aggression: It may drag on. Our compatriots may have to face new sacrifices in property and life. Whatever may happen, we must keep firm our resolve to fight the U.S. aggressors till total victory.

Our rivers, our mountains, our people will always be;
The American aggressors defeated, we will build a country ten times more beautiful.

Whatever difficulties and hardships may be ahead, our people are sure of total triumph. The U.S. imperialists shall have to quit. Our Fatherland shall be reunified. Our compatriots in the North and in the South shall be reunited under the same roof. We, a small nation, will have earned the unique honor of defeating, through a heroic struggle, two big imperialisms—the French and the American—and making a worthy contribution to the national liberation movement.

About the world communist movement: Having devoted my whole life to the revolution, I am proud of the growth of the international communist and workers' movement as well as grieved at the dissensions now dividing the fraternal parties.

I hope that our Party will do its best to contribute effectively to the restoration of unity among the fraternal parties on the basis of Marxism-Leninism and proletarian internationalism, in a way which conforms to both reason and sentiment.

I am sure that the fraternal parties and countries will have to unite again.

About personal matters: All my life, I have served the Fatherland, the revolution and the people with all my heart and strength. If I should now depart from this world, I would regret nothing, except not being able to serve longer and more.

When I am gone, grand funerals should be avoided so as not to waste the people's time and money.

Finally, to the whole people, the whole Party, the whole army, to my nephews and nieces, the youth and children, I leave my boundless love.

I also convey my cordial greetings of our comrades and friends, to the youth and children of the world.

My ultimate wish is that our whole Party and people, closely joining their efforts, build a peaceful, unified, independent, democratic and prosperous Vietnam, and make a worthy contribution to the world revolution.

SOURCE: A copy appears in Gettleman and others (eds.), *America and Vietnam*, pp. 440–441.

In the fall of 1969, Richard Nixon found himself in a bind. His strategies for ending the war having failed, he had to confront the Hobson's choice of either capitulating or escalating the war. Unwilling to do either, he sought a third choice, Vietnamization, inherited from the now-departed Johnson administration. He would gradually withdraw U.S. combat troops from Vietnam while at the same time helping the South Vietnamese build up their forces to where they could survive the VC/NVA attacks on their own. On November 3, 1969, President Nixon spoke to the American people. His main goals were to attack the antiwar movement strongly and to rally Americans in support of Vietnamization.

DOCUMENT 49. President Nixon's Speech on "Vietnamization," November 3, 1969.

Good evening, my fellow Americans:

Tonight I want to talk to you on a subject of deep concerns to all Americans and to many people in all parts of the world—the war in Vietnam.

I believe that one of the reasons for the deep division about Vietnam is that many Americans have lost confidence in what their Government has told them about our policy. The American people cannot and should not be asked to support a policy which involves the overriding issues of war and peace unless they know the truth about that policy.

Tonight, therefore, I would like to answer some of the questions that I know are on the minds of many of you listening to me.

How and why did America get involved in Vietnam in the first place?

How has this administration changed the policy of the previous administration?

What has really happened in the negotiations in Paris and on the battlefront in Vietnam?

What choices do we have if we are to end the war?

What are the prospects for peace?

Now, let me begin by describing the situation I found when I was inaugurated on January 20.

—The war had been going on for 4 years.

—31,000 Americans had been killed in action.

—The training program for the South Vietnamese was behind schedule.

—540,000 Americans were in Vietnam with no plans to reduce the number.

—No progress had been made at the negotiations in Paris and the United States had not put forth a comprehensive peace proposal.

—The war was causing deep division at home and criticism from many of our friends as well as our enemies abroad.

In view of these circumstances there were some who urged that I end the war at once by ordering the immediate withdrawal of all American forces.

From a political standpoint this would have been a popular and easy course to follow. After all, we became involved in the war while my predecessor was in office. I could blame the defeat which would be the result of my action on him and come out as the peacemaker. Some put it to me quite bluntly: This was the only way to avoid allowing Johnson's war to become Nixon's war.

But I had a greater obligation than to think only of the years of my administration and of the next election. I had to think of the effect of my decision on the next generation and on the future of peace and freedom in America and in the world.

Let us all understand that the question before us is not whether some Americans are for peace and some Americans are against peace. The question at issue is not whether Johnson's war becomes Nixon's war.

The great question is: How can we win America's peace?

Well, let us turn now to the fundamental issue. Why and how did the United States become involved in Vietnam in the first place?

Fifteen years ago North Vietnam, with the logistical support of Communist China and the Soviet Union, launched a campaign to impose a Communist government on South Vietnam by instigating and supporting a revolution.

In response to the request of the Government of South Vietnam, President Eisenhower sent economic aid and military equipment to assist the people of South Vietnam in their efforts to prevent a Communist takeover. Seven years ago, President Kennedy sent 16,000 military personnel to Vietnam as combat advisers. Four years ago, President Johnson sent American combat forces to South Vietnam.

Now, many believe that President Johnson's decision to send American combat forces to South Vietnam was wrong. Any many others—I among them—have been strongly critical of the way the war has been conducted.

But the question facing us today is: Now that we are in the war, what is the best way to end it?

In January I could only conclude that the precipitate withdrawal of American forces from Vietnam would be a disaster not only for South Vietnam but for the United States and for the cause of peace.

For the South Vietnamese, our precipitate withdrawal would inevitably allow the Communists to repeat the massacres which followed their takeover in the North 15 years before.

—They then murdered more than 50,000 people and hundreds of thousands more died in slave labor camps.

—We saw a prelude of what would happen in South Vietnam when the Communists entered the city of Hue last year. During their brief rule there, there was a bloody reign of terror in which 3,000 civilians were clubbed, shot to death, and buried in mass graves.

—With the sudden collapse of our support, these atrocities of Hue would become the nightmare of the entire nation—and particularly for the million and a half Catholic refugees who fled to South Vietnam when the Communists took over in the North.

For the United States, this first defeat in our Nation's history would result in a collapse of confidence in American leadership, not only in Asia but throughout the world.

Three American Presidents have recognized the great stakes involved in Vietnam and understood what had to be done.

In 1963, President Kennedy, with his characteristic eloquence and clarity, said: ". . . we want to see a stable government there, carrying on a struggle to maintain its national independence.

"We believe strongly in that. We are not going to withdraw from that effort. In my opinion, for us to withdraw from that effort would mean a collapse not only of South Viet-Nam, but Southeast Asia. So we are going to stay there."

President Eisenhower and President Johnson expressed the same conclusion during their terms of office.

For the future of peace, precipitate withdrawal would thus be a disaster of immense magnitude.

—A nation cannot remain great if it betrays its allies and lets down its friends.

—Our defeat and humiliation in South Vietnam without question would promote recklessness in the councils of those great powers who have not yet abandoned their goals of world conquest.

—This would spark violence wherever our commitments help maintain the peace—in the Middle East, in Berlin, eventually even in the Western Hemisphere.

Ultimately, this would cost more lives.

It would not bring peace; it would bring more war.

For these reasons, I rejected the recommendation that I should end the war by immediately withdrawing all of our forces. I chose instead to change American policy on both the negotiating front and battlefront. . . .

We Americans are a do-it-yourself people. We are an impatient people. Instead of teaching someone else to do a job, we like to do it ourselves. And this trait has been carried over into our foreign policy.

In Korea and again in Vietnam, the United States furnished most of the money, most of the arms, and most of the men to help the people of those countries defend their freedom against Communist aggression.

Before any American troops were committed to Vietnam, a leader of another Asian country expressed this opinion to me when I was traveling in Asia as a private citizen. He said: "When you are trying to assist another nation defend its freedom, U.S. policy should be to help them fight the war but not to fight the war for them." . . .

Well, in accordance with this wise counsel, I laid down in Guam three principles as guidelines for future American policy toward Asia:

—First, the United States will keep all of its treaty commitments.

—Second, we shall provide a shield if a nuclear power threatens the freedom of a nation allied with us or of a nation whose survival we consider vital to our security.

—Third, in cases involving other types of aggression, we shall furnish military and economic assistance when requested in accordance with our treaty commitments. But we shall look to the nation directly threatened to assume the primary responsibility of providing the manpower for its defense.

After I announced this policy, I found that the leaders of the Philippines, Thailand, Vietnam, South Korea, and other nations which might be threatened by Communist aggression, welcomed this new direction in American foreign policy.

The defense of freedom is everybody's business—not just America's business. And it is particularly the responsibility of the people whose freedom is threatened. In the previous administration, we Americanized the war in Vietnam. In this administration, we are Vietnamizing the search for peace.

The policy of the previous administration not only resulted in our assuming the primary responsibility for fighting the war, but even more significantly did not adequately stress the goal of strengthening the South Vietnamese so that they could defend themselves when we left.

The Vietnamization plan was launched following Secretary Laird's visit to Vietnam in March. Under the plan, I ordered first a substantial increase in the training and equipment of South Vietnamese forces.

—After 5 years of Americans going into Vietnam, we are finally bringing men home. By December 15, over 60,000 men will have been withdrawn from South Vietnam—including 20 percent of all of our combat forces.

—The South Vietnamese have continued to gain in strength. As a result they have been able to take over combat responsibilities from our American troops.

Two other significant developments have occurred since this administration took office.

—Enemy infiltration, infiltration which is essential if they are to launch a major attack, over the last 3 months is less than 20 percent of what it was over the same period last year.

—Most important—United States casualties have declined during the last 2 months to the lowest point in 3 years.

Let me now turn to our program for the future.

We have adopted a plan which we have worked out in cooperation with the South Vietnamese for the complete withdrawal of all U.S. combat ground forces, and their replacement by South Vietnamese forces on an orderly scheduled timetable. This withdrawal will be made from strength and not from weakness. As South Vietnamese forces become stronger, the rate of American withdrawal can become greater.

I have not and do not intend to announce the timetable for our program. And there are obvious reasons for this decision which I am sure you will understand. As I have indicated on several occasions, the rate of withdrawal will depend on developments on three fronts.

One of these is the progress which can be or might be made in the Paris talks. An announcement of a fixed timetable for our withdrawal would completely remove any incentive for the enemy to negotiate an agreement. They would simply wait until our forces had withdrawn and then move in.

The other two factors on which we will base our withdrawal decisions are the level of enemy activity and the progress of the training programs of the South Vietnamese forces. And I am glad to be able to report tonight progress on both of these fronts has been greater than we anticipated when we started the program in June for withdrawal. As a result, our timetable for withdrawal is more optimistic now than when we made our first estimates in June. Now, this clearly demonstrates why it is not wise to be frozen in on a fixed timetable.

We must retain the flexibility to base each withdrawal decision on the situation as it is at the time rather than on estimates that are no longer valid.

Along with this optimistic estimate, I must—in all candor—leave one note of caution.

If the level of enemy activity significantly increases we might have to adjust our timetable accordingly.

However, I want the record to be completely clear on one point.

At the time of the bombing halt just a year ago, there was some confusion as to whether there was an understanding on the part of the enemy that if we stopped the bombing of North Vietnam they would stop the shelling of cities in South Vietnam. I want to be sure that there is no misunderstanding on the part of the enemy with regard to our withdrawal program.

We have noted the reduced level of infiltration, the reduction of our casualties, and are basing our withdrawal decisions partially on those factors.

If the level of infiltration or our casualties increase while we are trying to scale down the fighting, it will be the result of a conscious decision by the enemy.

Hanoi could make no greater mistake than to assume that an increase in violence will be to its advantage. If I conclude that increased enemy action jeopardizes our remaining forces in Vietnam, I shall not hesitate to take strong and effective measures to deal with that situation.

This is not a threat. This is a statement of policy, which, as Commander in Chief of our Armed Forces, I am making in meeting my responsibility for the protection of American fighting men wherever they may be.

My fellow Americans, I am sure you can recognize from what I have said that we really only have two choices open to us if we want to end this war.

—I can order an immediate, precipitate withdrawal of all Americans from Vietnam without regard to the effects of that action.

—Or we can persist in our search for a just peace through a negotiated settlement if possible, or through continued implementation of our plan for Vietnamization if necessary—a plan in which we will withdraw all our forces from Vietnam on a schedule in accordance with our program, as the South Vietnamese become strong enough to defend their own freedom.

I have chosen this second course.

It is not the easy way.

It is the right way.

It is a plan which will end the war and serve the cause of peace—not just in Vietnam but in the Pacific and in the world.

In speaking of the consequences of a precipitate withdrawal, I mentioned that our allies would lose confidence in America.

Far more dangerous, we would lose confidence in ourselves. Oh, the immediate reaction would be a sense of relief that our men were coming home. But as we saw the consequences of what we had done, inevitable remorse and divisive recrimination would scar our spirit as a people.

We have faced other crises in our history and have become stronger by rejecting the easy way out and taking the right way in meeting our challenges. Our greatness as a nation has been our capacity to do what had to be done when we knew our course was right.

I recognize that some of my fellow citizens disagree with the plan for peace I have chosen. Honest and patriotic Americans have reached different conclusions as to how peace should be achieved.

In San Francisco a few weeks ago, I saw demonstrators carrying signs reading: "Lose in Vietnam, bring the boys home."

Well, one of the strengths of our free society is that any American has a right to reach that conclusion and to advocate that point of view. But as President of the United States, I would be untrue to my oath of office if I allowed the policy of this Nation to be dictated by the minority who hold that point of view and who try to impose it on the Nation by mounting demonstrations in the street.

For almost 200 years, the policy of this Nation has been made under our Constitution by those leaders in the Congress and the White House elected by all of the people. If a vocal minority, however fervent its cause, prevails over reason and the will of the majority, this Nation has no future as a free society.

And now I would like to address a word, if I may, to the young people of this Nation who are particularly concerned, and I understand why they are concerned, about this war.

I respect your idealism.

I share your concern for peace.

I want peace as much as you do.

There are powerful personal reasons I want to end this war. This week I will have to sign 83 letters to mothers, fathers, wives, and loved ones of men who have given their lives for America in Vietnam. It is very little satisfaction to me that this is only one-third as many letters as I signed the first week in office. There is nothing I want more than to see the day come when I do not have to write any of those letters.

—I want to end the war to save the lives of those brave young men in Vietnam.

—But I want to end it in a way which will increase the chance that their younger brothers and their sons will not have to fight in some future Vietnam someplace in the world.

—And I want to end the war for another reason. I want to end it so that the energy and dedication of you, our young people, now too often directed into bitter hatred against those responsible for the war, can be turned to the great challenges of peace, a better life for all Americans, a better life for all people on this earth.

I have chosen a plan for peace. I believe it will succeed.

If it does succeed, what the critics say now won't matter. If it does not succeed, anything I say then won't matter.

I know it may not be fashionable to speak of patriotism or national destiny these days. But I feel it is appropriate to do so on this occasion.

Two hundred years ago this Nation was weak and poor. But even then, America was the hope of millions in the world. Today we have become the strongest and richest nation in the world. And the wheel of destiny has turned so that any hope the world has for the survival of peace and freedom will be determined by whether the American people have the moral stamina and the courage to meet the challenge of free world leadership.

Let historians not record that when America was the most powerful nation in the world we passed on the other side of the road and allowed the last hopes for peace and freedom of millions of people to be suffocated by the forces of totalitarianism.

And so tonight—to you, the great silent majority of my fellow Americans—I ask for your support.

I pledged in my campaign for the Presidency to end the war in a way that we could win the peace. I have initiated a plan of action which will enable me to keep that pledge.

The more support I can have from the American people, the sooner that pledge can be redeemed; for the more divided we are at home, the less likely the enemy is to negotiate at Paris.

Let us be united for peace. Let us also be united against defeat. Because let us understand: North Vietnam cannot defeat or humiliate the United States. Only Americans can do that.

Fifty years ago, in this room and at this very desk, President Woodrow Wilson spoke words which caught the imagination of a war-weary world. He said: "This is the war to end war." His dream for peace after World War I was shattered on the hard realities of great power politics and Woodrow Wilson died a broken man.

Tonight I do not tell you that the war in Vietnam is the war to end wars.

But I do say this: I have initiated a plan which will end this war in a way that will bring us closer to that great goal to which Woodrow Wilson and every American President in our history has been dedicated—the goal of a just and lasting peace.

As President I hold the responsibility for choosing the best path to that goal and then leading the Nation along it.

I pledge to you tonight that I shall meet this responsibility with all of the strength and wisdom I can command in accordance with your hopes, mindful of your concerns, sustained by your prayers.

Thank you and goodnight.

SOURCE: *Public Papers of the Presidents of the United States: Richard Nixon, 1969*, pp. 901–909.

In the spring of 1970, the Vietnam war suddenly expanded. In neighboring Cambodia, pro-American officials overthrew the neutralist leader, Prince Norodom Sihanouk. Sihanouk had allowed the Vietcong and North Vietnamese to use areas in his country bordering South Vietnam as staging areas for attacks on South Vietnam. He had also permitted the North Vietnamese to use the port of Sihanoukville as a major supply depot. Sihanouk had also kept a discreet silence about secret U.S. bombing of these bases that had been going on since 1969.

The new Cambodian leader, Lon Nol, promptly ordered the North Vietnamese and Vietcong forces to vacate his country. Because these bases were crucial to their conduct of the war in South Vietnam, they refused to leave. Instead, they began a military campaign to overthrow Lon Nol and supported an indigenous revolutionary Marxist group, the Khmer Rouge. The deposed Sihanouk quickly cast his lot with the Communists and received the backing of China.

President Nixon, responding to these developments in Cambodia, authorized an allied invasion of Cambodia. For some time, military advisers had been urging an attack on the staging areas, which had also served as sanctuaries for VC and NVA forces fleeing U.S. assaults. On the evening of April 30, 1970, Nixon told the American people of his decision to widen the war. The next day, American and South Vietnamese forces invaded Cambodia.

DOCUMENT 50. President Nixon's Speech on Cambodia, April 30, 1970.

Good evening my fellow Americans:

Ten days ago, in my report to the Nation on Vietnam, I announced a decision to withdraw an additional 150,000 Americans from Vietnam over the next year. I said then that I was making that decision despite our concern over increased enemy activity in Laos, in Cambodia, and in South Vietnam.

At that time, I warned that if I concluded that increased enemy activity in any of these areas endangered the lives of Americans remaining in Vietnam, I would not hesitate to take strong and effective measures to deal with that situation.

Despite that warning, North Vietnam has increased its military aggression in all these areas, and particularly in Cambodia.

After full consultation with the National Security Council, Ambassador Bunker, General Abrams, and my other advisors, I have concluded that the actions of the enemy in the last 10 days clearly endanger the lives of Americans who are in Vietnam now and would constitute an unacceptable risk to those who will be there after withdrawal of another 150,000.

To protect our men who are in Vietnam and to guarantee the continued success of our withdrawal and Vietnamization programs, I have concluded that the time has come for action.

Tonight, I shall describe the actions of the enemy, the actions I have ordered to deal with that situation, and the reasons for my decision.

Cambodia, a small country of 7 million people, has been a neutral nation since the Geneva agreement of 1954—an agreement, incidentally, which was signed by the Government of North Vietnam.

American policy since then has been to scrupulously respect the neutrality of the Cambodian people. We have maintained a skeleton diplomatic mission of fewer than 15 in Cambodia's capital, and that only since last August. For the previous 4 years, from 1965 to 1969, we did not have any diplomatic mission whatever in Cambodia. And for the past 5 years, we have provided no military assistance whatever and no economic assistance to Cambodia.

North Vietnam, however, has not respected that neutrality.

For the past 5 years—as indicated on this map that you see here—North Vietnam has occupied military sanctuaries all along the Cambodian frontier with South Vietnam. Some of these extend up to 20 miles into Cambodia....

In cooperation with the armed forces of South Vietnam, attacks are being launched this week to clean out major enemy sanctuaries on the Cambodian-Vietnam border.

A major responsibility for the ground operations is being assumed by South Vietnamese forces....

There is one area, however, immediately above Parrot's Beak, where I have concluded that a combined American and South Vietnamese operation is necessary.

Tonight, American and South Vietnamese units will attack the headquarters for the entire Communist military operation in South Vietnam. This key control center has been occupied by the North Vietnamese and Vietcong for 5 years in blatant violation of Cambodia's neutrality.

This is not an invasion of Cambodia. The areas in which these attacks will be launched are completely occupied and controlled by North Vietnamese forces. Our purpose is not to occupy the areas. Once enemy forces are driven out of these sanctuaries and once their military supplies are destroyed, we will withdraw....

We take this action not for the purpose of expanding the war into Cambodia but for the purpose of ending the war in Vietnam and winning the just peace we all desire. We have made—we will continue to make every possible effort to end this war through negotiation at the conference table rather than through more fighting on the battlefield. . . .

The action that I have announced tonight puts the leaders of North Vietnam on notice that we will be patient in working for peace; we will be conciliatory at the conference table, but we will not be humiliated. We will not be defeated. We will not allow American men by the thousands to be killed by an enemy from privileged sanctuaries. . . .

My fellow Americans, we live in an age of anarchy, both abroad and at home. We see mindless attacks on all the great institutions which have been created by free civilizations in the last 500 years. Even here in the United States, great universities are being systematically destroyed. . . .

If, when the chips are down, the world's most powerful nation, the United States of America, acts like a pitiful, helpless giant, the forces of totalitarianism and anarchy will threaten free nations and free institutions throughout the world.

It is not our power but our will and character that is being tested tonight. . . .

I have rejected all political considerations in making this decision. . . .

Whether my party gains in November is nothing compared to the lives of 400,000 brave Americans fighting for our country and for the cause of peace and freedom in Vietnam. Whether I may be a one-term President is insignificant compared to whether by our failure to act in this crisis the United States proves itself to be unworthy to lead the forces of freedom in this critical period in world history. I would rather be a one-term President and do what I believe is right than to be a two-term President at the cost of seeing America become a second-rate power and to see this Nation accept the first defeat in its proud 190-year history. . . .

SOURCE: *Public Papers of the Presidents of the United States: Richard Nixon, 1970*, pp. 405–409.

Although President Nixon apparently anticipated some outcry and criticism of his controversial decision to invade Cambodia and widen the war, he did not anticipate the furious protests, strikes, and demonstrations that erupted on scores of college campuses across the land. Kent State University in Ohio was one of the most disorderly campuses, and the governor had ordered the National Guard to the campus. On May 4, protesters gathered on the university Commons. After they refused orders to disperse, National Guard troops moved in to disperse them. Protesters began to taunt the troops, threw rocks, and advanced toward them. A squad of Guardsmen then opened fire, killing four protesters and wounding nine others.

On May 14, students rioted at Jackson State College, a historically black college in Jackson, Mississippi. That night, students pelted passing white motorists with rocks and bottles and set fire to a truck. Firefighters, called to put out the blaze, were also harassed by the students. City and state police, called in to protect the firefighters, started shooting at the students. They fired a fusillade into a girls' dormitory, killing two students and wounding 12 others.

DOCUMENT 51. Excerpts from *The Report of the President's Commission on Campus Unrest*, 1970.

On April 30, 1970, President Nixon announced that American and South Vietnamese forces were moving against enemy sanctuaries in Cambodia. Minutes after this announcement, student-organized protest demonstrations were under way at Princeton and Oberlin College. Within a few days, strikes and other protests had taken place at scores of colleges and universities throughout the country.

The expanding wave of strikes brought with it some serious disturbances. One of these was at Kent State University in Ohio, and approximately 750 Ohio National Guardsmen were sent to quell the disorders there.

On May 2, the ROTC building at Kent State was set afire. On May 4, Kent State students congregated on the university Commons and defied an order by the Guard to disperse. Guardsmen proceeded to disperse the crowd. The students then began to taunt Guard units and to throw rocks. . . .

Many guardsmen said they had hard going as they withdrew up the hill. Fassinger said he was hit six times by stones, once on the shoulder so hard that he stumbled.

Fassinger had removed his gas mask to see more clearly. He said the guardsmen had reached a point between the Pagoda and Taylor Hall, and he was attempting to maintain them in a reasonably orderly formation, when he heard a sound like a shot, which was immediately followed by a volley of shots. He saw the troops on the Taylor Hall end of the line shooting. He yelled, "Cease-fire!" and ran along the line repeating the command.

Major Jones said he first heard an explosion which he thought was a firecracker. As he turned to his left, he heard another explosion which he knew to be an M-1 rifle shot. As he turned to his right, toward Taylor Hall, he said he saw guardsmen kneeling and bringing their rifles to their shoulders. He heard another M-1 shot, and then a volley of them. He yelled, "Cease-fire!" several times, and rushed down the line shoving rifle barrels up and away from the crowd. He hit several guardsmen on their helmets with his swagger stick to stop them from firing.

General Canterbury stated that he first heard a single shot, which he thought was fired from some distance away on his left and which in his opinion did not come from a military weapon. Immediately afterward, he heard a volley of M-1 fire from his right, the Taylor Hall end of the line. The Guard's fire was directed away from the direction from which Canterbury thought the initial, nonmilitary shot came. . . .

Canterbury, Fassinger, and Jones—the three ranking officers on the hill—all said no order to fire was given.

Twenty-eight guardsmen have acknowledged firing from Blanket Hill. Of these, 25 fired 55 shots from rifles, two fired five shots from .45 caliber pistols, and one fired a single blast from a shotgun. Sound tracks indicate that the firing of these 61 shots lasted approximately 13 seconds. The time of the shooting was approximately 12:25 P.M. Four persons were killed and nine were wounded. . . .

During the six days after the President's announcement of the Cambodian incursion, but prior to the deaths at Kent State, some twenty new student strikes had begun each day. During the four days that followed the Kent killings, there were a hundred or more strikes each day. A student strike center located at Brandeis University reported that, by the 10th of May, 448 campuses were either still affected by some sort of strike or completely closed down.

Ten days after the events at Kent State there were disturbances at Jackson State College, a black school in Jackson, Mississippi. On the night of May 14, students threw bricks and bottles at passing white motorists, a truck was set ablaze, and city and state police, called to protect firemen, were harassed by the crowd. Some policemen fired a fusillade into a girls' dormitory. Two blacks were killed, and at least twelve were wounded.

Other schools joined the student strike, and many temporarily suspended classes in memory of those killed at Jackson State. By the end of May . . . nearly one third of the approximately 2,500 colleges and universities in America had experienced some kind of protest activity. The high point of the strikes was during the week following the deaths at Kent State. . . .

SOURCE: *The Report of the President's Commission on Campus Unrest*, 1970.

By the spring of 1971, most Americans yearned for an end to the seemingly interminable war in Vietnam. But Americans once more were anguished by the war when a military court convicted Lieutenant William J. Calley of mass murder for his role in the My Lai massacre several years earlier. A few days later, a group of disillusioned Vietnam veterans, some of them maimed and crippled, staged a poignant demonstration in the nation's capital. The veterans, one-by-one, came forward and threw their war ribbons and medals onto the steps of the capitol building. Three weeks later, a spokesman for Vietnam Veterans Against the War, John Kerry, testified before the Senate Foreign Relations Committee. Kerry, a Navy veteran, later entered politics. In 1984, he was elected a U.S. Senator from Massachusetts.

DOCUMENT 52. John Kerry's Testimony Before the Senate Foreign Relations Committee, April 22, 1971.

Thank you very much, Senator Fulbright, Senator Javits, Senator Symington, Senator Pell. I would like to say for the record, and also for the men behind me who are also wearing the uniform and their medals, that my sitting here is really symbolic. I am not here as John Kerry. I am here as one member of the group of 1,000 which is a small representation of a very much larger group of veterans in this country, and were it possible for all of them to sit at this table they would be here and have the same kind of testimony.

I would simply like to speak in very general terms. I apologize if my statement is general because I received notification yesterday you would hear me and I am afraid that because of the court injunction I was up most of the night and haven't had a great deal of time to prepare for this hearing.

I would like to talk on behalf of all those veterans and say that several months ago in Detroit we had an investigation at which over 150 honorably discharged, and many very highly decorated, veterans testified to war crimes committed in Southeast Asia. These were not isolated incidents but crimes committed on a day to day basis with the full awareness of officers at all levels of command.

It is impossible to describe to you exactly what did happen in Detroit— the emotions in the room and the feelings of the men who were reliving their experiences in Vietnam. They relived the absolute horror of what this country, in a sense, made them do.

They told stories that at times they had personally raped, cut off ears, cut off heads, taped wires from portable telephones to human genitals and turned up the power, cut off limbs, blown up bodies, randomly shot at civilians, razed villages in fashion reminiscent of Genghis Khan, shot cattle and dogs for fun, poisoned food stocks, and generally ravaged the countryside of South Vietnam in addition to the normal ravage of war and the normal and very particular ravaging which is done by the applied bombing power of this country.

We call this investigation the Winter Soldier Investigation. The term Winter Soldier is a play on words of Thomas Paine's in 1776 when he spoke of the Sunshine Patriots and summer time soldiers who deserted at Valley Forge because the going was rough.

We who have come here to Washington have come here because we feel we have to be winter soldiers now. We could come back to this country, we could be quiet, we could hold our silence, we could not tell what went on in Vietnam, but we feel because of what threatens this country, not the reds, but the crimes which we are committing that threaten it, that we have to speak out.

I would like to talk to you a little bit about what the result is of the feelings these men carry with them after coming back from Vietnam. The country doesn't know it yet but it has created a monster, a monster in the form of millions of men who have been taught to deal and to trade in violence and who are given the chance to die for the biggest nothing in history; men who have returned with a sense of anger and a sense of betrayal which no one has yet grasped.

As a veteran and one who feels this anger I would like to talk about it. We are angry because we feel we have been used in the worst fashion by the administration of this country.

In 1970 at West Point Vice President Agnew said "some glamorize the criminal misfits of society while our best men die in Asian rice paddies to preserve the freedom which most of those misfits abuse," and this was used as a rallying point for our effort in Vietnam.

But for us, as boys in Asia whom the country was supposed to support, his statement is a terrible distortion from which we can only draw a very deep sense of revulsion, and hence the anger of some of the men who are here in Washington today. It is a distortion because we in no way consider ourselves the best men of this country; because those he calls misfits were standing up for us in a way that nobody else in this country dared to; because so many who have died would have returned to this country to join the misfits in their efforts to ask for an immediate withdrawal from South Vietnam; because so many of those best men have returned as quadriplegics and amputees—and they lie forgotten in Veterans Administration Hospitals in this country which fly the flag which so many have chosen as their own personal symbol—and we cannot consider ourselves America's best men when we are ashamed of and hated for what we were called on to do in Southeast Asia.

In our opinion, and from our experience, there is nothing in South Vietnam which could happen that realistically threatens the United States of America. And to attempt to justify the loss of one American life in Vietnam, Cambodia or Laos by linking such loss to the preservation of freedom, which those misfits supposedly abuse, is to us the height of criminal hypocrisy, and it is that kind of hypocrisy which we feel has torn this country apart.

We are probably much more angry than that, but I don't want to go into the foreign policy aspects because I am outclassed here. I know that all of you talk about every possible alternative for getting out of Vietnam. We understand that. We know you have considered the seriousness of the aspects to the utmost level and I am not going to try to dwell on that. But I want to relate to you the feeling that many of the men who have returned to this country express because we are probably angriest about all that we were told about Vietnam and about the mystical war against communism.

We found that not only was it a civil war, an effort by a people who had for years been seeking their liberation from any colonial influence whatsoever, but also we found that the Vietnamese whom we had enthusiastically molded after our own image were hard put to take up the fight against the threat we were supposedly saving them from.

We found most people didn't even know the difference between communism and democracy. They only wanted to work in rice paddies without helicopters strafing them and bombs with napalm burning their villages and tearing their country apart. They wanted everything to do with the war, particularly with this foreign presence of the United States of America, to leave them alone in peace, and they practiced the art of survival by siding with whichever military force was present at a particular time, be it Viet Cong, North Vietnamese or American.

We found also that all too often American men were dying in those rice paddies for want of support from their allies. We saw first hand how monies from American taxes were used for a corrupt dictatorial regime. We saw that many people in this country had a one-sided idea of who was kept free by our flag, and blacks provided the highest percentage of casualties. We saw Vietnam ravaged equally by American bombs and search and destroy missions, as well as by Viet Cong terrorism, and yet we listened while this country tried to blame all of the havoc on the Viet Cong.

We rationalized destroying villages in order to save them. We saw America lose her sense of morality as she accepted very coolly a My Lai and refused to give up the image of American soldiers who hand out chocolate bars and chewing gum.

We learned the meaning of free fire zones, shooting anything that moves, and we watched whiie America placed a cheapness on the lives of orientals.

We watched the United States falsification of body counts, in fact the glorification of body counts. We listened while month after month we were told the back of the enemy was about to break. We fought using weapons against "oriental human beings." We fought using weapons against those people which I do not believe this country would dream of using were we fighting in the European theater. We watched while men charged up hills because a general said that hill has to be taken, and after losing one platoon or two platoons they marched away to leave the hill for reoccupation by the North Vietnamese. We watched pride allow the most unimportant battles to be blown into extravaganzas, because we couldn't lose, and we couldn't retreat, and because it didn't matter how many American bodies were lost to prove that point, and so there were Hamburger Hills and Khe Sanhs and Hill 81s and Fire Base 6s, and so many others. . . .

We are asking here in Washington for some action; action from the Congress of the United States of America which has the power to raise and maintain armies, and which by the Constitution also has the power to declare war.

We have come here, not to the President, because we believe that this body can be responsive to the will of the people, and we believe that the will of the people says that we should be out of Vietnam now.

We are here in Washington also to say that the problem of this war is not just a question of war and diplomacy. It is part and parcel of everything that we are trying as human beings to communicate to people in this country—the question of racism which is rampant in the military, and so many other questions such as the use of weapons; the hypocrisy of our taking umbrage at the Geneva Conventions and using that as justification for a continuation of this war when we are more guilty than any other body of violations of those Geneva Conventions; in the use of free fire zones, harassment interdiction fire, search and destroy missions, the bombings, the torture of prisoners, the killing of prisoners, all accepted policy by many units in South Vietnam. That is what we are trying to say. It is part and parcel of everything.

An American Indian friend of mine who lives in the Indian Nation of Alcatraz put it to me very succinctly. He told me how as a boy on an Indian reservation he had watched television and he used to cheer the cowboys when they came in and shot the Indians, and then suddenly one day he stopped in Vietnam and he said "my God, I am doing to these people the very same thing that was done to my people," and he stopped. And that is what we are trying to say, that we think this thing has to end.

We are also here to ask, and we are here to ask vehemently, where are the leaders of our country? Where is the leadership? We are here to ask where are McNamara, Rostow, Bundy, Gilpatric and so many others? Where are they now that we, the men whom they sent off to war, have returned? These are commanders who have deserted their troops, and there is no more serious crime in the laws of war. The Army says they never leave their wounded. The Marines say they never leave even their dead. These men have left all the casualties and retreated behind a pious shield of public rectitude. They have left the real stuff of their reputations bleaching behind them in the sun in this country.

Finally, this administration has done us the ultimate dishonor. They have attempted to disown us and the sacrifices we made for this country. In their blindness and fear they have tried to deny that we are veterans or that we served in Nam. We do not need their testimony. Our own scars and stumps of limbs are witness enough for others and for ourselves.

We wish that a merciful God could wipe away our own memories of that service as easily as this administration has wiped away their memories of us. But all that they have done and all that they can do by this denial is to make more clear than ever our own determination to undertake one last mission—to search out and destroy the last vestige of this barbaric war, to pacify our own hearts, to conquer the hate and the fear that have driven this country these last ten years and more, so when 30 years from now our brothers go down the street without a leg, without an arm, or a face, and small boys ask why, we will be able to say "Vietnam" and not mean a desert, not a filthy obscene memory, but mean instead the place where America finally turned and where soldiers like us helped it in the turning.

Thank you.

One major consequence of the long American war in Vietnam was the decline of the U.S. Army that began in 1968 and got progressively worse during 1969 to 1971. The Army's morale, discipline, and fighting spirit eroded. There were many causes of its deterioration including the ambiguities inherent in Nixon's Vietnamization policy, an unfair conscription system, a decline in the quality of commissioned and noncommissioned officers, dubious Army personnel policies, declining public support for the war, black-white racial tensions, and a contagion of drug use.

DOCUMENT 53. Excerpts from Colonel Robert D. Heinl, Jr.'s Analysis of the Decline of the U.S. Armed Forces, June 7, 1971.

The morale, discipline and battleworthiness of the U.S. Armed Forces are, with a few salient exceptions, lower and worse than at any time in this century and possibly in the history of the United States.

By every conceivable indicator, our army that now remains in Vietnam is in a state approaching collapse, with individual units avoiding or having refused combat, murdering their officers and noncommissioned officers, drug-ridden, and dispirited where not near-mutinous.

Elsewhere than Vietnam, the situation is nearly as serious.

Intolerably clobbered and buffeted from without and within by social turbulence, pandemic drug addiction, race war, sedition, civilian scapegoatise, draftee recalcitrance and malevolence, barracks theft and common crime, unsupported in their travail by the general government, in Congress as well as the executive branch, distrusted, disliked, and often reviled by the public, the uniformed services today are places of agony for the loyal, silent professionals who doggedly hang on and try to keep the ship afloat.

The responses of the services of these unheard-of conditions, forces and new public attitudes, are confused, resentful, occasionally pollyanna-ish, and in some cases even calculated to worsen the malaise that is wracking them.

While no senior officer (especially one on active duty) can openly voice any such assessment, the foregoing conclusions find virtually unanimous support in numerous non-attributable interviews with responsible senior and midlevel officers, as well as career noncommissioned officers and petty officers in all services.

Historical precedents do exist for some of the services' problems, such as desertion, mutiny, unpopularity, seditious attacks, and racial troubles. Others, such as drugs, pose difficulties that are wholly new. Nowhere, however, in the history of the Armed Forces have comparable past troubles presented themselves in such general magnitude, acuteness, or concentrated focus as today.

By several orders of magnitude, the Army seems to be in worst trouble. But the Navy has serious and unprecedented problems, while the Air Force, on the surface at least still clear of the quicksands in which the Army is sinking, is itself facing disquieting difficulties.

Only the Marines—who have made the news this year by their hard line against indiscipline and general permissiveness—seem, with their expected staunchness and tough tradition, to be weathering the storm.

To understand the military consequences of what is happening to the U.S. Armed Forces, Vietnam is a good place to start. It is in Vietnam that the rearguard of a 500,000-man army, in its day (and in the observation of the writer) the best army the United States ever put into the field, is numbly extricating itself from a nightmare war the Armed Forces feel they had foisted on them by bright civilians who are now back on campus writing books about the folly of it all.

"They have set up separate companies," writes an American soldier from Cu Chi, quoted in the *New York Times*, "for men who refuse to go out into the field." It is no big thing to refuse to go. If a man is ordered to go to such and such a place he no longer goes through the hassle of refusing; he just packs his shirt and goes to visit some buddies at another base camp. Operations have become incredibly ragtag. Many guys don't even put on their uniforms any more....

"Frag incidents" or just "fragging" is current soldier slang in Vietnam for the murder or attempted murder of strict, unpopular, or just aggressive officers and NCOs. With extreme reluctant (after a young West Pointer from Senator Mike Mansfield's Montana was fragged in his sleep) the Pentagon has now disclosed that fraggings in 1970 (209) have more than doubled those of the previous year (96).

Word of the deaths of officers will bring cheers at troop movies or in bivouacs of certain units.

In one such division—the morale-plagued Americal—fraggings during 1971 have been authoritatively estimated to be running about one a week.

Yet fraggings, though hard to document, form part of the ugly lore of every war. The first such verified incident known to have taken place occurred 190 years ago when Pennsylvania soldiers in the Continental Army killed one of their captains during the night of 1 January 1781.

Bounties, raised by common subscription in amounts running anywhere from $50 to $1,000, have been widely reported put on the heads of leaders whom the privates and Sp4s want to rub out.

Shortly after the costly assault on Hamburger Hill in mid-1969, the GI underground newspaper in Vietnam, "GI Says," publicly offered a $10,000 bounty on LCol Weldon Honeycutt, the officer who ordered (and led) the attack. Despite several attempts, however, Honeycutt managed to live out his tour and return Stateside. . . .

The issue of "combat refusal," an official euphemism for disobedience of orders to fight—the soldier's gravest crime—has only recently been again precipitated on the frontier of Laos by Troop B, 1st Cavalry's mass refusal to recapture their captain's command vehicle containing communication gear, codes and other secret operation orders. . . .

"Search and evade" (meaning tacit avoidance of combat by units in the field) is now virtually a principle of war, vividly expressed by the GI phrase, "CYA (cover your ass) and get home!"

That "search-and-evade" has not gone unnoticed by the enemy is underscored by the Viet Cong delegation's recent statement at the Paris Peace Talks that communist units in Indochina have been ordered not to engage American units which do not molest them. The same statement boasted—not without foundation in fact—that American defectors are in the VC ranks.

Symbolic anti-war fasts (such as the one at Pleiku where an entire medical unit, led by its officers, refused Thanksgiving turkey), peace symbols, "V"-signs not for victory but for peace, booing and cursing of officers and even of hapless entertainers such as Bob Hope, are unhappily commonplace.

As for drugs and race, Vietnam's problems today not only reflect but reinforce those of the Armed Forces as a whole. In April, for example, members of a Congressional investigating subcommittee reported that 10 to 15% of our troops in Vietnam are now using high-grade heroin, and that drug addiction there is "of epidemic proportions."

Only last year an Air Force major and command pilot for Ambassador

Bunker was apprehended at Tan Son Nhut air base outside Saigon with $8-million worth of heroin in his aircraft. This major is now in Leavenworth.

Early this year, an Air Force regular colonel was court-martialed and ca-shiered for leading his squadron in pot parties, while, at Cam Ranh Air Force Base, 43 members of the base security police squadron were recently swept up in dragnet narcotics raids.

All the foregoing facts—and many more dire indicators of the worst kind of military trouble—point to widespread conditions among American forces in Vietnam that have only been exceeded in this century by the French Army's Ni-velle mutinies of 1917 and the collapse of the Tsarist armies in 1916 and 1917.

It is a truism that national armies closely reflect societies from which they have been raised. It would be strange indeed if the Armed Forces did not today mirror the agonizing divisions and social traumas of American society, and of course they do.

For this very reason, our Armed Forces outside Vietnam not only reflect these conditions but disclose the depths of their troubles in an awful litany of sedition, disaffection, desertion, race, drugs, breakdowns of authority, abandon-ment of discipline, and, as a cumulative result, the lowest state of military morale in the history of the country.

Sedition—coupled with disaffection within the ranks, and externally fo-mented with an audacity and intensity previously inconceivable—infests the Armed Services:

 • At best count, there appear to be some 144 underground newspapers published on or aimed at U.S. military bases in this country and overseas. Since 1970 the number of such sheets has increased 40% (up from 103 last fall). These journals are not mere gripe-sheets that poke soldier fun in the "Beetle Bailey" tradition, at the brass and the sergeants. "In Vietnam," writes the Ft Lewis-McChord Free Press, "the Lifers, the Brass, are the true Enemy, not the enemy." Another West Coast sheet advises readers: "Don't desert. Go to Vietnam and kill your commanding officer."

 • At least 14 GI dissent organizations (including two made up exclusively of officers) now operate more or less openly. Ancillary to these are at least six antiwar veterans' groups which strive to influence GIs. . . .

Racial conflicts (most but not all sparked by young black enlisted men) are erupting murderously in all services.

At a recent high commanders' conference, General Westmoreland and other senior generals heard the report from Germany that in many units white soldiers are now afraid to enter barracks alone at night for fear of "head-hunting" ambushes by blacks.

In the quoted words of one soldier on duty in West Germany, "I'm much more afraid of getting mugged on the post than I am of getting attacked by the Russians."

Other reports tell of jail-delivery attacks on Army stockades and military police to release black prisoners, and of officers being struck in public by black soldiers. Augsburg, Krailsheim, and Hohenfels are said to be rife with racial trouble. Hohenfels was the scene of a racial fragging last year—one of the few so far recorded outside Vietnam.

In Ulm, last fall, a white noncommissioned officer killed a black soldier who was holding a loaded .45 on two unarmed white officers.

Elsewhere, according to *Fortune* magazine, junior officers are now being attacked at night when inspecting barracks containing numbers of black soldiers.

Kelley Hill, a Ft Benning, Ga., barracks area, has been the scene of repeated nighttime assaults on white soldiers. One such soldier bitterly remarked, "Kelley Hill may belong to the commander in the daytime but it belongs to the blacks after dark." ...

The drug problem—like the civilian situation from which it directly derives—is running away with the services. In March, Navy Secretary John H. Chafee, speaking for the two sea services, said bluntly that drug abuse in both Navy and Marines is out of control.

In 1966, the Navy discharged 170 drug offenders. Three years later (1969), 3,800 were discharged. Last year in 1970, the total jumped to over 5,000.

Drug abuse in the Pacific Fleet—with Asia on one side, and kinky California on the other—gives the Navy its worst headaches. To cite one example, a destroyer due to sail from the West Coast last year for the Far East nearly had to postpone deployment when, five days before departure, a ring of some 30 drug users (over 10 percent of the crew) was uncovered.

Only last week, eight midshipmen were dismissed from the Naval Academy following disclosure of an alleged drug ring. While the Navy emphatically denies allegations in a copyrighted article by the *Annapolis Capitol* that up to 1,000 midshipmen now use marijuana, midshipman sources confirm that pot is anything but unknown at Annapolis.

Yet the Navy is somewhat ahead in the drug game because of the difficulty in concealing addiction at close quarters aboard ship, and because fixes are unobtainable during long deployments at sea.

The Air Force, despite 2,715 drug investigations in 1970, is in even better shape: its rate of 3 cases per thousand airmen is the lowest in the services.

By contrast, the Army had 17,742 drug investigations the same year. According to Col. Thomas B. Hauschild, of the Medical Command of our Army forces in Europe, some 46 percent of the roughly 200,000 soldiers there had used illegal drugs at least once. In one battalion surveyed in West Germany, over 50 percent of the men smoked marijuana regularly (some on duty), while roughly half of those were using hard drugs of some type.

What those statistics say is that the Armed Forces (like their parent society) are in the grip of a drug pandemic—a conclusion underscored by the one fact that, just since 1968, the total number of verified drug addiction cases throughout the Armed Forces has nearly doubled. One other yardstick: according to military medical sources, needle hepatitis now poses as great a problem among young soldiers as VD.

At Ft Bragg, the Army's third largest post, adjacent to Fayetteville, N.C.

(a garrison town whose conditions one official likened to New York's "East Village" and San Francisco's "Haight-Ashbury") a recent survey disclosed that 4% (or over 1,400) of the 36,000 soldiers there are hard-drug (mainly heroin and LSD) addicts. In the 82nd Airborne Division, the strategic-reserve unit that boasts its title of "America's Honor Guard," approximately 450 soldier drug abusers were being treated when this reporter visited the post in April. About a hundred were under intensive treatment in special drug wards. . . .

In 1970, the Army had 65,643 deserters, or roughly the equivalent of four infantry divisions. This desertion rate (52.3 soldiers per thousand) is well over twice the peak rate for Korea (22.5 per thousand). It is more than quadruple the 1966 desertion-rate (14.7 per thousand) of the then well-trained, high-spirited professional Army.

If desertions continue to rise (as they are still doing this year), they will attain or surpass the WWII peak of 63 per thousand which, incidentally, occurred in the same year (1945) when more soldiers were actually being discharged from the Army for psychoneurosis than were drafted.

The Air Force—relatively uninvolved in the Vietnam war, all-volunteer, management-oriented rather than disciplinary and hierarchic—enjoys a numerical rate of less than one deserter per thousand men, but even this is double what it was three years ago.

The Marines in 1970 had the highest desertion index in the modern history of the Corps and, for that year at least, slightly higher than the Army's. As the Marines now phase out of Vietnam (and haven't taken a draftee in nearly two years), their desertions are expected to decrease sharply. Meanwhile, grimly remarked one officer, "Let the bastards go. We're all the better without them."

Letting the bastards go is something the Marines can probably afford. "The Marine Corps Isn't Looking for a Lot of Recruits," reads a current recruiting poster, "We Just Need a Few Good Men." This is the happy situation of a Corps slimming down to an elite force again composed of true volunteers who want to be professionals.

But letting the bastards go doesn't work at all for the Army and the Navy, who do need a lot of recruits and whose reenlistment problems are dire.

Admiral Elmo R. Zumwalt, Jr, Chief of Naval Operations, minces no words. "We have a personnel crisis," he recently said, "that borders on disaster."

The Navy's crisis, as Zumwalt accurately describes it, is that of a highly technical, material oriented service that finds itself unable to retain the expensively-trained technicians needed to operate warships, which are the largest, most complex items of machinery that man makes and uses. . . .

The trouble of the services—produced by and also in turn producing the dismaying conditions described in this article—is above all a crisis of soul and backbone. It entails—the word is not too strong—something very near a collapse of the command authority and leadership George Washington saw as the soul of military forces. This collapse results, at least in part, from a concurrent collapse of public confidence in the military establishment. . . .

But the fall in public esteem of all three major services—not just the

Army—is exceeded by the fall or at least the enfeeblement of the hierarchic and disciplinary system by which they exist and, when ordered to do so, fight and sometimes die. . . .

SOURCE: Robert D. Heinl, Jr., "The Collapse of the Armed Forces," *Armed Forces Journal* (June 7, 1971), pp. 30–37.

As 1972 began, both the battlefields of Vietnam and the American home front were calm. Because of Vietnamization only about 20,000 U.S. combat soldiers remained in Vietnam and they too would soon come home. As the U.S. combat role diminished and the number of U.S. casualties dwindled, the antiwar movement disintegrated. The war had outlasted its organized opposition. The Paris peace talks remained deadlocked. The sticking point was U.S. insistence that the Thieu government in the South remain in power; the Communists insisted that Thieu had go to.

Suddenly, in the spring of 1972, the war resumed, larger than ever, when the North Vietnamese launched a major invasion of South Vietnam along three fronts. The offensive was eventually stopped primarily by the use of massive American bombing, and President Nixon's bold decision to mine Haiphong and the other North Vietnamese ports. South Vietnam had survived its most serious challenge since the American intervention in 1965.

DOCUMENT 54. Excerpts from a Senate Foreign Relations Committee Report on the 1972 Communist Spring Offensive, May 1972.

The overall effect of the North Vietnamese offensive, its "success or failure" and the relative strength of the South Vietnamese Government's position, cannot be calculated solely in terms of cities lost or successfully defended, casualty figures or sortie rates. The security situation in the countryside—or, to put it another way, the impact of the offensive on pacification—must also be taken into account in any overall assessment of the current situation.

Among other comments on the security situation made in the course of our briefings were these:

(a) Not since the Tet offensive of 1968 has there been such a large decline in security during a one-month period.

(b) The enemy offensive was accompanied by record levels of terrorism, particularly in Military Region I.

(c) A great number of young people were abducted by the enemy during March and April, particularly in Military Regions I and II, since the local Viet Cong need manpower.

(d) The effect of the offensive on refugee resettlement and return-to-village programs has been "disastrous" with virtually all regular refugee programs in the 23 provinces in which new refugees have been generated halted and all efforts concentrated on emergency relief.

While Hamlet Evaluation System (HES) statistics are no longer taken with any great seriousness by American officials in either Washington or Saigon—some give them less credence than heretofore because the reporting is now done by the Vietnamese—the HES statistics are said to be considered to be useful in gauging broad trends in the security picture. Following are some of the measurements of change which took place during the first full month of the offensive.

In February of this year, 83% of the population was considered to be in category A or B—that is, under government control. As of April 30, this percentage had declined to 70.6%....

Whether or not the Viet Cong strength in the rural areas will continue to grow apparently depends on several factors: the current strength of the Viet Cong local and main forces and the Viet Cong infrastruture; the ability of the ARVN to contain Viet Cong initiatives; and the potential of the South Vietnamese Government to reverse the inroads made by the Viet Cong in recent months [ARVN is the U.S.-trained army of South Vietnam.] ...

Most American officials believed that as a result of the Tet offensive of 1968 and intensive efforts during the last 4 years, the Viet Cong infrastructure had been seriously damaged, although no official was willing or able to support this view with precise statistics. Some officials, both civilian and military, believed that the most convincing evidence of the Viet Cong's ineffectiveness was what they regarded as the absence of any significant Viet Cong participation in the current offensive. To support this view, they referred to various North Vietnamese directives and captured documents calling upon the Viet Cong to "rise" and to take various specific actions, few of which they have done. Their overall conclusion was that the Viet Cong had not "risen" because it no longer existed as a significant force.

Some Americans with long experience in Vietnam, the CIA officers who specialize in this subject and most Vietnamese to whom we talked disagreed. They said that, unlike the situation in the Tet offensive of 1968, there had been no call for a "general offensive, general uprising," the term used at that time. They pointed out that COSVN Directive 43 of March 1972 (COSVN is the Central Office for South Vietnam which is the Viet Cong field headquarters believed to be located at Kratie in Cambodia) stressed that the Viet Cong should lay the groundwork for "spontaneous uprisings" in South Vietnam in 1972, that there has been no call for a "general offensive, general uprising" in the course of this offensive and that they did not expect one because the Viet Cong were badly hurt in 1968 and would not surface again unless they were certain that the areas in which they did rise would not be recaptured by government forces. (COSVN Directive 43 and other COSVN directives and resolutions have, however, complained of a failure on the part of the Viet Cong cadre to establish a close relationship with the people in order to motivate them to rise up when the call does come and have also complained of the failure on the part of the Viet Cong to coordinate their activities with the successes achieved by main force elements.) According to these officials, the COSVN directives showed that the current offensive was regarded as an attempt to redress the balance of forces by inflicting heavy casualties on South Vietnamese army units, seizing base areas and weakening the government's pacification efforts. . . .

Over the long term it is not only the question of new areas brought under communist control, but also the overall psychological shock that has resulted from the impact of the North Vietnamese offensive, that is significant in considering the security situation in the countryside. In many of the areas we visited we were told that the people had again become fearful that the government was incapable of protecting them. In some areas, particularly along the coastal area of Military Regions I and II, many Vietnamese apparently believed that the United States had deliberately allowed the North Vietnamese to advance as part of a deal involving the cession of territory. . . .

Almost every advisor with whom we spoke identified "the question of leadership" as South Vietnam's greatest single problem. In the course of our two week stay, the quality of ARVN leadership, in both civil and military capacities and at every level from President Thieu on down, was criticized or at least questioned by everyone with whom we spoke—both Vietnamese and Americans. It is an important aspect of the problem of security in the countryside because all Regional Commanders, Province Chiefs and District Chiefs are ARVN officers.

Most observers believe that the problem begins at the top of the government. It is said that President Thieu has picked his key commanders and provincial officials primarily on the basis of their loyalty to him, rather than on the basis of integrity or military ability. Despite the present serious situation, there are apparently no indications that Thieu intends to make the sweeping changes which many American and Vietnamese observers believe are needed to transform the ARVN into a well led army and to enhance the effectiveness of the government's control over the countryside. . . .

SOURCE: United States Senate, Committee on Foreign Relations, *Report*, May 1972, pp. 14–19.

Washington and Hanoi, having failed to break the diplomatic stalemate by military means during the spring and summer of 1972, moved in the fall of that year to break the military stalemate by diplomacy. The North Vietnamese, for the first time since American involvement in the war began, appeared to want a diplomatic solution if it did not contravene their long-range goal of achieving national reunification. By late October, Henry Kissinger and the North Vietnamese emissary, Le Duc Tho, had forged the essentials of an agreement. But General Thieu, the South Vietnamese leader, refused to accept it. He was especially concerned about a provision allowing the North Vietnamese to keep a large contingent of troops in the South after the Americans had withdrawn.

Nixon, who shared some of Thieu's concerns, backed the South Vietnamese leader. When subsequent efforts to renegotiate the agreement foundered, Nixon broke off the talks. In an effort to get better terms and perhaps seriously cripple the war-making ability of North Vietnam, Nixon launched the largest aerial assault of the war against military and industrial targets in the vicinity of Hanoi and Haiphong. The bombing lasted from December 18 to December 29, 1972. When Hanoi indicated that it would resume negotiations if the U.S. stopped its bombing, Nixon relented. Talks resumed in Paris on January 8, 1973, and an agreement was quickly reached on all substantive issues. The agreement was similar in all important aspects to the one reached previously. Thieu again objected, but this time Nixon, figuring this was the best agreement he was likely to get under the circumstances, forced Thieu to sign it. To make the agreement more acceptable to General Thieu, the United States significantly increased the amount of economic and military aid going to South Vietnam. President Nixon also wrote Thieu a personal letter in which he promised him that the United States "will respond with full force" should North Vietnam violate the terms of the settlement.

DOCUMENT 55. President Nixon's Letter to President Nguyen Van Thieu, January 5, 1973.

This will acknowledge your letter of December 20, 1972.

There is nothing substantial that I can add to my many previous messages, including my December 17 letter, which clearly stated my opinions and intentions. With respect to the question of North Vietnamese troops, we will again present your views to the Communists as we have done vigorously at every other opportunity in the negotiations. The result is certain to be once more the rejection of our position. We have explained to you repeatedly why we believe the problem of North Vietnamese troops is manageable under the agreement, and I see no reason to repeat all the arguments.

We will proceed next week in Paris along the lines that General Haig explained to you. Accordingly, if the North Vietnamese meet our concerns on the two outstanding substantive issues in the agreement, concerning the DMZ and the method of signing, and if we can arrange acceptable supervisory machinery, we will proceed to conclude the settlement. The gravest consequences would then ensue if your government chose to reject the agreement and split off from the United States. As I said in my December 17 letter, "I am convinced that your refusal to join us would be an invitation to disaster—to the loss of all that we together have fought for over the past decade. It would be inexcusable above all because we will have lost a just and honorable alternative."

As we enter this new round of talks, I hope that our countries will now show a united front. It is imperative for our common objectives that your government take no further actions that complicate our task and would make more difficult the acceptance of the settlement by all parties. We will keep you informed of the negotiations in Paris through daily briefings of Ambassador Lam.

I can only repeat what I have so often said: The best guarantee for the survival of South Vietnam is the unity of our two countries which would be gravely jeopardized if you persist in your present course. The actions of our Congress since its return have clearly borne out the many warnings we have made.

Should you decide, as I trust you will, to go with us, you have my assurance of continued assistance in the post-settlement period and that we will respond with full force should the settlement be violated by North Vietnam. So once more I conclude with an appeal to you to close ranks with us.

SOURCE: A copy of Nixon's secret letter was printed in the *New York Times*, May 1, 1975, p. 16.

The Paris Peace Accords signed January 27, 1973, officially ended the Vietnam war for America. The agreement was signed by delegates representing the four principals, North Vietnam, South Vietnam, the United States, and the Provisional Revolutionary Government (PRG), which was formed by the National Liberation Front in 1969. The peace treaty had two main divisions, a military agreement and a political section. The essence of the military agreement called for the United States to remove all its remaining forces within 60 days. In exchange, Hanoi agreed to return all American prisoners of war within 60 days. North Vietnam was also allowed to keep an estimated 150,000 troops in South Vietnam. The essence of the political agreement called for both the Thieu government and the PRG to be accorded a political status in the South. South Vietnam was declared a free and independent nation.

DOCUMENT 56. Excerpts from the Paris Accords, January 27, 1973.

Article 1

.... The United States and all other countries respect the independence, sovereignty, unity, and territorial integrity of Viet-Nam as recognized by the 1954 Geneva Agreements on Viet-Nam. . . .

Article 2

A cease-fire shall be observed throughout South Viet-Nam as of 2400 hours G.M.T., on January 27, 1973.

At the same hour, the United States will stop all its military activities against the territory of the Democratic Republic of Viet-Nam by ground, air and naval forces, wherever they may be based, and end the mining of the territorial waters, ports, harbors, and waterways of the Democratic Republic of Viet-Nam. The United States will remove, permanently deactivate or destroy all the mines in the territorial waters, ports, harbors, and waterways of North Viet-Nam as soon as this Agreement goes into effect.

The complete cessation of hostilities mentioned in this Article shall be durable and without limit of time. . . .

Article 4

The United States will not continue its military involvement or intervene in the internal affairs of South Viet-Nam.

Article 5

Within sixty days of the signing of this Agreement, there will be a total withdrawal from South Viet-Nam of troops, military advisers, and military personnel, including technical military personnel and military personnel associated with the pacification program, armaments, munitions, and war material of the United States and those of the other foreign countries mentioned in Article 3(a). Advisers from the above-mentioned countries to all paramilitary organizations and the police force will also be withdrawn within the same period of time.

Article 6

The dismantlement of all military bases in South Viet-Nam of the United States and of the other foreign countries mentioned in Article 3(a) shall be completed within sixty days of the signing of this Agreement.

Article 7

From the enforcement of the cease-fire to the formation of the government provided for in Article 9(b) and 14 of this Agreement, the two South Vietnamese parties shall not accept the introduction of troops, military advisers, and military personnel including technical military personnel, armaments, munitions, and war material into South Viet-Nam. . . .

Article 8

(a) The return of captured military personnel and foreign civilians of the parties shall be carried out simultaneously with and completed not later than the same day as the troop withdrawal mentioned in Article 5. The parties shall exchange complete lists of the above-mentioned captured military personnel and foreign civilians on the day of the signing of this Agreement.

(b) The Parties shall help each other to get information about those military personnel and foreign civilians of the parties missing in action, to determine the location and take care of the graves of the dead so as to facilitate the exhumation and repatriation of the remains, and to take any such other measures as may be required to get information about those still considered missing in action.

(c) The question of the return of Vietnamese civilian personnel captured and detained in South Viet-Nam will be resolved by the two South Vietnamese parties on the basis of the principles of Article 21(b) of the Agreement on the Cessation of Hostilities in Viet-Nam of July 20, 1954. The two South Vietnamese parties will do so in a spirit of national reconciliation and concord, with a view to ending hatred and enmity, in order to ease suffering and to reunite families. The two South Vietnamese parties will do their utmost to resolve this question within ninety days after the cease-fire comes into effect. . . .

Article 11

Immediately after the cease-fire, the two South Vietnamese parties will:
—achieve national reconciliation and concord, end hatred and enmity, prohibit all acts of reprisal and discrimination against individuals or organizations that have collaborated with one side or the other;
—ensure the democratic liberties of the people: personal freedom, freedom of speech, freedom of the press, freedom of meeting, freedom of organization, freedom of political activities, freedom of belief, freedom of movement, freedom of residence, freedom of work, right to property ownership, and right to free enterprise. . . .

Chapter V
The Reunification of Viet-Nam and The Relationship
Between North and South Viet-Nam

Article 15

The reunification of Viet-Nam shall be carried out step by step through peaceful means on the basis of discussions and agreements between North and South Viet-Nam, without coercion or annexation by either party, and without foreign interference. The time for reunification will be agreed upon by North and South Viet-Nam.
Pending reunification:

(a) The military demarcation line between the two zones at the 17th parallel is only provisional and not a political or territorial boundary, as provided for in paragraph 6 of the Final Declaration of the 1954 Geneva Conference.

(b) North and South Viet-Nam shall respect the Demilitarized Zone on either side of the Provisional Military Demarcation Line.

(c) North and South Viet-Nam shall promptly start negotiations with a view to reestablishing normal relations in various fields. Among the questions to be negotiated are the modalities of civilian movement across the Provisional Military Demarcation Line.

(d) North and South Viet-Nam shall not join any military alliance or military bloc and shall not allow foreign powers to maintain military bases, troops, military advisers, and military personnel on their respective territories, as stipulated in the 1954 Geneva Agreements on Viet-Nam. . . .

Article 21

The United States anticipates that this Agreement will usher in an era of reconciliation with the Democratic Republic of Viet-Nam as with all the peoples of Indochina. In pursuance of its traditional policy, the United States will contribute to healing the wounds of war and to postwar reconstruction of the Democratic Republic of Viet-Nam and throughout Indochina.

Article 22

The ending of the war, the restoration of peace in Viet-Nam, and the strict implementation of this Agreement will create conditions for establishing a new, equal and mutually beneficial relationship between the United States and the Democratic Republic of Viet-Nam on the basis of respect of each other's independence and sovereignty, and non-interference in each other's internal affairs. At the same time this will ensure stable peace in Viet-Nam and contribute to the preservation of lasting peace in Indochina and Southeast Asia. . . .

The Return of Captured Military Personnel and Foreign Civilians

Article 1

The parties signatory to the Agreement shall return the captured military personnel of the parties mentioned in Article 8(a) of the Agreement as follows:
—all captured military personnel of the United States and those of the other foreign countries mentioned in Article 3(a) of the Agreement shall be returned to United States authorities;
—all captured Vietnamese military personnel, whether belonging to regular or irregular armed forces, shall be returned to the two South Vietnamese parties; they shall be returned to that South Vietnamese party under whose command they served.

Article 2

All captured civilians who are nationals of the United States or of any other foreign countries mentioned in Article 3(a) of the Agreement shall be returned to United States authorities. All other captured foreign civilians shall be returned to the authorities of their country of nationality by any one of the parties willing and able to do so.

Article 3

The parties shall today exchange complete lists of captured persons mentioned in Articles 1 and 2 of this Protocol.

Article 4

(a) The return of all captured persons mentioned in Articles 1 and 2 of this Protocol shall be completed within sixty days of the signing of the Agreement at a rate no slower than the rate of withdrawal from South Viet-Nam of United States forces and those of the other foreign countries mentioned in Article 5 of the Agreement.

(b) Persons who are seriously ill, wounded or maimed, old persons and women shall be returned first. The remainder shall be returned either by returning all from one detention place after another or in order of their dates of capture, beginning with those who have been held the longest. . . .

With Regard to Dead and Missing Persons

Article 10

(a) The Four-Party Joint Military Commission shall ensure joint action by the parties in implementing Article 8(b) of the Agreement. When the Four-Party Joint Military Commission has ended its activities, a Four-Party Joint Military team shall be maintained to carry on this task.

(b) With regard to Vietnamese civilian personnel dead or missing in South Viet-Nam, the two South Vietnamese parties shall help each other to obtain information about missing persons, determine the location and take care of the graves of the dead, in a spirit of national reconciliation and concord, in keeping with the people's aspirations. . . .

SOURCE: U.S. Secretary of State (ed.), *United States Treaties and Other International Agreements*, 1974, *passim*.

Shortly after the signing of the Paris treaty, President Nixon wrote another secret letter to a Vietnamese official. This time his letter was addressed to Pham Van Dong, Prime Minister of the DRV. In his letter, President Nixon committed the United States to aiding in the postwar reconstruction of North Vietnam, pledging in the range of $3.25 billion. No money was ever paid.

DOCUMENT 57. President Nixon's Letter to Prime Minister Pham Van Dong, February 1, 1973.

The President wishes to inform the Democratic Republic of Vietnam of the principles which will govern United States participation in the postwar reconstruction of North Vietnam. As indicated in Article 21 of the Agreement on Ending the War and Restoring Peace in Vietnam signed in Paris on Jan. 27, 1973, the United States undertakes this participation in accordance with its traditional policies. These principles are as follows:

1. The Government of the United States of America will contribute to postwar reconstruction in North Vietnam without any political conditions.

2. Preliminary United States studies indicate that the appropriate programs for the United States contribution to postwar reconstruction will fall in the range of $3.25 billion of grant aid over five years. Other forms of aid will be agreed upon between the two parties. This estimate is subject to revision and to detailed discussion between the Government of the United States and the Government of the Democratic Republic [of] Vietnam.

3. The United States will propose to the Democratic Republic of Vietnam the establishment of a United States-North Vietnamese Joint Economic Commission within 30 days from the date of this message.

4. The function of the commission will be to develop programs for the United States contribution to reconstruction of North Vietnam. This United States contribution will be based upon such factors as:
(a) the needs of North Vietnam arising from the dislocation of war;
(b) The requirements for postwar reconstruction in the agricultural and industrial sectors of North Vietnam's economy.

5. The Joint Economic Commission will have an equal number of representatives from each side. It will agree upon a mechanism to administer the program which will constitute the United States contribution to the reconstruction of North Vietnam. The commission will attempt to complete this agreement within 60 days after its establishment.

6. The two members of the commission will function on the principle of respect for each other's sovereignty, noninterference in each other's internal affairs, equality and mutual benefit. The offices of the commission will be located at a place to be agreed upon by the United States and the Democratic Republic of Vietnam.

7. The United States considers that the implementation of the foregoing principles will prompt economic, trade and other relations between the United States of America and the Democratic Republic of Vietnam and will contribute to insuring a stable and lasting peace in Indochina. These principles ac-

cord with the spirit of Chapter VIII of the Agreement on Ending the War and Restoring Peace in Vietnam which was signed in Paris on Jan. 27, 1973. . . .

SOURCE: Porter (ed.), *Vietnam: The Definitive Documentation*, Vol. 2, Document 324, "Letter from Nixon to Pham Van Dong," February 1, 1973.

The war in South Vietnam went on despite the signing of the Paris accords, only now it continued without direct American participation. Neither side observed the cease-fire and both ignored or deliberately violated many of the other terms of the agreement. Neither side made a serious effort to seek a political settlement to the long war. South Vietnam, dependent on U.S. economic and military aid since birth, struggled to survive after the Americans had departed. President Nixon, increasingly engulfed by the Watergate scandals from March 1973 until his forced resignation from office in August 1974, could not keep the promises of support and protection that he had made to General Thieu. Congress restricted the president's power to intervene militarily in the Indochina war. Congress cut off all funding for bombing in Cambodia effective August 15, 1973 and in November Congress enacted the War Powers Act, which was aimed at preventing Nixon from reintroducing U.S. combat troops into South Vietnam.

DOCUMENT 58. Excerpts from the War Powers Resolution, November 7, 1973.

. . . The President in every possible instance shall consult with Congress before introducing United States Armed Forces into hostilities or into situations where imminent involvement in hostilities is clearly indicated by the circumstances, and after every such introduction shall consult regularly with the Congress until United States Armed Forces are no longer engaged in hostilities or have been removed from such situations.

§ 1543. Reporting Requirement

   (a) *Written report; time of submission; circumstances necessitating submission; information reported*
   In the absence of a declaration of war, in any case in which United States Armed Forces are introduced—

   (1) into hostilities or into situations where imminent involvement in hostilities is clearly indicated by the circumstances;

   (2) into the territory, airspace or waters of a foreign nation, while equipped for combat, except for deployments which relate solely to supply, replacement, repair or training of such forces; or

   (3) in numbers which substantially enlarge United States Armed Forces equipped for combat already located in a foreign nation;

the President shall submit within 48 hours to the Speaker of the House of Representatives and to the President, pro tempore of the Senate a report, in writing, setting forth—

(A) the circumstances necessitating the introduction of United States Armed Forces;

(B) the constitutional and legislative authority under which such introduction took place; and

(C) the estimated scope and duration of the hostilities or involvement.

(b) Other information reported

The President shall provide such other information as the Congress may request in the fulfillment of its constitutional responsibilities with respect to committing the Nation to war and to the use of United States Armed Forces abroad.

(c) Periodic reports; semiannual requirement

Whenever United States Armed Forces are introduced into hostilities or into any situation described in subsection (a) of this section, the President shall, so long as such armed forces continue to be engaged in such hostilities or situation, report to the Congress periodically on the status of such hostilities or situation as well as on the scope and duration of such hostilities or situation, but in no event shall he report to the Congress less often than once every six months.

§ 1544. Congressional action

(a) Transmittal of report and referral to Congressional Committees; joint request for convening Congress

Each report submitted pursuant to section 1543(a)(1) of this title shall be transmitted to the Speaker of the House of Representatives and to the President pro tempore of the Senate on the same calendar day. Each report so transmitted shall be referred to the Committee on International Relations of the House of Representatives and to the Committee on Foreign Relations of the Senate for appropriate action. If, when the report is transmitted, the Congress has adjourned sine die or has adjourned for any period in excess of three calendar days, the Speaker of the House of Representatives and the President pro tempore of the Senate, if they deem it advisable (or if petitioned by at least 30 percent of the membership of their respective Houses) shall jointly request the President to convene Congress in order that it may consider the report and take appropriate action pursuant to this section.

(b) Termination of use of United States Armed Forces; exceptions; extension period

Within sixty calendar days after a report is submitted or is required to be submitted pursuant to section 1543(a)(1) of this title, whichever is earlier, the President shall terminate any use of United States Armed Forces with respect to which such report was submitted (or required to be submitted), unless the Congress (1) has declared war or has enacted a specific authorization for such use of

United States Armed Forces, (2) has extended by law such sixty-day period, or (3) is physically unable to meet as a result of an armed attack upon the United States. Such sixty-day period shall be extended for not more than an additional thirty days if the President determines and certifies to the Congress in writing that unavoidable military necessity respecting the safety of United States Armed Forces requires the continued use of such armed forces in the course of bringing about a prompt removal of such forces.

(c) Concurrent resolution for removal by President of United States Armed Forces
    Notwithstanding subsection (b) of this section, at any time that United States Armed Forces are engaged in hostilities outside the territory of the United States, its possessions and territories without a declaration of war or specific statutory authorization, such forces shall be removed by the President if the Congress so directs by concurrent resolution.

SOURCE: From the *United States Legal Code*, Vol. 11, 1976, pp. 1926–1927.

During 1974 and the beginning of 1975, the power balance of Indochina shifted in favor of North Vietnam. Cutbacks in American aid contributed to the decline of South Vietnam. Even so, it came as a shock to Americans when South Vietnam's military forces began to collapse in the face of a North Vietnamese offensive in the spring of 1975. The beginning of the end of South Vietnam occurred in March when General Thieu, in a desperate effort to save half his country, ordered his armies to withdraw from the central highlands and northern provinces. The withdrawal quickly turned into a rout, and by mid-April, North Vietnamese forces closed in on Saigon. As the end of South Vietnam approached, President Gerald R. Ford (who became president following Nixon's resignation) tried to persuade Congress to approve $722 million in emergency aid to try to save America's imperiled client. Secretary of State Henry Kissinger appeared before the Senate Appropriations Committee to try to convince reluctant senators that they should support the administration's aid request. He failed. The senators knew that there was virtually no popular support in the nation for further U.S. involvement in Indochina, and they believed that they would just be throwing good money after bad if they funded the aid request. Besides, most senators believed that America had already expended far too much of its blood and treasure in Vietnam and they were loath to contribute any more money to a lost cause.

DOCUMENT 59. Excerpts from Secretary of State Henry A. Kissinger's Testimony Before the Senate Appropriations Committee, April 15, 1975.

SECRETARY KISSINGER: At the time of the Paris accords it was my belief that the South Vietnamese with the existing balance in South Vietnam would be able to maintain their security, and if the North Vietnamese had lived up to the Paris accords, which prohibited the infiltration of additional personnel or material, the military situation in South Vietnam could have been maintained indefinitely.

SENATOR MONTOYA: Now, on April 5 in your press conference at Palm Springs, you stated that at that time there had been infiltration by North Vietnam into South Vietnam with approximately 18 divisions. Now why did that happen, if you say that we had military parity or perhaps you can tell us when that military parity started to disintegrate.

SECRETARY KISSINGER: The military parity began to disintegrate during the course of last year, when the accumulated cuts in American aid, some of which were due to inflationary pressures and to the rise in oil prices, began to force the South Vietnamese into a static defensive position while the North Vietnamese continued their infiltration. . . .

SENATOR MONTOYA: In your statement you tell us that you want $396 million to sustain South Vietnam for 60 days and of course the other $326 million of the $722 million is for the purpose of organizing ranger units and training more manpower for self-defense. Now, in the light of this budgetary request, what happens after the 60 days? Are you going to come in and ask for more millions of dollars to sustain them?

SECRETARY KISSINGER: Senator, after the 60 days, depending of course upon the military situation and assuming there has been no negotiation, we would be requesting from the Congress the sum that we have already submitted, which is $1.3 billion. . . .

SENATOR MONTOYA: In all seriousness, do you think that the expenditure of the money contained in this budget request will help the situation in South Vietnam and create an atmosphere whereby a political settlement can be made?

SECRETARY KISSINGER: In all seriousness, Senator, I recall no set of discussions between the President and his senior advisers that were more prayerfully conducted than these . . . [It is] his judgment—with which I fully concurred— that whatever prediction you make about the future, we will be better off with this sum than without this sum. . . .

SENATOR HUDDLESTON: So the American people want to know whether or not after all these years this additional funding will actually lead toward any conclusion that is any better than what is going to happen whenever we do stop. Is there an answer to that?

SECRETARY KISSINGER: There is no certain answer to that question. I wish there were.

SOURCE: United States Senate, *Appropriations Committee Hearings*, April 15, 1975, *passim*.

Saigon fell to the Communists on April 30, 1975. The final American effort in Vietnam consisted of a hastily organized airlift that flew thousands of U.S. military and civilian officials, their dependents, "third country" personnel, and South Vietnamese, who had worked for or cooperated with the Americans and now feared for their lives, out of the country. The last helicopter departed the U.S. embassy grounds just hours ahead of the Communist takeover. Americans understood that their long crusade to determine the political destiny of South Vietnam had ended in disaster, for us, and a *fortiori*, for the people whom we had tried so hard so long to help. As South Vietnam passed into the dustbin of history, thoughtful Americans tried to sum up the Indochina enterprise that had engaged the nation for 25 years.

DOCUMENT 60: Finale: A Brief History of a Long War, by Leslie Gelb, May 1, 1975.

News Analysis

In Franz Kafka's "The Trial," a priest sets out to explain the mysteries of life to a character called K. They discuss a parable of the law and disagree on its meaning.

"No," says the priest, "it is not necessary to accept everything as true, one must only accept it as necessary."

"A melancholy conclusion," K responds. "It turns lying into a universal principle."

From Truman to Ford, six Presidents felt that they had to do and say what was necessary to prevent a Communist takeover of Vietnam. For all, perhaps with the exception of Mr. Ford, Indochina was their initiation into American foreign policy. While other threats to peace came and went, Vietnam was always there—a cockpit of confrontation, a testing place.

And there were always two battles going on for those 25 years: one out there and one back here.

There, it was the Promethean clash of colonialism, nationalism, Communism and Americanism. Here, it was the clash of imperatives not to "lose" a country to Communism and not to fight Asian land wars—how to walk the line between not winning and not getting out.

The battle would be endless in Vietnam until it finally was no longer viewed as necessary in Washington.

Memo to Truman

On the day after his inauguration, President Harry S. Truman received a memorandum from the State Department outlining the principal problems in the world.

The second item concerned France. It argued for restoring French morale even though the French have "put forward requests which are out of all proportion to their present strength and have in certain areas, notably in connection with Indochina, showed unreasonable suspicions of American aims and motives."

On Nov. 18, 1952, President-elect Dwight D. Eisenhower was briefed by the outgoing Secretary of State, Dean G. Acheson, on "only the most important problems." Mr. Acheson told the new President of the war weariness in France over fighting in her Indochinese colonies, of "the fence–sitting" by the people of Indochina, and of the fact that Washington was paying about half the cost of the war. He concluded, "This is an urgent matter upon which the new Administration must be prepared to act."

On Jan. 19, 1961, the day before the inauguration of John F. Kennedy, Mr. Eisenhower told the new President of "the deteriorating situation in Southeast Asia."

He said that Laos was the immediate problem, that it must be defended, and that "our unilateral intervention would be our last desperate hope in the event we were unable to prevail upon" allies to join.

On Nov. 23, the day after Mr. Kennedy's assassination, President Lyndon B. Johnson listened to his new advisers and later wrote, "Only South Vietnam gave me real cause for concern." They offered very different estimates of the situation there, but all agreed on the need for continuity of policy.

President Richard M. Nixon had his Vietnam strategy worked out before he took office, but his first action on foreign affairs was to ask the bureaucracy for a detailed study of the prospects in Vietnam.

It will be some time before the memoirs and documents of President Ford emerge, but from what is known Vietnam quickly became his albatross as well.

The historical forces that set the Vietnamese civil war in motion started over a century ago, as European powers sought new territories and France claimed Indochina as her domain. World War II set loose many independence movements and, in Vietnam, the Communist laid claim to the mantle of nationalism. American Presidents pursued a course of diplomacy aimed at shaping the world in the image of American democracy, at or least, making sure that it was not shaped in the image of Communist idols.

There was only a brief time in the beginning when this American impulse was not paramount. During the years right after World War II President Truman walked a tightrope between the French, trying to reassert their hold on the Indochinese colonies, and the Vietnamese—a collection of Communists and nationalists—fighting for independence. Only after the Communist take-over in China did he clearly choose sides.

Essential to Security

In 1950, soon after Moscow and Peking recognized the Democratic Republic of Vietnam led by Ho Chi Minh, Mr. Truman recognized the French-controlled state of Vietnam headed by Emperor Bao Dai. Then after the outbreak of the Korean war, he cast the American security net over Indochina.

The Presidentially approved National Security Council policy paper of June 25, 1952, said it all. It called Indochina "of great strategic importance in the general international interest rather than in the purely French interest, and as essential to the security of the free world, not only in the Far East but in the Middle East and Europe as well." The American object was "to prevent the countries of Southeast Asia from passing into the Communist orbit." This thinking was not a secret, for President Truman had announced to the nation that the loss of Indochina "would mean the loss of freedom for millions of people, the loss of vital raw materials, the loss of points of critical strategic importance to the free world."

Five successive Administrations were to pay public and secret obeisance to this domino theory—including that of Mr. Ford. Five successive Presidents were to seek an independent non–Communist South Vietnam.

This basic American commitment was set—in fact, although not in law—as early as 1950. Over the next two decades, American involvement would deepen in an effort to prevent a Communist take-over.

The question of whether American leaders would have started down this road had they foreseen the loss of more than 50,000 American lives and the expenditure of billions upon billions is historically irrelevant. The point is that each President was prepared to pay the immediate costs.

What drove them was a combination of three factors: a strategic mode of thought that held that peace was indivisible; a domestic paranoia centered around a right-wing McCarthyite reaction, and, in time, a bureaucratic monster that wanted to prove and improve itself and do the job of stopping Communism.

President Eisenhower and his Secretary of State, John Foster Dulles, fell into this pattern, although not completely. By 1954, the United States was providing almost $3-billion in aid to the war effort in Indochina, or about 80 per cent of the total French cost. But Mr. Eisenhower faced his moment of truth in the spring of 1954, when French forces were surrounded by the Vietminh at Dien Bien Phu. He knew that if the French garrison fell, the psychological shock would knock France out of the war.

Only American intervention could save the French. Mr. Dulles, Vice President Nixon and the Chairman of the Joint Chiefs of Staff, Adm. Arthur W. Radford, said go. Other members of the Joint Chiefs and a group of bipartisan Congressional leaders, including Senator Lyndon Johnson, said no—unless America's allies would help and Paris would grant true independence to Vietnam. President Eisenhower tried to meet these conditions and failed.

France then found a Premier—Pierre Mendès-France—who had the political courage to say "enough," and thus began the Geneva conference. The conferees—France, China, the Soviet Union, the Vietminh, and Bao Dai's representatives, and the United States as an observer—divided Vietnam at the 17th Parallel, with the prospect of reunification within two years through free elections. Neither Washington nor, in time, the new Saigon strongman, Ngo Dinh Diem, agreed to these political terms. Saigon and Hanoi held opposing positions and a new war was about to begin.

From 1955 to 1961, President Eisenhower was to pour about $200-million in military aid into Saigon annually, making South Vietnam the largest recipient of American arms after South Korea.

President Eisenhower left this legacy: He kept America out of war and put America into Vietnam. When President Kennedy took office, 685 American military men were in South Vietnam; when he died, 16,000 Americans were fighting a clandestine war there.

During President Kennedy's Thousand Days American television viewers witnessed self-immolations by Buddhists in protest against the Diem regime; the United States almost sent marines into Laos before a coalition government was established, and Indochina became steady front-page news, with Secretary of Defense Robert S. McNamara, pointer in hand, explaining the maps on television, and Secretary of State Dean Rusk never tiring of warning of the Chinese Communist menace.

It was the heyday of the Green Berets, for the young President saw them as praetorians against the new kind of Communist threat—guerrilla warfare. As President Kennedy privately warned of the hopelessness of a white man's war and kept calling it "their" war, he escalated American involvement and lent his public prestige to the cause.

Weeks before his assassination, he told a television audience: "I don't agree with those who say we should withdraw. That would be a great mistake. I know people don't like Americans to be engaged in this kind of an effort. Forty-seven Americans have been killed in combat with the enemy, but this is a very important struggle."

Basic Patterns Emerge

It was during the Kennedy years that the basic patterns of the war were to emerge.

The Saigon Government and its military forces always were reported to be getting better, but they never got good enough. Something was wrong somewhere; something always was wrong. For military power without political cohesiveness and support proved to be an empty shell. The non-Communist groups could never unify and gain legitimacy.

Hanoi and its Vietcong allies in the South always were reported to be taking heavier and heavier losses, but they kept coming back. Something always went right for them. Their leadership remained unified, their nation and armed forces disciplined, and organized, and it was they who held the banner of nationalism.

Victory would have been theirs on many occasions except for the pattern of increasing American involvement. Whenever Saigon was in immediate danger of losing, America would do more to redress the balance.

The upshot was a military stalemate. From time to time, negotiating efforts were begun. They got nowhere, underlining the fact that this was a civil war, a war that could not be ended by compromise, but only by force of arms. As each side tried for force, the other would match it, and death became a way of life in Vietnam.

Back in Washington, the credibility gap was emerging. As President Kennedy's press secretary, Pierre Salinger, was later to put it, Mr. Kennedy "was not anxious to admit the existence of a real war." Later President Johnson was not eager to tell Americans that the "light at the end of the tunnel" was very far away, though he and his aides were well aware of it.

The basic policy problems that were to confront President Johnson were rooted in these patterns. They concerned how to build a Saigon Government able to stand on its own and how much American military power to use in the war.

President Johnson, like his predecessors, knew that the war could not be ended unless the Saigon Government reformed, so he made reforms a condition for further American aid. But, again like his predecessors, he violated his own condition. The problem was this: If the United States did not deliver first and the situation further deteriorated, reforms would become academic. The more Washington did, the less Saigon would be likely to do. The less Washington did, the more likely Saigon would be to lose. In this way, it became an American war, and American planes began the bombing of North Vietnam and American troops levels climbed to a peak of almost 550,000.

As President Johnson and his advisers later explained, they felt that if they used maximum force and tried to end the war by destroying North Vietnam, they would run the risk of igniting World War III.

A Middle Way Chosen

If they were to deal with Vietnam as President Truman handled China in 1949, and let it fall, they would run of the risk of another round of McCarthyite attack.

Mr. Johnson chose the middle way, a policy of gradualism, similar to that used in Korea. He would hope to outlast the adversaries, to get them to stay on their side of the line. To avoid the nightmare of world war and McCarthyism, Mr. Johnson chose prolonged limited war.

The American public went along with this approach until the Communists launched their Lunar New Year offensive of early 1968. If Hanoi could launch such an offensive after so many years, more and more people thought, then America's Vietnam policy was a failure, and we had to get out. Thus began the agonizingly slow process of de-Americanizing the war. Under President Nixon and Henry A. Kissinger this policy—phasing out American forces slowly enough not to jeopardize the battlefield situation but rapidly enough to assuage American political opinion—was labeled Vietnamization.

In January, 1973, after the war spilled over into Cambodia, and after Mr. Nixon ordered the mining of Haiphong harbor and the carpet-bombing of Hanoi, a peace accord was signed in Paris. The essence of this agreement was that all American forces were to be withdrawn in return for the release of American prisoners of war, and that Hanoi's forces could stay in the South.

The accords also called for a cease-fire leading to free elections in South Vietnam. Few expected this would happen, and to insure against future American military intervention, Congress legislated a ban on American military reinvolvement.

Little to Choose From

Over the years, given the goal of a non-Communist South Vietnam, the United States faced three historical dilemmas.

At first, American leaders realized that there was no chance of defeating the Vietminh unless France granted independence to Vietnam, but that if France granted independence, she would not remain and fight the war. So, the United States could not win with France and it would not win without her.

Then, American leaders recognized that Mr. Diem was losing popular support, but that at the same time he represented the only hope of future political stability. So the United States could not win with him and could not win without him.

Later, the leaders concluded that the Saigon regime of President Nguyen Van Thieu would not reform with more American aid and could not survive without American involvement, and that Hanoi's effort seemed able to survive despite American efforts. So again, the war could not be won with American might—but it could be lost without it.

When the last American soldiers left Vietnam, most analysts believed that it would be only a matter of time before the Saigon Government collapsed. That time came in the spring of 1975. The Ford Administration pulled out all stops to avoid the collapse, with warnings of bloodbaths and falling dominoes. As one senior Administration official privately put it, they tried to "feed the vegetable intravenously" with another dose of military aid. This time, entreaties to Congress were to no avail. The Saigon armed forces had lost the will to fight.

Vietnam now will know a kind of peace. What will happen in the United

States—whether the nation will tear itself apart in assessing guilt or adjust with compassion and develop a new sense of purpose—is another matter.

SOURCE: Leslie Gelb, "Vietnam, Test of Presidents, Was Distant War and Battle at Home," *New York Times*, May 1, 1975, p. 18.

BOOK II Essays

A MYTH FOR ALL SEASONS: THE DOMINO THEORY AND AMERICA'S LONGEST WAR

by Paul Conway

We begin our essay section with Paul Conway's perceptive analysis of the domino theory, the reigning U.S. Cold War foreign-policy myth that propelled and sustained America's Indochina intervention that culminated in the longest war in U.S. history. Conway finds the genesis of the logic that energized the domino theory in the American response to a political crisis preceding World War II; specifically, the domino logic represented a postwar application of the "lesson of Munich" to the Soviet Union. Perceiving the Soviets to be the new Nazis in the aftermath of their takeover of Eastern Europe during 1945/1946, American officials resolved to contain Soviet expansionism, to protect the security and freedom of the United States and its allies, and to avoid World War III. In Conway's etiology, the domino theory evolved as a component of the U.S. Cold War ideology of containment of Communism in Europe in 1947.

During 1949/1950, in the aftermath of the Chinese revolution and the outbreak of the Korean war, increased concern about Asian affairs compelled American officials to extend the containment ideology and its domino logic to Asia. China must be prevented from expanding into Southeast Asia just as the Soviet Union had been stopped from expanding into southern Europe. President Truman and Secretary of State Dean Acheson redefined an ongoing French war in Indochina, a war meant to reimpose colonialism on the Vietnamese people; they incorporated the French effort into the free world's effort to contain the global spread of Communism. The United States began sending military and economic aid to the French and loyalist Vietnamese. The source of the expansionist contagion threatening Southeast Asia was identified as the Moscow-Beijing axis extending through their

181

putative agents in Vietnam, namely Ho Chi Minh and his revolutionary nationalists, the Vietminh. When the French war effort failed, despite massive U.S. economic, military, political, and moral support, American officials, in thrall to the logic of the domino theory, intervened to pick up the sword the French had dropped. As the French departed from Vietnam, Americans were busily at work creating a new nation in southern Vietnam to turn back the red tide.

One of the most useful parts of Paul Conway's analysis is his demonstration of the various phases through which the domino argument passed on its way to political and strategic disaster in Vietnam. In its Asian application, the logic of the domino was not immutable; it was not a unitary metaphor. In its pristine formulation by President Eisenhower during an April 7, 1954, press conference, Vietnam was understood to be a conduit for Communist expansion. If the Vietnam domino fell, then so would Laos, Cambodia, Thailand, and Burma. In time, Indonesia and the Philippines would also fall. By implication, India, Pakistan, Australia, and New Zealand would one day follow suit. Come the apocalypse and America itself, the ultimate domino, weakened and isolated, would succumb to its horrid logic. Communism would dominate the world. The Eisenhower version of the domino theory also stressed the importance of preserving Indochina as a source of rice and raw materials and as a trading area for Japan and America's European allies.

John F. Kennedy and his New Frontier came into office in January 1961. The new administration was eager to confront the Communists at crucial points around the globe, confident that Americans would demonstrate that Communist-inspired wars of "national liberation" could not succeed, that Communism was not the wave of the future in Southeast Asia. Vietnam would be a test case for American counterinsurgency strategies. In the Vietnamese cockpit, Americans would pass the test and the Communists would fail it. Kennedy and his men stressed the political and strategic consequences of falling dominoes for the United States and its free-world friends. Lyndon Johnson, who succeeded Kennedy on November 22, 1963, following Kennedy's tragic murder in Dallas, embraced the Kennedy version of the domino theory, emphasizing the strategic and political consequences of the fall of South Vietnam rather than its economic results.

The third phase of the domino theory promulgated during Richard Nixon's presidency in 1969/1970 suggests that its logic had worn thin. Years of rising costs and casualties in a stalemated war, a war that Americans could neither win nor abandon, undermined the propagandistic power of the theory. Nixon was forced to defend the seemingly perpetual American war by emphasizing the need to avoid a humiliating defeat, a defeat that would demoralize Americans, dismay our allies, embolden our enemies, and unhinge the international order. Nixon insisted that even if the United States could not win a military victory, it must avoid losing the war, and South Vietnam must survive. Nixon also warned that if South Vietnam fell, there would be a bloodbath of nightmare proportions that would forever stain the American conscience. Conway suggests that these arguments, in effect, amount to an abandonment of the domino theory, because it was no longer credible. It had ceased to be a viable myth. The domino theory itself turned out to be one of the dominoes that fell during the course of the lengthy Vietnam debacle.

The final part of Conway's essay is concerned with post-Vietnam efforts to revive the domino theory, efforts to demonstrate that Soviet foreign-policy gains around the world during the late 1970s flowed from the American defeat in Vietnam. Conway succeeds in demonstrating that these arguments are simplistic and generally specious, that the causes and consequences of international behaviors, whether foreign-policy advances or retreats, are much too complex to be explained by such a simplistic notion as the domino theory. These arguments represent failed efforts to resuscitate a failed theory. Conway concludes that the domino myth was "ahistorical in perspective" and implied a prescience about international events that never once proved true beyond Indochina itself. The aftermath of the Vietnam war exposed the domino theory as the logical fallacy that it always was. It deserved to be swept into the dustbin of discredited ideologies.

In our own time, when the Cold War has become history and Vietnam a dimming memory, when the Soviet Union is in retreat internationally as it struggles to solve severe internal economic and political problems, threats to American security, if they arise at all, are much more likely to come from internal problems or perhaps from serious economic, financial, or ecological imbalances in the world. Conway's timely article will help us shuck useless ideological baggage such as the domino myth with its spurious logic that always oversimplified and distorted complex relations among nations, a meretricious logic that lured us into the greatest foreign-policy disaster in our history.

> There was no corner of the known world where some interest was not alleged to be in danger or under actual attack. If the interests were not Roman, they were those of Rome's allies; and if Rome had no allies, the allies would be invented.
>
> Joseph Schumpeter

As many anthropologists have demonstrated, human societies cannot exist without myths to sustain them.[1] Myths may be grandiose folktales or simpleminded generalizations. Political myths are significant assumptions widely shared and rarely questioned within a society. According to Murray Edelman, each myth itself has consequences, although not the ones it literally proclaims.[2] Another possibility, considered elsewhere, is that of a self-fulfilling prophesy.[3]

Throughout America's longest war one myth—the domino theory—sustained the ongoing commitment of money, materiel, and human beings. It was endorsed by every president and repeated by countless officials in a variety of public pronouncements. One respected scholar said it was "perhaps the most important single reason for America's involvement."[4] Another called it "the theoretical justification for American involvement in the Vietnam War."[5]

There were three distinct patterns in the development of the domino theory. During the earliest phase, American policymakers warned that "if Indochina [the former French colonies of Vietnam, Laos and Cambodia] were to fall," the entire region's valuable raw materials would be lost to Japan, America's foremost Asian ally in the struggle with the Soviet Union. During the second phase, which was most of the 1960s, the domino theory usually suggested that the fall of Vietnam would, in a mechanistic, sequential fashion, lead to the loss of Laos, Cambodia, and numerous other Asian states to Communist subversives aligned with China. Economic variables were hardly mentioned during that decade. During the last phase of the Vietnam war, after the Tet-68 offensive, and especially during the administrations of Richard Nixon and Gerald Ford, the warnings were amorphous. The loss of Vietnam would, it was then argued, lead to a bloodbath, humiliation, disrespect, and consequently a host of disasters throughout the world. In the wake of the war there were several efforts to revive the domino theory as well as arguments about whether Vietnam had proved or disproved its validity.

BACKGROUND

Perhaps it has always been reassuring for people to believe that they are God's chosen people and that their enemies are somewhat less than deserving. Such a moralistic perspective often includes the assumption that adversaries are inherently evil and less civilized; thus, "the only language they understand is force."[6] Americans have often been prone to such conceit, as the history of U.S. foreign relations illustrates. For almost two centuries the United States had never lost a major war. A relatively religious people in a traditional sense, many Americans found it easy to presume that God was on their side.

In the twentieth century particularly, superior American technology promised to resolve any conflicts that threatened American values abroad.[7] The United States emerged from World War II with a revitalized economy, a nuclear monopoly, and boundless optimism. A deeply rooted sense of political mission, faith in God, and technological prowess were then the bedrock of America's political culture.

Although the United States emerged from World War II as the most powerful nation on earth, it was not without a sense of vulnerability. The Soviet Union posed an ideological challenge. Implicitly, Moscow seemed a long-term political and economic threat if not an immediate military nemesis.

The Soviet dictator, Joseph Stalin, was demonstrably ruthless and opportunistic, a difficult, if not impossible, adversary with which to deal. An early confrontation occurred in 1946 when Soviet troops refused to evacuate territory they had occupied as a result of the war in Iranian Azerbaijan. Stalin decided to withdraw the troops only after Harry Truman's implicit threat to use force, perhaps the first exercise of American nuclear dilomacy following Nagasaki.

The American president, unlike his predecessor, had little sympathy for nationalistic, anti-colonial leaders such as Ho Chi Minh in Vietnam. Washington was preoccupied with Europe. The French effort to regain control of its colonial empire in Indochina was viewed primarily in terms of the ideological clash with expansionistic Soviet communism.

The logic of dominoes grew out of World War II. The "lesson" of Munich—never to acquiesce to the territorial demands of an aggressive, militaristic dictator—seemed undeniable in relation to the Soviet threat. Stalin was the moral equivalent of Hitler. Diplomatically he had engineered the transformation of most of Eastern Europe into the Soviet Communist orbit. International Communism was then indeed a monolithic movement, except for Yugoslavia's nascent deviation under Tito. The policy of "containment," political, diplomatic and economic, was a logical response to Soviet adventurism in Europe.[8]

Early in 1947, two fragile nations in particular seemed essential to the stability of the West: Greece and Turkey. As then Undersecretary of State Dean Acheson explained, if either state should fall into Moscow's sphere of influence, neighboring states would be undermined as well. The Middle East, and even South Asia and Africa, would be vulnerable to Soviet subversion. The U.S. response was decisive. Unprecedented aid, materiel as well as economic, went to pro-U.S. factions in Athens and Ankara.

Explaining the Truman administration's decision to intervene in Greece and Turkey, Acheson used the metaphor of rotten apples: just one in a barrel could quickly contaminate the rest.[9] The logic of U.S. intervention was in place— later the metaphor would change.

Intervention was dramatically successful. Covert aid to Italian as well as French conservatives had a stabilizing effect in Rome and Paris. The highly publicized Marshall Plan revitalized West European economies. Stalin's blockade of West Berlin was thwarted by a combination of resolve and nuclear diplomacy.

Despite the sense that containment was succeeding in Europe, America's sense of vulnerability was exacerbated during the Truman years. The Soviets tested their first nuclear bomb in 1949. The victory of Mao Zedung's Communist forces in China dramatized the ideological threat to U.S. interests. Thereafter, Ho Chi Minh's revolutionary struggle in Vietnam would appear even more sinister to Americans.[10]

The Korean conflict brought the Cold War to a crescendo. North Korea's aggression against South Korea in June of 1950 was not viewed as an isolated, independent action. It was viewed, reasonably, as a Soviet-sponsored act. The focus of containment policy thus shifted sharply to Asia, where a military presence seemed imperative and where clear lines again had to be drawn to deter future aggression. Ironically, Chinese intervention in the Korean war in November 1950—partly the consequence of Washington's inconsistency and hubris— reinforced the sense of a monolithic threat orchestrated in Moscow. Truman feared that if "Russian satellites" were to succeed in Korea,[11] "it would be Indochina, then Hong Kong, then Malaya."[12] Acheson then warned that Japan and the Philippines might be next.[13] While the war in Korea raged, the United States made its first commitment of military advisers to help the French in Vietnam. "Rice, rubber and tin" were part of the rationale in a 1951 State Department publication.[14] Even before a new Republican administration was to take office "the domino theory was firmly rooted as a principle of American foreign policy."[15]

PHASE ONE: "IF INDOCHINA FALLS . . ."

> You have broader considerations that might follow what you would call the fall-
> ing domino principle . . . the possible sequence of events, the loss of Indochina,
> of Burma, of Thailand, of the peninsula and Indonesia. . . . It turns the so-called
> defensive chain of Japan, Formosa, of the Philippines and to the southward; it
> moves in to threaten Australia and New Zealand . . . that region Japan must have
> as a trading area.
>
> Dwight Eisenhower, April 7, 1954, press conference

The first expression of the domino analogy occurred just prior to the dramatic defeat of French forces at Dien Bien Phu.[16] More than a year before the press conference where Eisenhower enunciated the domino theory, the essence of the idea was stated quite clearly by Secretary of State John Foster Dulles. On January 23, 1953, he pronounced the new administration's view of the situation in Asia:

> The Soviet Russians are making a drive to get Japan, not only through what they
> are doing in Korea but also through what they are doing in Indochina. If they
> could get this peninsula of Indochina, Siam, Burma, and Malaya, they would
> have what is called the Rice Bowl of Asia.[17]

Thus, Soviet control of the rice bowl, Dulles added, would lead to Soviet control of Japan and India as well. Richard Nixon, then vice-president, elabo-rated months later. Beginning with the phrase "if Indochina falls . . . ," Nixon explained that Thailand, Malaya (with its rubber and tin), and Indonesia would be helpless.[18] When Eisenhower first used the analogy of falling dominoes to justify American intervention in Vietnam, the logic and rhetoric was already part and parcel of the administration's *Zeitgeist*. He too referred to the region's raw materials, "tin, tungsten, [and] rubber," in relation to Japan's needs.[19]

Nixon reiterated the same perspective several days later but with a new twist. His warning of direct military intervention, the first of its kind, was perhaps a rhetorical probe or trial balloon. "It is hoped that the U.S. will not have to send troops there but if this government cannot avoid it, the administration must face up to the situation and dispatch forces. . . . If Indochina went Communist, Red pressures would increase on Malaya, Thailand, and Indonesia and other Asian nations. The main target of the Communists in Indochina, as it was in Korea, is Japan. Conquest of areas so vital to Japan's economy would reduce Japan to an economic satellite of the Soviet Union."[20] Later, Eisenhower rebuffed the notion that U.S. forces would supplant the French, but the rationale for intervention was in place.

Disregarding the spirit of the Geneva accords that at least allowed the French to evacuate the region, the Eisenhower administration enthusiastically moved into the vacuum. Extravagant American economic aid and political assist-ance formally divided Vietnam by helping to create a new state under Ngo Dinh Diem. It was never to be a peaceful state. The organization of a subversive political force, The National Liberation Front, encouraged by Hanoi, and a resuscitated Vietminh (renamed, pejoratively, the Vietcong) occurred in the years leading up to John F. Kennedy's election.

Surprisingly, it was not Vietnam, but Laos, that most worried the outgoing president in 1961. Eisenhower's last-minute advice to the young president-elect was to use American power to prevent the fall of Laos—"the key to the entire area of Southeast Asia." Warning that "if Laos were to fall to the Communists, then it would just be a question of time until South Vietnam, Cambodia, Thailand, and Burma would collapse," Ike implicitly seemed to acknowledge the tenuous accomplishments of U.S. political intervention during his previous eight years in office.[21]

THE SECOND PHASE: "IF VIETNAM FALLS . . ."

Diplomatic initiatives and covert activities defused the 1961 crisis in Laos but the political situation in Vietnam rapidly deteriorated. John F. Kennedy and his advisers introduced new "flexible" techniques such as Special Forces (Green Berets), chemical agents, and helicopters. They defined the political conflict in Vietnam as predominantly a military problem. Not only the burgeoning guerrilla insurgency but the fact that it elicited overt diplomatic encouragement and limited, surreptitious aid from Beijing and Moscow led Washington to assume that this war of liberation, above all others, might be a model for Communist insurgencies elsewhere. Indeed, Soviet and Chinese leaders encouraged this idea. Vo Nguyen Giap, the Vietnamese hero of Dien Bien Phu, explicitly projected a kind of domino theory from the other side: "If the special warfare that the U.S. imperialists are testing in South Vietnam is overcome, then it can be defeated everywhere in the world."[22] Thus by the early 1960s there were magnified "mirror images" of Vietnam's strategic significance.[23] In the minds of Cold War adversaries, Vietnam became a test case, despite the fact it was a unique situation. Although it initially had little to do with the Cold War, the significance of the conflict in Vietnam was widely exaggerated.

Some have alleged that Kennedy initially had doubts about the domino theory. However, there is little in his record as legislator or president to support that view. He was surrounded by advisers who assumed that Vietnam was a vital strategic link in the region. In his public rhetoric he totally embraced the metaphor of dominoes. Back in 1956 he had called Vietnam "the cornerstone of the free world in Southeast Asia . . . the finger in the dike."[24]

Kennedy's most influential adviser was, arguably, Secretary of Defense Robert McNamara. McNamara's November 1961 memorandum to Kennedy expressed his enthusiasm for the domino metaphor. "The joint chiefs, Mr. Gilpatrick, and I have reached the following conclusions: the fall of South Vietnam to Communism would lead to the fairly rapid extension of Communist control, or complete accommodation to Communism, in the rest of Southeast Asia and in Indochina. The strategic implications worldwide . . . would be extremely serious."[25]

Vice-President Lyndon Johnson's orientation to foreign-policy issues was even less sophisticated than was Kennedy's. Johnson was sent on a highly publicized fact-finding mission to Saigon in 1961. His conclusions were not startling, but characteristic of the Cold War hyperbole of the 1960s. "Asian Communism is compromised and contained by the maintenance of the free nations on the subcontinent. Without this inhibitory influence the island outposts—Philippines, Japan, Taiwan—have no security and the vast Pacific becomes a Red Sea."[26]

Kenney's last warnings before his assassination were monotonous affirmations of the domino metaphor: "If we withdraw, the Communists would control Vietnam, pretty soon Thailand, Cambodia, Laos, Malaya, would go, and all of Southeast Asia would be under the control of the Communists, the Chinese. If South Vietnam went, it would not only give them [China] an improved geographic position for an assault on Malaysia, but it would also give the impression that the wave of the future in Southeast Asia was China and the Communists. So I do believe it."[27]

During the Kennedy and Johnson administrations the formulation of the domino theory that was most often expressed predicted a mechanistic sequence of military events that was rather simplistic. Virtually no economic variables were stressed as they had been during Eisenhower's administration. Subsequently, the economies of Indochina were ravaged by conflict and inflation. Bombing eventually destroyed most of the industrial base in North Vietnam. In the South, rubber plantations were eliminated. A nation that had exported rice became dependent upon foodstuffs imported from abroad. By the end of the decade even America's economy was being undermined by the war. Wall Street investors were especially encouraged by diplomatic initiatives to end the conflict.[28] Many radical critics who assumed the war was "imperialistic" in a Leninist sense would have been surprised by the economic naivete of American leaders throughout the decade.

Back in 1964, President Lyndon Johnson asked the CIA to analyze the domino theory itself. The CIA response was that "with the possible exception of Cambodia it is likely that no nation in the area would quickly succumb to Communists as a result of the fall of Laos and South Vietnam."[29] Although the sparsely populated, fragile state of Laos would inevitably be dominated by a united Vietnam, Sihanouk's Cambodia was a more stable system during the 1960s. Cambodia was economically viable with the capability to feed itself. Prince Norodom Sihanouk's adroit, nonaligned diplomacy kept his country out of the war. The CIA anslysis did not anticipate the long duration of conflict in the region and the significant changes that occurred at the end of the decade. By then Sihanouk's accommodation to increasingly intrusive North Vietnamese military units and Richard Nixon's secret bombing of Cambodia (in 1969) led to intense opposition to Sihanouk's government in Phnom Penh. Cambodia then began to unravel. The 1970 coup by disgruntled military officers quickly led to an invasion by American and ARVN (South Vietnamese) troops. That incursion and subsequent bombing operations facilitated the growth of a Marxist (Khmer Rouge) insurrection. Previously the Khmer Rouge had been a negligible force. Sihanouk, in an effort to regain power, lent his name to the rebel cause. The pro-U.S. junta, led by Lon Nol, was corrupt and ineffectual. The ultimate victory of the radical Maoist clique resulted in the murder and starvation of over a million people. Under the leadership of Pol Pot and the Khmer Rouge, what was left of Cambodia's traditional social order was ravaged in the renamed state of Kampuchea.

Some critics, such as William Shawcross, argue that Cambodia's devastation was America's fault. It resulted from a self-fulfilling American prophesy, a consequence rather than validation of the domino theory.[30] Others such as Henry Kissinger would later argue that the penetration of North Vietnamese and Viet Cong forces into Cambodia's interior during the late 1960s was the primary cause of the horrendous genocide that occurred under the Khmer Rouge.[31] Ironically perhaps, the same Hanoi leadership that precipitated the U.S. intervention and the collapse of Sihanouk's regime, itself intervened in 1978 to oust Pol Pot's pro-Chinese government. A pro-Soviet, Vietnamese hegemony then prevailed in Indochina.

The 1964 CIA analysis represents the only internal study of the domino theory extant during the Vietnam war. Its conclusion, that "a continuation of the spread of Communism in the area would not be inexorable," clearly disparaged the use of the domino metaphor.[32] The analysis was balanced. Evidently, the study was ignored.

On the other hand, there were deliberate efforts to bolster the myth. One government claim was that the U.S. presence in Vietnam encouraged right-wing elements to squelch a planned Communist coup in Indochina in 1964. Bernard Brody and others disparaged such propaganda.[33] There was simply no evidence to support it.

As an outsider and prominent spokesman for the Republican party, Richard Nixon enthusiastically supported the intensification of U.S. military operations in Vietnam, warning that a victory for the Vietcong "would mean ultimately the destruction of freedom of speech for all men for all time, not only in Asia but in the United States as well."[34] One of his many statements from that period is worth repeating here, particularly in light of his subsequent efforts to rationalize developments that occurred after the war ended.

> On the fate of South Vietnam depends the fate of all of Asia. For South Vietnam is the dam in the river. A Communist victory there would mean inevitably and soon that the flood would begin; next would come the loss of Laos, Cambodia, Thailand, Malaysia and Indonesia, which is only 45 miles from the Philippines and next door to Australia. Can anyone seriously suggest that in such a circumstance the United States would not have to engage in a major war to save the Philippines from the same fate as Vietnam? And what of Japan? . . .
>
> Overnight, the United States would cease to be a power on the world's greatest ocean. Our ships and planes could thereafter circumnavigate the globe only with Communist permission . . . Encouraged by our retreat the Communists will increase their aggressive action not only in Asia but in Africa, Latin America, and the Near East.[35]

Was Vietnam inevitably hostile to U.S. interests? Historically the Vietnamese had been the most assertive, expansionist population in Indochina, a fact that had nothing to do with Communist ideology. Ho Chi Minh was a popular nationalistic leader, albeit authoritarian, and a committed Marxist. Given his personal history he might have been enthusiastic about commerce and diplomacy with the United States had Truman or even Eisenhower accepted his legitimacy. We will never know. But given the *Weltanschauung* of the first two decades of the Cold War, Ho was presumed to be a Soviet "puppet" by such people as Acheson and Dulles. Centuries of conflict between Vietnam and China were irrelevant given the dearth of solid Asian expertise and the ahistorical perspective of policy-makers in Washington.

During the mid-1960s American media elites and thus the general public seemed to endorse the domino theory. Even influential journalists such as Neil Sheehan and David Halberstam, who were critical of military tactics, reiterated the premises behind U.S. intervention. Sheehan, for instance, argued that "the fall of Southeast Asia to China . . . would amount to a strategic disaster."[36] Halberstam viewed Vietnam as "a strategic country in a key area, . . . perhaps one of only five or six nations [that is] truly vital to U.S. interests. Withdrawal means that throughout the world, enemies of the West will be encouraged to try insurgencies like the one in Vietnam."[37]

By the time the United States began to commit itself to a major military effort, the demise of monolithic Communism, particularly the Sino-Soviet split, was highly publicized and widely appreciated. Only a few high-level officials in Washington could ignore that reality. Some, such as Secretary of State Dean Rusk, seemed preoccupied with China rather than with the Soviet Union. The spread of China's influence and Communist ideology in Asia was seen as a grave threat to U.S. security, no less so than it would be if it were under the influence of a Stalinist regime in Moscow. The split between China and the Soviet Union was recognized, but it didn't matter.

Not until the split almost erupted in open warfare (and involved sporadic violence along the Sino-Soviet frontier) did U.S. policymakers come to view it as an opportunity. Nixon and Kissinger then believed it could be exploited for broad strategic purposes as well as to extricate U.S. forces from Vietnam. They began to play what became known as the "China card" in 1970, initiating a process of rapprochement with Beijing, in an effort to increase their leverage in Moscow. Realistically the Soviet Union was perceived as the primary threat to American security; thus China was potentially an ally.

Soviet military aid to Hanoi had been insignificant prior to the Gulf of Tonkin "crisis" and even well after it. Back in the late 1940s Stalin had refused to recognize Hanoi's government. Ho Chi Minh's failure to get significant help from the Soviet Union in the late 1950s, with Khrushchev even willing to accept the admission of South Vietnam into the United Nations, was hardly acknowledged in Washington. Thus another kind of self-fulfilling prophesy unfolded in regard to Soviet involvement.[38]

Only gradually was U.S. support to Diem and his successors in Saigon countered by Soviet military aid to North Vietnam. By the late 1960s, anti-aircraft weapons, particularly surface-to-air missiles (SAMs) as well as other conventional arms, became more and more indispensable to Hanoi's war effort. Although Moscow's contribution to North Vietnam (and the total combined assistance from Communist states, including China) never approached the massive level of U.S. aid to South Vietnam, it allowed some level of protection from U.S. bombing raids over North Vietnam. The total value of arms imports to North Vietnam surpassed $1 billion only in 1972. Over the next two years combined Soviet military aid totaled less than $300 million, far less than the United States sent to Saigon during that anticlimactic period.[39]

Soviet aid certainly made the Spring 1972 offensive possible. It was Russian tanks that were used in that major North Vietnamese operation, which occurred four years after the Tet offensive. It was the last major watershed in the military struggle. After that offensive was repulsed by Nixon's bold actions, both sides made major concessions. For the first time since the second Indochina war had begun, the antagonists made serious efforts to negotiate a cease-fire in the South.[40]

The domino theory was subjected to intensive criticism after the initiation of sustained bombing operations over North Vietnam and the introduction of U.S. combat forces in the South. Thereafter, myth was rebutted by several prestigious, authoritative intellectuals. Highly respected political scientist Hans Morgenthau argued "the so-called domino theory was a slogan born of fear and of a misconception . . . unsupported by any historic evidence."[41] A specialist in the history of the region, George Kahin, argued that the rationalization was absurd in light of historical tensions between China and Vietnam.[42] Most significantly, the author of "containment" policy himself protested that his overall notion of U.S. strategy direction vis-à-vis the Soviet Union was perverted by an overemphasis on military aspects of containment. George Kennan told the Fulbright committee: "It is difficult to believe that any decisive developments in the world situation would be influenced by the unification of Vietnam under Ho Chi Minh."[43]

Although American policymakers seemed most concerned about China during the 1960s, the policy of escalation led, ironically, to the spread of Soviet influence. In Southeast Asia no dominos fell beyond Indochina itself.[44]

"IF AMERICA WITHDRAWS . . .": THE LAST PHASE

By the time Richard Nixon became Commander in Chief, purportedly with a secret plan to get the United States out of Southeast Asia, the war in Vietnam was a political disaster at home. The mounting American casualties, the sense of military stalemate, an increasingly negative international reaction, and climactically, the traumatic effect of the first days of the Tet offensive, made the war too costly for many Americans to support. Moreover, the domino theory had lost much of its plausibility as an effective justification to continue the war. Increasingly the official rationale for the ongoing military effort emphasized concerns that previously had been implicit, if not secondary. In effect, the domino theory was superseded by warnings of a "bloodbath" in the event of a U.S. withdrawal and, finally, a general "humiliation" of the United States if it failed to stay the course in Vietnam.

The bloodbath predicted if and when U.S. forces withdrew was a powerful argument. On one hand, tales of thousands of atrocities that occurred in North Vietnam after the Geneva accords, although greatly exaggerated, were widely accepted. Even more salient were credible reports of approximately 3,000 murders that occurred while the Communists occupied the city of Hue during the first weeks of the Tet offensive in 1968. When approximately a million desperate Vietnamese fled and many perished at sea in the years after the war, many saw the bloodbath thesis validated. Some Americans also viewed the genocide in Cambodia as *post hoc* evidence for America's military commitment in Southeast Asia.

The last reformulation of the domino theory emphasized the fear of humiliation and its general consequences that came to the fore during the Nixon and Ford years. But this had been a real concern as early as 1965. It was first expressed quietly in John McNaughton's memo to Robert McNamara, later revealed only because of the unauthorized publication of the *Pentagon Papers*. McNaughton's point was that 70 percent of the U.S. motivation then was probably to avoid a humiliating defeat.[45] One interpretation suggests a grotesque irony: American officials confronting an Asian enemy often stereotyped as having less regard for human life and too much concern for "saving face," subsequently dispatched hundreds of thousands of American troops, over 50,000 of whom would die, primarily to avoid a "humiliating" loss of face.

Henry Kissinger's formulation of the domino theory was grounded in a balance of power perspective and a concern for America's reputation abroad. Even before he was appointed Richard Nixon's National Security Adviser, Kissinger warned that a "victory by a third-class Communist peasant state over the United States will strengthen the most bellicose factions in the internecine Communist struggle around the world. We are fighting for ourselves and for international stability."[46] Although he acknowledged the disintegration of monolithic Communism, Kissinger implied that the humbling of America's military image would be disastrous to world order. (During the war he was vague about what specific disasters might occur, but when reversals later occurred in Ethiopia, Angola, and Iran he was quick to suggest that they were the inevitable dominoes.)

Implicitly, the prospect of defeat suggested specific political consequences in Washington. As James Thomson, a National Security Council staffer, put it: "The final domino in the domino sequence is not some Asian country. It is the President himself."[47] The insight was logical. Certainly no president wanted to lose Vietnam while he was in office; to do so would be politically disastrous to the party in power. Nixon acknowledged such concerns yet denied his own vulnerability to presidential politics in April 1970. His effort to justify the invasion of Cambodia provided what is perhaps his best-remembered statement on the war. "If when the chips are down the world's most powerful nation—the

United States of America—acts like a pitiful helpless giant, the forces of totalitarianism and anarchy will threaten the world. . . . I would rather be a one-term President than see America become a second-rate power and . . . accept the first defeat in its proud 190-year history."[48]

The humiliation of an incumbent administration was thus both a domestic and a diplomatic concern. Daniel Ellsberg was perhaps the first to enunciate the argument that Washington never really anticipated the possibility of "victory" in Vietnam, yet democratic politics compelled the president to avoid a defeat. Ellsberg called it the "stalemate thesis."[49] His analysis disparaged genuine optimism on the part of leaders such as Johnson, Nixon, and General Westmoreland, all of whom at various stages clearly expressed (and seemed to believe) the possibility of an American military victory in Vietnam. Leslie Gelb and Richard K. Betts also argued that "the [democratic] system worked" in that respect. Most recently, Gelb argued that the "essential domino" was public opinion.[50] Their point was that a lack of patience on the part of Americans, exacerbated by the unprecedented duration of a war with heavy casualties, made it impossible for the United States to succeed militarily.

Throughout his political life Richard Nixon's tendency toward hyperbole was always extreme. Nonetheless, there is no reason to disbelieve his often repeated faith that Vietnam and Indochina were of enormous strategic importance to the security of the United States. As vice-president, perennial presidential candidate, as president, and even as president emeritus, Nixon expressed an unwavering belief that America's intervention in Vietnam was vitally necessary. Even as late as 1972 he probably believed, as Bernard Brody persuasively argued, that the United States could "win" militarily.[51]

Nixon's policy of "Vietnamization" was arrived at through trial and error. Direct negotiations with Hanoi, simultaneous phased withdrawals of American armed forces from Vietnam, and punishing bombing raids, which had a Clausewitzian as well as a tactical orientation, were the essence of his approach. What is noteworthy again is that Nixon did not make a major concession in negotiations with Vietnam until May 1972. Before then he expected Hanoi to respond to Soviet or Chinese diplomatic pressures if not American military initiatives.

Nixon's promise to support President Nguyen Van Thieu in the event that the 1973 cease-fire arrangement broke down suggests Nixon's conviction that an anti-Communist regime in Saigon might be preserved indefinitely.[52] He was wrong. The Treaty of Paris proved even less politically viable than the Geneva agreements 19 years earlier.

Kissinger, along with Nixon's designated successor, Gerald Ford, alluded to dominoes in a last desperate effort to gain congressional support for increased aid to Cambodia in 1975. "If we have one country after another—allies of the United States—losing faith in our word . . . the first one to go could vitally affect the national security of the United States,"[53] President Ford stated.

During the 1980s, attempts to revive the domino theory and revitalize its logic with new metaphors had limited success. Ronald Reagan's effort to reverse the consolidation of Nicaragua's revolution under the Sandinista government was most noteworthy. "We are the last domino," Reagan said in 1980, although by 1986 the metaphor of spreading cancer was used in his presidential warning that to "ignore the malignancy in Managua will allow its spread and become a mortal threat to the entire New World."[54] The "Kissinger Commission," allegedly bipartisan, had also warned of the prospect that "other countries of Central America" would fall after Nicaragua, bringing with it the spectre of the Marxist domination of the entire region."[55]

AFTERMATH: THE EFFORTS TO PROVE THE DOMINO THEORY

The most vigorous defenders of the domino theory, Nixon and Kissinger, remained steadfast in their conviction that history had proven them correct. "It is fashionable, today, to deride the domino theory, but any sophisticated observer of foreign policy recognizes that on the world scene when one domino falls others do not fall immediately or even adjacently. What happens is more like a move in chess than a move in checkers."[56] So far, so good, one might respond to Nixon, although he certainly had implied that a game like checkers was in progress during the mid-1960s. Nixon's formulation reiterated Kissinger's words uttered back in 1978: "I know it is fashionable to sneer at the words *domino theory.*" Both argued essentially that, during the postwar period, events beyond Indochina confirmed their worst fears. Kissinger stated that "the much maligned domino theory . . . turned out be correct."[57] Nixon warned:

> Our defeat sparked a rash of totalitarian conquests around the world as we retreated into a five-year, self-imposed exile. In crisis after crisis in Africa, the Mideast, and Central America, critics of American involvement abroad brandished "another Vietnam" like a scepter, an all-purpose argument stopper. . . . While we rung our hands and agonized over our mistakes, over 100 million people were lost to the west in the vacuum left by our withdrawal from the world stage.[58]

For a period of several years after the war, American interests were indeed set back by developments in Ethiopia, Angola, Iran, South Yemen, and Nicaragua. But China was not the beneficiary. On the other hand, Soviet influence was extended as a result of chance and opportunism. Almost all of the setbacks were blamed on the so-called Vietnam syndrome and the Carter administration's vacilation. In the last month of 1979, the USSR invaded Afghanistan. That event and the 1980 "hostage crisis," when over 50 Americans were held captive in the U.S. embassy in Teheran, encouraged an assertive, nationalistic mood associated with Ronald Reagan's election. As time passes, these complex developments may be less difficult to analyze from a global perspective. Two questions are relevant here: Would those developments have occurred had the United States maintained an anti-Communist government in Saigon? Second, was the restraint of U.S. policymakers who responded to those disparate events appropriate?

Internal upheavals that occurred in Ethiopia, Iran, and Nicaragua seemed, arguably, well beyond America's capacity to manage politically. In the first case, the establishment of a Marxist regime in Ethiopia precipitated the loss of a major U.S. strategic communications intercept facility. By the middle of the decade a strong Soviet and Cuban presence was established there. Never did Washington policymakers express a sense that U.S. intervention could prevent or reverse those developments.

In the populist revolution that deposed the Shah of Iran in 1979, there was an enormous backlash against the United States, particularly against policies that the Nixon administration had intensified early in the decade. The Soviets did not benefit directly from the expulsion of Americans in Iran, but it was a traumatic loss to U.S. policymakers. The Soviet Union did benefit from a 1978 coup in South Yemen. The Soviets also increased their influence in both Angola and Nicaragua. The intervention of Cuban troops in Angola ensured the 1976 triumph of a Marxist faction as Congress precluded any resuscitation of U.S. covert actions there. Assuming that such operations could have counterbalanced Soviet military initiatives with tens of thousands of Cuban proxies, this situation was perhaps the most plausible argument that the backlash from defeat in Vietnam caused a domino to fall far beyond Indochina. There was little possibility that American troops or surrogates, analogous to Cuban forces, could have successfully intervened in Angola, especially with South African soldiers already supporting the anti-Marxist faction there. Similarly, direct U.S. interventions in Nicaragua and Iran were unlikely options (given the lack of any evidence that policymakers discussed such alternatives). When, during the last month of the decade, the USSR intervened directly in neighboring Afghanistan, the Soviets were impervious to American threats. That aggression ultimately proved damaging to the mismanaged Soviet economy and the inflated image of the Red Army as well as devastating to Afghanistan itself.

In retrospect, American interests suffered short-term losses over a span of five years after Vietnam. Because of those losses, some believed that the domino theory had been validated. But to which version did they refer? In those cases that represented setbacks to U.S. interests, there were very few opportunities that had a reasonable potential for the effective utilization of American threats, much less force. As William Bundy's analysis of international developments during the 1970s concluded: "In no case was there a reasonably clear-cut or promising use-of-force option as the situation stood at the time for decision."[59]

Nixon's argument that "our defeat in Vietnam paralyzed America's will to act," encouraging aggression in the Third World and "causing stunning reversals" over the subsequent five years, was overly simplistic.[60] Certainly America's capacity to intervene was circumscribed by years of exasperating stalemate in Vietnam. This was evident even by 1973, with the passage of the War Powers Act. By then America's defeat, as such, was almost superfluous. As for aggression and subsequent "stunning reversals" to U.S. interests, they might well have happened if the United States had prevailed in Vietnam, an unlikely outcome at best.

CONCLUSIONS

Joseph Schumpeter's thoughts about the mind-set of Roman policymakers[61] suggests a tendency toward exaggeration that characterized Washington elites throughout much of the Cold War. As a rationalization, the domino theory was plausible because it was based on truisms that transcended Cold War politics. The myth that one's most threatening adversaries "only understand the language of force" seems universal. Significant shifts in big-power relationships with lesser states do cause adversaries to reassess their policies. Sometimes they encourage additional political initiatives in contiguous areas. In a shrinking world of mass communications technology the sequence or chain of reactions to dramatic events may be very widespread. But political behavior is unpredictable, motivated by nationalism, insecurity, ideology, and a variety of complex considerations. Unfortunately, there may always be a tendency for moralistic leaders with a balance-of-power political perspective to misperceive distant, unique circumstances. The logic of intervention by powerful states persists, whatever the metaphors.

The militarization of containment policy led to commitments in many places where no American interests initially were at stake. One implicit assumption was that leaders in Moscow (and later Beijing) had a strategic plan, not simply an ideological motivation, to establish Communist states everywhere in the world. That assumption ensured a zero-sum-game mentality. One apologia published a dozen years after Nixon left the presidency implicitly expressed that assumption: Referring to a lesson he learned from former Soviet spy Whitaker Chambers and the latter's observation that "for the Communists the war in Korea is not about Korea, it is a war about Japan," Nixon went on to say, "I tried to analyze the war in Vietnam the same way [it] was not just about Vietnam, but about Cambodia, Laos, Indonesia, Angola, Ethiopia and Nicaragua."[62] With hindsight, the loss of all but one of those countries now seems less significant; the relatedness of developments in those countries (apart from Indochina) is even less apparent. There was indeed opportunism on the part of America's adversaries, but also limited coordination and, almost certainly, no plan.

America's longest war was followed by the Khmer Rouge devastation of Cambodia; Vietnam's 1978 invasion and occupation of that country; China's military incursion into Vietnam in 1979; economic stagnation, political repression, and unprecedented mass emigration from the region. Soviet influence pervades what was Indochina. All of these developments were shaped by a variety of factors in addition to U.S. intervention.

Now Vietnam is peripheral to American security interests, just as it was prior to the war. The entire peninsula of Indochina is insignificant to the American economy and even, for the moment, to Japan's. One of many ironies now is that Japan and the United States, with competitive economies, may vie for Indochina's resources and markets in the near future. Whatever the outcome of such competition, it is hardly critical to either country's national survival.

There is no denying that Americans experienced a crisis of confidence in their political institutions and their sense of global purpose during the years following Saigon's fall. Some "lessons" have been institutionalized.[63] Legislation to restrict covert operations and limit presidential war-making powers is still in effect from that period, although sometimes ignored. The so-called Weinberger Doctrine sets Pentagon restraints on military initiatives abroad. Policymakers are less likely to squander resources in an effort to control complex events in far-off lands.

No doubt much of what happened through defeat was educational and beneficial to the American people in general. Presumably, the public is less susceptible to the lure of domino-like logic. The limitations of militaristic super-power politics were demonstrated in Afghanistan as well. Americans now have a more realistic perspective on the limited military and economic capabilities of the USSR as well as their own country. With the advent of Mikhail Gorbachev's major effort to reform the Soviet system, Americans are even less likely to support a militarized containment policy in remote, obscure places.

The domino theory, as it was initially expressed, proved to be false; nonetheless, because it was redefined, almost imperceptibly, during the war, it not only endured but also seemed validated by the outcome of the conflict. The myth of the domino theory had a life of its own, sustaining a web of images, events, and the political culture of America during the Cold War.

Myths may generate self-fulfilling prophecies as well as consequences quite different from the ones they proclaim. So it was with America's domino theory. That myth was ahistorical in perspective and implied a prescience about international events that has never been justified. As "theory" it was always shoddy. Perhaps, as George Moss has written, the last domino to fall was America's mythic conception of its destiny.[64] Even so, historians may come to view the Vietnam war more as a symptom than as a significant cause of America's decline as a dominant superpower.

Beyond Indochina, no specific predictions of falling dominoes ever came to pass. Less than two decades after an unprecedented defeat, there are widespread perceptions that America's national insecurity has much less to do with the spread of Communism or specifically the Soviet military threat than before. In relation to those perceived threats, the United States now seems more secure—especially in light of the recent astonishing developments within the USSR and Eastern Europe that were not anticipated. Problems at home, such as widespread drug abuse, crime, and environmental pollution, now seem far more ominous. One might guess that emerging myths about these threats may have already begun to mislead American policymakers.

NOTES

1. For example, see Joseph Campbell, *Primitive Mythology: The Masks of God* (New York's Viking/ Penguin Books, 1959), p. 4. The term describes a well-known, sacred narrative which links supernatural, spiritual beliefs to empirically observed conditions within a given culture. So-

cial scientists tend to use the term casually. Most agree that the truth of a myth is irrelevant; widely shared beliefs that represent perceived truths become "myths" because of their social significance.

2. Murray Edelman, *The Symbolic Uses of Politics* (Urbana: University of Illinois, 1964), p. 4.

3. If a (false) belief or expectation leads people to behave in ways that confirm those expectations it is a self-fulfilling prophesy. The concept is associated with sociologist Robert K. Merton, among others. See Jon M. Shepard *Sociology*, 3rd ed. (St. Paul, Minn.: West Publishing Co., 1987), p. 362.

4. Ralph K. White, *Nobody Wanted War: Misperception in Vietnam and Other Wars* (New York: Doubleday/Anchor, 1970), p. 142.

5. Henry T. Nash, *American Foreign Policy: Changing Perspectives on National Security* (Homewood, Ill.: Dorsey Press, 1978), p. 35.

6. The generalization is familiar to Americans in reference to Soviet political leaders. Ironically, a remarkably similar generalization appears in Strobe Talbott's translation of *Krushchev Remembers* (Boston: Little, Brown, 1970) in reference to Chinese leaders (p. 478). It has also been overheard in the rhetoric of Palestinians and Israelis and other sets of enemies. Perhaps it is a universal myth reflected in the mirror images of historical adversaries.

7. H. Bruce Franklin, *War Stars: The Superweapon and the American Imagination* (New York: Oxford University Press, 1988), provides a brilliant overview of America's longstanding preoccupation with technological solutions to complex international problems.

8. George F. Kennan ("X"), "The Sources of Soviet Conduct," *Foreign Affairs* (July 1947), pp. 566–582.

9. Acheson warned, "If the USSR could seize control of Turkey they would almost inevitably extend their control over Greece and Iran. If they controlled Greece, Turkey would sooner or later succumb, with or without a war, and then Iran . . . From (the Eastern Mediterranean and the Middle East) the possibilities for penetration of South Asia and Africa were limitless." See. Joseph M. Jones, *The Fifteen Weeks* (New York: Viking, 1955), p. 140.

10. John G. Stoessinger, *Nations in Darkness: China, Russia, and America*, 3rd ed., revised (New York: Random House, 1981), pp. 58–60.

11. Walter LaFeber, *America, Russia and the Cold War*, 4th ed. (New York: John Wiley, 1980), p. 120.

12. Ibid.

13. U.S. Department of State, *Indochina: The War in Southeast Asia* (Washington, D.C.: 1951), pp. 1–7, cited in Ibid., p. 120.

14. Ibid., p. 110.

15. George C. Herring, *America's Longest War: The United States and Vietnam 1950–1975*, 2nd ed. (New York: Random House, 1986), p. 22.

16. U.S. Government, *Public Papers of the Presidents of the United States: Dwight D. Eisenhower*, 1954 (Washington, D.C.: 1958), pp. 381–390.

17. Department of State *Bulletin*, February 9, 1953, p. 213.

18. Radio and television address, December 23, 1953, in Ibid., January 4, 1954, p. 12.

19. *Public Papers*, Eisenhower.

20. *New York Times*, April 17, 1954, cited in Marvin E. Gettleman and others, *Vietnam and America: A Documented History* (New York: Grove Press, 1985), p. 52.

21. Clark Clifford Memorandum of September 29, 1967, reprinted in Mike Gravel (ed), *The Pentagon Papers*, (Boston: Beacon Press, 1971), Vol. II, pp. 635–637.

22. Cited in White, *Nobody Wanted War*, p. 148.

23. An article by Chinese Marshal Lin Paio in the September 1965 *Foreign Language Press* was viewed as a revolutionary "blueprint for world conquest" by some officials in Washington. Stoessinger, *Nations in Darkness*, pp. 78–79, was perhaps the first to suggest "mirror imagery" in regard to perceptions of the war at that stage.

24. "America's Stake in Vietnam," *Vital Speeches*, 22 (August 1, 1956), pp. 617–619.

25. November 8, 1961 (Memorandum) in *New York Times* edition of the *Pentagon Papers* (New York: Bantam Books, 1971), pp. 148–149.

26. Ibid., p. 128.

27. Gravel (ed.), *Pentagon Papers*, Vol. II, p. 828. Also, the NBC-TV interview with David Brinkley on September 30, 1963.

28. Betty C. Hanson and Bruce Russett, "Testing Some Economic Interpretations of American Intervention: Korea, Indochina and the Stock Market," in Steven J. Rosen and James R. Kurth (eds.), *Testing the Theory of the Military Industrial Complex* (Lexington, Mass.: D.C. Heath, 1974), esp. pp. 240–244.

29. *Pentagon Papers* (*Times* edition), p. 254.

30. William Shawcross, *Sideshow: Kissinger, Nixon, and the Destruction of Cambodia* (New York: Simon & Schuster, Pocket Books, 1979).

31. Henry Kissinger, *Years of Upheaval* (Boston: Little, Brown, 1982), pp. 335–369.

32. *Pentagon Papers*, (*Times* edition), *op cit.*

33. Bernard Brody, *War and Politics* (New York: Macmillan, 1973), pp. 149–150. Shawcross, *Sideshow: Kissinger, Nixon, and the Destruction of Cambodia*.

34. Ibid., p. 153.

35. "Needed in Vietnam: The Will to Win," *Reader's Digest*, August 1964, p. 39.

36. Neil Sheehan, "Much Is At Stake in Southeast Asian Struggle," *New York Times*, August 16, 1964, p. 4E.

37. David Halberstam, *The Making of a Quagmire* (New York: Knopf, 1964), p. 177.

38. Janos Radvanyi's perception was that "Stalin did not trust him (Ho) and Khrushchev despised him." See "Vietnam War Diplomacy: Reflections of a Former Iron Curtain Official," in Lloyd J. Matthews and Dale E. Brown (eds.), *Assessing the Vietnam War* (New York: Permagon-Brassey, 1987), p. 58.

39. Arms Control and Disarmament Agency, *World Military Expenditures and Arms Transfers: 1969–1978*, Publication 108, December 1980, p. 156.

40. Tad Szule, "How Kissinger Did It: Behind the Vietnam Cease-Fire Agreement," *Foreign Policy* 15 (Summer 1974), p. 42.

41. Hans Morgenthau, "Russia, the U.S., and Vietnam," *New Republic* (May 1, 1965), p. 13.

42. Marcus G. Raskin and Bernard B. Fall (eds.), *The Vietnam Reader* (New York: Random House, 1965), p. 294.

43. George F. Kennan, Testimony to the Senate Foreign Relations (Fulbright) Committee: February 10, 1966, in *New Republic* (February 26, 1966), pp. 19–30.

44. Dan Oberdorfer, "Rather Than Fall After Vietnam, the Dominoes Have Prospered," *Washington Post* (National Weekly Edition, August 13, 1984), p. 16.

45. "McNaughton's November Draft . . . ," in *Pentagon Papers* (*Times* ed.), p. 432.

46. "What Should We Do Now?" *Look* (August 9, 1966), pp. 20–22.

47. See "LBJ Goes to War," in *Vietnam: A Television History*, produced by Stanley Karnow for Public Broadcasting System.

48. *The New York Times*, May 1, 1970.

49. "The Quagmire Myth and the Stalemate Machine," *Public Policy* (Spring 1971), pp. 217–274.

50. Leslie Gelb and Richard K. Betts, "Vietnam: The System Worked," in *Foreign Policy* (Summer 1971), pp. 140–167; and "The Essential Domino: American Politics and Vietnam," *Foreign Affairs*, 50 (April 1976), p. 466.

51. Brody, *War and Politics*, pp. 157–222.

52. "Letter From Nixon to Thieu," January 5, 1973, in Gareth Porter (ed.), *Vietnam: A History in Documents* (New York: Meridian, 1981), p. 424.

53. *New York Times,* March 18, 1975, quoted in Nash, *American Foreign Policy,* p. 246.

54. Jerome Slater, "Dominoes in Central America: Will They Fall? Does It Matter?" *International Security,* 12:2 (Fall 1987), pp. 105–134.

55. *New York Times,* March 17, 1986, p. 12 cited in Ibid.

56. Richard Nixon, "Lessons of the Alger Hiss Case," *New York Times,* January 8, 1986, p. A23.

57. Kissinger also wrote that "each new upheaval tends to start a rock slide." In reference to nonaligned states, he stated, "They have seen that Communist advances led by Moscow are irreversible," *For the Record: Selected Statements 1977–1980* (Boston: Little, Brown, 1981), pp. 288, 271.

58. Richard Nixon, *No More Vietnams* (New York: Arbor House, 1985), p. 13.

59. William Bundy, "The Relative Importance of Force," in George K. Osborn and others (eds.), *Democracy, Strategy and Vietnam* (Lexington, Mass.: D.C. Heath, 1987), esp. pp. 219–229.

60. Nixon, *No More Vietnams,* pp. 166, 212.

61. Joseph Schumpeter, *Imperialism and Social Classes* (New York: N.P., 1955), p. 51, cited in Arthur Schlesinger, *The Imperial Presidency* (Boston: Houghton Mifflin, 1973), p. 148.

62. Nixon, "Lessons of the Alger Hiss Case." On the other hand, Kissinger later acknowledged that the premise (of a centralized direction to guerrilla war in Indochina and elsewhere) was "mistaken." See Kissinger, *Years of Upheaval,* p. 82.

63. "The learning of a collective . . . [lesson] must be internalized in some enduring, objective, consistent, and therefore predictable way. They may be institutionalized . . . or take the form of new constraints or conditions that are added to the policy process." Earl C. Ravenal, *Never Again: Learning From America's Foreign Policy Failures* (Philadelphia: Temple University Press, 1978), pp. 27–28.

64. George Moss, *Vietnam: An American Ordeal* (Englewood Cliffs, N.J.: Prentice Hall, 1990), pp. 373–374.

NIXON AND VIETNAM: VIETNAM AND ELECTORAL POLITICS*

by Stephen E. Ambrose

We are privileged to offer, as the second article in our collection, Stephen E. Ambrose's lecture analyzing the ways Richard M. Nixon played politics with the Vietnam war issue during the 1968 and 1972 presidential campaigns. Ambrose's article, initially given as the third in a prestigious biennial series—The Dwight D. Eisenhower Lectures in War and Peace, held at Kansas State University in October 1988—also amounts to a stinging indictment of Nixon's Vietnam policy, a policy that Ambrose suggests only delayed the inevitable U.S. defeat for four years at grave cost in lives and dollars to both the American and Vietnamese people. In addition, Ambrose finds that Nixon's failed effort to achieve "peace with honor" in Vietnam ultimately destroyed his presidency. The genesis of the siege mentality that led to the excesses and scandals of Watergate can be found in Nixon's frustrations arising out of his failure to bring the Vietnam war to a rapid conclusion and to his willingness to countenance ruthless measures to squelch domestic political "enemies."

    Ambrose, who has recently completed the second of a projected three-volume biography of the former president, shows that Nixon did not propose, nor did he have, a "secret plan" for ending the stalemated Vietnam war in 1968. During that year's presidential campaign, Nixon mostly attacked Lyndon Johnson's failed war strategy of graduated escalation and promised, in general terms, that he would end the war and win the peace. On election eve, Nixon, fearful that Hubert H. Humphrey—whose candidacy was enhanced by Johnson's partial bombing halt and

*Source: Dwight D. Eisenhower Lectures in War and Peace, no. 3, © 1988, Department of History, Kansas State University and reprinted with permission.

indication that a peace agreement was imminent—might win the election, tried to sabotage the peace talks. Nixon also falsely accused President Johnson of betraying American soldiers fighting in Vietnam and he lied about North Vietnamese moving troops south after the bombing pause. In fact, according to Ambrose, both Humphrey and Nixon shamelessly played politics with the war during the 1968 campaign "in their single-minded pursuit of personal political victory at any cost." The Vietnam war undermined the democratic political process in 1968; the duplicitous remarks of the candidates denied the American electorate an opportunity to vote meaningfully on the great issue of war and peace.

As president, Nixon, unable to craft an effective war policy, was forced to fall back on Vietnamization, a plan already in place during the final months of Johnson's presidency. Although Nixon did not realize it, Vietnamization was inherently unworkable because the South Vietnamese government, a committee of generals who held power by virtue of their American connections and their willingness to support U.S. policies, could neither govern nor fight effectively on their own no matter how much money, weaponry, training, advice, and encouragement they got from the Americans. Meanwhile, U.S. troop withdrawals, politically necessary to appease domestic public opinion and the Congress, signaled to Hanoi that America did not have the political will either to win the war or to force a compromise settlement. But Nixon's bold use of air power managed to stave off an all-out NVA assault and save the South Vietnamese from conquest in the spring and summer of 1972 despite the withdrawal of most U.S. ground combat forces. The Vietnam stalemate continued and another presidential election approached.

Nixon, hoping to end the war before the 1972 election, in which he ran against George McGovern, made concessions that amounted to capitulation. He agreed to allow the North Vietnamese to keep 150,000 troops in South Vietnam and to accord the Provisional Revolutionary Government of the Vietcong political legitimacy. In addition, the United States would remove all its remaining troops in exchange for a return of the American POWs. The North Vietnamese were quite willing to cut a deal with Nixon because they understood that Washington's terms did not contravene their long-term goal of national reunification. They could tolerate the existence of the South Vietnamese government of Nguyen Van Thieu for a few years.

But General Thieu, who knew that Vietnamization had failed, who knew that his government could not survive an American withdrawal for very long no matter what President Nixon told the American people, refused to accept the settlement. Nixon, pressured by conservative supporters at home to hold out for better terms, supported Thieu. Nixon's special envoy and leading foreign-policy adviser, Henry Kissinger, who wanted Nixon to sign the peace agreement without Thieu's support, complicated Nixon's 1972 reelection efforts. A few days before election day, Kissinger announced that "peace was at hand." Fortunately for Nixon, his Democratic challenger, Senator George McGovern, had mounted an ineffectual campaign and posed no threat to Nixon despite Nixon's failure to end the war. The president told the American people on election eve that, although there would be a delay, a peace agreement, a good peace agreement, was coming soon. Nixon won reelection by an overwhelming landslide.

There followed the Christmas bombing and renewed negotiations. Finally, the Paris accords ending the Vietnam war were signed on January 27, 173. This time Nixon pressured Thieu, still reluctant, into signing. The terms were no better than the ones Thieu and Nixon had rejected in late October, but Nixon, fearing that the new Democratic Congress would soon cut off all funds for continued war in Indochina, took the best deal he could get. What he got, despite the brave rhetorical face that he and Kissinger put upon the Paris agreement, was a disguised defeat, delayed for a couple of years while the North Vietnamese geared themselves up for another offensive that would overwhelm South Vietnam's weak defenses in the aftermath of the U.S. withdrawal. Ambrose implies that Nixon could have gotten the same terms in 1969 and ended the war four years sooner. Some 15,000 additional Americans had to die in Vietnam because Nixon mishandled American policy in Vietnam in a vain effort to capture a chimera called "peace with honor."

When Dwight Eisenhower became President, in January 1953, he inherited an unpopular and expensive Democratic war on the Asian mainland. During the '52 campaign, he had been critical of Harry Truman's handling of the war, but careful not to commit himself on how he would conduct it. His options, once elected, were open. The Republicans, led by Vice President Richard Nixon, urged him to either march to the Yalu River with a reinforced U.N. army, or use atomic weapons against China. Instead, Ike decided that Korea was not worth the cost and the risk, and made peace within six months of taking office.

When Nixon became President, in January 1969, he inherited an unpopular and expensive Democratic war on the Asian mainland. During the '68 campaign, he had been critical of Lyndon Johnson's handling of the war, but careful not to commit himself on how he would conduct it. Unlike Ike in Korea, he had played a major role in getting America involved in Vietnam. Also unlike Ike, he could not threaten the Communists with escalation if they did not accept an armistice, because the Soviets could match him bomb for bomb in nuclear warfare, while on the ground he had to accept the fact that the American political system could not stand the strain of a larger war.

Nixon had to retreat. It was his fate, and a big part of his tragedy. For twenty years, he had been the most prominent and persistent advocate of taking the offensive against Communism around the world. In every crisis, his policy was to attack, with more firepower, now.

But in 1969 he had to preside over a retreat. He knew it, he accepted the fact, made his decision, and although he hated doing so, announced in June 1969, that a retreat was underway.

Fifteen years earlier, at a Cabinet meeting, during a discussion of a bill before Congress, Nixon had turned to Eisenhower and said, "As in any battle, you need a second line of retreat."

"No, Dick," Ike had replied. "You need two to attack, only one to retreat."

If Dick had chosen that single line, and gone about it with more dispatch, much would have been different. Suppose that in the summer of 1969 Nixon had withdrawn all American troops, as he finally did in early 1973. Think of the effect on the economy, on inflation, on the campuses, on the media's attitude towards Nixon, on a lasting detente and arms control and Nixon's whole structure of peace, on law and order (in and out of the White House), on everything. Think of the things that would not have happened—no Cambodian incursion, no Kent State tragedy, no 4 A.M. meeting with students at the Lincoln Memorial, no anti-war demonstrations, no Christmas bombing.

But all these things did happen, because Nixon mishandled the retreat, stretching it out at a terrible price in lives and treasure and his own reputation. Because the war went on, tension and division filled the land, and the Nixon-bashers went into a frenzy. It was the continuation of the Vietnam War that prepared the ground and provided the nourishment for the Watergate seed, which without the Vietnam war would never have sprouted.

It was fitting, however, that Vietnam was the ultimate cause of Nixon's downfall, because except for LBJ no other political leader in the nation had done so much to put America into Vietnam. The process began way back in 1954, when Nixon told Eisenhower he should use atomic weapons to rescue the French at Dien Bien Phu. When Ike refused, Nixon told a press conference that if sending American boys to Vietnam was the only way to prevent a Communist victory, "I personally would support such a decision." Ike would not, and a Communist North Vietnam was born at Geneva in 1954. Nixon then became the leading advocate of creating SEATO and extending its protection to South Vietnam.

Ten years and many events later, the South Vietnamese were under attack and demanding that America live up to its promises to provide protection. Nixon was in the forefront of those American politicians urging an all-out response. Through the first half of the sixties, Nixon was the number one critic of JFK's and LBJ's Vietnam policy, his criticism was not that they were getting involved, but rather that they were not getting involved deeply or quickly enough. And long before Johnson ever opened peace talks with the North Vietnamese, Nixon had denounced any and all possible negotiations as a disguised surrender. When Nixon later said, in 1969, that he had inherited a war not of his making, he was being too modest. From the time of the Gulf of Tonkin Resolution onward, Nixon spurred Johnson to ever greater involvement in Vietnam.

As Johnson escalated through 1965, Nixon stayed one step ahead of him, demanding more—more troops, more bombing raids, more firepower. He accused Johnson of allowing America to get "bogged down" in a long and costly ground war and said that military commanders should be allowed to bomb targets in and around Hanoi, and to put mines in Haiphong harbor.

In December 1965, Nixon published an article in *Reader's Digest* on the specifics of the war in Vietnam and on the general problem of how to relate to aggressive Communism in Asia.

Nixon said he would negotiate only on the basis of three minimum conditions; that North Vietnam stop its aggression; that South Vietnam's freedom and independence be guaranteed; that there be "no substitute for victory." In other words, no negotiations. Nixon was explicit on this point: "To negotiate in Vietnam would be negotiation of the wrong kind, at the wrong time, at the wrong place." To negotiate with the Viet Cong or North Vietnamese before driving them out of South Vietnam "would be like negotiating with Hitler before the German armies had been driven from France."

All this led up to Nixon's rock solid position on negotiations: "We should negotiate only when our military superiority is so convincing that we can achieve our objective at the conference table." To most people, that sounded more like a surrender than a conference table.

Nixon was as one with President Johnson on the question of what was at stake. "If the United States gives up on Vietnam,"Nixon wrote in the *Digest*, "the Pacific Ocean will become a Red Sea." He explained that "the true enemy behind the Viet Cong and North Vietnam is China. . . . If Vietnam is lost, Red China would gain vast new power." Indonesia, Thailand, Cambodia, and Laos would "inevitably fall under communist domination." Red China would be "only 14 miles from the Philippines and less than 100 miles from Australia."

But with a small investment now, in South Vietnam, America could hold the Reds back. Nixon wrote that the tide had turned in Vietnam, and "a real victory" was now possible. It would "take two years or more of the hardest kind of fighting. It will require stepped-up air and land attacks."

Thus, Nixon at the end of 1965 was harkening back to the war of his youth, using images and symbols and a basic frame of reference from World War II to describe and think about Vietnam. For Nixon, victory was possible. It was a question of will. He called for escalation, immediate and decisive.

Johnson then launched the great search and destroy offensive of 1966–1967, as General Westmoreland's force expanded to over a half-million men. But in late January, 1968, at Tet, the Communists launched a counter-offensive. They took fearful losses, but they nevertheless achieved their objective of making it obvious that the Americans were not winning, that the massive influx of American weapons and men into Vietnam had not turned the tide. And the panic reaction of the press, television, and the public all indicated that John Kennedy had been wrong when he said back in January, 1961, that the United States would "pay any price, bear any burden" to insure the survival of freedom, in Vietnam and elsewhere. There were limits, and they had quite possibly been reached, to what the Americans would pay, to the burden they would bear. Meanwhile, Johnson's policy of escalating the war while extending the Great Society programs while refusing to raise taxes to pay for either was threatening to create runaway inflation along with uncontrollable deficits.

In sum, the policy Nixon had advocated relentlessly for the past four years fell apart almost at the exact time he began his formal campaign for the Presidency. He needed time to think of a new approach.

His staff, however, was pressing him, insisting that *he* had to speak out on Vietnam. Herbert Brownell, formerly Ike's attorney-general and an unofficial advisor to the Nixon camp, said that Nixon had to say he would end the war, just as Ike had done back in 1952 with regard to Korea. Speechwriter Bill Safire told Nixon that people wanted hope, that he had an obligation to give it to them, and that as ending the war was what he wanted to do anyway, that was what he should promise.

On March 5, 1969 Nixon spoke out on Tet and its aftermath. "I pledge to you," he said, "new leadership will end the war and win the peace in the Pacific." He did *not* say, as was later reported and widely believed, that he had "a secret plan to end the war." In fact, he said the opposite: that he had no gimmick, "no push-button technique" to end the war. He insisted that he was not suggesting "withdrawal from Vietnam."

Over the next few days, Nixon repeated his pledge to "end the war and win the peace." Indeed, he added to it, reminding his audiences that he had been part of an Administration that had come to power in 1953 in the middle of "another war in Asia. We ended that war and kept the nation out of other wars for eight years. And that's the kind of leadership you'll be voting for this year if you support my ticket." As he continued this campaign, Democrats joined reporters in demanding to know some details of how he proposed to achieve his objectives. Nixon refused to provide any. He explained that to give out any details of how he would carry out his pledge would fatally weaken his bargaining position if he became President. "I'm not trying to be a coy or political," Nixon coyly said.

Although he refused to talk about his plan (which was non-existent anyway), Nixon was fairly specific about what he would not do. He said he would not seek an "unconditional surrender" by North Vietnam, "nor do I want Ho's head on a plate." He would work for an "honorable" bargain that would insure self-determination for South Vietnam, that could not be construed as a "defeat for the United States or a reward for aggression," and that would not lead to "further wars of liberation" in Asia. Hidden in all the verbiage was a clear-cut change in Nixon's thinking about Vietnam. No longer was he calling for victory. No longer was he calling for escalation. Never before had he suggested cutting a deal with the Russians. For the first time he was using the words "honorable peace," not "victorious peace." Never before had he used the word "withdrawal," and even though he denied that he intended to withdraw, that was the logical conclusion.

Johnson agreed. At the end of March, he announced that he was limiting the bombing of North Vietnam. He added that he was withdrawing from the Presidential race. He also decided that he would not meet Westmoreland's request for reinforcements, which meant he had decided to settle for something short of victory—although he did not say so. Escalation, as a policy, was dead as a result of Tet. Now the problem was how to extract the United States from Vietnam.

Complicating that process was the Presidential election. Nixon went into the campaign with a 30-point lead over Vice-President Hubert Humphrey, but by the last week in October the Democrats were gaining. Johnson gave the Humphrey campaign a terrific boost when he announced that in return for a complete bombing halt in North Vietnam, the Communists had agreed to come to peace talks in Paris. Nixon, very much afraid that an outbreak of peace would mean a Humphrey victory, contacted a dear friend of South Vietnamese President Thieu. Her name was Anna Chennault, and she passed a message to Thieu: refuse to go to the peace table, undercut the peace talks, and you will get a better deal from the Republicans after Nixon wins.

Thieu did just what Nixon wanted—he sabotaged the peace talks.

Over the years, as the details of the Chennault story began to emerge in the memoirs of the participants, it became one of the favorites of the Nixon bashers. They charged that he was so utterly cynical, so completely self-serving, so absolutely lacking in principle of any kind, that he deliberately sabotaged peace just to win the election.

Insofar as the charges imply that Nixon prevented peace in November 1968, they are false.

Not that Nixon did not want to, or try so, but he did not have to.

Nixon did not need Mrs. Chennault to persuade Thieu to refuse to go to Paris. Thieu had no trouble figuring that one out for himself, as the Johnson people well knew. In an unsigned, undated memorandum in the LBJ Library in Austin, with no salutation or other indication as to who it was directed to, Clark Clifford wrote by hand: "Reason why Saigon has not moved and does not want to move [on peace talks]. A). Saigon does not want peace.

1. Make better political settlement later.
2. In no danger because of U.S. troops.
3. No compulsion to help ARVN.
4. Wealth in country.
5. Personal corruption."

Clifford was absolutely right.

The Government of Vietnam (GVN) was a government without a country or a people. Its sole support was the U.S. government. Its sole raison d'etre was the war. For the GVN to agree to peace would be to sign its own death warrant. The 550,000 American soldiers in South Vietnam, plus the U.S. Navy off-shore, plus the American Air Force stationed in Thailand, the Philippines, Guam, and elsewhere, meant exactly what Clifford said, that the GVN was "in no danger."

There was no need to improve the ARVN when the Americans insisted on doing all the fighting anyway. The only wealth in the country, the only source of employment, was the U.S. Army and the American embassy. The personal corruption in the GVN was as bad as any in the world.

Under these conditions, why on earth should Thieu go to a peace table? He had everything to lose, nothing to gain.

And who created these conditions? Not Richard Nixon.

It is true that he had contributed, with his hawkish statements from 1954 right on through to 1968, but so did the Kennedy Administration and before that the Eisenhower Administration and after that the Johnson Administration. The GVN of 1968 was an all-American creation.

The big lie in 1968 was that there was a way to peace through a coalition government, one that could be achieved in peace talks in Paris. That implied that the GVN really was a government that really did represent something more than itself and a handful of corrupt high-ranking ARVN officers.

Nixon knew that Thieu would not go to Paris, with or without Mrs. Chennault whispering in his ear. Being Nixon, he worried, and could not keep himself from trying to influence Thieu through Chennault, so he was guilty in his motives and his actions, but he was not decisive. It was not Nixon who prevented an outbreak of peace in November, 1968. He merely exploited a situation he did not create.

He did so by mounting a calculated campaign to convince the American people that their President had sold out the people of South Vietnam, tried a tricky political deal and failed, capitulated to the Communists, deceived the GVN, and played politics with peace.

On his nation-wide television broadcast on Election Eve, Nixon seized his final opportunity to drive home the point that the bombing halt was a political decision taken at the expense of American boys fighting in Vietnam. He said that at first Johnson's order had appeared to offer real hope, "but then the negotiations came apart at the seams."

Nixon said he had heard "a very disturbing report" that in the past two days "the North Vietnamese are moving thousands of tons of supplies down the Ho Chi Minh Trail, and our bombers are not able to stop them."

He had heard no such report. He simply made that up.

The Democrats were monitoring the Nixon show. Humphrey was told about what Nixon had said. He immediately replied, telling his audience "there is no indication of increased infiltration." His aides had checked with the Pentagon, he said, and no one there had heard any such thing. "And let me say that it does not help the negotiations to falsely accuse anyone at this particular time." Of course, it also did not help the negotiations for the Democrats to pretend that serious peace talks were going to begin on Wednesday.

There was a remarkable similarity to the last days of the 1968 campaign and the last days of the 1972 campaign. In the first case, the Administration implied that peace was at hand. In the second case, the Administration said explicitly that peace was at hand. In each case, the President knew that the GVN had *not* agreed to the proposed peace formula, and that the North Vietnamese had *not* agreed to settle for something short of victory. In each case, in its quest for votes, the Administration treated the American people with cynical contempt.

In 1968 American politics had sunk to depths not reached since the Civil

War and Reconstruction. America's political leaders, Johnson and Humphrey, Nixon and Agnew, and most of the others, were just playing with people. The image they conjure up for this author is one of Charley Chaplin, acting the mad dictator, kicking around the globe as if it were a balloon. If they had the slightest feeling for the death and destruction that was devouring Vietnam, if they had any concern for the lives of the American soldiers in Vietnam, if they had the least commitment to a decent respect for the opinion of mankind, if they had the vaguest concern to meet their Constitutional obligation to promote domestic tranquility, if it ever even occurred to them to strive to provide the conditions that would allow the American people to pursue happiness, they managed to ignore it all, in their single-minded pursuit of personal political victory at any cost. It would take years, and many violent storms with hurricane-force winds, to clear the air of the loathsome stench of the last week of the 1968 campaign.

Nixon won the election, and took office in January, 1969. A couple of months later, the North Vietnamese Army (NVA) launched a major offensive in South Vietnam. Nixon responded by instituting a bombing campaign against the enemy supply line, known as the Ho Chi Minh Trail, in Cambodia and Laos. This was done secretly. In public, once the bombers had stopped the offensive, Nixon announced his plan to end the war. He called it Vietnamization, and it was a plan to continue the war with American air and sea power, while leaving the ground fighting, and the heavy casualties, to the Army of the Republic of Vietnam (ARVN).

Nixon said that his withdrawal policy would be based on the level of enemy action, the improvement in the ARVN, the progress in negotiations in Paris. That meant, in practice, that the withdrawal would be long and painful. Nixon was thus tempted to go for broke, and in the fall of 1969 began planning Operation DUCK HOOK. It was the hawk's dream—an all-out offensive, including a declaration of war against North Vietnam, an invasion and occupation of Hanoi, and atomic weapons along the Vietnamese-Chinese border. Nixon set an "or-else" deadline for Hanoi—either leave South Vietnam by November 1, or get ready for all-out war.

At the same time, the anti-war activists were mounting their biggest action ever, a Moratorium in mid-November. Nixon's advisors, led by Henry Kissinger, told the President he dared not escalate on the eve of the Moratorium; they feared DUCK HOOK would goad the anti-war demonstrators into acts of pure desperation and might throw the country into something like anarchy.

Nixon talked to the British guerrilla warfare expert, Sir Robert Thompson, who had played a leading role in defeating Communist insurrection in Malaysa in the 1950s.

"What would you think if we decided to escalate?" Nixon asked.

Thompson was opposed. He thought it would cause a worldwide furor without enhancing South Vietnam's long-term survival chances. Vietnamization, the improvement of the ARVN, was the right course. The analogy was Korea, where the improvement of the ROK forces, not a massive offensive against North Korea or a political settlement, had insured the survival of South Korea.

Vietnamization meant a continuation of American involvement in the war beyond Nixon's self-proclaimed target date on the end of 1970 or earlier. He asked Thompson if he thought it important for the United States "to see it through."

"Absolutely," Thompson replied. "In my opinion the future of Western civilization is at stake in the way you handle yourselves in Vietnam."

That was bombast, pure and simple, but Nixon agreed with Thompson's apocalyptic view. He also accepted Thompson's judgment, and Kissinger's recommendation, about DUCK HOOK. He felt that "the Moratorium had undercut the credibility of the ultimatum."

Put cynically, after having proclaimed that he would not let policy be made in the streets, Nixon let policy be made in the streets. Put positively, he had repressed his instinct to smash the enemy to choose a more moderate course with better long-term prospects. Put objectively, he had recognized that even though he was Commander in Chief of the world's most powerful armed forces, there were definite limits on his power.

Almost twenty years later, in April of 1988, Nixon said on "Meet the Press," that his decision against DUCK HOOK was the worst of his Presidency. He said that if he had implemented the offensive, he could have had peace in 1969. He did not explain why he thought so, or how that could have happened.

After deciding to let his November 1 deadline come and go without action, Nixon escalated the rhetoric.

On November 3, 1969, he made the most famous speech of his Presidency, concluding: "And so tonight—to you, the great silent majority of my fellow Americans—I ask for your support. . . .

"Let us be united for peace. Let us also be united against defeat. Because let us understand: North Vietnam cannot defeat or humiliate the United States. Only Americans can do that."

"Very few speeches actually influence the course of history," Nixon wrote in his memoirs. "The November 3 speech was one of them."

That was nonsense. Had Nixon announced DUCK HOOK, or had he announced a complete withdrawal by the end of the year, along with a unilateral cease fire, the speech might have changed the course of history. But by announcing that he was going to continue doing what he had been doing for nine months, all Nixon did was to divide the nation more deeply than ever. It was true that in the process he showed, at least temporarily, that support for his policies was greater than most people imagined.

Media criticism meanwhile, continued, which infuriated Nixon and his supporters. He wrote a note to himself, saying that he had surprised the press, and defeated the reporters, which delighted him.

It was almost as if the media, not Hanoi, was the enemy. He wrote, "The RN policy is to talk softly and to carry a big stick. That was the theme of November 3." Actually, the opposite was more nearly true; he had let the ultimatum deadline come and go without action, while he inflated the rhetoric. And for

Nixon to say that the survival of peace and freedom in the world depended on whether the American people supported him in his policy of keeping Thieu in power was simply ridiculous.

In his "silent majority" speech, Nixon had not set out to win support, but to show that it was there, he did not aim to convince, but to clobber the opposition; he was not attempting to reach out, to bring people together, but to isolate his domestic opposition. It worked, temporarily.

That same week, Nixon wrote a sentence that, in a real sense, summed up all the agony and pain and frustration and difficulty of the situation he found himself in with regard to Vietnam: "We simply cannot tell the mothers of our casualties and the soldiers who have spent part of their lives in Vietnam that it was all to no purpose."

There is power and truth and a beautiful simplicity in that sentence. But it poses this problem: could Nixon supply a purpose and justify the sacrifices that had been made by sending more boys over, by continuing the war, even after he had decided it would not be won?

In the Spring of 1970, Nixon launched the invasion of Cambodia. In announcing this action, Nixon grossly exaggerated, making it sound as if he were Ike on D-Day, or Caesar at the Rubicon. In fact, it was a rear-guard action designed to buy time for the long-drawn-out retreat. But it set off such a storm of protest, culminating at Kent State, that Nixon had to go back on TV to promise that he would have all American troops out of Cambodia within three weeks. That made the hawks furious, and illustrates nicely what an impossible position Nixon had put himself in with his policy of fighting a war while retreating from it without attempting to win it but refusing to admit that his country had lost it.

In the Spring of 1971, Nixon launched an invasion of Laos, this one without American ground troops but with American air cover. It was a spectacular failure. Meanwhile, the U.S. Air Force continued to pound Laos, Cambodia, and increasingly, North Vietnam.

In the Spring of 1972, however, the NVA had recovered sufficiently from the set-back of 1969 to begin its own offensive. It was a go-for-broke attack that came close to success. Massive American bombing missions just did manage to stop the communist offensive. Nixon, furious with the North Vietnamese, extended the bombing to Hanoi itself, and mined the harbor at Haiphong.

Simultaneously, he launched detente, capped by a trip to Peking and another to Moscow. In so doing, he had put himself in the damnedest position. The original rationale for the war was to stop Chinese expansion; now, while the killing went on in Vietnam, Nixon was exchanging toasts with Mao in Peking and with Brezhnev in Moscow, arranging for trade missions, signing arms agreements, and trying to bribe the Chinese and Russians into withdrawing their support from Hanoi.

Under the pressure of the bombing of Hanoi and the mining of Haiphong, and the pressure from their Communist backers to compromise, the North Vietnamese agreed to serious negotiations in the summer of 1972. These negotiations ran up against the American Presidential election date. Once again, the questions of peace talks and negotiations in Vietnam would be a major factor in the American election.

The North Vietnamese were willing to cut a deal, which, reduced to its essentials, was this: in return for a complete withdrawal of all American armed forces, Hanoi would give back the American POWs. The NVA would stay in South Vietnam (about 150,000 strong). There would be a National Council of Reconciliation to supervise new nationwide elections; its membership would be one-half Communist.

These terms amounted to capitulation by the Americans. Nixon himself had so characterized them, when the North Vietnamese first offered them in 1969. In late October of 1972, however, Nixon said they represented a "complete victory for the United States."

Unfortunately for Nixon, and for his chief negotiator, Henry Kissinger, President Thieu did not agree.

Thieu, who had been so helpful in 1968, proved in 1972 to be exceedingly difficult. Kissinger was beside himself. Having achieved so much, in his own view, he was being undercut by the very people he had saved. He compared the Vietnamese, North and South, to tigers balanced on stools in a cage, with himself as the animal trainer, cracking the whip to force them to go through the paces. "When one is in place, the other jumps off."

To Nixon, Kissinger said he was caught in a paradoxical situation "in which North Vietnam, which had in effect lost the war, was acting as if it had won; while South Vietnam, which had effectively won the war, was acting as if it had lost."

Had Thieu seen that message, he would have exploded in laughter or broken down into tears. How could Kissinger say such a thing? The accord gave the NVA the right to keep its troops in South Vietnam and the Communists the right to play a role in the political life of his country, because no matter how brilliantly Kissinger defended his National Council proposal, he could not cover the truth—it meant a coalition government, with Communist participation. Meanwhile, the Americans would be leaving.

Nixon began to realize that he had been premature in calling the agreement complete, and the doubts that he had had all along about the wisdom of settling before the election began to strengthen. Three developments reinforced those doubts.

First, General Alexander Haig told the President that the Communists were on the move militarily, seizing as much territory around Saigon as they could before the agreement was signed.

Second, Nixon was under pressure from the right wing in the United States. *National Review,* William F. Buckley's magazine, warned that any settlement must not be a cover for a coalition government, and must include a public pledge to continue all-out military aid to South Vietnam.

Third, General Westmoreland told Nixon he was opposed to the agreement. Although Westmoreland had recently completed his four-year tour as

Army Chief of Staff and retired, on October 20 Nixon called him to the White House for consultation. When the President finished briefing the General on the proposed settlement, Westmoreland urged him "to delay action on the new agreement and to hold out for better terms." He believed that more bombing of Hanoi and continued mining of Haiphong would force the Communists to make "meaningful concessions." He emphasized that it was "vital" that North Vietnamese troops be compelled to withdraw from South Vietnam. As to the National Council of Reconciliation, Westmoreland thought it was "impractical, almost absurd, nothing more than a facade."

Westmoreland was not the only high-ranking officer to oppose the agreement. The American military had fought long and hard in South Vietnam, under severe restrictions and at the cost of many a reputation. To a number of senior officers, the idea that the politicians were ready to make deals that they, like Thieu, believed would all but certainly lead to the eventual collapse of the Saigon government, was galling. Admiral Elmo Zumwalt made a bitter comment: "There are at least two words no one can use to characterize the outcome of that two-faced policy. One is 'peace.' The other is 'honor.'"

So even as he put pressure on Thieu to accept, even as he encouraged Kissinger to push the settlement, Nixon was drawn increasingly to the option Westmoreland had recommended, especially when Haig joined in. Haig said that after the election Nixon would be armed with a mandate that he could use to force concessions from Hanoi, because he would "be less constrained." Nixon noted in his diary, "Immediately after the election we will have an enormous mandate . . . and the enemy then either has to settle or face the consequences of what we could do to them."

But it was Thieu who refused to settle, not Hanoi. Kissinger's manipulations, and Nixon's policies, had put Nixon into a potentially embarrassing position. If Hanoi went public at this point, the negotiating record would show that the Communists had agreed to everything Nixon had required, and prove that Saigon, not Hanoi, was blocking peace. The tail was wagging the dog. Thieu had a veto power that he was determined to use. But if he used it, Nixon knew that the doves would stir up American public opinion against Saigon. The 93rd Congress would refuse to give the President any funds to continue the war. Hanoi would then win everything. All the sacrifices would have been in vain. Instead of peace with honor, there would be defeat with humiliation.

So what did the President want? A settlement, or a chance to bomb Hanoi into further concessions? Did he want Thieu to accept the Kissinger deal, or reject it? It is impossible to say, because he did not know himself. In any case, he had put himself into a position in which it was no longer his decision to make. After all those lives sacrificed, all those bombs, all that money spent, all that effort, the United States had lost control of events. It was up to the Vietnamese, North and South, to settle their war.

A week before the election, Hanoi went public. The Communists announced that they were ready to sign an agreement that Kissinger had accepted, but Thieu refused to go along.

To undercut the Communist propaganda, Kissinger then held a news conference. His purpose was "to undercut the North Vietnamese propaganda manuever and to make sure that our version of the agreement was the one that had greater public impact."

Kissinger had given hundreds of backgrounders by this time, and held dozens of on-the-record press conferences, but he had never before appeared live on television, because the White House press people were convinced that his heavy German accent would not play well in Middle America. But this occasion was so important that the decision was to go live.

The Briefing Room was jammed with reporters, confused and skeptical. Kissinger, calm and professional, appeared confident.

In his opening remarks, he declared, "We believe that peace is at hand. We believe that an agreement is within sight, based on the May 8th proposal of the President . . . which is just to all parties." Only minor details remained before the settlement was signed.

The phrase "peace is at hand" made banner headlines around the world. An enormous wave of relief swept over the country, tempered by skepticism from those who had gotten their hopes so high before, exactly four years earlier, when Johnson announced the bombing halt, only to have those hopes dashed. Still, overall, Kissinger's announcement created euphoria similar to that following Prime Minister Neville Chamberlain's post-Munich conference claim to have achieved "peace in our time."

Inside the White House, however, there was more anger than euphoria. Both Haldeman and John Ehrlichman, among others, felt that Kissinger was forcing his way into the center in an election that was already won. He had violated a cardinal rule, calling attention to himself and distracting it from Nixon. They suspected, rightly, that Kissinger had been saying in his private briefings that Nixon could not have achieved the breakthrough, that Kissinger had indicated that Nixon was so belligerent that he had failed to pick up the nuances of Le Duc Tho's position, that he had even accused Nixon of slowness of thought. Only Kissinger had the subtlety of mind to discern the changes in Hanoi's attitude. And if Kissinger had actually concluded an agreement, Haldeman and Ehrlichman wondered, where was it?

All the brilliance in the world, all the good PR notwithstanding, could not disguise Kissinger's duplicity. He had described as a dramatic diplomatic breakthrough what was in fact a diplomatic failure. In the process, he had put his boss into a highly vulnerable position, not necessarily for the election, but afterwards.

President Thieu made this clear on October 27, when he declared that South Vietnam would not be bound by any peace agreement that he did not sign. He repeated his demands, that North Vietnam withdraw its troops from the South and that Hanoi recognize South Vietnam as a sovereign nation without Communist participation in the government. He rejected the National Council out of hand.

Nixon was in a bind. He could not fire the popular Kissinger, or repudiate the agreement that he himself had called "complete." The President struggled to extract himself from a bad situation. On October 29 he stressed that he had achieved "peace with honor—not surrender—not begging." He spoke of the "historic year of 1972," in which he had given the world "a chance for peace for a generation."

That same day, he put pressure on Thieu. In a letter to the South Vietnamese President, Nixon defended the National Council idea, calling it "a face-saving device for the communists to cover their collapse on their demands for a coalition government and your resignation." He added a warning, "If the evident drift towards disagreement between the two of us continues . . . the essential base for U.S. support for you and your Government will be destroyed. In this respect the comments of your Foreign Minister that the U.S. is negotiating a surrender are as damaging as they are unfair and improper."

There was irony here: exactly four years earlier, Nixon had urged Thieu not to go to Paris for negotiations with the North Vietnamese; now he was trying to force Thieu to go to Paris to accept a settlement.

But Thieu would not cooperate. As a result, a backlash, similar to the one that had hit Humphrey in 1968, began to appear possible. As the details of the agreement began to sink in, Democratic nominee McGovern and others joined Senator Eugene McCarthy in demanding to know what had been gained that could not have been achieved four years earlier. McGovern's aides were cheering up at news that polls were indicating people had doubts as to how close peace really was. Mary McGrory wrote in the *Washington Star* that there was a "bewildering adverse reaction [to 'peace is at hand']. Canvassers reported even among the Silent Majority, there was indignation about the timing."

Nixon did what he did best. He counter-attacked. On November 2, in his first televised political broadcast of the campaign, he said he was determined that "the central points be clearly settled, so that there will be no misunderstanding which could lead to a breakdown of the settlement and a resumption of the war.

"We are going to sign the agreement when the agreement is right, not one day before—and when the agreement is right, we are going to sign without one day's delay."

The next day, in Rhode Island, Nixon again defended the settlement. He said "we have made a breakthrough in the negotiations which will lead to peace."

Nixon's speech was a tour de force. His explanation was satisfactory to a majority of the American people and rescued him from the potential trap Kissinger had created. He had solved his political problem.

And he won the election. But Thieu still would not sign, so Nixon undertook a new offensive. In order to get Saigon to do his will, he started bombing Hanoi, in a massive offensive unprecedented in the history of warfare. It did not cause Hanoi to crumble, but it did convince Thieu that Nixon would stand behind him, so in January the agreement that had been worked out three months earlier was finally signed. Nixon had finally achieved peace.

In the process, however, he had left a terrible taste in the mouths of many Americans. He had promised (or at least Kissinger had promised) that peace was at hand. As Haldeman and Ehrlichman knew, the promise was not necessary to win the election, but it was made, and when the next move was not peace but the Christmas bombing, people felt betrayed.

It was that sense of betrayal, so widely shared, that gave the Democrats the courage to go after Nixon with the opening gavel of the 93rd Congress in January of 1973. He had just won with 60% of the vote, but the Democrats figured—correctly, as it turned out—that they could drive him from office.

Usually, when bad things happened to Nixon, he had no one to blame but himself. In this case, however, when the ultimate catastrophe hit him, he could quite properly blame Henry Kissinger and President Thieu.

Two final points need to be made about Nixon and Vietnam. First, he was by no means a free agent. His policies did not reflect his best judgment about what should be done. His options were increasingly limited by the ever-growing strength of the doves, especially in Congress. Ironically, his success in driving the anti-war demonstrators off the streets contributed to this growth, by making the dove cause respectable. The result was that the 93rd Congress was not going to let him have one penny to carry on the war. He had to make peace before January 1973, or face the impossible situation of trying to carry on the war without funds.

Second, nearly all the names on the left-hand side of the Vietnam Wall in Washington commemorate men who died in action while Richard Nixon was their Commander in Chief, and they died after he had decided that the war could not be won.

NAPALM IN THE MORNING: THE VIETNAM WAR FILM

by Jack Colldeweih

When asked about Vietnam war films, "the average moviegoer would probably cite a few classics such as *The Deer Hunter* and *Apocalypse Now*," according to film analyst Jack Colldeweih. But Colldeweih's research has unearthed 134 films that treat, directly or indirectly, the subject of the Vietnam war, and, as he points out, more continue to be made. Vietnam remains an irresistible subject for fiction film-makers. Hollywood can be counted on to keep cranking them out for the foreseeable future. Colldeweih, who is writing a book about Vietnam-era films, has furnished us with the most up-to-date and comprehensive study of such films.

He has categorized the Vietnam films according to topic: Films of Prelude, Films of Engagement, Films of the Homefront, Films of the POW-MIA Problem, and Films of Politics About the War. Colldeweih has added deft critical commentaries about most films, which provide us with a sense of their content and their value (or lack of value) as artistic and historical creations, what they tell us about the war and how well they tell us. Colldeweih performs these critical tasks with great skill and learning.

Colldeweih finds that the Films of Prelude, those made prior to America's involvement in Vietnam, amount to little more than anti-Communist propaganda. They reinforce Cold War stereotypes and ideologies, and they are part of the American Cold War culture that bolstered official versions of international relations and U.S. foreign policy. These films reinforced the attitudes and beliefs that underlay America's Vietnam intervention.

Of the Films of Engagement, the two best are Francis Ford Coppola's *Apoca-*

lypse Now (1979) and Oliver Stone's *Platoon* (1986). Coppola's surrealistic retelling of Joseph Conrad's novella *Heart of Darkness* contains some of the most beautiful and powerful sequences in modern American cinematography. Despite its flawed ending, *Apocalypse Now* can rightfully claim the mantle of serious art. In a series of bizarre and powerful images, it reveals the essential horror and the craziness of the American descent into barbarism. *Platoon* is an earnest effort to capture the Vietnam war as experienced by the soldiers (the "grunts") who had to fight it. There are some gritty details of combat, and Stone tries to depict realistically the kinds of Americans who were sent to fight the war. But the film, essentially a series of action encounters, fails to offer viewers much insight into the meaning or the purpose of the war.

Most of the homefront films amounted to inane efforts that did not treat their subjects seriously or honestly. One of the better films was *Easy Rider* (1969), a low-budget classic that tells the story of two drug dealers who take a motorcycle trip across the country. Their bike trip is a countercultural odyssey; the America of the easy riders is a series of encounters with people who have either dropped out of, or have never been in, the mainstream. The two hippie bikers are eventually destroyed by violence within the American culture that parallels the violence of Vietnam.

Colldeweih finds that the films dealing with the Vietnam veterans and their problems are generally poorly done. Using a variety of genres and styles, these films focus on a recurring subject, the scarred veteran, the man who has been damaged psychologically by the war. He returns to civilian life a misfit. Most of these cinematic veterans end up either using their killers' skills to destroy "bad guys" or else they are neurotics and psychotics who murder and maim good people, and often destroy themselves. Two serious, albeit unsatisfying, films about veterans include *Coming Home* and *The Deer Hunter,* both released in 1978.

None of the POW-MIA films is very good, nor can any be taken seriously. Sylvester Stallone's *Rambo* films and Chuck Norris's violent fantasies belong to this genre. According to Colldeweih, the less said about these movies, the better for serious filmgoers or students of the Vietnam war.

For the final film category, the movies concerned with the politics of the war, a variety of strategies and genres have been employed. The Western has been used as a kind of political allegory with resonances and correspondences to Vietnam. The best of these "Vietnam Westerns" was *Little Big Man*. From an Indian's perspective, the white man's atrocities against Native Americans resemble U.S. war crimes against Vietnamese villagers.

Colldeweih views the *corpus* of Vietnam film literature as ultimately disappointing and unsatisfying. The war posed cinematic challenges that Vietnam filmmakers mostly failed to surmount. There has not been, perhaps there will never be, a great film made about America's role in Vietnam. Colldeweih suggests that a serious, honest filmic treatment of a national tragedy such as the American experience in Vietnam may not be possible. The film industry is, after all, a commercial mass entertainment medium. With few exceptions, filmmakers have furnished us rather thin gruel and a lot of bad movies about the Vietnam war. Colldeweih's plaint: "We want substance, and so far all we have gotten is shadow."

Asked about the Vietnam war film, the average moviegoer would probably cite a few classics such as *The Deer Hunter* and *Apocalypse Now,* and some recent examples on the order of *Full Metal Jacket, Good Morning, Vietnam,* and *Casualties of War.* Moviegoers might even recall a few more because of their appearance on network or cable television, or their availability on videocassette. In any case, to the majority of the film-going public, the war started when the United States became actively involved in Vietnam. Thus, to the average moviegoer, the first Vietnam war film was *The Green Berets* (1968).

However, many films had been made about the American involvement in Vietnam before 1968. If one includes the homefront film, which contained references to the war, both before and after the 1973 cease-fire, the list of films available becomes quite large.

Although our emphasis in this review is on the major "action" films, several other types will be included:

- homefront films depicting support and protest;
- films about veterans and their return to civilian life;
- films about America's involvement in Vietnam prior to 1964;
- films about POWs and MIAs;
- films where Vietnam is purely a locale;
- films using different time periods and settings as a disguised commentary on the war;
- important television and cable films.

PRELUDE

Although most Americans might not be able to locate either Indochina or Vietnam on a map, they have seen several films set there; furthermore, their initial attitudes were shaped by those films, as well as by American culture in general and the ideology of the Cold War.

Not until *A Yank in Indochina* (1952) were Americans shown in combat with guerrilla forces. Flying supplies to the French and Vietnamese fighting the Vietminh, the two Yanks subsequently lead a paratroop attack against the Communists, foreshadowing similar events that would lead the United States into full-scale involvement in the war. Aid in the form of money and supplies was inevitably followed by assistance in the form of advice and leadership, and then by large-scale military engagement. Released during the Korean War, the film supported the idea that Americans could stop Communism anywhere.

By late 1957 Communist insurgent activity in Vietnam began in earnest. That same year *The Quiet American* was released, based on Graham Greene's novel critical of our actions in Vietnam. The film version was the opposite: it was more anti-Communist than anti-American, dealing with a politically naive American (played by Audie Murphy) who comes to Vietnam with his own plans for settling the civil war.

The next two films provided especially vicious characterizations of the rebels, although they were led by non-Asians. In *Five Gates to Hell* (1959) a dedicated Communist (played by Neville Brand) abducts a group of French doctors and nurses to treat his sick warlord, planning to give the nurses to his men afterward. Attempting to escape, several of the nurses are killed. In *Brushfire* (1961) the rebels attacking peaceful planters are led by an ex-Nazi, thereby tarring the rebels with two brushes: Communism and Nazism.

In 1961 President Kennedy sent Special Forces advisers to Vietnam and began secret military warfare in Laos and North Vietnam. Although Americans were dying in Vietnam, the United States was officially still not at war in 1963 when *The Ugly American* was released. Based on the Burdick-Lederer novel, it is set in the fictional Sarkhan, to which a journalist-publisher (Marlon Brando) is sent as ambassador. His Cold-War suspicions and activities provoke the local pro-Communists, leading to civil unrest and disorder. Both *The Ugly American* and *The Quiet American* argued that a "neutral" third force was needed between the antagonists of Communism and Capitalism. Unfortunately, neither *The Ugly American* nor its message was well received.

That same year the topical *A Yank in Viet-Nam* was released, in which a Marine Corps major is captured by the Vietcong and subsequently rescued by friendly guerrillas. He accompanies the guerrillas on their raids, later assuming leadership, as in *A Yank in Indochina*.

These films, released before the 1964 Gulf of Tonkin resolution, had several implications: the enemy was vicious and dangerous; the enemy was bent on world domination; our chosen allies were brave and true, but needed military and financial aid; if we didn't stop the Communists in Vietnam, we would lose Southeast Asia, as President Eisenhower's 1954 "domino theory" maintained; finally, we could win "on the cheap" without sending large ground forces to fight the enemy directly. It all coincided nicely with the official line from Washington.

ENGAGEMENT

If we assume that America's official engagement in the war dates from the 1964 Gulf of Tonkin resolution, it is amazing that four years elapsed before the appearance of the first Vietnam combat film; it is even more amazing that a full decade passed before the release of the next one (see Table 1). Except for a few documentaries such as *The Anderson Platoon* (1966), *A Face of War* (1968), and *Hoa-Binh* (1971), the American public's perception of Vietnam came from television news reports and John Wayne's *The Green Berets* (1968).

Table 1. Annual Number of Vietnam War-Related Films (by category)

YEAR	ENGAGEMENT	HOMEFRONT	VETERANS	POW/MIA	POLITICS	TOTAL
1965	1			1		2
1966	1					1
1967		1	1		1	3
1968	1	1	2		2	6
1969		7	3		2	12
1970		6	3		5	14
1971		2	7	1	1	11
1972		4	3		1	8
1973		2	2			4
1974			1			1
1975						0
1976			2			2
1977			6	1	1	8
1978	2	2	2			6
1979	1	3			1	5
1980	1	1	2			4
1981		2	3		1	6
1982			2		1	3
1983		1		1		2
1984	2		1	1		4
1985		1	1	2		4
1986	1					1
1987	3	1		1		5
1988	7	1	3	1		12
1989	4	1	4	1		10
	24	36	48	10	16	134

On the other hand, perhaps it is not so amazing. First we must bear in mind that the American film industry is profit-oriented; it has also been the mouthpiece of American sentiments. Thus, the industry was in a bind when it came to Vietnam. While much of America supported the military effort in Vietnam, the young, who constituted the largest part of the film-going public (or the "film generation" it was called), were divided. As America's apologist, the industry might lose much of its audience and therefore its profits. On the other hand, it wanted to be seen as supporting "our boys fighting over there." The solution was to avoid the "fighting" war altogether and concentrate on the homefront.

In addition, Bernard Dick, in *The Star-Spangled Screen*, writes:

> Before it could achieve any artistic importance, the combat film had to evolve into something beyond battles and beachheads; but it could only do that when the war was winding down or over, when the war could be understood as a conflict that, for all its horrors, was able to reveal something about the combatants that would never have come out in peacetime.[1]

The Green Berets can in no sense be said to have achieved any "artistic importance." It is true that the film made money, both domestically and internationally, but that may be more attributable to "the popularity of John Wayne than [to] the breadth of public support for the war."[2] In any case, it is generally considered a poor film with stereotypical characters performing predictable actions and speaking preachy dialogue.

Martha Bayles describes the film as "set in the confident days of 1963, fashioned in the style of 1949, and lobbed like a grenade into 1968."[3] In the film, a journalist, skeptical of America's policies in Vietnam and the Green Berets' mission, is challenged to see for himself by a Green Beret colonel played by John Wayne. Once there, the journalist sees with stark clarity: it's the "good guys versus the bad guys." No question as to which is which: the bad Viet Cong, with outside help, are severely hurting the good anti-Communist South Vietnamese, who want and need American aid. After having seen the truth, the journalist intends to go back and tell it to a public that has been confused by the press. The colonel and his Green Berets will, of course, stay and continue to help the South Vietnamese.

It was not by chance that the film chose a *journalist* to go to Vietnam. Although journalists have a natural outlet for information and opinion, people are often confused by what they read in the press, especially when it does not coincide with what Washington has been telling them.[4] The colonel's charge in the *Green Berets*—that if the journalists went to Vietnam, they would see the truth—was sheer ignorance at best, disingenuous at worst. Reporters such as David Halberstam, Charles Mohr, Mert Perry, and Malcomb Browne had been there for years and were the sources of much of that contradictory information.

After a decade of avoiding the subject, the first of a series of Vietnam combat films appeared. Although *Apocalypse Now* (1979) was the first to begin production, *The Boys in Company C* (1978) and *Go Tell the Spartans* (1978) preceded it into the theaters. *The Boys in Company C* was a low-budget film with a tired storyline celebrating the American fighting man. Here, however, we have not the socioeconomic, geographic, and ethnic stew of the World War II movie, but rather a mix of contemporary cultural stereotypes such as the flower-child, ghetto street-tough, and writer. The film does provide an early, but not new, look at some of the more unsavory details of the war, such as drug dealing and smuggling, corruption within the Army of the Republic of Vietnam (ARVN), an unskilled and uncaring American officer corps, and illegitimate GI-Vietnamese children. The Vietcong (VC), though a constant threat, are little to be seen.

Go Tell the Spartans, an adaptation of Daniel Ford's novel *Incident at Muc Wa,* recalls the time when Americans were just "advisers" to the ARVN troops. The film's title refers to "Herodotus's acount in *The Histories* of the misguided idealism, tactical blunders, and suicidal heroism at the Battle of Thermopylae, where its defenders left the message, 'Go Tell the Spartans, thou that passeth by, that here, obedient to their laws, we lie.'"[5] A small group of U.S. advisers, South Vietnamese soldiers, and local mercenaries attempt to hold a small hamlet from VC attack. They fail, victims of the Vietcong and a group of Vietnamese refugees as well as of American policy, a point made clear by the major who describes a tour of duty in Vietnam as one for a sucker, one that is aimless and without goals or direction.

The first major combat film about Vietnam with some claim to artistic merit was Coppola's *Apolcalypse Now* (1979). The film is visually stunning and extremely well edited; where it fails is in its conception, which leads to an unsatisfying ending. Coppola was so unclear as to where he was going that he shot, and tried out before general release, three different endings, none of which was really satisfactory. He claimed that the film "would give its audience a sense of the horror, the madness, the sensuousness, and the moral dilemma of the Vietnam war."[6]

The film takes the form of a quest by a nearly burnt-out Special Forces assassin, Captain Willard (Martin Sheen) to go "up-river," find, and "terminate with extreme prejudice" the command of a rogue army colonel who has taken the war into his own hands. The power of the film is in the journey, which ends in Cambodia; it is at the destination, when Willard finds Colonel Kurtz (Marlon Brando), that the film sinks into the jungle and decays.

Inspired by Joseph Conrad's novella *Heart of Darkness,* the film has Willard journey up river (like Marlow of the novel) to find the legendary Kurtz (in both the film and the book). Willard (the Marlow of the novel) witnesses the decline of civilization and the emergence of primitive, even savage, behavior, reflecting the potential darkness of the human soul. It is during this journey that the images are the most bizarre and powerful. The beginning of the film is riveting; we see a broad expanse of jungle, and then hear the words, "This is the end ... " in the song by Jim Morrison and the Doors, as the jungle landscape suddenly explodes in sheets of flame and smoke, while helicopters (the eternal symbol of Vietnam) scoot to and fro. The sound of the helicopters becomes louder, and their rotating blades dissolve into the blades of the ceiling fan of a Saigon hotel room where we first see Willard: his face is upside down as he stares at the fan and, in voice-over, tells us who he is and how he got there. In fact, much of the film's information is presented in the form of Willard's interior monologue.

The film is like a golf course that progressively deteriorates the farther one gets from the first tee. The fairways get rougher and the greens shoddier and more distorted. The military base where Willard gets his assignment is the first tee. Here Willard has lunch with his superiors and is given an assignment "which does not exist nor will it ever exist." This type of assignment is not an altogether new experience for Willard. The fairway is the journey with his assigned boat crew to find Colonel Kilgore (Robert Duvall), who will use his helicopters to escort Willard to the mouth of the Nung river. The first hole on the course is finding Kilgore, who is mopping up in the aftermath of a raid on a Vietcong base. Kilgore is an odd sight, wearing a nineteenth-century cavalry hat and scarf, and using a similarly dressed bugler to signal his commands.

Kilgore is reluctant to carry out the mission for Willard until he learns that one member of the boat crew is a famous California surfer and that the VC village guarding the river's mouth has reportedly the best surf in the country. Believing that the surf is going to waste because "Charlie [the Vietcong] doesn't surf," Kilgore immediately organizes the mission. The subsequent raid on the village is one of the most visually striking battles in film history. Playing Richard

Wagner's "Ride of the Valkyries" from loudspeakers on helicopters painted with "Death from Above" on their noses, the squadron swoops in on the village from the seaward direction. In the midst of the carnage, Kilgore insists that the surfer, and two of his own men, take their surfboards and try the water. At battle's end, Kilgore ruminates on the experience: "I love the smell of napalm in the morning. It smells like ... victory." Willard is left to reflect that, "If that's how Kilgore fought the war, I began to wonder what they really had against Kurtz."

Other "golf holes" consist of the destruction of a sampan crew, an encounter with a tiger, a visit by Playboy bunnies to a supply base in the jungle, a nighttime battle at a bridge on the Cambodian border, and attacks by VC and Montagnard tribesmen along the rivers—each "hole" eerier than the one before. The course ends at Kurtz's camp at a ruined temple in Cambodia.

The film at this point simply cannot deliver what has been expected. As Kurtz, Marlon Brando had a thankless role, and there was little that he, or any other actor, could do to salvage it. Ultimately, in keeping with the myth of the slaying of kings as outlined in Sir James Frazer's *The Golden Bough*, Willard kills Kurtz because Kurtz wants it as much as any other reason. As Willard tells us, he himself was "no longer in their fucking army."

Regardless, the film succeeds at getting at what has troubled so many Vietnam veterans:

> Vietnam (the war rather than the country) is no more than the heart of that darkness, and endless psychodrama, half Theater of Cruelty, half Theater of the Absurd, in which impulses normally lurking just below or intermittently bursting through the crust of civilization are given free rein. . . . And Kurtz's Cambodian enclave was doubtless intended to symbolize the very heart of the heart, the inner sanctum of America's collective unconscious.[7]

In 1980, a year after *Apocalypse Now* was released, engagement with the enemy was serialized in a television movie made from Philip Caputo's best-selling memoir *A Rumor of War*. It relates the gradual transformation of Caputo (Brad Davis in the movie) from American college youth to gung-ho Marine officer to cynical veteran who is court-martialed for the murder of Vietnamese civilians, which he later attempts to cover up. Its battle scenes, while less bizarre than those of *Apocalypse Now*, were more realistic and provided some understanding of the pressures and frustrations faced by American ground forces.

Platoon (1986), however, was a highly touted and eagerly awaited film directed by Oliver Stone, a Vietnam veteran. The credits tell us the movie was dedicated to "those who fought and died in Vietnam." Many veterans, although bitter about Americans' lack of understanding of what they had been through, felt *Platoon* was fairly accurate. One who had served with Stone in Vietnam said that it illustrated the "waste, corruption, filth, napalm, blood, and guts, the destruction and absolute craziness of that war."[8] John Wheeler, chairman of the Vietnam Veterans Memorial Fund, called it "part of the healing process."[9]

The movie revolves around the experiences of three men: an idealistic newcomer named Taylor (played by Charlie Sheen), who has volunteered for Vietnam to "expand his experiences," and two battle-tested sergeants, Barnes (Tom Berenger) and Elias (Willem Dafoe) who compete for the allegiance of the members of the platoon. Barnes is a killing machine, perfectly suited to war: intelligent, charismatic, merciless, relentless, dominating, capable, and, above all, dangerous. His men feel safe with him in battle. Elias shares many of Barnes's traits, but is merciful, dominates through charisma rather than brute strength, and does not at all seem dangerous. Barnes drinks; Elias smokes pot; Barnes plays cards; Elias listens to rock music. Neither they nor their followers blend easily together. The audience, like Taylor, is expected to take sides, and Taylor eventually chooses Elias.

As in *Apocalypse Now*, much information is given through voice-over narration, in this case by Taylor. We even hear the contents of the letters that he writes home. In addition, Stone provided many gritty details of military life that are usually passed over in most combat films; he also gave an apparently truer depiction of the comparatively limited variety of Americans who were serving on the battlefield there, namely the underclass, who had neither the pull nor perhaps even the desire to get a deferment, join the National Guard, or flee to Canada.

A series of frustrations suffered by the platoon leads to an assault on a village in search of the elusive enemy that had brutally killed one of the GIs. The result is an orgy of destruction, rape, and murder by some who have lost self-control, including, momentarily, Taylor. The key moment comes in a violent confrontation between Elias and Barnes over Barnes's very real threat to murder a child to force information out of her father. This confrontation breaks the uneasy truce between the two, and between their respective followers. Their ultimate clash occurs during another firefight when Barnes goes after Elias, who has gone alone into the jungle to outflank the enemy. Barnes shoots him, leaving him for dead and telling the others that he was killed by the enemy. As the platoon is lifted out by helicopter, they see the wounded Elias emerge into the clearing, arms upraised in supplication, only to be killed by the onrushing enemy. Strongly suspecting Barnes of lying about the entire episode, Elias's followers futilely plot Barnes's assassination.

In the final cataclysmic battle, Taylor finally gets his chance to avenge the death of Elias. He finds the wounded Barnes the next morning and, at Barnes's challenge, kills him on the spot.

As Taylor, also wounded in the battle, is flown out we see the carnage below and hear his voice telling us that the enemy we were fighting was not external, but internal; it was within us, a sentiment that echoes *Apocalypse Now*, and yet says very little about the politics of the war. In fact, other than a few negative comments by Elias, no one discusses the meaning and purpose of the war. If the film had been made during or shortly after the war, this would not have been at all unusual. As Russell Shain points out, "Hollywood did not delve into the underlying causes of World War II. Only 2.7% of the 405 1939–1947 films examined the causes of the war to any major extent."[10] This movie, however, was released some 13 years after that controversial conflict and the director/scriptwriter was trying to make a statement. During his Oscar acceptance speech, Stone said,

> Through this award you really are acknowledging the Vietnam veteran and I think what you're saying is that for the first time you really understand what happened there, and I think what you're saying is that it should never happen again. And if it does, then these American boys died over there for nothing, because American learned nothing from the Vietnam war.[11]

Whatever its message or intent, the film's four-Oscar success was followed by a trio of Vietnam combat films of varying quality and intent in 1987: *Hamburger Hill*, *Full Metal Jacket*, and *Good Morning, Vietnam*, although the combat in the latter was directed more against bureaucratic officers who didn't understand rock and roll music than it was against the Vietcong.

Hamburger Hill, in focusing on a small group rather than one or two individuals, recalls some World War II films, such as *Battleground* (1949).[12] It tells of the attack by the 101st Airborne Division on a hill in the A Shau Valley in May 1969, a hill with no importance other than that the enemy was there. The action was widely criticized at the time because of heavy losses over ten days of repeated assaults, at the end of which the captured hill was abandoned and subsequently reoccupied by the enemy. The film follows a squad of fourteen who are reduced to three. Although the film is seemingly all battle action, it does give the civilian some sense of the incredible noise and confusion of combat.

Full Metal Jacket was anxiously awaited because of Stanley Kubrick's reputation as a major director and because of the newly whetted appetite for films that could get at the meaning of the Vietnam conflict. Kubrick is normally a reclusive director who labors meticulously over his films. The result is usually highly individualistic; in this case it was also generally disappointing.

There were really two films; the first was an icy examination of the recruit training experience, where civilians are stripped of their identity and remolded into the Marines' version of "American fighting men," a shocker to those who haven't been there. Using comparatively unknown actors, the first half of the movie focuses on three recruits: Joker (Mathew Modine), Cowboy (Arliss Howard), and Pyle (Vincent D'Onofrio), and their Marine drill instructor, Sgt. Hartman (a former real D.I., Lee Ermey). The methods of transformation are brutal, even vicious, but also effective—erratically effective in the case of Pyle who, on the eve of being shipped out to active service, kills Sgt. Hartman and himself. It seems almost understandable, after having heard Hartman extol, among others, the marksmanship of the ex-Marine who took over the tower on the campus of the University of Texas and who shot dozens of people before being slain in his sniper's nest.

The heightened expectations for the rest of the film dissipate in the second half, where we follow the exploits of Joker, assigned as a journalist to the military newspaper *Stars and Stripes*. The Marine company has been broken up, and the only other familiar character that we see again is Cowboy, an indecisive leader who is soon slain by a sniper. Other than a quick firefight at base camp during the 1968 Tet offensive, the only combat action shown is a patrol entering Hue during the battle to retake it. The action focuses on the attempt to find and kill the sniper who has shot Cowboy and several other members of the patrol. The intended high point is whether Joker will finish off the wounded female sniper, who is begging him to do so.

Joker's wise-guy wit is as off-putting to the audience as it is to the other characters. We tend to be as emotionally distanced from him as we are to the main characters in other Kubrick films such as *2001: A Space Odyssey* and *Clockwork Orange.* We note the absurdities and contradictions of the war, but in a detached, intellectual manner; we do not feel them. They are as abstract as a seminar on the War of 1812.

The year 1988 was a banner one for the war buff; no fewer than eight Vietnam combat films were released, most of them eminently forgettable. *Bat 21* was a standard drama of an intelligence officer trapped in enemy territory (there were no "enemy lines" to speak of), fighting his way back to rescue. It was well-acted, but familiar. An interesting view of the war was *84 Charley Mopic,* which was seen through the lens (literally) of a combat cameraman. We stumble, run for our lives, and dive for cover when he does. In that sense, it is reminiscent of the subjective camera technique of the 1946 drama *Lady in the Lake,* both involving and disorienting.

Iron Triangle is interesting because it is the only film released here to reflect the Vietcong's viewpoint. It was, unfortunately, not very effective, but it did put a more humane face on a generally unseen enemy. *Off Limits* was essentially a detective movie that happened to be set in Saigon. The last three films, *The Expendables, 'Nam Angels,* and *Platoon Leader,* were cheap knockoffs of little virtue. No movie that has an American officer recruit Hell's Angels to ride their bikes into the jungle against a former Nazi SS officer and his Montagnard native followers to rescue his men can be all good (*'Nam Angels*). Besides, it was imitative of *The Losers* (1971), which used four bikers for a similar mission. As Bernard Dick writes, "Eventually, Hollywood gets around to making a movie about everything. . . ."[13] *The Expendables* was merely an updated version of *The Dirty Dozen.* One memorable scene did appear in *Platoon Leader,* however: a "cherry" lieutenant is trying to make conversation with an experienced enlisted man as they ride in a helicopter. He asks the GI, "What's it like?" The GI stares at him silently for a few moments and then replies, "It's good. You go out on patrol and you kill a few of them. And then they kill a few of yours. Then you go back to base. Eat. Sleep. Next day, same thing. Before you know it you're either dead or going home. It's good."

Casualties of War (1989) reduced the Vietnam war to a much narrower but deeper dimension. Whereas *Apocalypse Now* examined the war and its moral meaning for America from an overall perspective, and *Platoon* looked at its atrocities on a village level, this film focuses on a single squad of five men and its abduction, rape, and murder of one Vietnamese girl. This is atrocity at its most elemental level. It is based on a real incident in 1966, in the early phase of American military involvement in Vietnam, a few years before the much larger-scale atrocity of My Lai. But the real-life results were similar in terms of the attempts by the military to overlook or cover up the incident and in the punishment meted out to those involved. The story was told in an article by Daniel Lang in the October 18, 1969, issue of the *New Yorker* and subsequently made into a book.

In essence, this Brian De Palma film follows a five-man squad, consisting of the young but experienced macho sergeant Meserve (Sean Penn); two regular squad members; the "cherry" replacement Eriksson (Michael J. Fox); and the more experienced transferee, Diaz. Denied the opportunity to "party" in town the night before leaving for a reconnaissance mission, the squad follows Meserve into a village and kidnaps a young girl to use as "R & R" during their journey.

The men repeatedly rape the girl, Diaz reluctantly so. Only Eriksson re-fuses. The film revolves around Eriksson's futile attempts to save the girl, and his agony over his failure. Battered and bloody, the girl is ultimately stabbed and shot to death.

Eriksson is more successful in his persistent attempts to have the other four squad members brought up on charges, despite attempts on his life and the Army's reluctance to pursue the case. In the film the men are convicted and sentenced to many years of hard labor. In reality, the sentences were greatly re-duced and the men freed in a comparatively short time. Elia Kazan made a 16mm film in 1972, *The Visitors*, perhaps a fictional follow-up of the same incident, in which two Vietnam veterans, released from prison, come to exact revenge on a third, whose testimony against them in a rape and murder trial helped convict them.

Whether seen as a report of a true incident or as a metaphor for the entire American involvement in Vietnam, it is an effective film on a very personal level, if nearly unwatchable in some scenes. Pauline Kael wrote, "The director has isolated us from all distractions. There are no plot subterfuges; war is the only metaphor. The soldiers hate Vietnam and the Vietnamese for their frustra-tions, their grievances, their fear, and they take their revenge on the girl."[14] The film's role in the so-called healing process is indeterminate. Gavin Smith noted that, "Vietnam vets might say that these war atrocities were committed by a min-ute percentage of soldiers—but that's irrelevant. The baby-killing GI psycho is a stereotype produced and perpetuated because it permits denial of historical responsibility. It was the crazies, not *us.*"[15]

Two additional films of engagement came out in 1989: *Last Stand at Lang Mei*, based on a real incident, is a tale of men trapped behind enemy lines; *Born on the Fourth of July*, by Oliver Stone, is based on the life of Marine Ron Kovic, "who entered the war as a gung-ho patriot and finished it as a paraplegic war protester."[16]

The decade-long hiatus referred to above between films of military en-gagement with the enemy was not one in which no films were made with refer-ence, or relevance, to the war. In fact, nearly half of all the nonengagement mov-ies referring to the war that were made between 1965 and 1989 were released in that period (see Table 1). All but three of the films that make specifically political comments about the war were released before 1973. Life in the United States during the Vietnam war and problems concerning the returning veteran made up the majority of war-related subjects.

THE HOMEFRONT

The complex social crosscurrents that wove the fabric of the 1960s have not yet been fully sorted out, but a few threads stand out clearly. These include substantial national prosperity, worldwide liberation movements, and a "youth culture" questioning the values and mores of the older generation—the "generation gap." Prosperity, of course, is what allowed the young such indulgence, and the political liberation gave it focus, however tenuous.

The Vietnam war was therefore a natural target for youth-oriented films, but a target seldom aimed at directly. Movies were mostly about impediments to self-actualization, which often boiled down to having sex and avoiding routinized employment. The military draft, leading to the most routinized and controlling employment of all, was another story.

Windflowers (1967) and *Greetings* (1968) were early independent productions dealing with draft-avoidance and its potential consequences, *Windflowers* melodramatically, *Greetings* comically. *The Gay Deceivers* (1969) followed up on the comic potential of pretending to be homosexual to avoid military service. In this case, however, unable to live with the social embarrassment of seeming to be gay, two young men try to enlist, only to be rejected by two homosexual recruiting officers who long for an entirely gay army. *Hair* (1979), directed by Milos Forman a decade after the musical opened in New York, also included a musical scene in which multiracial examining officers express their interracial homosexual longings for the draftees lined up before them.

The most important of these confrontational draft-avoidance films was *Alice's Restaurant* (1969), directed by Arthur Penn. It focused on Arlo Guthrie's real experiences as related in his lengthy hit record of the same title. Guthrie drops out of college, drifts to New York and then to Stockbridge, Massachusetts, where he falls in with an incipient hippie commune. Discarding the trash following a Thanksgiving dinner there, he is arrested for littering. Later, called in for a pre-induction physical, he fails in his attempt to outwit the psychiatrist by pretending to be an unbalanced killer. He is finally rejected as morally unfit; this is because of his prior criminal record as a litterbug. While the story itself is slight, the detailed portrayal of the counterculture gives the film some substance.

Other films dealing with draft dodging involved the question of hiding out, either in this country or in Canada, or fighting the draft, and hence the war, directly. Films in this group include *Cowards* (1970), *Summertree* (1971), adapted from the Off-Broadway play, *Outside In* (1972), and *Duty Bound* (1973). An interesting combination of themes appeared in *Journal Through Rosebud* (1972). Although not one of director Tom Gries' better efforts, the movie follows a young draft dodger who seeks sanctuary on the Rosebud Indian Reservation in South Dakota.

The film is as much about the plight of present-day American Indians as it is about avoiding the draft. (The connection between American Indians and the Vietnam war occurs several times and will be dealt with in greater detail in the section on politics.)

Some films did feature those who stayed home to oppose the war directly, such as *The Activist* (1969), *Homer* (1970), *Prism* (1971) and *The Trial of the Catonsville 9* (1972), based on Daniel Berrigan's play.

Many of the films of the period, however, were inane exercises meant primarily to cash in on the "youth market" solidly identified by *Easy Rider* (1969). Although not directly related to the war or homefront protests, *Easy Rider* seemed to capture some of the social malaise that many young people were feeling, and its profits were large enough to convince Hollywood this was a market worth pandering to, especially since Hollywood's "blockbusters," aimed at middle-class adults, were *losing* money.

A number of mainstream productions quickly followed *Easy Rider*. *Zabriskie Point* (1970), directed by Michelangelo Antonioni, was one of the biggest in terms of expectations, following his critical success with *Blow-Up* (1966), and in terms of artistic failure. The film deals with the brief adventures of a college student, who may or may not have shot a policeman during a campus demonstration, and the secretary he picks up along the way. In the act of returning a small plane, he is shot down by massed firepower at the airport. Hearing the news, the girl imagines, in slow-motion detail, the repetitious destruction of her employer's desert mansion and, symbolically, America.

Other films dealing with campus demonstrations and protests against "the Establishment" included *Getting Straight* (1970) about a Vietnam veteran pursuing a graduate degree. Confronting the university president, the graduate student sets him straight about the demonstrations. He tells him that revolution is created by repression. Referring to an undergraduate shouting "Pigs go home!" as an example, he says that not long ago the kid was concerned with getting laid and now he's primed to destroy the school, that the wiser course would have been to ease off and let him get laid. The graduate student later throws a rock through a window and has sex himself. The film premiered a few days after the student killings at Kent State University in Ohio, an event that highlighted the film's emptiness.

The Strawberry Statement, based on James Kunen's book about the 1968 Columbia University riots, appeared the same year. It was an equally fatuous exercise in audience exploitation. Two other early protest films tried different approaches. *Hail, Hero* (1969) had a clean-cut hippie protesting the war, but ultimately deciding to go into the military anyway. *The Revolutionary* (1970), on the other hand, portrays a college student named A (shades of Kafka), in an unspecified time and place, gradually developing into a bomb-throwing revolutionary.

Later youth films, such as *American Graffiti* (1973) and its sequel *More American Graffiti* (1979), *Big Wednesday* (1978), *A Small Circle of Friends* (1980), *Four Friends* (1981), and *This Time Forever* (1981), emphasized friendship and love rather than the war itself. *Hair* (1979) did the same thing, but as a musical celebrating the "Age of Aquarius."

Only one film dealt with what should have been a natural subject for Hollywood: the wives of POWs and MIAs. Apparently when Hollywood set "women's pictures" aside in the 1950s, it meant it. *Limbo* (1972) was a melodrama about such women, three in particular, and their efforts to cope with the uncertainty of the status of their husbands. The critical reaction to the movie was perhaps the reason for its singularity. Pauline Kael's evaluation is representative:

> This "women's picture" is so exploitive it's some sort of classic—a salute to banality. . . . There's not a single false note of originality. The cliches come at you full face. . . . This is one of the few films that attempt to touch on the war directly, but it comes out of a morally exhausted popular culture: the moviemakers can find no drama in their subject, no characters and nothing to reveal. The movie never really gets into the hell of not knowing whether your husband is alive or dead. . . . The movie doesn't get into anything; it mentions things, but no thought is developed. . . . Nobody would ever guess from this movie that there had ever been public protests against the Vietnam war; *Limbo* allows itself only the merest hints of malfunctioning in the democratic system.[17]

Oddly enough, it was *Friendly Fire* (1979), a television movie, that faced the war's effect on the homefront. Television is usually the least likely medium to handle dramatic material without fudging it, but *Friendly Fire* took head-on the issue of death in Vietnam by other than enemy action.

Based on a real incident, and the book written about it by C.D.B. Bryan, the film follows a midwestern couple's quest to discover exactly how their son died. Because his death was accidental, caused by "friendly fire," the son's name was omitted from published casualty lists. The parents' constant inquiries provoke the government to resort to telephone taps and mail censorship. The parents' attitude toward the war changes from one of general support to active participation in the Washington Peace March. Their obsession with the case and their antiwar activities gradually alienate them from the rest of the town. It is another instance of the war's divisiveness.

An end title claims that between 1968 and 1973, at least 10,303 Americans died in Vietnam through "friendly fire"; that is, about 20 percent of American fatalities there. No source for that assertion is identified, however.

Who'll Stop the Rain? (1978) dramatized yet another way the Vietnam war was brought home to America. Adapted from Robert Stone's novel, *Dog Soldiers,* it follows the activities of a journalist in Vietnam who arranges to have a quantity of heroin smuggled back into the United States. There is little mention of the war itself. Rather, the film deals symbolically with the importation of Asian-style corruption as a result of the war. Albert Auster and Leonard Quart observed:

> Vietnam is used as a metaphor for America's capacity for violence and self-annihilation. Its landscape is literally and figuratively a desert, a void where people

lead vague, drifting lives or become vicious murderous men. The United States, like Vietnam, is a country where killing has become as normal as eating.[18]

A few other more recent films about the homefront are worthy of note. *Streamers* (1983), directed by Robert Altman and based on David Rabe's stage play, explored the social attitudes of a group of soldiers in an army barracks a few days before being sent to Vietnam. *Alamo Bay* (1985) looked at a more contemporary conflict between Vietnamese refugees from the war and Gulf Coast fishermen who resent their presence. Finally, there is *Gardens of Stone* (1987), directed by Francis Coppola, which examined the war's effect on the military that remained in the United States—specifically, the Old Guard burial unit, stationed at Arlington National Cemetery, which had to face the stream of coffins arriving daily from Vietnam. In the end, the unit had to confront the death of one of its own who finally succeeded in getting transferred to Vietnam, believing that "the right man in the right place at the right time can change the course of history."

The homefront films contained very little that either a citizen or Hollywood could take pride in. They were generally exploitative, examining few of the issues surrounding the war or the controversies dividing the nation.

THE VETERAN

There was another aspect of the homefront films: the plight of the veteran. The major themes were the veteran's wounds in combat and his adjustment to civilian life. These have been a mainstay of Hollywood since World War I. Prime examples might be *I am a Fugitive from a Chain Gang* (1932), *Pride of the Marines* (1945), *The Best Years of Our Lives* (1946), *The Men* (1950), and *Home of the Brave* (1949). The early Vietnam veteran movies were, unfortunately, not in their league; they were instead mostly continuations of the "motorcycle" films with an added fillip: the returned veteran with enhanced fighting abilities to add to the violence and mayhem endemic to these movies.

The Born Losers (1967), for example, featured Billy Jack (Tom Laughlin) as a former Green Beret, at that time considered the epitome of the military fighting man. He was also a "half-breed" Indian as well as a disillusioned Vietnam veteran, although the reasons for that disillusionment are not made clear. He lives outside a small town in the Southeast where a number of young women have been raped by a motorcycle gang and threatened with further violence should they testify against their attackers. Despite being a proponent of nonviolence, Billy Jack uses a great deal of it to destroy the members of the gang. Although audiences accustomed to seeing the bikers triumph over their persecutors may have been disappointed, they were at least satisfied with the glorious mayhem.

The Billy Jack character reappeared in several sequels: *Billy Jack* (1971), *The Trial of Billy Jack* (1974) and *Billy Jack Goes to Washington* (1977). *Billy Jack* built on the themes of *The Born Losers*. Here he has taken on the role of defender of

The Free School, a nontraditional, counterculture institution run by his girl-friend. But this time his antagonists are not motorcycle gang members but cit-izens of the town who oppose the school.

When the son of an affluent family rapes Billy Jack's girlfriend and mur-ders one of the students, Billy Jack takes his revenge and prepares to fight the town to his death. At this point the movie comes to grips with one of the themes running through not only the Billy Jack films but also other protest films of the era: What does it mean to be a proponent of peace and nonviolence, and under what provocations can one maintain it? Billy Jack's girlfriend argues that if she can swallow her hatred while being raped, he should be able to do so now; that if he means what he says about believing in peace, he should practice it. Although not fully convinced, Billy Jack commits himself to the cause of the school.

The follow-up film, *The Trial of Billy Jack*, is chiefly significant for its allu-sion to nearly every atrocity from Wounded Knee to My Lai and Kent State. During the trial we are told of Billy Jack's experiences in Vietnam, which in-cluded a My Lai-style massacre, and the reasons for his disillusionment. The disil-lusionment and anger, whether turned inward or outward, have continued to be the primary thread running through most of the veterans' movies since *Billy Jack*. Billy Jack's solution was to turn those feelings into social commitment, a solution that not every veteran could accept.

Angels from Hell and *The Angry Breed*, released a year after *Born Losers*, both had veterans with nothing more on their minds than getting involved with biker gangs and displaying contempt for the system that sent them to Vietnam. The veteran in *Satan's Sadists* (1969), however, used his combat skills *against* a motorcy-cle gang; and in *Chrome and Hot Leather* (1971) the Vietnam veteran and three of his buddies, all Green Beret instructors, not only use their combat skills but also rockets, tear gas, and grenades. They destroy the rapist bikers the same way they destroyed the Vietcong. Coming home, it seems, did not necessarily mean leaving death and destruction behind.

This point was emphasized in a different kind of motorcycle film, *The Hard Ride* (1970). Here, an ex-sergeant accompanies the body of his dead black buddy home for burial. He tries to get his dead friend's girlfriend and the Indian leader of his motorcycle gang to attend the funeral. At the end, there is a double funeral for both the ex-sergeant and his buddy. Similarly, in *Tracks* (1977), another sergeant accompanies a friend's body home. The obviously disturbed sergeant (Dennis Hopper) is even more disturbed when there is no one to meet him upon his arrival. When no one appears at the grave side burial service, the sergeant snaps, cracks open the lowered casket, and takes out automatic weapons to "waste" anyone he sees.

The disturbed-veteran theme came early in the Vietnam films and has persisted, though in different guises. The "disturbance" is not the same as the World War II "shell-shock" themes or the psychological torture associated with Korea. For those who suffer it, it is a sense of displacement, anomie, and guilt that may manifest itself in physical and/or psychological withdrawal, or in vio-lence—self-destructive or otherwise.

In some films, like *The Big Bounce* (1969) and *Norwood* (1970), the veterans become drifters, wandering from adventure to adventure. *Heroes* (1977) has the veteran escaping from a psychiatric hospital and traveling across the country searching for his golden rainbow, falling in love in the process. The psychologically disabled ex-officer in *Americana* (1981)[19] finds his goal in a small Kansas town. Spying a broken-down carousel in the middle of town, he proceeds to repair it for no reason other than therapy. Opposed by a suspicious community that can't understand him, he picks up and spends his hitherto neglected disability checks to finance the repair.

The most famous of the drifter vets was Rambo, introduced in *First Blood* (1982). After visiting the family of a buddy who died of cancer apparently induced by exposure to Agent Orange, John Rambo (Sylvester Stallone), an ex-Green Beret, drifts into a small community in the Pacific Northwest. Although told to get out of town by the local sheriff, Rambo returns only to be promptly arrested and beaten by sadistic guards. In a scene that includes flashbacks to his torture by the Vietnamese, Rambo loses self-control and turns on his captors, beating them up and then escaping to the forest where he feels at home. He then uses his military training to defeat his pursuers, who range from police to the National Guard, helicopters, and dogs. He eventually returns to town to find the sheriff and causes mayhem in his efforts to flush him out. Only his former Green Beret commander is able to persuade Rambo to surrender, after listening to Rambo's tirade about those in America who "sold us out" in Vietnam.

Rambo is next seen in *Rambo: First Blood Part II* (1985), to be discussed in the next section on the POW/MIA movies, and then in *Rambo III* (1988). In the latter, he turns up in Asia where he engages in stick-fighting to earn money for the local monks. Here he is persuaded to go on a special mission to Afghanistan to rescue his old mentor and friend, Colonel Trautman. Rambo has taken on the virtues of the gunfighter hero of the Western, who comes into town to right a wrong but then must leave, because he doesn't fit in with civilized folk. Think of him as a super-economy-size Shane.

The perceived wrongs of some veterans were not righted in so salutary a fashion, however. *Welcome Home, Soldier Boys* (1972) followed four ex-Green Berets (again) on their way to California. Finding hostility and trouble wherever they go, they react by, among other things, gang-raping a girl and burning down the town of Hope, New Mexico.

Another form of drifting was depicted in *Riders of the Storm* (1988), in which a team of psychological-warfare veterans crisscross the United States in an elaborately equipped B-52. Their final mission is to sabotage the campaign of a right-wing female candidate for president who turns out to be a man.

The veteran in *The Stunt Man* (1980)[20] was more of a fugitive than a drifter. Fleeing the police, he is accidentally involved in the death of a movie stunt man during the shooting of a film. Since the veteran has been filmed as well, he is persuaded to replace the stunt man in exchange for being hidden from the police. What he did to cause the police and FBI to pursue him is a recurring theme. Suspicious, hostile, and paranoid, he could have done anything. Yet, we are told, his "crime" was comparatively minor. Feeling betrayed by his boss at an ice cream parlor and by his unfaithful wife, the protagonist decides to take revenge on his boss. Instead, he mistakenly freezes the nose and ears of a policeman with a tub of ice cream: criminal assault.

Some of the movie Vietnam veterans were not drifters, although no better adjusted to civilian life. In *Hi! Mom* (1969), Brian DePalma has his hero (Robert De Niro) return from the war to become a maker of pornographic films and a bomber of apartment houses. In *Slaughter* (1972) and its sequel *Slaughter's Big Rip-Off* (1973) another ex-Green Beret goes after the drug syndicate that murdered his parents, again using the methods learned in the military. A similar theme appears in *Gordon's War* (1973), where an ex-Green Beret, discovering that his wife is a victim of the drug plague, organizes the local citizenry to clean up Harlem. In *Clay Pigeon* (1971) a disenchanted veteran gets involved with a Los Angeles drug gang until he has a change of mind and rubs them out. *Special Delivery* (1976) has a gang of veterans getting together to rob a bank and facing the consequences of having both the police and a gang of killers after them.

Some movie veterans were neither drifters nor men with a purpose, but were men of "opportunity." Martin Scorcese's *Taxi Driver* (1976) opens with a psychopathic former Marine, Travis Bickle (Robert De Niro), driving a taxi through a hellish-looking New York. After meeting an attractive campaign worker, he comes close to assassinating her political candidate. And after meeting a teenage prostitute, he kills her pimp and the pimp's associates and returns the girl to her midwestern family. The public mistakenly lauds him for what was really a psychopathic act. He was going to kill someone; the targets just happened to be so repulsive that the act was applauded.

Another man of "opportunity" appeared in John Frankenheimer's *Black Sunday* (1977). A former POW, who now pilots the TV blimp shooting the Super Bowl, is recruited by a terrorist organization to drop an anti-personnel bomb on the crowd during the game. He has no interest in the terrorists' goals; his motive is revenge on the country that caused him to become a POW.

For some veterans, things just "happened." In *Glory Boy* (1971)[21] an ex-serviceman returns to his father's farm with two friends, trying to come to terms with the atrocities he had committed in Vietnam. Instead, in the ensuing tense atmosphere, rape and murder result. And in *Rolling Thunder* (1977) an ex-POW returns home to his family after eight years of torture. The grateful townspeople give him a silver dollar for every day of captivity. This sizable hoard provokes a gang of thieves to rob him, to grind his hand in a garbage disposal, and to kill his family. The remainder of the film depicts his pursuit of the killers and his vengeance.

The American Indian ex-serviceman in *Johnny Firecloud* (1977) returns from Vietnam intent upon helping his father, only to face a real-estate developer with designs on his father's land and a population that still habors prejudice against Indians. The black ex-POW in *Some Kind of Hero* (1982) fares no better. He has lost his wife to another man, and all his savings, which they took with them; he can't get his veteran's benefits because the Defense Department considers him a traitor; and his mother is being evicted from a nursing home. It is interesting that this sequence of events was taken from a novel by James Kirkwood about his own homecoming from Korea. Some experiences are apparently timeless.

For many of the film vets, postwar adjustments meant coming to terms with themselves—their psychic and physical wounds—not external circumstances and events. In *The Ravager* (1970), a soldier, traumatized by witnessing a rape and murder by the Vietcong, continues to be haunted by the memory after his return home. The veteran in *Jud* (1971) is so scarred that he can no longer handle civilian life at all. The ex-POW in *Welcome Home, Johnny Bristol* (1971) is startled to discover that the ideal Vermont hometown he was fighting for no longer exists; in fact, it never existed. It was an illusion, created to sustain him during his ordeal, which was more worthwhile than his real but ordinary Philadelphia neighborhood.

Other films about veterans with disabling psychic wounds include *The Ninth Configuration* (1980), *Medal of Honor Rag* (1982), *Birdy* (1984), *Cease Fire* (1985), *Distant Thunder* (1988), *Jackknife* (1989), *In Country* (1989), *Welcome Home* (1989), and *Vietnam, Texas* (1989). The veteran in *The Ninth Configuration* is so traumatized that he has assumed the identity of another man killed in Vietnam, an Army psychiatrist. As part of his treatment he is ostensibly put in charge of a group of government psychiatric cases in an isolated castle in the Pacific Northwest. *Medal of Honor Rag*, adapted from a 1975 play, portrays the psychiatric treatment of a Medal of Honor winner (taken from a real case) suffering from survivor's guilt and receiving public honors for going berserk in combat. *Birdy* examines the relationship of two veterans, one in a catatonic state, who are reunited after the war in a psychiatric hospital.

The veteran in *Cease Fire* refuses to acknowledge that he even has a problem, despite the fact that 15 years after the war he nearly kills his wife when he sees her as one of the enemy. The veterans in the more recent films are much less dangerous, although still haunted by their experiences. In *Distant Thunder* the ex-soldier has taken to living in the wilderness. *Jackknife* has one veteran helping a buddy overcome his grief over the death of a mutual friend in Vietnam. Not a great deal happens in the film in terms of action, yet it is very moving and realistic. Another "quiet" film is *In Country*, in which a teenage girl comes to terms with her father's death in the war and helps her uncle, with whom she lives, finally resolve his feelings about his experiences there. The film ends with a visit by the girl, her uncle, and her grandmother to the war memorial for Vietnam veterans in Washington, D.C.

Welcome Home (1989) is less effective in portraying the plight of an escaped POW who doesn't return home for 17 years, having built a new life with a Vietnamese woman. Forcibly separated from his Asian family, he returns home to find his wife remarried and a son who doesn't know him. A subplot implies the government doesn't want to acknowledge either his presence or that of other "missing" servicemen still living in Vietnam. Another film, unreleased as of this writing, titled *Vietnam, Texas*, depicts "a priest tormented by the guilt of leaving behind a beautiful Vietnamese woman and their child."[22]

The two films by which subsequent veteran movies are usually measured are *Coming Home* and *The Deer Hunter,* both released in 1978 and both receiving several Oscars. It is unclear how well each would fare today.

Coming Home revolves around three people: Sally Hyde (Jane Fonda), her Marine Corps husband, Capt. Bob Hyde (Bruce Dern), and Luke Martin (Jon Voight), a paraplegic veteran she meets while doing volunteer work in the military hospital. While Bob Hyde is off fighting a war he can neither understand nor describe, Sally and Luke help each other adjust to civilian life. She becomes sexually functional for the first time and he becomes an active antiwar protester. When Bob returns from the war with a foot wound and in need of compassion, he gets little from his wife. When last seen, he is stripping off his uniform on the beach and wading into the water to end his life. Bob was unable to "come home again," in contrast to Luke and to Sally, who knew what was important in life.

The Deer Hunter traces the fortunes of four friends, steelworkers in a small Pennsylvania town. Although the beginning is impressive, the film begins to fragment when three of the four, Michael (Robert De Niro), Nick (Christopher Walken), and Steven (John Savage), go off to Vietnam. Virtually none of the war is seen, nor is the enemy, except for their Viet Cong captors. Instead, the audience is treated to an extended sequence of Russian roulette that the three are forced to play for the enjoyment of their captors. The three escape, but are separated. Nick recuperates in a Saigon hospital but then remains in Saigon where he becomes a professional player of Russian roulette. After Steven's broken legs are amputated, he refuses to see his wife. Michael goes home, but then returns to Saigon to locate Nick. The men play Russian roulette, the only way in which Michael can make contact with Nick. Nick loses and Michael returns home with Nick's body.

It was not Hollywood's finest hour. What the film promotes are the sanctity of small-town America, the glory of the hunt, and the comparative purity of American values as opposed to those of Asia; it is "Yellow Perilism," Vietnam style. Gilbert Adair commented:

> Its attempts to reaffirm the viability of a heroic posture in an unheroic age, revivify the frontier myth when it was being most vigorously contested and, above all, salve the nation's uneasy conscience make it prime exhibit in any dossier of American attitudes to the war. At the same time, however, a movie should be more than the servile barometer of its audience's aspirations. . . . What is required *now* for the generation that fought or lived through Vietnam is a movie to challenge our perceptions instead of reinforcing them, dismantle our prejudices instead of indulging them.[23]

Cutter's Way (1981), an adaptation of Newton Thornburg's novel, *Cutter and Bone,* was a richer and more complex exploration of a veteran and his friendships, although on a much smaller scale. While there is a plot about bringing a crooked tycoon to justice, the focus of the film is on Cutter (John Heard), a one-eyed, paraplegic wheelchair-bound veteran, and his relationship with Bone (Jeff

Bridges), a "laid-back" Ivy League pal. Not only is Cutter not haunted by his war experiences, but this cynical bundle of aggressive energy is out to engage the world. Bone's function is to deal with him nonjudgmentally and to hold him within bounds.

Two films dealt with deserters in a surprisingly objective way: *Summer Soldiers* (1971), about deserters hiding in Japan; and *Two People* (1973), depicting a repentant deserter who returns home to face the consequences. Finally, just to show that there was no leaving the war behind, *Search and Destroy* (1981) featured two veterans who are stalked in the United States by a vengeful former Vietnamese official skilled in Oriental martial arts.

THE POW-MIA PROBLEM

Not all GIs in Vietnam had the opportunity to return to civilian life, at least not immediately. Comparatively few films were made about prisoners of war (POWs) or those considered missing in action (MIA); most of these films appeared in the Reagan years, when POWs and MIAs were popular political subjects.

Nearly all of the films were about attempted rescues, the first one, *To the Shores of Hell,* appearing in 1965. The explanation for such an early date, despite the fact that the United States had relatively few troops in Vietnam, lies in the nature of American involvement at that time. Civilians had been working there since the 1950s. The POW to be rescued in the film was a civilian doctor held captive by the Vietcong, a perfectly logical premise for a film. The rescuer was his brother, a Marine Corps major. It was perhaps the last logical premise in any of the subsequent films about the subject.

In the above-mentioned *The Losers,* two veterans are sent to Vietnam with three friends as a five-man motorcycle squad to rescue an American presidential adviser from a Chinese prison camp. In *Good Guys Wear Black* (1977), the movies still haven't gotten around to rescuing GIs. This film has former commando, now political science professor, John Booker (Chuck Norris) trying to discover who set up his earlier raid to rescue CIA personnel from a Vietnamese prison so that it would fail. Of course, it turns out to be a high government official, the Secretary of State-designate. This, as we shall see, is a recurring plot device in this kind of film.

Uncommon Valor (1983) was, as the promos used to say, "ripped from the day's headlines." In late 1982, a raid into Laos to rescue captive Americans was attempted by an ex-Green Beret colonel and a small group of associates; it proved a failure. Hollywood, of course, has greater creativity and resources. The film's raid is organized by a captive's father, a Marine colonel (Gene Hackman), and the team consists of five former members of the captive's platoon plus the colonel. The foray manages to free a number of POWs, but the son had already died in the camp. Why does the father have to do all this himself? Because, the movie insists, America is no longer interested—we lost.[24]

Missing in Action (1984) and its successors, *Missing in Action 2—The Beginning* (1985) and *Braddock: Missing in Action III* (1988) made about as much sense as the order and numerals of their titles. In the first, Col. Braddock (Chuck Norris), a Vietnam ex-POW, had been missing in action for seven years. Learning of a congressional delegation to Vietnam, Col. Braddock returns there to find some MIAs to present to the delegation. He did have the help of an old friend, however, so the slaughter of hundreds of the enemy would not seem implausible. The sequel, which includes Braddock's Vietnam experiences, has him surviving such tortures in his Vietnamese prison as would make Torquemada blanch. He is able, singlehandedly, to escape, destroy both the camp and hundreds of Vietnamese soldiers, and free the prisoners held there. As for the last film in the series, let it simply be said that Col. Braddock returns yet again to Vietnam, this time to search for his wife. Let us pray that she was an orphan.

Rambo: First Blood Part II (1985) seemed to cap the POW rescue cycle of films, for there have been none since. This film picks up on John Rambo (Sylvester Stallone) doing hard time for his last outburst. His former commander, Colonel Trautman, arrives at the prison to offer Rambo a deal: undertake a photographic mission in Vietnam and get off the rockpile. It is, of course, a trap, meant to fail so that the United States' government can get on with other issues. Rambo nevertheless succeeds in defeating the Vietnamese and their Soviet advisers, freeing the American POWs, and exposing the plot to make the mission fail. The process by which he does so is not worth mentioning, although it is the point of the film. Throughout the film, charges are made that the American servicemen and the American public alike were sold out by a spineless government.

A variation on this theme appeared in a 1989 made-for-cable movie, *The Forgotten*. Seventeen years after the war ended for American troops, six Green Beret POWs are repatriated—not to the United States, but to Germany for deprogramming. After interminable delays, the men get suspicious and escape their handlers, only to discover that they are being hunted and shot at by unknown government agents.

Only a single film focused on the prisoners themselves and what they endured: *Hanoi Hilton* (1987), which, unfortunately, did not serve them well. The story follows a group of American POWs in their captivity by the North Vietnamese. The beatings, torture, and other inhuman treatment are carefully detailed, as are the soldiers' bravery and resourcefulness. However, the film's clichéd dialogue and tired situations do not sustain the viewer's interest. No real understanding of the plight of the POWs emerges.

Albert Auster and Leonard Quart write of these films:

> The films provided a rationale for the loss of the war (irresponsible or corrupt politicians), a popular war-film hero, and a perfidious and demonic enemy. They also reversed the tactical and historic roles of the Americans and Vietnamese— it is the Americans who are both the victims and the guerrillas here—while ignoring the real circumstances of the war. No mention or images of carpet bombing,

the use of Agent Orange, search-and-destroy missions, or strategic hamlets disrupt the familiar war-film heroics of these works.[25]

POLITICS

Though few in number, a variety of films made political comments on the war, or at least were interpreted as doing so. They ranged in time from the nineteenth century to an unspecified future; from France and the Caribbean to Mexico, the United States, and South Africa. The first, *Live for Life* (1967), took the form of a romance between a married French journalist and an American woman. It is through the journalist that the viewer sees a number of mini-documentaries of violence around the world, including a realistic battle in Vietnam. The documentary form allows for political commentary, much of it critical.

Medium Cool (1969) dealt with the political consciousness-raising of another journalist, this time an American television reporter whose primary passion is to shoot film. By falling in love with a woman whose husband is serving in Vietnam, he also gets involved with the antiwar demonstrators at the Chicago Democratic National Convention in 1968. (Remarkably, director Haskell Wexler shot the climax in the city park where the protesters were encamped when the Chicago police rampaged through it, assaulting whomever they found.) Because the political commentary comes through the story rather than through set speeches, it is more effective.

A more interesting film was *Burn!* (1970) by Marxist director Gillo Pontecorvo. A British agent, Sir William Walker (Marlon Brando), is sent to provoke a black slave revolt on a Portuguese-held island in the Caribbean Sea so that the British government can obtain more favorable trade terms for cane sugar. Having succeeded, he sets up a puppet government more amenable to British interests, and then departs for Indochina (on a presumably similar mission). Ten years later, he is recalled from retirement: the blacks have revolted again, this time on their own. In the process of dealing with the guerrilla war, Walker burns all the cane fields, destroying the island's economy (recalling the American officer's comment during the Tet-68 offensive in Vietnam: "It became necessary to destroy the town to save it"). When the leader of the puppet government tries to regain control from Walker to negotiate with the rebels, Walker has him brought before a firing squad. In the end, having successfully suppressed the revolt, Walker prepares to leave the island but is assassinated by an unreconstructed rebel. The resonance with Vietnam is compelling and intended.

The American Western was also used for political commentary on Vietnam. *The Wild Bunch* (1969) ostensibly dealt with a gang of outlaws who were chased out of the United States into Mexico during the Mexican Revolution of 1910. The climactic battle is a scene of prolonged bloodshed and destruction (lasting about 20 minutes in the original film) in which most of the victims are civilians. The leader of the gang is finally killed not by the enemy troops but by a prostitute and a child. David Cook wrote of this film: "But a year before the revelation of the My Lai massacre, the outraged critics could not know that they were watching an allegory of American intervention in Vietnam."[26]

Two other Westerns equated the treatment of American Indians by the United States with the treatment of the Vietnamese. *Soldier Blue* (1970), set within the context of a romance between a young cavalryman and a repatriated female, who was a captive of the Indians, detailed a long string of abuses by the white society and its government against the Indians, destroying many generally held myths in the process. The film ends with the massacre of an entire Indian village, historically based, it is said, on both the Sand Creek Massacre of 1864 and the battle of Wounded Knee in 1890. The brutality of the sequence makes it virtually unwatchable.

The other Western was the epic *Little Big Man,* released the same year. Director Arthur Penn's film follows the adventures of Jack Crabb (Dustin Hoffman) through the "winning" of the West, as he bounces to and fro between white and Indian societies. Picked up as a refugee by the Cheyennes after his parents are killed by the Pawnees, he is adopted into the tribe. We therefore see the settlement of the West from both sides of the conflict. It is soon apparent whose side the film is on. The Indians are noble, honest, and honorable; the whites are not.

> The atrocities in *Little Big Man* are staged with deliberation and clarity; in retrospect, given the eventual revelations about Vietnam regarding My Lai, the saturation bombing of the Plain of Jars in Laos and numerous other atrocities, Penn's recognition of Vietnam's precedent in the Indian wars is accurate right down to the Napoleonic psychosis with which he endows Custer.[27]

Southern Comfort (1981) transferred Vietnam to the Deep South where some National Guardsmen are going through summer field exercises. They "borrow" some Cajun canoes to cross a body of water rather than trudge through the swamp. A guerrilla war of sorts breaks out between the canoe owners and the Guardsmen. The Guardsmen have only blanks, however, and the Cajuns are shooting live ammunition.

Of the film in this category, only two specifically referred to Vietnam. The first, *Twilight's Last Gleaming* (1977), took place not on the battlefield in Vietnam, but at a missile silo in the United States. An ex-Air Force general, falsely imprisoned by the military, escapes with a band of confederates and takes over a silo containing nine nuclear ballistic missiles. He has promised his associates a large bundle of money and flight out of the country if they will assist him. He wants no money, but rather a public presidential statement about America's Vietnam involvement that says, in part, "the objective of this war is to demonstrate to the Russians a brutal national will, that we have the willingness to inflict and suffer untold punishment. That no matter what the cost in American blood, we would perpetrate a theatrical holocaust." It is, essentially, the "madman" policy of Richard Nixon. The threat from the ex-general is that if he doesn't get such a statement, he will launch his missiles and start World War III. It was not a good film, but at least it did broach the subject of American *policies* in Indo-china, a subject generally ignored.

The second of these two Vietnam-based political films was *Don't Cry, It's Only Thunder* (1982). Based on a true story, the film follows the attempts by a female doctor and an army medic to get help for an orphanage that is desperately needed for the abandoned mixed-race children of American GIs.

The remaining films in this category are all displacements to other wars. *M*A*S*H* (1970), although set during the Korean war, is Vietnam in content, attitudes, and style. The title refers to mobile surgical hospitals set up near the front lines to treat casualties on an emergency basis. Its hip comedy demonstrated total irreverence for the government. It hooted down displays of sentimentality and super-patriotism, yet it dealt seriously and graphically with the real purpose of such hospitals.

No Drums, No Bugles (1971) looked back to the Civil War to relate the legend of a conscientious objector from West Virginia who preferred to spend three years living alone in a cave rather than violate his vow not to fight. In contemporary terms, he chose jail rather than do what he did not believe in.

Ironically, it was an Australian film about the Boer War in South Africa that most specifically dealt with a political issue of the Vietnam war—the behavior of American troops in the field and the "Vietnam syndrome" when they return home. *Breaker Morant* (1979) is about the court-martial of three Australian officers of the Bushveldt Carbiniers, a group organized to combat the Boer guerrilla bands roaming through the South African countryside. They are on trial for three specific counts of murder: the execution of a Boer, the execution of a group of Boers who had surrendered, and the ambush slaying of a German missionary suspected of being a Boer spy. The film opens with the trial and then uses flashbacks to fill in details of the plot.

The trial is not for the victims; it is being staged because convictions will help end the war earlier. Although highlighting the opportunism of the British government at the time, the true point of the film is made by the defense counsel in his summation:

> When the rules and customs of war are departed from by one side, one must expect the same sort of behavior from the other.... Now I don't ask for proclamations condoning distasteful methods of war, but I do say we must take for granted that it does happen.... The fact of the matter is, that war changes men's natures. The barbarities of war are seldom committed by abnormal men. The tragedy of war is that these horrors are committed by normal men in abnormal situations—situations in which the ebb and flow of everyday life have departed and been replaced by a constant round of fear and anger, blood and death. Soldiers at war are not to be judged by civilian rules—even though they commit acts which, calmly viewed afterwards, could only be seen as unchristian and brutal. And if, in every war, particularly guerrilla war, all the men who committed reprisals were to be charged and tried as murderers, court-martials like this one would be in permanent session, would they not? I say that we cannot hope to judge such men unless we ourselves have been submitted to the same pressures, the same provocations as these men, whose actions are on trial.

CONCLUSION

The films of the Vietnam war are, on the whole, unsatisfying. Perhaps that is inevitable; perhaps asking for more from the films than from the rest of society is unreasonable. But we do. Seth Cagin and Philip Dray observe:

> The war was a cinematic challenge. For the first time in history, filmmakers had to depict a conflict whose vocabulary of images was one with which most Americans were already familiar. Television coverage of the war had been exhaustive, and Hollywood was hard put to top it for immediacy, poignancy or interest. This may be one reason the best contemporary Vietnam films were those that did not attempt a fictionalization of the war, but addressed it either allegorically or in the form of a documentary.[28]

Although movies are essentially entertainment, on issues important to us we wish for something more: an image that resonates with truth. Television is too practical and ordinary; seen through that little box, even the news is a commercial product. The movies can draw us in, connect with us on a more fundamental level. Hollywood has not done for Vietnam what it did for World War I with *All Quiet on the Western Front* or for World War II with *The Bridge on the River Kwai*. We want substance, and so far all we have gotten is shadow.

NOTES

1. Bernard Dick, *The Star-Spangled Screen* (Lexington: University of Kentucky Press, 1985), p. 142.
2. Gilbert Adair, *Vietnam on Film* (New York: Proteus Publishing Co., 1981), p. 52.
3. Martha Bayles, "The Road to Rambo III," *The New Republic*, 199 (1988), p. 30.
4. But see Daniel Hallin, *The Uncensored War* (New York: Oxford University Press, 1986) for an extensively documented rebuttal to the oft-repeated charge that the media "lost the war."
5. Albert Auster and Leonard Quart, *How the War Was Remembered* (New York: Praeger, 1988), p. 52. The authors' approach is interesting, but the execution is flawed. The book has numerous errors and should be read with caution. Their analysis of *Go Tell the Spartans*, however, is right on target.
6. Adair, *Vietnam on Film*, p. 145.
7. Ibid., pp. 154–155.
8. Quoted in Auster and Quart, *How the War Was Remembered*, p. 140.
9. Ibid., p. 131.
10. Russell Earl Shain, *An Analysis of Motion Pictures About War Released by the American Film Industry 1930–1970* (New York: Arno Press, 1976), p. 286. Shain's work must be read with caution because much of his information is based on film reviews rather than the films themselves, and there are many errors.
11. Quoted in Auster and Quart, *How the War Was Remembered*, p. 139.
12. See Dick, *Star-Spangled Screen*, pp. 143–145.
13. Ibid., p. 243.
14. Pauline Kael, "A Wounded Apparition," *The New Yorker* (August 21, 1989), p. 79.
15. Gavin Smith, "Body Count," *Film Comment* (July-August 1989), p. 51.

16. Rob Medich, "C'est la Guerre," *Premiere* (October 1989), p. 31.

17. Pauline Kael, "Out of Tragedy, Suds," in *Reeling* (New York: Warner Books, 1972), pp. 154–159.

18. Auster and Quart, *How the War Was Remembered,* p. 58.

19. Produced in the mid-1970s.

20. Based on the 1970 novel by Paul Brodeur, and announced as a 1971 release.

21. Re-released under the title *My Old Man's Place* in 1972.

22. Medich, "C'est la Guerre."

23. Adair, *Vietnam on Film,* p. 142.

24. See Auster and Quart, *How the War Was Remembered,* pp. 99–103, for an interesting analysis of the film.

25. Ibid., p. 107.

26. David A. Cook, *A History of Narrative Film* (New York: W.W. Norton & Co., Inc., 1981), pp. 632–633.

27. Seth Cogin and Philip Dray, *Hollywood Films of the Seventies* (New York: Harper & Row, 1984).

28. Ibid., pp. 257–258.

NEWS OR NEMESIS: DID TELEVISION LOSE THE VIETNAM WAR?

by George Donelson Moss

Most everyone knows that the Vietnam war was the first major foreign war that the United States ever lost. Most everyone also knows that the Vietnam war was history's first televised war. Millions of Americans believe that the way television journalists covered the Vietnam war was a major cause of the American defeat in Vietnam. That is, Americans believe that their country lost history's first televised war *because* it was televised. The quite remarkable fact about this widely held and deeply believed theory of television's impact on the outcome of the Vietnam war is that it is not true. There is no available evidence to sustain it. There is an abundance of data, arguments, and theories that challenge the notion that television news coverage of the war was a decisive cause of the U.S. failure in Vietnam. That notion is one of the reigning myths of our time, one of the false lessons learned from the war, a set of beliefs that cannot withstand critical scrutiny and scientific analysis.

The long essay "News or Nemesis: Did Television Lose the Vietnam War?" represents my best effort to refute the belief that television lost the war, to expose it for the myth that it is. To refute the myth, I have crafted a strategy that draws upon all the available evidence, the work of other media analysts, and a variety of theories and research methodologies.

In the introduction, I state the theory that television lost the Vietnam war fully and fairly; in fact, by constructing a composite version, I probably endow the theory with greater coherence and cogency than it possesses in the minds of those individuals who embrace it.

Part I of my article calls attention to some of the problems that face serious television news analysts, particularly the paradox of having both too much and too little data with which to work. I also cite journalists, media analysts, and historians who have challenged the television myth.

Part II of the essay provides a brief history of the evolution of television news to establish the significant historical reality that the coming of age of television news coincided with America's going to war in Vietnam. It is also important to understand that, contrary to conventional wisdom, it is not true that most Americans got most of their news about the Vietnam war from television newscasts. There was much less news about the Vietnam war carried on television than appeared in the contemporaneous print media. Television news coverage was much more likely to reinforce people's pre-existing attitudes toward the war than to change them. Hawks tended to think that the news anchors were hawks; doves tended to think that they were doves. Viewers were more likely to impose their political views on them. Finally, the commercial television networks did not want to and probably could not strike an adversarial stance against government policies during the Vietnam war era.

The arguments that I adduce in Part III are particularly damaging to believers in the television myth. Relying on the findings of a prominent political scientist, John E. Mueller, I show that the Korean war, fought between 1950 and 1953, became as unpopular as the Vietnam war did between the years 1965 and 1968. But during the Korean war, television news coverage of war was in its infancy, most Americans did not watch television newscasts, the news from Korea was heavily censored, and the correspondents covering the war all supported the American effort. Television news coverage does not make a war unpopular. It is the perception of mounting costs and casualties linked to the perception that the war is not being won. Both of these perceptions, in turn, are joined with a loss of faith in national leaders. If people perceive that their leaders are neither competent nor trustworthy, they are unlikely to support their war policies.

Part IV also undermines the belief that television news lost the war. Using data-based arguments derived from content analyses of television news coverage of the war, I show that, contrary to what people think they remember about news coverage of Vietnam, most television news stories did not show U.S. troops dying in combat. Remarkably little American blood was ever shed on television. Reviews of videotapes and kinescopes of the television news stories about Vietnam disprove the oft-repeated charge that the American viewing public got a nightly dose of blood and gore, which in time turned them against the war. Television coverage of the war was not unfavorable much of the time. In fact, for the first three years, news coverage was overwhelmingly favorable; most television journalists supported the American effort. News coverage of the war only became more critical *after* public opinion had turned against it.

In Part V, I refute the claim that biased and graphic television coverage of the surprise Communist Tet-68 offensive caused a massive fall-off in public support for the war and forced President Johnson to abandon his strategy of graduated escalation. Believers in the television myth have insisted that in the years following Tet, America was forced to withdraw its troops from Vietnam because popular support for the war declined. They believe that U.S. troop withdrawals opened the door to

Communist victory and that popular support for America's involvement in Vietnam vanished because of television coverage of Tet and its aftermath.

I use a complex analysis to show that television news coverage of the events of Tet and its aftermath did not turn Americans against the war nor cause Lyndon Johnson to abandon his strategy of military escalation. Tet brought on a political crisis in the United States that had been building for a year. During this crisis, a coterie of elite advisers convinced Johnson that he must abandon his strategy because it was not working. The strategy was politically and strategically bankrupt, it was dividing the American people, and it threatened to harm the national interest. Television news coverage did not create this political crisis or significantly influence the discussions that induced Johnson's policy change.

In Part VI of my article, I refute one of the correlative arguments of the television myth, namely that television coverage of the antiwar movement strengthened the forces opposed to the war, enhanced public opinion against the war, demoralized U.S. troops fighting in Vietnam, and helped to undermine the political will of Presidents Johnson and Nixon to persevere in Vietnam. Television coverage of the radical antiwar movement was always hostile, and coverage of the liberal antiwar movement was at best neutral. I also show that the antiwar movement did not turn the American public against the war. In fact, the organized left-wing, campus-based, vocal antiwar movement appears to have had little, if any, impact on public opinion or on the war policies of the Johnson and Nixon administrations.

In the concluding section of my essay I analyze the reasons for America's defeat in Vietnam. Defeat derived mainly from political failures and not from television news coverage of the war. But television news became a scapegoat. It got blamed for losing a war when it only carried the message that we lost the war. It is important to understand why the United States lost in Vietnam. It is also important that we absolve the media, particularly television news, of the false charge that the media contributed decisively to that defeat.

Vietnam was the first televised war, the first war to be shown night after night in our living rooms. Color video brought Americans the sights and sounds of war— troops on patrol, occasionally in combat, the whirring of helicopter rotors, and the boiling flames of napalm bombs igniting a jungle-canopied hillside. The Vietnam war was also the first that the United States ever lost. Despite committing 543,000 troops, waging the largest aerial war in history, and expending $150 billion of their wealth, Americans were forced to leave Vietnam in 1973 having failed to defeat the forces of the National Liberation Front and the People's Army of North Vietnam trying to overthrow the government of South Vietnam. Two years later, Saigon fell and Hanoi completed its conquest of southern Vietnam.

Many Americans believe that television was a major cause of the American defeat in Vietnam, that is, the United States lost history's first televised war precisely *because* it was televised. It has been given to Robert Elegant, a novelist and journalist who covered Southeast Asia for years, to state the case against television baldly:

For the first time in modern history, the outcome of a war was determined, not on the battlefield but on the printed page and, above all, on the television screen. Looking back coolly, I believe that it can be said that American forces actually won the limited military struggle. They virtually crushed the Vietcong in the South, . . . and thereafter they threw back the invasion by regular North Vietnamese divisions. Nonetheless, the war was finally lost to the invaders *after* [emphasis his] the U.S. disengagement because the political pressures built up by the media had made it quite impossible for Washington to maintain even the minimal ma terial and moral support that would have enabled the Saigon regime to continue effective resistance.[1]

Many former American civilian and military leaders of the Vietnam era share Elegant's view that television coverage cost America a war it could have won. So do a sizable number of television and print journalists themselves. Lyndon Johnson went to his grave convinced that the media, particularly television, prevented American victory. Richard Nixon shares his view. General William Westmoreland, the military commander in Vietnam from 1964 to 1968, is sharply critical of television coverage, which he believes played into enemy hands, gravely harming the American effort.[2] The late General Maxwell Taylor, who served as Chairman of the Joint Chiefs of Staff under Presidents Kennedy and Johnson, and who was the U.S. Ambassador to Saigon when Johnson made his fateful decisions to Americanize the Vietnam war in 1965, later said: "In Vietnam there was the feeling on the part of some of the press that their task was to destroy the American command and to work against what was being done."[3]

Among journalists who share such views, Keyes Beech, an old Asia hand, has written, ". . . the media helped lose the war . . . because of the way the war was reported. What often seems to be forgotten is that the war was lost in the U.S., not in Vietnam."[4] At the time Saigon fell to the Communists, James Reston, the distinguished *New York Times* columnist, wrote an obituary to the failed American effort in which he observed that

the reporters and the cameras were decisive in the end. They brought the issues of the war to the people, before the Congress and the courts, and forced the withdrawal of American power from Vietnam.[5]

It is regarded as axiomatic among the ranks of the professional military that the way television covered the Vietnam war rendered a U.S. victory impossible. General Douglas Kinnard interviewed over 100 generals who held command positions during the war. Nearly all of them were critical of television coverage of the war, which they pronounced "counterproductive to the war effort."[6] Many Vietnam veterans share these views. The belief has become embedded in the matrix of national memory; it is part of the conventional wisdom. Many Americans believe that the formidable television camera, nightly conveying its indelible images of men at war in all its raw violence and horror, sickened us, in time turning us against the war and forcing the withdrawal of American forces from Vietnam, which then cleared the way for the Communist takeover.

Those embracing the notion that television coverage of the war caused the eventual American defeat also believe its correlatives. In addition to their nightly coverage of martial blood and gore, television reporters, cameramen, and anchormen, those who opposed the war, contrived to present stories and made editorial comments casting the U.S. war effort in an unfavorable light, compelling sympathy for our enemies, fueling domestic opposition, undermining popular support, and lowering the morale of American troops in Vietnam. Further, television provided extensive coverage to the vocal antiwar movement that promoted its growth, inflated its appeal, and circulated its antiwar propaganda. Exploiting opportunities provided by history's first uncensored war, a powerful adversarial medium worked in various ways to undermine public support for the American military effort in Vietnam.

Reinforcing these widely held beliefs is the understanding that the Vietnam war coincided with an era in national life when television had become an all-encompassing cultural force. The 1960s were a television age. Television not only furnished Americans with a flood of information about the war but it also provided us with our knowledge of the world in general, most of our popular entertainment, our buying cues to a vast panoply of consumer goods, and even told us how to vote. Television's ability to influence our attitudes toward the Vietnam war represented but a dimension of its pervasive influence on our lives and thoughts, on consciousness itself.

For all those who accept it, the belief that television ultimately determined the outcome of the Vietnam war also accounts for an otherwise nearly inexplicable historical catastrophe—the failure of the mightiest nation in the history of the planet, with immense wealth, power, and sophisticated military technology, to crush a much poorer, smaller, and far less technologically advanced foe.

The quite remarkable fact about this widely held and deeply believed theory of television's impact on the outcome of the Vietnam war is that it is spurious. There is no available evidence that sustains it. All available data challenge the idea that television coverage was a decisive cause of the American failure in Vietnam.

I   Television News and Public Opinion

Since public opinion is supposed to be the prime mover in democracies, one might reasonably expect to find a vast literature. One does not find it. There are excellent books on government and parties, that is on the machinery which in theory registers public opinions after they are formed. But on the sources from which these public opinions arise, on the processes by which they are derived, there is relatively little.

Walter Lippmann, *Public Opinion*, 1922

Walter Lippman wrote *Public Opinion* to prod political scientists into studying the forces creating and shaping public opinion in the aftermath of World War I, a war in which nations, including the United States, had systematically used propaganda to impel their citizenry to sacrifice for a holy cause and to view their enemies as barbarians. In the early 1920s, war-bred idealism gave way to disillusionment with its outcome, and in Lippman's view, with democracy itself. Further, public relations firms, following the wartime government propagandists, were shaping the news and manipulating public opinion for their corporate clients. Lippman, fearing these new agencies, attempted to call forth a new science of public opinion that would understand the sources of mass irrationalism and develop mechanisms to preserve democracy in a postwar world where democracy appeared more imperiled than ever.

Lippman's post–World War I lament aptly describes the lack of systematic study of how and by what processes television news influenced public opinion during the Vietnam war era. Considering the intrinsic importance of the subject, its implications for the functioning of democratic political processes, the conduct of foreign policy, and the outcome of war, it is surprising to find that there are few analyses of television's effect on public opinion. There exist few laboratory or field studies of how, by what mechanisms, and to what extent television newscasts influenced popular attitudes during the Vietnam era. No systematic inventories of audiences were made; no before-and-after experiments, to determine the effects of newscasts on popular attitudes, were conducted.

No doubt a major reason why we have comparatively few such studies is that we have scant empirical data identifying those who watched television news and how frequently they watched it during the Vietnam war years. Nor do we know much about how viewers perceived television news or how it influenced them. Did the news provide background noise for dinner conversation or were viewers absorbed by the electronic imagery and the accompanying sonorous commentary of news anchors? What registered in people's minds when they absorbed a flood of visual images accompanied by a voice-over coming out of a 19-inch screen? Did people from different backgrounds, harboring different experiences, ideologies, and views of the war all understand and interpret war news in similar ways? Was there any difference between the way a dovish liberal arts college professor and a hawkish construction worker viewed the same battle scenes on the tube? Did they absorb and use that information similarly? Are some individuals more impressionable than others, more likely to be influenced by television newscasts than others? If so, who are these impressionable folks and why are they susceptible? Did the impact of television coverage of the war depend on whether one had intense feelings about the conflict or was relatively indifferent to it? How does one separate out the influence of television news from the influence of other news media, and, for that matter, other factors such as age, gender, race, education, religion, occupation, status, income, political affiliation, and world view, all of which might have shaped an individual's opinion about the Vietnam war? How does one measure the effects of the war itself on public opinion as distinct from television's mediated version of the war? Does television news generally follow and reflect public opinion or does it often shape and create opinions? It is difficult, often impossible, to discover answers to these kinds of questions because we have only scattered and fragmentary data "on the sources from which these public opinions arise, on the processes by which they are derived," as Walter Lippmann observed almost 70 years ago.

There is a more subtle challenge facing those who study the impact of television news on the perceptions, ideas, and attitudes of its audience. Some media analysts theorize that the deepest impact of television news coverage is subliminal, especially in the case of the Vietnam war, because television news coverage of the conflict tended to be repetitive over a lengthy time interval. If such theories of unconscious learning are valid, relatively low-level mass learning occurred at the deepest structural levels, below the threshold of conscious recall or remembrance. The social sciences possess no research techniques for reclaiming or measuring such learning or even demonstrating empirically that such processes occurred. There is no way to excavate elusive memory traces that the audience itself is not aware of much less describe their effects.

In addition to the lack of empirical evidence available, another problem we quickly encounter as we try to determine what role television played in the formation of public opinion in the Vietnam era is, paradoxically, too much data. Vietnam was the number-one news story for over seven years, from the summer of 1965, when the Johnson administration committed U.S. ground combat forces to Vietnam, until the January 1973 peace agreement, which ended American military involvement in Vietnam. There was more news coverage of the war, both print and electronic, than for any other story in American journalistic history. Television coverage included not only the national network news stories but also features, specials, documentaries, interview programs, press conferences, and elections in which Vietnam issues were central topics. There was also a vast national radio network that covered the war. All local television and radio stations also carried much Vietnam news during the years between 1965 and 1973.

The print media coverage of the war was much vaster, not only in the prestige national press like the *New York Times* and the *Washington Post,* but also in all newspapers, from large metropolitan dailies to small-town weeklies. These papers carried a lot of war news. Then there were the weekly news magazines— *Time, Newsweek,* and *U.S. News and World Report*—all of which contained huge amounts of war reportage for years. Not to mention the monthly periodicals such as the *Atlantic* and *Life,* or the important magazines of political opinion like *The New Republic, The Nation,* and *National Review.* All these magazines devoted much space to Vietnam and Vietnam-related stories. No investigator or team of investigators can read, watch, or listen to more than a small sample of this vast media literature. We have access to massive media reportage; we can find comparatively little information enabling us to understand how, in what ways, or even if this vast news output influenced the thinking of the public who consumed it.

Despite having to face the twin problems of having too much and too little data available, journalists and scholars have not allowed the myth that television lost the Vietnam war to go unchallenged. Among journalists, Peter Arnett, a former Associated Press correspondent who spent eight years covering the war, has defended the accuracy, objectivity, and professionalism of war correspondents.[7] Morley Safer, who reported the war for CBS television news, has rightly

attacked Robert Elegant for impugning the patriotism of journalists and for failing to back up his accusations with facts.[8] Charles Mohr, a former *Time* and *New
York Times* reporter who spent years covering the war in Vietnam, considered by
his peers the best journalist on a difficult beat, has stated that wars are not lost
in newspaper columns or television booths and those who made such charges
have created a myth.[9] Michael Arlen, who wrote a series of elegant pieces on
television for the *New Yorker* during the late 1960s, suggested that the way television covered the war domesticated it. He suggested that television transformed a
real war into a "living-room war," by which he meant the nightly footage shown
in miniature on a 19-inch tube tamed the war. The televised war became part of
the homey ambiance, part of life's daily routine.[10] Television interviewer Ted
Koppel bluntly observed: "People don't need television to tell them a boy has
gone to Southeast Asia and not come back."[11]

Along with a few journalists, a handful of social scientists representing a
variety of disciplines has refuted the notion that television coverage of the Vietnam war decisively influenced its outcome. Mass-communication analysts Lawrence Lichty and George Bailey have written numerous articles describing television coverage of the war. They have relentlessly asserted that there is simply no
evidence linking that coverage to public opinion. They argue that those who persist in making such linkages are relying on anecdotes, impressions, and false assumptions about the power of television.[12] Oscar Patterson III conducted a content analysis of the three national network news telecasts covering the war over
a span of eight years and demonstrated that the combat footage shown nightly
on the news rarely showed graphic images of wounded or dead Americans, or
any other violent scenes.[13] Political scientist John Mueller has challenged the
claim that television made the Vietnam war unpopular by using polling data to
show that a similar war to stop Communist aggression in Asia fought a decade
earlier in Korea became equally unpopular even though it was not televised.[14]
Political scientist Michael Mandelbaum has refuted the television myth with a
fine article that appeared in the fall 1982 issue of *Daedalus*, titled "Vietnam: The
Television War." Using a variety of sources and arguments, he unravels one-by-
one the various strands in the myth's flimsy tapestry. He speculates that the Vietnam war would have run its course pretty much as it did had the cathode ray
tube never been invented.[15]

The scholar who has mounted the most telling critique of the myth in a
series of articles and a thoroughly researched book, *The Uncensored War*, is Daniel
C. Hallin. Drawing upon the complete body of *New York Times* coverage of the
war from 1961 to 1965, and from over 1,500 television newscasts of the war from
1965 to 1973, Hallin delineates the many ideological and institutional restraints
operating to prevent the national television news networks from functioning as
adversaries of governmental policy. Using content analyses of television news
programs, he shows how television provided mostly favorable coverage of the
war through its first three years. Sometime in 1969, about the time President
Nixon began withdrawing American troops, television coverage of the war became more negative, but only after public opinion and many government leaders

had turned against the war. Even during these later years when television coverage was more critical, the Nixon administration was usually able to manipulate the news networks, control the flow of war news, and retain public support for its war policies. Hallin proves that television news did not play any important part in undermining popular support for the war.[16]

Prominent historians of the Vietnam conflict also reject the idea that television lost the war. George Herring, author of the best short history of the Vietnam war, *America's Longest War,* argues that the assertion can never be proven, "and it can be argued as plausibly that television generated support for the war or even caused apathy."[17] Stanley Karnow, who has written a lengthy book, *Vietnam: A History,* joins Herring in giving the television argument short shrift when he observes that media coverage of the war "tended to follow rather than lead the U.S. public."[18]

Even more damaging to the credibility of the myth, which is widely held by professional soldiers among others, is the findings of a scholar affiliated with the Southeast Asia Branch, U.S. Army Center of Military History. William M. Hammond has refuted the myth and is currently engaged in writing a two-volume official Army history of the relationships among the military and the media during the Vietnam war. He has subjected the myth to critical analysis and has found that the charge that the media in general or television news in particular lost the Vietnam war is groundless.[19]

II   A Short History and Politics of Television News

Mass television broadcasting owns a comparatively brief history and television newscasts have even shorter genealogies. Television became a mass medium in the early 1950s while television news broadcasts remained "of slight importance and of slighter quality."[20] In fact, television executives were more or less forced to develop the modern news format in the aftermath of TV quiz show scandals, which broke in the late 1950s, outraging viewers and compromising the integrity of the entire industry. Until the scandals, these quiz shows had ruled prime-time television. The worst offender turned out to be NBC's "Twenty-One," the top-rated weekly show on which bright, knowledgeable contestants competed against each other for big-money prizes.

These quiz show revelations triggered a "fin de fifties" orgy of cultural self-laceration and calls for reform, which fed into a larger enterprise, the search for national goals and a reaffirmation of national identity. Political leaders and national pundits both believed Americans required such reaffirmations to maintain Cold War commitments in the face of rising Soviet challenges and to stem the moral decay from within that was symbolized by crooked television shows.[21]

Television executives, shaken by the scandals threatening both their public image and pocketbooks, undertook a thorough house cleaning. They pulled the big-money quiz shows off the air and increased the number of hours devoted to news. They also ran more television specials and produced more documentaries that had serious news value. By no means an inevitable development, television news quickly established itself as a popular and profitable form of programming. In September 1963, national television news programs expanded from 15 minutes to 30 minutes, the present-day format.[22]

The coming of age of television news coincided with America's going to war in Vietnam during the mid-1960s. Appropriately, events in Southeast Asia would dominate television news coverage until the phase-out of the American combat role early in 1973. Public opinion polls indicated that television had become "pre-eminent in home entertainment in 1960, and became adults' primary source of news in 1970."[23] Presidents, generals, and other civilian and military leaders, as well as television executives and journalists, all acted upon the assumption that most Americans depended on television news for their information about the war and doubtless assumed television newscasts greatly influenced popular attitudes toward the war.

But there exists considerable evidence available to scholars challenging the assumption that the public relied on television for most of its information about the Vietnam war. Massive annual surveys conducted by the Simmons Market Research Bureau that used a variety of techniques to measure audience size for all the major media have shown that far more Americans read newspapers than watched television news during the years of the American presence in Vietnam, 1965 to 1972. John Robinson, affiliated with the Survey Research Center at the University of Michigan, using the Simmons data, found that 78 percent of the adult population read a newspaper daily while only 24 percent watched a televised network news broadcast on an average day in 1969. The number of households that watched national television network evening news on a regular basis (three or four times/week) was minuscule.[24]

It was apparently not true that popular celebrity-anchormen such as Walter Cronkite built up large personal followings during the Vietnam war era, a constituency that faithfully watched his nightly newscasts, hung on his every word, which they believed devoutly, and who were especially suggestible to his occasional editorial opinions. Nor was it true that the more dramatic electronic medium, with its glowing imagery supposedly more appropriate to the spirit of the times, pushed out staid newspapers as major news sources. Further, there was much overlap and duplication on the three evening network news shows. They duplicated about half their major stories each night. There was much more duplication of stories on television broadcasts than in newspapers or news magazines.[25] Other Vietnam news programming such as television documentaries and specials on the Vietnam war drew much smaller audience than the regular newscasts.

Economic pressures imposed severe time constraints on national television newscasts. A half-hour news program contained only 22 minutes of news, the other 8 minutes being devoted to commercials. During the years when the fighting in Vietnam was most intense, war news typically occupied about 3 to 4 minutes of the evening news, amounting to a few hundred spoken words synchronized to video clips of varying lengths.[26] By contrast, a typical front-page, single-column story in the *New York Times* about the Vietnam war, which would usually be continued on an inner page, ran at least 700 words and often more than 1,000 words. Each issue of the *Times* during the years when the war was the top news issue would contain several Vietnam news stories, features, series, editorials, and Op-Ed letters amounting to thousands of words. Additionally, the national news magazines devoted sizable coverage each issue to the Vietnam war for its duration. Add to these media the huge daily flow of Vietnam stories in the rest of the nation's daily, weekly, and monthly newspapers and newsmagazines and it becomes clear that the volume of Vietnam news available to the three-fourths of American adults who read a newspaper daily and those who read a newsmagazine each week overwhelmed the comparatively small amount of war news appearing on national television watched on a regular basis by a relatively small number of households. Richard Nixon, noted for his hostile preoccupation with the media, particularly "liberal" television journalists, once observed: "Television news is to news as bumper stickers are to philosophy."

Four important points flow from these findings:

1. Regardless of what they told pollsters, most Americans apparently got more of their news about the war from newspapers than from television news.

2. The number of Americans who relied on television news as their major source of information about the war in Vietnam on a regular basis was, contrary to the conventional wisdom, quite small, during 1965 to 1972.

3. Scholars who have studied the effects of mass communications on viewers have found that, because of the phenomenon of "selective perception," the media presentations often only reinforced people's pre-existing attitudes. Daniel Hallin states:

> There is evidence that this process was at work in the case of television coverage of Vietnam: a 1968 study found that 75% of respondents who considered themselves "hawks" on the war thought Walter Cronkite was also a "hawk." Somewhat more thought that [Chet] Huntley and [David] Brinkley were "hawks." But a majority of "doves" thought that each of the three anchors was a "dove."[27]

According to Hallin, people saw what they wanted to see and selectively interpreted televised news to conform with what they already believed. If that is so, it is difficult to understand how television newscasts might change very many minds or shape very many opinions about the war. People don't suspend their preconceptions in the process of tuning in the evening news; their minds are not *tabulae rasae* as they watch the screen and listen to the voice-over. The supposed powers of visual imagery and anchor's charisma to shape opinions about the war have been vastly exaggerated.

4. The politicians, military commanders, and journalists who assumed that television was a major source of news and a strong influence on public opinion during the Vietnam era and acted accordingly were misled by commercial polls and their own erroneous assumptions. This point can also serve as a cautionary tale for those who believe television news to have been a powerful influence on public opinion about the war. People may not know, may not be able to articulate the sources of their knowledge of the war. They may very well mistakenly attribute it to television news when its sources were newspapers and newsmagazines as the above evidence suggests.

Those who believe that television lost the Vietnam war exaggerate the power television news can wield within the framework of our political culture. In brief, they misunderstand the politics of television news. It was extremely difficult, probably impossible, for the television news networks as organized, as constituted, given the personnel they employed to gather and dispense the news, to take an independent, adversarial stance against the national government during the era of Vietnam. It was a political role that they did not seek and probably could not have attained had they tried because a host of external and internal restraints, both ideological and institutional, operated at all times on the television networks that precluded the adversarial option.

In 1968 or 1970, if someone had told harried officials in Washington—frustrated by their inability to win an increasingly unpopular war—that the essential political function of major television network newscasts was not adversarial journalism, but furnishing news that informed the public, supported American political processes and policies, and validated existing institutional arrangements, and that major television network news was an integral part of the established political order, these officials would probably have reacted in angry disbelief. They would react that way because they confused the exercise of political power with the forms through which political power was exercised. They also tended to blur distinctions between particular personnel trying to implement particular policies and the processes of governance. They further convinced themselves that most critics of their war policies were enemies of the government and were aiding the Communists and did not warrant television news coverage. Such attitudes reflected an amalgam of conceit and paranoia that appears to have flourished in high political places during the stresses and strains of the late 1960s and early 1970s.

Formally, of course, the television networks are not part of the federal government. They are organized social forms that function in a government-regulated and government-protected part of the private sector. But the networks perform their political functions informally, even inadvertently. They became part of the political system because of an unintended consequence of their commitment to the ideology of professional journalism.[28] Professional television journalists pride themselves on their objectivity. They hold that the proper form of television news is politically neutral factual reportage, a format from which they rarely strayed when reporting Vietnam war news. "Disinterested facticity" not only contributes to the fulfillment of the ancient Jeffersonian ideals of open governance and an informed citizenry, but it legitimates government policy and also legitimates television news coverage of government policy.

Because reporters must rely mainly on their access to government sources for straight news, and anchors normally read this news on the air without editorial commentary, television news often shows the news source, sometimes the president himself, defining and defending the chief executive's policies. If the issues are domestic matters, such as the budget, equal time is furnished to a congressional leader of the loyal opposition to present a policy alternative. Hence, television news provides us with a portrait of democracy in action, of governing processes promoted by an integral part of the same political process. By so doing, television vindicates its right to present the news.

Television news also focuses public attention on the White House. Often the national political news on the evening telecasts consists solely of what the president did during a news day. Television news also takes politics seriously, much more seriously than many of our apathetic citizenry caught up in the affairs of their daily lives and prone to regard the activities of official Washington as inconsequential. Television news reminds Americans that government is important and that politics is important. It reminds us that the president is important, as chief executive hired to do a job, as national leader, as conductor of our foreign policy, as commander-in-chief of the armed forces, and as the personification of the American nation. Television news takes national politics seriously because it is itself part of national politics as well as an information source, an ongoing civics lesson, and a primer in democratic citizenship. By taking politics seriously, television news becomes serious politics and also confirms its role as disinterested expert.

The television political process–news system has worked especially well for presidential conduct of foreign policy because there is often no representative of stature available for the "other side" and because there usually has been bipartisan support for the conduct of foreign policy in time of war or national emergency. Administrations have controlled both the flow and content of news coverage of their important policies by using the dependence of television news on access to them as major news sources and by relying on journalists to report the news straight, without interpretive commentary. On occasions, administrations have appealed to the patriotism of journalists or the imperatives of national security to kill inconvenient stories and to maintain political control over the news. News management or manipulation is one of the ways the American political game is played within our democratic system.

Journalists are wary about being used by presidents and other politicians, alert to detect misinformation or disinformation, but the conventions of professional journalism operate to favor government officials most of the time. Both the Johnson and Nixon administrations were able to control the flow and content of television news of the Vietnam war most of the time despite the eventual emergence of widespread opposition to their policies and the advent of fissures in the bipartisan consensus that had supported the war in its early years.

Many people assume that the politics of television news entails bias; in fact, that is probably the only political dimension of television news that they consider when talking about the media's influence on public opinion during the Vietnam era. Many conservatives, convinced that television news cost us the war, insist that network coverage of Vietnam reflected a liberal and dovish bias. Frank J. Shakespeare, a former CBS vice-president and director of the U.S. Information Agency in the Nixon administration, charged television news was "clearly liberally oriented" because most of the people who went into the news side of television tended to be liberally oriented.[29] Certainly former Vice-President Spiro Agnew thought so. His denunciations of the media, particularly television network news, were grounded upon his perception that a small group of liberal correspondents imposed their personal ideologies on the news as they tried to subvert the Nixon administration's agenda both at home and abroad.[30]

Their charges are by no means self-evidently true. Studies suggest that television reporters most likely derive their political values from the requisites of news organizations, not from their "personal ideologies." Producing television news is, above all, a group effort. Editors and producers, usually more professional and moderate in their views than correspondents, serve to check the latter. Producers especially are more committed to presenting both sides of a public-policy dispute, not resolving it in favor of one side or the other. They just want to air it out, not decide it. Edward Jay Epstein's survey of television producers and news editors showed that more than two-thirds felt that television had little effect in turning public opinion against the war.[31]

The news organization itself prevents reporters from taking clear stands on issues because of the fear that they might offend viewers. The television networks have no wish to annoy, or worse, alienate any sizable segment of their audience. Marketplace imperatives reinforce built-in network inclinations to offer a news product offensive to no one. Television networks, which are corporate organizations in the business of returning a profit on stockholders' investments, have a single source of income. The networks are paid by advertisers to air their commercials to the broadcast audience. The prices networks can charge advertisers is directly keyed to audience size. Further, there are institutional restraints, guidelines and policies that people adhered to. Above all, there is the professional reporter's commitment to objective reporting, to giving the viewers only the politically neutral facts, and eschewing journalistic editorializing.

Television news correspondents are not so much liberal as cynical in their basic orientation toward politics and politicians. They don't like or respect most politicians. Above all, they don't trust them. They suspect politicians to be motivated solely by the desire to get and keep public office. During Vietnam, they didn't like either Richard Nixon or George McGovern: the reason—both were politicians; their war policies were irrelevant. In addition, they resented the fact that politicians got a lot of news time for defending their policies and programs, using the evening news to influence the audience.[32] Clearly, we are dealing with a kind of bias here, even with hostility, but it was not a partisan or ideological bias favoring idealistic, liberal doves over realistic hawks when it came to war in Vietnam. The attitudes of TV reporters suggest more fundamental professional biases, biases against a type, against a class, against members of an oft-maligned profession. Such cynical, anti-political journalists were not given to favoring any particular political personality, issue, or cause over another. News coverage often took forms analogous to the Muslim view of the Reformation—namely a curse on both your houses—than one promoting dovish war views. Such anti-political views were congruent with biases widely shared by the American public during the Vietnam–Watergate era. A political unknown, Jimmy Carter, rode the streetcar of anti-politics to the White House in 1976.

The most important point to make is that television reporters, whatever constitutes their biases, are not free to impose their values on the final news product seen by mass audiences. This is because of built-in institutional restraints, external commercial pressures, and their own professional standards. The organization of the entire news operation prevented individual reporters and anchors from imprinting Vietnam war stories with their personal views.

There was also a more powerful restraint operating than history, institutional politics, economic pressures, and professional ideologies during the Vietnam era that made it extremely difficult for television journalists to oppose the American role in Vietnam or for them to become genuine adversaries of their government's policies—the Cold War ideology. Cold War ideological imperatives, more than all other factors, propelled the United States to war in Vietnam by stages. The Cold War consensus reigned unchallenged in the United States during the mid-1960s, influencing politicians, military officers, and journalists alike. It determined the way they viewed the developing American role in Vietnam. No one in government or in the mainstream of the news industry ever questioned the consensus, challenged its assumptions, or doubted its goals.

Bipolar conflict between the United States and the Soviet Union was the defining reality of global politics during the 1950s and early 1960s. Enmeshed in the ideological consensus that had fastened itself onto the American mind, Americans saw the Soviet Union as an aggressive, expansionist, ruthless power competing globally with the United States for strategic superiority and control of markets. American understanding of the global conflict was expressed in charged, moralistic rhetoric: The forces of freedom had engaged a powerful totalitarian foe and its clients. A Soviet Cold War victory would cost us not only hegemony, prestige, and wealth but could also mean the end of American civilization—a way of life based on middle-class democracy, free enterprise, and popular culture. A Soviet triumph would trigger a new Dark Age. Some earnest souls among us spouted "Better Dead than Red," appearing to prefer an atomic holocaust to life under Soviet commissars.

Their thinking dominated by the themes of consensus Cold War ideology, political leaders and journalists alike defined the civil war that began in the late 1950s in Vietnam, an underdeveloped Third World country emerging from the clutches of French colonialism, as a necessary opportunity for the United States to fight a limited war to prevent the expansion of Communism into southern Vietnam. Cold War ideological influences also conditioned American political leaders and journalists to perceive clearly only part of the Vietnam political reality. The Americans saw mostly Communist aggression; they failed to understand that Communism in this political context also represented a nationalistic, modernizing drive for emancipation from the vestiges of Western colonialism and a fundamental overhaul of the social structure that appealed to large numbers of impoverished Asian peasants living in southern Vietnam.

The domino correlative to the Cold War ideology greatly strengthened the American urge to intervene militarily in Vietnam by suggesting that the loss of the southern half of that small country to an expansionist Chinese Communism spearheaded by its proxies, Ho Chi Minh and the Vietnamese Communist Party, would imperil the strategic security of other Southeast Asian nations including Laos, Cambodia, Thailand, Burma, Indonesia, Malaysia, and the Philippines. Ultimately, the security of the United States could be threatened.[33] The domino theory greatly raised the stakes. When President Lyndon Johnson committed the United States to combat in Vietnam, television journalists also went to war to provide the American people with news coverage of the U.S. effort to contain Communism in Southeast Asia. There is no evidence suggesting that these journalists did not believe in the American cause or expect the United States to prevail within a few years.

But within a few years the United States did not prevail and the Cold War consensus eroded. A growing number of American political leaders concluded that the costs of the war required to assure the survival of a non-Communist government in southern Vietnam outweighed any conceivable benefits that the United States could hope to obtain from it. They called for American officials to seek a negotiated settlement that would allow the United States to extricate itself from a military stalemate. By the late-1960s, the Cold War ideological consensus may have cracked, but it did not entirely lose its power to influence the attitudes of many people toward the war. Dovish politicians, with few exceptions, never pushed beyond the confines of the consensus. Their quarrels with the Johnson and Nixon administrations were over means, not ends; methods, not goals. They challenged their military strategies, not their long-range goals of securing a non-Communist South Vietnamese nation. Most never questioned the premise that American involvement in Vietnam was a legitimate effort to contain Communist expansion, as long as the cost was not too high. They were prepared to abandon imperialism in Southeast Asia because it had become too deadly, too costly, too destructive, and too divisive. To my knowledge, no television journalist moved further than these doves, and most never moved as far in their views on the war.

During the early years of the American presence in Vietnam, while the consensus remained in place, television coverage of the war was ovewhelmingly favorable. Favorable coverage continued to mid-1969, about the time President Nixon announced his Vietnamization policy. From mid-1969 until the American role ended in January 1973, television coverage of the war became more critical. During these latter years of the war, television news programs featured proportionally more negative stories about the war. But this negative coverage mainly reflected the views of dovish congressional critics of the war and public opinion that had turned solidly against the war. Critical television news stories typically took the form of interviewing a prominent dove, usually a current or former political leader. Television journalists were not creating opposition to the war;

they were merely reporting it. Put another way, as the Cold War consensus crumbled, as the containment ideology eased its grip, television news coverage of Vietnam expanded to include propaganda critical of the war as well as propaganda favoring the conflict. Television news coverage of the war in Vietnam did not create the crack in the Cold War consensus.

III   The Untelevised War

The Vietnam war has been remembered as the nation's first televised war,[34] and many people believe that television coverage led to the American defeat. I want to pose another challenge to that belief by comparing the American experience in the Vietnam war, the nation's first televised war, with our experience with its predecessor, the Korean war, which was not televised.[35] Specifically, I want to compare trends in public opinion in both wars. These trends turn out to have been remarkably similar and therein lies a tale that the believers in the television myth may find instructive.

The two wars share many characteristics. American intervention into both countries was driven by Cold War ideologies and exigencies. Both were limited wars fought on the mainland of Asia to stem the advance of Communism. Both were undeclared wars fought in small countries far away whose outcomes posed no direct threat to American security interests. Both wars were initiated by liberal Democratic presidents, neither of whom sought reelection while the wars were still being fought, in effect, resigning. The conduct of both wars became entangled in domestic politics.[36]

One major difference between the two conflicts—the Korean war had an obvious, dramatic beginning: on June 26, 1950, North Korean forces suddenly attacked across the 38th parallel, invading South Korea. President Truman, within a matter of hours, committed U.S. forces to try to save South Korea from being overrun. There is no obvious date or event marking America's entry into full-scale war in Vietnam. The Kennedy and Johnson administrations gradually escalated the American military role in southern Vietnam, increasing the U.S. commitment while at the same time playing down the growing U.S. involvement for domestic political reasons. Historians of the causes of the Vietnam war generally consider a series of escalations occurring between March–July 1965, to be the beginning of the American war. During these months, the Johnson administration, fearful that troops of the National Liberation Front would soon defeat the South Vietnamese army unless the United States intervened in force, committed massive numbers of U.S. ground combat troops to Vietnam and simultaneously authorized the American commander, General William Westmoreland, to instigate combat operations anywhere in South Vietnam as he saw fit. By August 1, 1965, the United States was fighting another land war in Asia. It was also that summer that most Americans learned about a place called Vietnam. Polls show that prior to mid-1965, most Americans knew little about Southeast Asia, nor had they shown much previous concern with American activity in that region. For the purpose of comparing public-opinion trends, we will consider the

American war in Vietnam to have begun in August 1965, and the Korean war in late June 1950.

There was also a dramatic difference in the amount of openly expressed opposition to the two wars as measured by demonstrations, speeches, petitions, newspaper commentary, and political campaigns.[37] On the surface, it would appear that for these two similar kinds of wars, Vietnam was vastly more unpopular. It was certainly true that there was almost no vocal opposition to the Korean war.[38]

The American Left supported the Korean war either because of anti-Stalinism or else were cowed into silence by the threat of McCarthyism. By the time the American role in Vietnam came along in the mid-1960s, both the international and domestic political situation had altered appreciably. McCarthyism and Stalinism had vanished. American left-wingers did not perceive the Soviet Union to pose a direct threat to American interests in Southeast Asia. Further, the Sino-Soviet split had occurred and the Indonesian army had liquidated a potential Maoist revolution on Java in 1965. A year later, the lunatic Cultural Revolution was in full sway in China, plunging that country into political chaos. Leftists who had been militant Cold War warriors in 1950 loudly opposed the U.S. military buildup in Vietnam because they perceived no serious threat to American vital interests from the civil war raging in that country.[39]

In comparing trends in popular support for both wars, we use a Gallup poll that measured public responses to similar questions asked during both the Korean and Vietnam eras. For Korea, the question asked was: "Do you think that the United States made a mistake in going into war in Korea or not?" Gallup's Vietnam version of that query was: "In view of the developments since we entered the fighting in Vietnam, do you think the United States made a mistake sending troops to fight in Vietnam?" These questions can measure general support, or its lack, for the war. They do not, however, give us any indication of what alternative policy preferences respondents who thought the present war policy mistaken might prefer at any given time. They don't tell us who might be "hawks" and who might be "doves."

Polls show that initially there was strong popular support for Truman's intervention to counter the North Korean invasion. The first poll indicated 66 percent of Americans favored his actions. Support remained high through the fall as United Nations' forces drove north toward a seemingly inevitable victory in Korea. Americans were enjoying what they expected to be a short war that would end before Christmas not only with aggression against South Korea repulsed, but also with the liberation of a Communist satellite from Communist tyranny. Then came the Chinese armies smashing into northern Korea, driving UN forces back across the 38th Parallel and about two-thirds of the way down the Korean peninsula. The first poll following the Chinese intervention showed a dramatic drop in popular support for the Korean effort, from 66 percent to 39 percent, as all thoughts of a quick, easy victory were dashed.[40]

What is most interesting about popular support for the Korean War after it takes a precipitous plunge in response to the Chinese incursion is that it stays between 36 and 47 percent for the remaining two and a half years of war, despite mounting costs and casualties, double-digit inflation on the home front, the Truman-MacArthur controversy, the on-and-off peace talks, the stalemated battle-field near the 38th Parallel, McCarthyism raging at home, and the bitterly partisan 1952 election. Apparently, after the enormous shock created by Chinese intervention had registered, other events had no impact on public opinion. There appears to be a hard core of supporters averaging 42 percent of the population which backs the war effort regardless of political or military developments until a negotiated settlement of the war was reached in August 1953.[11] For nearly all its duration, nearly 60 percent of Americans believed that it was a mistake to get involved in Korea. Despite the almost total absence of vocal dissent, the Korean conflict was an unpopular war for most of its duration.

We find that when U.S. troops went to war in Vietnam during the summer of 1965, there was a strong level of popular support for the war, 65 percent, almost identical with the level of support at the beginning of the Korean war. This high level of support held for about a year. By the summer of 1966, it had slipped to 53 percent. Within that first year, expectations for a brief war had diminished, casualties were growing, and dissent was rising. From mid-1966 on, there is a steady, incremental erosion of popular support for the war.[12]

Like Korea, public-opinion trends for the Vietnam war do not correlate with major occurrences in the war or with domestic political events. Especially remarkable is the small impact on public opinion of a series of momentous events that took place in early 1968, events that determined the eventual course of the war—the Tet offensive, the replacement of General Westmoreland, President Johnson's decision not to seek reelection, the partial bombing halt, the beginning of peace talks, Johnson's decision to abandon his policy of gradual escalation, and the emergence of Senators Eugene McCarthy and Robert Kennedy, both of whom mounted challenges to Johnson. The combined impact on public opinion of all these events was quite small.[13] Both the Korean and Vietnam wars generated the same high level of popular support at the outset. That initial popular support for both wars expressed a rally-around-the-flag syndrome coupled to expectations of quick victories. It also reflected support for national leaders who had taken the nation to war.

Support declined for both wars after initial strong support. In the case of Korea, there was a sharp drop following Chinese intervention and then support held steady for the duration of the war. There was no comparable event in the Vietnam war to the Chinese intervention, so the pattern of declining support was gradual. It was not until mid-1969, after the war had been going on for four years, that popular support for it dropped below the low point for Korea.[14] It is important to understand that Korea was not a more popular war; often it was less popular than was Vietnam: "While the opposition to the war in Vietnam may have been more vocal than in Korea, it was not more extensive."[15] What has misled those who argue that Vietnam was a uniquely unpopular war that divided the American people more seriously than any event since our own Civil War was that the vocal opposition to Vietnam was vastly greater than for Korea.

The fallacy was to equate the absence of vocal opposition with the absence of all opposition or else to assume that if vocal opposition is absent, whatever latent opposition may exist in the culture is politically impotent. That is not true. It was the Korean war, more than any other factor, that cost the Democrats the 1952 election. It discredited Truman and gave Joseph McCarthy, Richard Nixon, and, above all, Dwight Eisenhower their major issue with which to hammer the Democrats. Shortly before the 1952 election, pollster Elmer Roper concluded that Korea was "clearly Eisenhower's strongest asset."[46] Pollster Louis Harris observed: "If one were to find a single, basic root cause out of which the impatience and protest of 1952 grew, it would have to be the failure of the Administration to bring the Korean fighting to a successful close."[47] Burton I. Kaufman, one of the ablest historians of the Korean War, accounting for widespread opposition to the Korean War in 1952, could well have been describing Vietnam when he wrote of a seemingly endless, costly war, with no prospect of victory in sight; of rising inflation and casualties coupled to a massive loss of faith in the nation's leadership.[48] Richard Nixon replicated Ike's successful 1952 Korean strategy when he promised war-weary Americans "peace with honor" in Vietnam to win narrowly the 1968 election over Hubert Humphrey and George Wallace.

There is another poll question from both the Korean and Vietnam eras that we can use, the presidential popularity question: Do you approve or disapprove of the way the president is handling his job? This question was asked repeatedly throughout both wars. If one assumes that respondents' answers were strongly influenced by their attitudes toward the war, the Korean war was less popular than was the Vietnam adventure because Truman scored consistently lower in these popular polls than did Johnson.[49]

A comparative study of public-opinion trends during the Korean and Vietnam wars challenges the assumption that it was television coverage of the Vietnam conflict that was driving down public support for the war. Whatever impact television had, it was not enough to reduce popular support below levels attained during the Korean war, the untelevised limited war to stop Communist aggression in Asia. The crucial question to ask is, What caused popular support for the two wars to decline? Television did not. There was little television coverage of the Korean war, comparatively few American households owned television sets in 1950, most did not watch what little televised news there was, and tight censorship was imposed on news from Korea.

Popular support for both wars declined as people reacted to the accumulating costs of the war. American casualties in Korea skyrocketed when the Chinese intervened. Casualties rose steadily in Vietnam from the summer of 1965 through 1968. Rising costs were perceived mainly in the form of increasing casualties, but also as rising taxes, inflation, curtailed social programs, and (in the case of Vietnam) rising levels of social conflict and domestic violence. These perceptions of rising costs were themselves framed by a set of assumptions, expectations, and understandings about the wars: about the purposes these limited wars served, what was at stake in both, how long the wars ought to last, how much should they cost in lives and dollars, when could they be expected to end, was the United States winning these wars, was the leadership doing a good job, were the leaders admired and trusted, and how was the country faring generally? All these concerns and others formed an interactive context between the particular impact that these wars had on individuals and the way it influenced public opinion about both wars. No doubt there was considerable variation in the frames of reference of individuals and how they perceived these war costs; no doubt the timetable for the forming of a dissenting or oppositional stance varied significantly. In time, the perceived costs of the wars dashed individual expectations for short, cheap wars, raised serious doubts about the performance of leaders, about the possibility of victory, and about outcomes that bore any rational relation to the costs entailed in achieving them. In time, individual perceptions multiplied to form groups comprising sizable majorities of our citizens who came to believe that it was a mistake for the United States to get involved in both Korea and Vietnam.

Opposition formed quickly in Korea because of the Chinese intervention; it emerged gradually in Vietnam because cost levels of the war rose gradually and it took time for the perception that the United States was not winning to become widespread. Television news coverage played no significant role in these processes of opinion formation that turned people against both wars. The public did not need television to inform them that war costs were rising and their government was not winning. Television did not make the wars unpopular.

IV   The Televised War

Close analysis of scripts, kinescopes, and videotapes of surviving news telecasts of the Vietnam war between August 1965 and January 1973 enables us to answer empirically two crucial and related questions about television coverage of the war: What did television show us of the war? and How did it show it? We can look at both the content and formal characteristics of television coverage, what the viewing audience saw of the war and the way television journalists framed what viewers saw. Answers yielded by the data to these questions further damage the credibility of the television myth.

Three media scholars have provided content analyses of television coverage of Vietnam and they have all reached similar findings.[30] They have shown that over half the televised news stories of the war featured U.S. troops in combat. Combat stories largely comprised the "television war" beamed nightly into the nation's living rooms. These stories represented the typical television account of the war—American troops shown in small-scale ground combat with NLF forces in some remote jungle or rice paddy in South Vietnam. Most of these stories were gathered by television news teams traveling with American GIs in the field.[31] Stories about the air war were also frequently shown on the nightly news, but not live-action films because neither the Air Force nor the Navy permitted television crews to accompany pilots on their missions. Other stories focused on the instruments of war, on U.S. military technology being used in Vietnam.[32] The rest of the television news stories usually presented different kinds of political stories such as quoting or paraphrasing remarks made by government officials in Washington or Saigon.

Contrary to what those who argue that television lost the war because of its coverage of the brute realities of modern warfare believe, most television news stories did not show actual combat. Only one in five combat stories depicted live action, and many of these live-action stories showed only scattered small-arms fire or an air strike in the distance.[53] Only about one in three of the live-action combat stories featured graphic coverage of wounded, dying, or dead soldiers shown on camera.[54] Given the strong emphasis that television news networks gave to military action in Vietnam and the large number of American casualties incurred in the real war, remarkably little American blood got spilled on the tube. The belief that television coverage of the war fed the American public a nightly dose of blood and gore is refuted by reviewing videotapes of the newscasts. It never happened.

Not only did television not show much live action or many casualties, it also failed to provide comprehensive coverage of the war. Most combat in the real war featured small-scale firefights of brief duration between highly mobile small units. Often the areas in which these quick, small battles occurred were inaccessible to television crews, or else they arrived after the skirmishes were over to record only their aftermath. Television journalists had no chance to record most of the battles that constituted the ground war in Vietnam. Most battles that got covered took place in areas 20 to 50 miles northeast of Saigon, the northern provinces just south of the DMZ, and in the Mekong Delta region to the south of Saigon. Battles elsewhere were often not covered. Most combat involving South Vietnamese or Allied forces never got television coverage unless they fought with American troops. Night battles were not covered on television. Most of the action by the Special Forces went uncovered. The naval war also went largely uncovered. Enemy actions were never covered. Television viewers never had any sense of the NLF forces as organized military units with an order of battle, a chain-of-command, and tactics and strategies of their own. Television news depicted them as faceless, sinister, elusive forces hiding in the jungles who often ambushed, killed, and maimed American boys. Much more of the war never made the tube than did.

Even when television cameras recorded men in combat, they could not capture the intensity of the combat experience conveyed by good print reporters or articulate soldiers.[55] The intense noise level of real combat came over the television audio systems in muted form—the sounds of small-arms fire, mortars, and bombs registering many decibel levels below their real intensity. Television could not depict what combat felt like or what it smelled like. Television never conveyed the grime, the fatigue, or the terror of men fighting for their lives. Nor could it capture the shock and pain of being wounded, or the horror of watching a buddy blown away by enemy fire. Nor could it relate the confusion, the craziness, the adrenalin rush, the manic excitement, the incredible intensity of all feelings and perceptions, the "high" that soldiers experienced in the midst of a firefight, which was often akin to sexual excitement. These were experiences and feeling states that soldiers remembered and wrote about after their combat experiences or else described to journalists who recorded them.[36] Electronic imagery transmitted a relatively neat, clean version of war that could not convey even a hint of the powerful feelings and experiences of men in violent and deadly conflict.

Critics who believe that television lost the war in Vietnam have assumed that television is a literal medium, conveying direct, powerful, and unmediated images of men at war. They believe that television nightly exposed people to the hideous realities of modern warfare, eventually turning large numbers against the war in Vietnam. They also believe that because television presents war in the raw, any war carried on television will soon become intolerable to most people because they cannot take much war straight.

Such views rest on a series of misconceptions. First, quantitative analyses of television news coverage of the war have proven that television provided only a partial, sanitized view of combat, rarely portraying any graphic scenes that would horrify or disgust viewers. Secondly, critics have made simplistic, McLuhanesque assumptions that coverage of the war determined viewers' responses to it. They were unaware of a basic political reality, that the reasons why people support or oppose wars have little, if anything, to do with how those wars are presented in the media.

Those who believe that television lost us a war in Southeast Asia also need to be reminded that television is not a literal medium. Television imagery of war does not flow direct from the battlefield to the living room. It does not give us war firsthand, in all its raw reality. Every television image of the Vietnam war shown nightly in the nation's living rooms was not simply a form of technology; it was also a cultural artifact.[57] Viewers saw what the camera operator and a host of other industry professionals wanted them to see. Viewers watched video clips of the Vietnam war 36 to 48 hours after they had been taken and processed by a team of reporters, writers, editors, producers, and anchors in Saigon, Tokyo, and New York. The processing incorporated considerations of timing, formatting, taste, politics, professional standards, and technical quality. Viewers of television news received partial glimpses of the war, which reflected the medium's technical limitations and its sociocultural context, not direct-to-the-viewer reality. The edited segment of action finally viewed by the public probably had about as much relation to battlefield reality in Vietnam as a battle scene shot in Hollywood. In fact, combat veterans of Vietnam have described the simulated combat scenes staged in fiction films like *Hamburger Hill* as more realistic than television news coverage of the war.

Michael Arlen has observed another limit of television's reporting of the war. He found coverage to be incoherent. Viewers saw helicopters hovering over a rice paddy, a patrol boat sailing slowly up a river, jet bombers taking off from the deck of an attack carrier, infantrymen walking single file along a trail, and perhaps a burst of action as a tactical bomber napalmed a piece of jungle in the distance. The televised war came across as a series of routine patrols, none of which connected to any other, nor to any overall strategy. These 30-second glimpses of war were torn from a complex sequence of experience, of causation, of consequences not shown and that the viewer cannot know. Arlen called this kind of television treatment "keyhole coverage"; viewers perceived fragments of an unintelligible whole akin to the experience of a person seeing movement and hearing voices while peering through a keyhole.[58]

What then do these 30 seconds' worth of combat images mean to the millions of viewers watching them? No one knows for sure. We do not know very much about how audiences construct meanings for what they see on television. Hallin suggests that viewers generally accept what they are told by narrators. They see what they are told they are seeing by reporters and anchors.[59] If Hallin's surmise is valid, his implication is that television's supposedly powerful visual imagery, far from conveying potent, dramatic, irresistible, and instantly intelligible pictorial messages, is essentially meaningless until interpreted for the viewer by the narrator. Such would be the case, I would think, for news from a remote, exotic, mysterious place like Vietnam. Most television news watchers knew nothing about the history, culture, politics, and geography of Vietnam. They also knew little about the tactics and techniques of modern warfare. Any meaning that the images of a strange war in a strange place could have for viewers would have to come from the narration, which was synchronized to the visual images flitting across the 19-inch screen. It would be the meaning conveyed in words which gave most television images whatever potency they had. Take away the words, and the images of a typical Vietnam war story would be meaningless, a 30-second video clip suspended from time, space, from history itself, a decontextualized pictorial congeries in search of significantion.

The point must also be made emphatically that contrary to what the believers in the television myth remember or think that they remember of television coverage of the war, content analyses prove that coverage of Vietnam from August 1965 to January 1973 was not unfavorable much of the time, either as straight news or as editorial commentary. During the first few years of the war, "television coverage was lopsidedly favorable to American policy in Vietnam, often so explicitly favorable."[60] Whatever might be the story during the later years of war, it is important to understand that television coverage of the war in the first few years probably contributed to the United States becoming involved in the Vietnam conflict and maintained public support for it. It embraced and reinforced the Cold War consensus ideology. Television coverage became more critical after Tet, and by the summer of 1969.

> But television's turnabout on the war was part of a larger change, a response to as well as a cause of the unhappiness with the war that was developing at many levels, from the halls of the Pentagon to Main Street, U.S.A. and the fire bases of Quang Tri Province.[61]

Television coverage of the war more often followed than formed public opinion. It changed with it, reflecting as well as shaping; the interaction between medium and audience is complex. Those who believe that television lost a war assume a simplistic technological determinism belied by the evidence. Even during the later years of the war, when television footage included more critical stories, many aspects of the war continued to get favorable coverage. Ground combat continued to be reported favorably; U.S. troops continued to win most of the firefights and inflict heavier losses on the enemy than they sustained. The air war always got favorable coverage right to the end. Stories about the air war usually focused on the personal experiences of pilots or else on the sophisticated technology at their command.[62]

Content analyses also show that television news gave more coverage to atrocities committed by the NLF than to those committed by the American side. Even during the later years of coverage, when television was more critical of the war, enemy atrocity stories were the second most frequent television war story, second only to American combat stories.[63] There was also an important difference in the way American atrocity stories were covered and the way enemy atrocity stories were presented. Whether it was the slaughter of civilians by platoons at My Lai or individual atrocities committed under duress by enraged or frightened soldiers, no television story ever suggested the United States might have a policy of targeting civilians or that civilian casualties would inevitably come from counterinsurgency tactics, the huge amount of firepower employed by American forces, or the racist nature of the war. Television news never hinted that atrocities might flow from soldiers' attitudes, which routinely portrayed Vietnamese people as "dinks," "slopes," "slants," or, most commonly, "gooks." Each atrocity got presented as an isolated experience. It happened at the moment for reasons that were never examined. Invariably, however, NLF atrocity stories were presented as flowing from a deliberate policy of calculated terror as an instrument of intimidation and control. Atrocities by Americans were always discrete occurrences. Enemy atrocities were always systemic, part of a brutal political process. Ours just happened. Theirs were always planned.[64]

Although analyses can provide us with a clear sense of the amount and kind of television news stories about Vietnam that were shown to the public, we have only a few empirical studies that give us any indication of how television news coverage of the war might have influenced public attitudes toward that conflict. The results of the only public-opinion poll that ever asked people how television news coverage of the Vietnam war influenced their attitudes toward the war were printed in the July 10, 1967, issue of *Newsweek*. Eighty-three percent of respondents said that they felt *more hawkish* after watching the news.[65] At the time this poll was taken, other polls were showing that more than 50 percent of Americans believed that U.S. entry into the war had been a mistake.[66] The most obvious inference one could draw from these data is that opposition to the war in Vietnam was rising despite, not because of, television coverage.

Other studies have shown that viewers can remember very little from having watched television newscasts. One researcher found that fewer than 10 percent of viewers could recall any story they had seen on the television news the day before. News stories from the print media were remembered much better. One explanation for the better retention of information from newspapers than from television news broadcasts is that knowledge from print media accumulates, it builds upon previous learning, whereas television news stories wash over the brain electronically, like waves upon a beach, erasing any previous knowledge. Another reason might have to do with the pattern of television war coverage: the tendency to show repetitious, formulaic stories night after night on the tube, the generic 30-second video clip that all the networks used over and over again to frame their accounts from Vietnam. If this finding about the evanescence of television news retention is valid, that news stories about the war did not stick in the minds of viewers, if they could not even remember having watched it the night before, it is highly unlikely that accounts about the war had much influence on the public's thinking or attitudes about the war.[67]

A more substantial study of patterns of recall among television news watchers was done in 1971 by Russell Neuman when news about Vietnam was still the most frequent weekly category of news story shown. He and his assistants polled a standard sample of news viewers a few minutes to 3 hours after they had watched all or part of a network television news program. Most respondents fell into a large undifferentiated mass of typical American news watchers who just happened to catch the news that night on television. They did not tune into television news regularly, had no special interest in the news or in being well-informed, nor did they evince any unusual interest in the war. Without prompting, these viewers could recall only 5 to 10 percent of the stories they had just watched. With prompting they could recall about 20 percent of the stories. For this study, Neuman had categorized the news into ten story types. The most frequently recalled stories were about the weather and human-interest items. Frequency of recall of Vietnam stories ranked sixth among the ten categories.[68]

Neuman portrayed the typical television news viewer as relatively uneducated, tired after a day's work, slumped in a chair, staring at the television set as news and entertainment came by in a steady stream of words and pictures. The typical viewer probably made little distinction between television news and the prime-time entertainment fare that followed it, may even have considered the nightly news part of the evening's television entertainment. It is unlikely that Vietnam news stories or any other news stories except perhaps weather and local scandals stayed with this viewer or influenced the viewer's thinking.[69]

Psychiatrist Frederick Wertham, writing in the *New York Times* in 1966, stated his belief that television coverage of combat does not necessarily cause people to sicken or tire of war and call for its end. Dr. Wertham thought that television coverage of Vietnam could have the opposite effect on viewers, that it caused people to accept war, to become hardened to it, and to find it a part of the routine of life. A 1972 *Newsweek* readers' survey suggesting that the public was developing a tolerance to Vietnam news telecasts[70] would tend to confirm Dr. Wertham's hypothesis.

Television coverage of combat, especially coverage depicting American soldiers in combat over many years, which did not show much live action, which rarely showed dead or wounded soldiers, and which was usually framed by a melodramatic, black-and-white interpretation of our good guys against their bad guys, would more likely have the effect of legitimizing combat in Vietnam than delegitimizing it. The evidence suggests that television coverage of the war more often elicited popular support for the conflict than caused people to reject or oppose it.

In my view, continual exposure to televised war most likely made most Americans apathetic about the killing occurring on the other side of the world. It turned them off emotionally; in time it became impossible for most Americans to have any kind of response to what they were seeing. Seemingly interminable, miniaturized pictures of men at war flitting across the 19-inch screen—inextricably blended with fictional images from entertainment programs shown nightly, frequently interrupted by intrusive commercial messages—became part of the prime-time pabulum nightly ingested by many Americans.

V   Then Came Tet

The Tet offensive, which took place in January-February 1968, turned out to be the crucial campaign of the Vietnam war as far as America was concerned. Tet was a major turning point in that long conflict. After Tet, it proved impossible for the United States to escalate the ground war. Lacking both public and congressional support for the war, this meant that America and its allies could not achieve military victory in Southeast Asia. In time, the United States was forced to withdraw its forces, leaving the South Vietnamese vulnerable to a Communist takeover. Those who believe that television coverage of the war contributed significantly to the American defeat often cite media coverage of Tet and its political aftermath to prove their case that biased, distorted coverage of the war undermined popular support, cost Americans a victory and ultimately the war. In reality, Tet and its aftermath prove that television coverage was a minor factor in a complex sequence of events that determined the eventual outcome of the war.

As 1967 was coming to an end, the American public had the general sense that militarily the war in Vietnam was going well for the United States. The air war was being waged at its highest level of intensity to date; there were nearly 500,000 U.S. troops in South Vietnam. President Lyndon Johnson had brought General Westmoreland home to make speeches in which the field commander stated that the enemy was losing men at a greater rate than it could replace them.[71] Johnson made an effective defense of his war policy and it gained in the polls as 1967 ended.[72]

Then came Tet-68. Violating a truce that had been declared to permit the Vietnamese people to participate in the country's most important holiday, Tet, or the lunar New Year, some 84,000 NLF and PAVN (People's Army of Viet Nam) forces simultaneously attacked Saigon, provincial capitals, and district towns all across South Vietnam. They caught the ARVN and U.S. forces by surprise. They also caught Washington politicians and American journalists by surprise. The enemy suddenly had brought the war home to urban populations hitherto secure from the ravages of battle. The enemy showed both numbers and military capabilities that American intelligence officers did not believe they had. Although surprised, both ARVN and American troops recovered quickly from their initial confusion and dismay. They fought back effectively. Within a few days, ARVN and U.S. forces had retaken all the cities and towns that the Communists had captured with the exception of Hue, where fighting lasted almost a month before the enemy was finally expelled.[73]

In the months after Tet, public support for the war declined, and the antiwar movement became more active. Political leaders and media editorials became outspokenly critical of Lyndon Johnson's war policies. Within the administration, a conflict between Johnson's dovish and hawkish advisers raged with rising intensity. The president himself was confused, uncertain as to what course of action to pursue in response to Tet.

Critics of television have made three points about its Tet coverage. The first is that television reportage brought the events of Tet home to viewers with dramatic vividness and immediacy. Video clips showed an NLF suicide squad penetrating the American embassy in Saigon, the very citadel of American power. There was also a sizable increase in news stories depicting military casualties on both sides. Coverage of the fighting at Hue, which dragged on for weeks, was especially graphic. It depicted American Marines pinned down by sniper fire, suffering heavy casualties amidst the burning rubble that once was Vietnam's most beautiful city. Daniel Hallin has observed that it was television's Tet coverage that first revealed the brutality of the war on a regular basis.[74]

While Americans viewed the battles of Tet on the evening news, the networks also gave extensive coverage to the battle for Khe Sanh waged simultaneously. Khe Sanh was a Marine outpost near the Laotian border just south of the DMZ blocking a major infiltration route for PAVN forces entering South Vietnam. Two North Vietnamese divisions besieged Khe Sanh for 77 days. For a time reporters feared that Khe Sanh might be a reprise of the French disaster at Dien Bien Phu. Dramatic television footage showed the Marines, under heavy fire, suffering casualties, trying to survive. In fact, Khe Sanh's survival was never in doubt. American artillery and bombers inflicted thousands of casualties on the enemy before they abandoned the siege in April of 1968.

Media critics have faulted the networks for their coverage of the siege of Khe Sanh as well as for their coverage of the Tet offensive. They have accused journalists of exaggerating both the threat of defeat and the importance of a campaign that was peripheral to the main thrust of the Tet campaign. But television journalists covering Khe Sanh were simply mirroring official concern for its survival. General Westmoreland, fooled by the planners of Tet, initially thought the North Vietnamese were making their major effort at Khe Sanh and he believed that the attacks on Saigon were a feint.[75] Westmoreland hoped to lure the PAVN forces besieging Khe Sanh into a main force battle *a la* Dien Bien Phu where superior U.S. airpower and artillery fire, coupled to American air assault and supply capabilities, would enable American forces to prevail. President Johnson, aware of the French fate and dreading the possibility of a reprise at Khe

Sanh, had a model of Khe Sanh constructed in the White House war room. He called General Westmoreland daily about the progress of the campaign.[76]

The most famous television footage of the war came out of Tet. On the evening of February 2, 1968, NBC television news anchor Chet Huntley introduced correspondent Howard Tuckner reporting from Saigon on the fighting in the capital city. The last 52 seconds of Tuckner's report consisted of a film showing the chief of South Vietnam's National Police, General Nguyen Ngoc Loan, drawing his pistol, pointing it at the head of a captured Vietcong commando, and shooting him to death. The body of the dead VC instantly slumped to the pavement while blood spurted from his head and formed a slowly spreading dark pool on the cobbled street. The film sequence ended at this point without further commentary.[77] Believers in the myth that television cost America a war it could have won have argued that General Loan's televised summary execution of a Vietcong terrorist shocked and confused American television viewers, thereby alienating public support for the war.

Perhaps, but we really don't know much about how the millions of American news watchers who witnessed the brutal execution reacted nor how it may have affected their attitudes toward the war. NBC news received many letters protesting the showing of this controversial sequence. Most letter writers accused NBC of bad taste in showing the film. Their next most common criticism was that children might have watched it. Few of the letter writers even mentioned the war and none questioned the truthfulness of the network's news coverage or the controversial film sequence. None gave any indication that the execution footage or television coverage of Tet generally had any influence on their attitudes toward American conduct of the Vietnam war. Although powerful and shocking, the shooting of the VC terrorist evidently had no impact on public opinion about the war, only on public opinion about what should be shown on television about Vietnam.[78]

The second point that critics of television coverage of Tet-68 make is that American journalists at first reported the Communist assaults as victories thereby adding to the public's perception that Tet was a great disaster for our side. By the time the journalists got it right and began reporting the American and South Vietnamese victories, it was too late. The damage had been done and efforts by government officials to portray Tet for what it really was—a military disaster for Hanoi and the NLF—were ineffective. There is a lot of data to test the validity of their charges. The Tet-68 offensive is one of the most extensively studied events of the war. There also exist studies of the media coverage of Tet, most notably Peter Braestrup's massive *Big Story*.[79] Many who argue that television contributed significantly to the eventual loss of the Vietnam war often cite Braestrup.

Braestrup charged the media with distorted coverage and erroneous interpretations of the initial fighting, which caused the American public to regard Tet as a Communist victory when it was not.[80] But he is at pains to point out that he did not charge either print or television journalists with bias. He merely pointed out that because of the unique circumstances prevailing at Tet—

the complete surprise attained by the enemy, the fast-paced, quick-breaking military action that was hard to follow and to understand at first—there occurred an uncharacteristic, one-time lapse of media professionalism that resulted in distorted coverage by some journalists of the Tet fighting.[81] He never said that Tet coverage by either print or television journalists turned public opinion against the war. Indeed, he pointed out that such claims are impossible to substantiate: "No empirical data exist to link news coverage with changes in public opinion."[82]

Braestrup contended that skewed media coverage exacerbated a growing political crisis in Washington that would have occurred even if journalistic accounts of Tet had been accurate. He also pointed out that Lyndon Johnson's indecisive behavior in the aftermath of Tet was a much more important contributor to the crisis than media coverage. Braestrup stated that it was probably Johnson's inept leadership that caused the drop in public support for the war. Whatever changes occurred in public attitudes toward the Vietnam war following Tet were caused by failures of political leadership, not by television news coverage of the campaign.[83]

When Robert Elegant charged in the November 1982 issue of *Encounter* that television caused Americans to lose a war that it had actually won—which I quoted in my introduction—Braestrup challenged him vigorously, again pointing out that

> there is no empirical evidence that shows any firm link between media coverage and trends in public opinion. We simply do not *know* [emphasis his] much about the causes of change in public opinion.[84]

The third point that the critics have made of television coverage of Tet is that hostile television commentaries both eroded public support for the war and encouraged its opponents. They have often cited the most influential of the television news anchors, Walter Cronkite, who delivered a personal editorial to his viewers on the evening of February 23, 1968, at the end of his report. Cronkite, hitherto a supporter of the American role in Vietnam, that evening declared the war a stalemate and called for negotiations:

> It seems now more certain than ever that the bloody experience of Vietnam is to end in a stalemate. . . . The only rational way out [of Vietnam] is to negotiate, not as victors, but as an honorable people who had lived up to their pledge to defend democracy, and did the best they could.[85]

Lyndon Johnson, dismayed by Cronkite's editorial, reportedly told aides that if he had lost Cronkite's support for the war, then he must also have lost the support of the great American heartland for his war policy of gradual escalation.

There is no direct evidence to sustain the allegations that television's realistic coverage of the fighting during Tet, its erroneous interpretation of some of the early battles that showed the Communists winning when they were not, or television editorial comments challenging optimistic official statements about the war's progress undermined public support for the war. There is much surface evidence that challenges such charges. Public-opinion polls show about the same levels of support for the war at the end of March 1968, two months after Tet, as had been the case at the beginning of the year a month before Tet. In fact, public opinion at the end of March 1968 was similar to where it had been in October 1967, long before Tet.[86] The first poll taken after Tet showed a 5 percent jump in support for the war.[87] The post-Tet drop-off in public support for the war does not come until April 1968, after the president had made an important speech announcing that he was abandoning his policy of gradual escalation and would not seek reelection.[88]

These polls raise the question of just how much of a shock Tet-68 caused the American public. Few were that well-educated with a good grasp of American history and knew much about Vietnam. Even fewer were passionately politicized by the war, watched the television evening news avidly to get the latest information on the course of the war, or heard the speeches of Lyndon Johnson and General Westmoreland in November 1967. The typical person polled was more likely to be poorly educated, poorly informed, and not much engaged in the affairs of state or a war going on in a remote corner of the world. He or she did not have strongly held views concerning U.S. policy in Vietnam. Most people when polled made simplistic and generalized suggestions such as "let's go in and hit them hard; do what we have to do to win and get out." Or, "let's stop the killing and make a negotiated agreement." These responses were not reactions to particular events in the war, even dramatic ones like Tet, because most people were not following events closely enough to react to particular occurrences. Many were probably turned off by the war long before Tet and were no longer following the course of the war. Their responses to pollsters' questions derived from accumulated experiences and impressions formed over the years.

The Tet-68 offensive shocked President Johnson, his close civilian and military advisers, and journalists both in Vietnam and Washington. Official Washington had apparently believed its own optimistic propaganda about the progress of the war. But Tet-68 shocked most Americans far less. If one carefully charts public opinion, one sees that Tet-68 has little impact. As measured by its immediate effect on public attitudes, Tet-68 hardly caused any shift at all except for a brief strengthening of the public's support for the war. Americans did not have much of a reaction to Tet or to television's initial portrayal of the campaign as a great disaster for the United States and its South Vietnamese clients. It didn't appear to matter how television portrayed Tet, whether journalists reported it with clinical accuracy and detachment or got it all backwards and told Americans that we were losing when in fact we were winning tactically.

People probably took their cues on how to respond to the events of Tet-68 from the performance of administration officials. Johnson, surprised and confused by the Tet offensive, did not assert leadership and did not take control of the crisis situation. Meanwhile, congressional opponents of Johnson's war policy spoke out, and media editorials challenging the administration's views of the war effort proliferated. Periodicals hitherto supportive of the war effort now challenged the administration and called for negotiations. The growing divisions within Johnson's government over what course of action to take intensified. There was an interim political vacuum during which the president lost control of the flow of news and the ability to define and interpret his war policy for the people. Not until March 31, 1968, when he made his speech, which had been carefully publicized in advance to ensure a large audience, did he regain the initiative, but with an altered policy. The shift in public opinion, showing a sharp rise in dove sentiment, coincided with Johnson's speech announcing major changes in his Vietnam policy.[89]

There had been a much more significant shift in public opinion concerning a limited war in Asia than the one that occurred following Johnson's address to the nation. It occurred during the Korean war following the intervention of the Chinese on November 26, 1950, just when it appeared that UN troops were on the verge of liberating Korea and coming home victorious. Public suport for the Korean war dropped precipitously—by 27 percentage points.[90] And that fall-off following the Chinese intervention cannot be blamed on television news coverage or biased journalism since there was little television war news in 1950, most Americans did not have television sets at that time, and war correspondents were all patriotic supporters of the UN war effort. Compared to the drop in public support for the Korean conflict in 1950, the small fall-off in public support for the war in the aftermath of Tet-68 is minuscule.

Let us suppose that Lyndon Johnson had ordered a major escalation of the war in the aftermath of Tet-68. There is evidence that his first instinct was to strike hard at the enemy because of its perfidy and because U.S. and ARVN forces were inflicting heavy losses on the NLF and PAVN troops. His military advisers and some of his senior civilian advisers urged him to do just that. How would public opinion have responded to a strong escalation of the fighting immediately after Tet? There would, of course, have been considerable opposition in the streets, in the halls of Congress, and in the media as costs and casualties rose dramatically. However, I believe that the approval rating for Johnson and his war policy would have risen dramatically in the short run. The public was still more hawkish than dovish at that time. Johnson also probably understood that if he did make a decisive move, it would have caught the support of the broad mass of the American public and a majority in Congress. The historic pattern revealed by polling has been for public opinion to rally in support of a leader's initiative, whether it is escalatory or de-escalatory.[91] It is the leader perceived as taking decisive actions that draws popular support, not the action per se.

Had Johnson escalated the war after Tet as I have suggested, public support would have begun to drop within a few months had the policy been perceived not to be effective.[92] I further believe that however television covered my hypothetical American post-Tet offensive, whether accurately or inaccurately, favorably or unfavorably, as straight news or with accompanying editorializing, television news coverage would have had little effect on public opinion as long as the U.S. effort appeared to be succeeding and as long as President Johnson was perceived to be a strong leader.

The surprisingly strong showing in the New Hampshire primary in March 1968 of antiwar candidate Senator Eugene McCarthy, followed four days later by Robert Kennedy's declaration that he too would seek the Democratic presidential nomination running on an antiwar platform, apparently were considerations in Lyndon Johnson's decision not to seek reelection.[93] But it is also important to understand that public opinion in March 1968 was still more hawkish than dovish despite Walter Cronkite's editorial pronouncement, and Johnson was aware of that political reality.[94] He was much more concerned about placating hawkish opponents than doves at that time because the hawks were powerful senior senators on the Armed Services and Foreign Relations committees. Polls taken in March 1968 show that large segments of the public were expressing dissatisfaction with Johnson's policy of gradual escalation, but a majority of these malcontents wanted further escalation of the war. They acknowledged that getting into the war was a mistake, but now that the United States had committed much blood and treasure, they favored doing whatever had to be done to win. Not until 1969, long after Tet and the departure of Lyndon Johnson, did doves outnumber hawks.[95]

Johnson was extremely reluctant to abandon his war policy after having invested so much in it for so long. In early 1968, he most likely continued to believe that gradual escalation could bring military victory in Vietnam. He also believed that he could still get the Democratic nomination and could probably beat either of the likely Republican candidates, Richard Nixon or Ronald Reagan, and win reelection. But he knew it would be rough. His own party would be split and his broad base of support, the consensus that he had cultivated so successfully, had eroded considerably from the heyday of the Great Society in 1964–1965. He could still win but only at a cost of exacerbating the deep fissures within American society.

The most important consideration in Johnson's decision to abandon his policy of gradual escalation and not to run again was insider, establishment pressures. (Johnson was not influenced by the vocal antiwar movement in March 1968 when he made his announcement. He knew that the doves lacked power, had little popular support, were comparatively few in number, and were hated by most Middle Americans more than those folks hated the increasingly unpopular war.) Johnson changed course after Tet mainly because Secretary of Defense Clark Clifford, after conducting a thorough investigation of Johnson's war policy, concluded that escalation had reached its tolerable limits and must be abandoned to avoid national disaster. Clifford arranged for Defense Department analysts, who believed that Johnson's war policy was failing, to brief a group of distinguished former senior military and civilian leaders. The analysts convinced these men, led by former Secretary of State Dean Acheson, of the need for Johnson to change policies.[96] This informal advisory group, dubbed the "Wise Men," had met previously with Johnson in November 1967, at that time endorsing his Vietnam policy of gradual military escalation. But during the interim, serious political and economic crises were building, catalyzed by Tet. The Wise Men told Johnson that the war in Vietnam could not be won at any reasonable cost acceptable to the nation. They told him that the main reason for loss of popular support for his policy was the seemingly endless war. They called his attention to the growing divisions within the country, to rising inflation, and to mounting budget deficits caused by his failure to raise taxes or to trim domestic social spending to finance the increasingly costly war. They also told him that America's international balance-of-payments was showing a deficit for 1967, the dollar was declining in value, and speculators were draining U.S. gold reserves.[97]

It was the weight of the advice that Johnson got from Clifford and the Wise Men, luminaries who had shaped the foreign policies of the Truman, Eisenhower, and Kennedy administrations, as well as Johnson's, that keyed the president's change. It was not media coverage, poll-readings, the speeches of dovish critics, or public opinion that did it. The Wise Men confronted Johnson with painful political and economic facts of life, and they were ultimately effective. The president, angry and frustrated, after thinking about the political situation he confronted, accepted recommendations to change his war policy.[98]

Johnson's dramatic pronouncements at the end of March did not signal the abandonment of his goal of securing an independent South Vietnamese government, only that he understood that his current policy of gradual escalation was no longer politically tenable. He was maneuvering to buy time, to evolve a new policy that would defuse the opposition and restore the faltering consensus. Neither Johnson nor the other participants in the making of his decision to abandon his war policy of gradual escalation intended or foresaw that it was to be a historic turning point in American involvement in Southeast Asia. The president was not changing American goals or repudiating past strategies. He still believed that the United States could and should prevail, that America should honor its commitments and meet its responsibilities in Vietnam. Johnson was shifting strategies to regain the political high ground to continue the war and win it.[99]

Johnson had, in fact, following Clark Clifford's advice, reverted to what Richard Nixon's Secretary of Defense, Melvin Laird, would call "Vietnamization" a year later. And Vietnamization was little more than a return to the policy of the Kennedy years when American advisers helped ARVN forces fight the NLF during 1961 to 1963.[100] But it is likely, however, that much of the public, both hawks and doves, at the time Johnson made his speech, interpreted the president's announced policy changes as tantamount to abandoning his efforts to seek a military victory in Vietnam, that he had converted to dovishness and was making greater efforts to achieve a negotiated settlement. Probably one of the major causes of the upsurge in antiwar feeling following Johnson's speech was because people, assuming Johnson's conversion to dovishness, joined the president. They reasoned that if the president had become dovish, it was all right to be a dove too.

Another reason why people blame television news for the loss of Vietnam is that they did not understand Communist strategies and tactics at the time of Tet-68. Television critics assumed that since Tet turned out to be a political and psychological disaster for the United States, that the Communists planned it that way. They believed that Hanoi was willing to sacrifice NLF forces and suffer major military defeats to inflict a decisive psychological and political blow against the Americans. In their view, the Communists succeeded, aided and abetted by television journalists inadvertently playing into Red hands with their distorted and opinionated coverage of Tet-68, which ultimately undermined public support for the war and forced Lyndon Johnson to abandon his Vietnam policy. These television critics have fallen prey to the *post hoc, ergo propter hoc* fallacy and Communist propaganda.

The Tet campaign was planned by Vo Nguyen Giap, PAVN's brilliant military strategist. As with all his campaigns, Giap sought both military and political objectives, with political goals paramount.[101] Tet-68 also has to be understood within the framework of Giap's grand strategy. His strategy paralleled Westmoreland's attrition strategy. Giap's long-range goal was to inflict enough losses on the Americans that they would agree to a political settlement satisfactory to Hanoi, which entailed stopping all acts of war against North Vietnam, replacing the South Vietnamese government with a coalition government, and getting American troops out of Vietnam.[102]

Seen from within Giap's grand strategic frame, Tet was one more campaign in a long war of attrition. From Giap's perspective, the Vietnam war would last as long as Americans were willing to die for Saigon. Giap expected that the Tet offensive would reduce, perhaps end, U.S. enthusiasm for the cause. Hanoi's more important Tet goal was a political one—to undermine the South Vietnamese government and to drive a wedge between Saigon and its American protectors. The Communist leaders convinced themselves that the South Vietnamese people were ripe for revolution. Tet-68 was designed to show the people in the South that U.S. forces could not protect them even within their urban shelters and that ARVN forces could not fight. Such revelations would trigger an uprising of soldiers, peasants, religious factions, students, and other groups who would overthrow the Saigon "puppets" and demand that the Americans leave. By taking the war to the urban populations, hitherto relatively immune from the plague of war, Hanoi intended to shatter the people's sense of safety and trigger a rebellion.[103]

Hanoi was trying to influence Vietnamese public opinion; it tried to inflict a decisive psychological and political blow on the South Vietnamese people, not on the American people. For Giap, South Vietnam was the vital political arena, not the United States. Success hinged upon shifting the power balance in Saigon, not in Washington. Ho Chi Minh, working with Giap, also added a diplomatic initiative to Tet-68, both for propaganda purposes and because he expected Americans, in the aftermath of Tet, to be more willing to negotiate on his terms.[104]

Let us also look at the results of Tet from the Communist perspective. The Communists made military and political errors that hurt their cause. They were astonished at the fighting capabilities displayed by the ARVN troops. They failed to accomplish a single tactical objective, and they suffered their heaviest casualties of the war, losing all their crack NLF units. Where PAVN regulars joined the fighting, they also got blown away. Never again would NLF main force units be a significant military presence in the South. PAVN forces had to be sent south to replace them, so after Tet the war in South Vietnam became more of a conventional war between main-force PAVN troops and U.S./ARVN forces.[105] The Communists also suffered serious political setbacks during Tet. In many provinces they lost the revolutionary infrastructures painstakingly built over the years.[106] Worse, the expected uprising never occurred. In fact, many South Vietnamese turned against the NLF for its having violated the Tet truce and because the ARVN soldiers fought with unexpected effectiveness.[107]

The Communists did not anticipate the great uproar that the Tet-68 campaigns provoked within the United States. Gradually they came to understand that although they had been beaten militarily at Tet and failed to accomplish their major political objectives, the American reaction amounted to a devastating political defeat for our side, which turned out to be the beginning of the end for the American effort to stop Communist expansionism in southern Vietnam. Tet ended up confirming Giap's long-range strategy even though it thwarted his immediate plans. The American reaction to Tet was not planned by clever Communist strategists who got help from television journalists, antiwar activists, and dovish politicos; it was a serendipitous by-product of a campaign that had other, failed goals. If the political outcome of Tet confirmed anything, it was the historical law of unintended consequences.

Tet-68 created a crisis within the foreign policy-making elite of this nation. They perceived that Johnson's war policy, which they had all supported until the Tet campaigns, to have failed. It could not accomplish its limited political goals at any acceptable cost. It was also weakening U.S. diplomatic and strategic policy in the world; it was working to the advantage of our global rival, the Soviets; it was weakening the economy; and it was causing serious domestic turmoil. The Wise Men convinced Johnson that they were correct, that the national interest could best be served by a change of policy in Vietnam.

It also served the president and his advisers' political purposes to blame both the media and public opinion for their decision. They would not have to consider that the policy that they had conceived, implemented, and pursued vigorously for two and a half years might be inherently unworkable. They had grievously underestimated the determination and fighting ability of both the NLF and PAVN. They had seriously underestimated the duration and cost of the war. They had overestimated the willingness of the American people to go on passively paying in lives and dollars for their military adventure in Southeast Asia in the service of containment ideology and its correlatives.

Johnson could also avoid having to take responsibility for his decision by taking refuge in political inevitability—he could claim that he had no choice thanks to what television and dovish politicians had done to public opinion. But television news and public attitudes are minor players in this dramatic decision, which was made of, by, and for the elite foreign-policy leaders of the nation. The failure of political nerve occurred first at the upper reaches of Wall Street and Washington, not at CBS News or in the American heartland.

VI   The Enemies of War

Tet and its aftermath proved to be a unique period in television reportage of the war, a departure from the routines of coverage. Graphic portrayals of brutal fighting were beamed into living rooms nightly for months. But by midsummer 1968, television journalism had reverted to its established patterns of war coverage. Few graphic scenes of war thereafter found their way into viewers' homes. The typical news story once again showed U.S. troops on patrol or engaged in sporadic combat. But proportionately fewer combat stories were reported and the television networks gave more attention to the political dimensions of the conflict, particularly the peace talks floundering along in Paris. Post-Tet television coverage of the war also became more critical. The reportage stressed the increasing costs of the war, especially as measured by large-scale American casualties. News story wrapups were no longer so upbeat, no longer implied that victory was inevitable, or even likely. Reports included stories about the decline of troop morale and the attendant problems of drug use, racial conflict, and refusals by some GIs to fight. Whereas television accounts of the war had portrayed American troopers in the 1965–1967 era as gung-ho warriors believing in the cause and confident of victory, television coverage during 1969 to 1972 increasingly portrayed American soldiers as reluctant conscripts, cynical about the outcome of the war, fighting to survive their year in the jungle.

The shift in television news coverage of Vietnam occurring after Tet reflected the changed attitudes of soldiers and their views of the war.[108] In the early stages of coverage, when the nation supported the war and confident soldiers believed in the cause, television gave the war mostly positive coverage. After 1968, when most Americans no longer supported the war and increasing numbers of conscripted GIs neither understood nor believed in the cause, nor expected to win because they perceived their government to be pursuing a no-win policy, television coverage became increasingly negative. Examples of such negative coverage appeared in a CBS television documentary, "The World of Charlie Company," filmed in May-June 1970, during the Cambodian incursion, the last major campaign involving American ground combat forces. CBS journalists accompanied a rifle company that was part of the invading force and recorded the troops' thoughts and actions. Some soldiers wore peace symbols and refused to fight or fire their weapons unless directly attacked by PAVN forces. They viewed fighting and risking their lives for a cause they did not believe in nor was supported by the American people as pointless. They refused direct orders to march down a road they viewed to be dangerous and, unbeknownst to their officers, reinterpreted orders to go on patrol to minimize the risks of combat. Charlie Company riflemen, aware of Nixon's policy of withdrawing American combat troops, saw their military role as a holding action rather than an attempt to win the war. No one in Charlie Company wanted to be the last American soldier killed in Southeast Asia. Television did not influence the course of the war; the course of the war influenced television's coverage of the war. Television did not turn soldiers' attitudes against the war; the war itself turned soldiers' attitudes against it.

Public opinion had turned against the war in Southeast Asia by the time Richard Nixon came to office in January 1969. Nixon began his presidency amidst a backdrop of domestic discord and violence symptomatic of a deeply divided electorate. Although the discord and violence of the late 1960s were fed from many sources, the controversial, stalemated war in Vietnam was the most potent single cause of disorder and appeared to impart a special intensity to the other causes. Nixon owed his margin of electoral victory more than anything else to the increasingly unpopular war in Vietnam that Hubert Humphrey, as Johnson's vice-president and hand-picked successor, could not shake. Nixon, a shrewd reader of the public pulse, offered the voters a plan to end the war, which he did not disclose, insisting that it had to remain secret to be effective.[109] Television news presented Nixon's presidential bid and the early months of his presidency on his terms; they portrayed him as a leader who understood that the war must be ended, who made phasing out the conflict in Southeast Asia a top foreign-policy priority, and had the plan to do it.

But Nixon and his chief foreign-policy adviser, National Security Adviser Henry Kissinger, soon discovered that Hanoi rejected his program of more realistic negotiating terms linked to threats of further escalation of the war if Hanoi did not quickly adopt a negotiating stance acceptable to the United States. Stymied, Nixon then embraced the essentials of Lyndon Johnson's policy that had been in place upon his accession to the presidency, a policy that Nixon's Secretary of Defense, Melvin Laird, labeled "Vietnamization"—a phased withdrawal of American combat troops at the same time expanding and improving the fighting effectiveness of the ARVN forces to prepare them to assume major combat responsibilities against the NLF and PAVN forces once American forces had departed. These military strategies were tied to increased efforts to move the stalled peace negotiations forward toward a cease-fire and political settlement. All the while, Nixon continued to seek the original U.S. objective of creating an independent, non-Communist South Vietnamese government. No more than Lyndon Johnson or John Kennedy before him would Nixon allow himself to be the first American president to lose a war.[110] Both futile negotiations and the war went on.

There was a contradiction at the heart of Nixon's Vietnamization policy. On the one hand he was winding down the American ground combat role in response to domestic political pressure. On the other hand, he escalated the naval and air wars against North Vietnam, and he ordered invasions and bombings of Laos and Cambodia, two neutral nations contiguous to Vietnam, in pursuit of American political objectives in Southeast Asia. His simultaneous efforts to get out and to make his opponents back down in the face of American power meant in reality that Nixon was pursuing a fundamentally irrational policy with incompatible objectives; he was trying to get out of a war and yet win it.

Nixon garbed his contradictory war aims with the rhetoric of "peace with honor," which disguised their incompatibility and spoke to the contradictory aspirations of most Americans who yearned to get out of Vietnam but did not want to lose a war. In time, to Nixon's bitter disappointment and frustration, the contradiction was resolved. The United States got out of Vietnam in early 1973, then lost the war two years later when the Communists captured Saigon and South Vietnam fell. In August 1974, Nixon himself was forced to resign from office because of accumulating evidence against him in the Watergate scandal. Nixon's bunker mentality that made Watergate possible mainly grew out of his frustrations with his Vietnam policy, his failure to end the war quickly, and his criminal efforts to stifle domestic opponents, whom he viewed to be undermining his efforts to protect national security.

The most important argument made by those who share Mr. Nixon's anguish over the outcome of the Vietnam war, and who strongly believe that television news coverage of that conflict was largely responsible for its tragic denouement, is that television journalists gave extensive coverage to the domestic critics of the war. They charge that television coverage of antiwar activities inflated their significance, widely disseminated their antiwar propaganda, and helped them recruit members. Because they believe that it significantly enhanced the antiwar movement's efforts and impact, they argue that television news sizably increased the number of Americans opposing the war and encouraged more politicians to take antiwar stances, thereby helping to undermine the political will of both the Johnson and Nixon administrations to persevere in Vietnam. Television's aid to the enemies of war also contributed to the demoralization of American troops and encouraged NLF and PAVN forces to continue resisting American military pressures.

These powerful indictments form the vital heart of the case that critics of television's coverage of the Vietnam war make against that electronic news medium. Their charges also raise a number of important questions: Did television news coverage in fact enhance the efforts of antiwar activists, enabling them to accomplish all the tasks claimed by the medium's critics? What were the achievements of the antiwar movement, its power allegedly enhanced by television coverage? Did antiwar activities turn large numbers of Americans against the war? Did they significantly inhibit the war policies of the Johnson and Nixon administrations? Did they undermine the morale of our soldiers in Vietnam and encourage our enemies to persist until victory was theirs? Are the activities of antiwar activists a major cause of the U.S. defeat? Because television did not enhance the effectiveness of the antiwar movement, which itself managed only a slight impact on public opinion, on government war policies, on troop morale, and thus on the course and outcome of the war, the argument that television lost the Vietnam war loses much of its cogency and credibility. Television's critics apparently do not understand that the heart of their argument depends for its lifeblood on two very slender sources.

Opposition to Lyndon Johnson's war policy began in early 1965. It included both doves who opposed the bombing of North Vietnam and the commitment of American ground combat troops as well as hawks who favored an allout effort from the outset to defeat Communist expansionism. Initially, antiwar activists operated outside established political channels, outside the established arenas of debate.[111] One of the major weaknesses of the antiwar organizations, which seriously limited their effectiveness, was their inability to unite on such matters as goals, rhetoric, tactics, and strategies in pursuit of a common cause. Intra-group and inter-group tensions and factional conflicts often impaired their various antiwar efforts. Opponents of the war included mostly radicals and liberals, but their ranks also included a scattering of libertarian conservatives and traditional isolationists. Mainly, antiwar activists were recruited from the political Left—Old Leftists, religious pacifists, the student-based New Left, elements from the civil rights movement, and assorted others. What these organizations and networks of organizations shared were a principled opposition to the war, a vocal activism, a desire to influence public opinion, and the goal of changing the government's war policies.[112]

Television news discovered the antiwar movement as the American war was beginning in 1965, although much early antiwar activity never got television coverage, never made the evening network news.[113] The first antiwar protest to get television coverage occurred in April 1965, when SDS (Students for a Democratic Society) organized a demonstration attended by about 15,000 protesters in the nation's capital. But contrary to those who believe television aided the antiwar movement, television coverage of this demonstration and most antiwar demonstrations in the 1965 to 1967 period was not favorable or even neutral. Television journalists framed their stories about antiwar activities in hostile terms. They did not adhere to their credo of "disinterested facticity." News coverage stressed the protesters' relatively small numbers and their ineffectiveness. Demonstrators were presented as marginal, extremist, a radical fringe causing traffic jams and posing problems of order. Rarely were antiwar activists allowed to speak on television news either to explain why they were protesting the conflict or to state their antiwar views and alternative policy proposals. If news anchors wanted commentary about antiwar activities, they normally went to government officials who inevitably disparaged the demonstrators, usually stressing their futility and reiterating that their words and actions would have no effect on the government's conduct of the war, and often reminding viewers that most Americans supported the U.S. commitment in Vietnam. Television coverage of antiwar activities often highlighted their theatrical, exotic, or occasionally violent dimensions. News commentators also emphasized the presence of Communists among the demonstrators. They also called attention to the presence of pro-war right-wing groups who often staged counterdemonstrations. Highlighting the presence of pro-war demonstrators also suggested that antiwar activity promoted social division and political polarization. Both Right and Left came across as extremist fringe groups unrepresentative of mainstream political culture.

Television coverage was both negative and distorted, usually making the demonstrations appear smaller, more radical, more bizarre, more violent, and more irresponsible than they were. Typically, television newscasters contrasted the antiwar activists, often college students protesting the war, with the troops fighting and dying in Vietnam in the defense of freedom. Such dichotomies were usually presented in simplistic, melodramatic good guy/bad guy stereotypes in which soldiers were portrayed as young heroes sacrificing themselves for the good of the nation and the protesters were depicted as traitors undermining the war effort and aiding the nation's enemies. Media coverage of antiwar protests during these years stressed two themes—their futility and their danger. Either the demonstrations were ineffective, or if effective, they posed a threat to internal security and aided the enemy. In either case, they were presented as subversive, deviant, outside the sphere of legitimate controversy.[114]

Some examples taken from content analyses of television news stories of antiwar activity demonstrate empirically the negative reportage that characterized coverage of protest demonstrations during the first few years of the war. ABC newsman Peter Jennings covered a protest by the radical May Second Movement in October 1965. He opened his report with the charged statement:

> While Americans fight and die in Vietnam, there are those in this country who sympathize with the Vietcong.[115]

CBS television once gathered a group of troopers at a firebase in Vietnam to show them a filmed lecture on draft resistance attended by college students in the States. Reporter Morley Safer then solicited the soldiers' reactions: "You're getting shot at," Safer said to one soldier. "Five of your buddies were killed down the road the other day. How do you feel watching that film?" The CBS news piece closed by quoting a soldier who wished that the young men attending the draft resistance lecture had walked that fatal road.[116]

A CBS news story by reporter Bruce Morton covering an SDS antiwar demonstration in Washington that was aired on the evening of November 27, 1965, typified television coverage of antiwar activities early in the war. Morton's narrative stressed the futility of protest, its marginality, and public fatigue with antiwar activities. He stated that the demonstrations would have no impact on President Johnson's policy and that they aided the enemy. No one from SDS was quoted. To prove his contention that the protests were aiding the enemy, Morton read statements from two sources—Secretary of State Dean Rusk and the *Peking People's Daily*.[117] Television's negative and distortive framing of most antiwar activities, particularly during 1965 to 1967, may be a reason why youthful antiwar activists were hated by most of the public, often by people who themselves had come to oppose the war.[118]

Significant and growing popular opposition to the war was evident by the summer of 1967, two years after Lyndon Johnson had Americanized the war. After Tet-68, popular opposition to the war swelled, and by the time Richard Nixon became president, a majority of Americans opposed the war. When the American role in Vietnam finally ended in January 1973, most Americans had come to oppose the war. But never did public opinion support antiwar demonstrations or demonstrators. "Although the war became increasingly unpopular, the antiwar movement was always *more* [emphasis his] unpopular."[119]

Television news functioned as a political instrument to contain and to discredit activist efforts to oppose the Vietnam war. Television news accomplished these political purposes by framing its coverage of much antiwar activities to spotlight their relatively small numbers, deviance, disloyalty, extremism, futility, and violence. Such negative framing represented a deliberate political strategy, crafted and implemented by journalists who viewed most antiwar organizations to be outside the sphere of legitimate controversy.

Part of the confusion on the part of those who persist in erroneously linking television coverage of the antiwar movement with the growing unpopularity of the Vietnam war, which led ultimately to the American defeat in Southeast Asia, lies in their failure to distinguish between two discrete antiwar currents flowing in the body politic. One, much the smaller of the two currents, consisted of the organized, vocal antiwar organizations recruited mostly from left-wing political elements, radicals and, after Tet, many liberals as well. What gave these antiwar activists what unity they possessed was the shared belief that the fighting in Vietnam was wrong and that the United States should cease all acts of war and withdraw immediately from that region.

The other, vastly larger antiwar current, constituted more disparate elements than the antiwar activists; it represented a rough cross section of the American populace and eventually included a majority of the citizenry. These groups were not vocal, not organized, nor were they usually given to demonstrating their concerns publicly. Their opposition was passive, not active; pragmatic, not principled. It might have registered in a public-opinion poll, a vote for an antiwar ballot measure, or a vote for a dovish candidate for public office. It was confined mostly to the private realms of life, diffuse and inarticulate. It was rooted in the calculus that the nation was paying too high a price in lives, dollars, inflation, increased taxes, shrunken social programs, political polarization, and social disorder to go on supporting a war that appeared increasingly to be an endless, escalating stalemate.[120] Many of these "pragmatics" despised the left-wing, vocal antiwar activists. They hated college protesters worse than they did the increasingly unpopular war.[121] These two antiwar factions did not join together in a common cause to oppose a war that they both hated. They did not identify with each other nor did they share an antiwar rhetoric or modes of discourse. They inhabited different political cultures; they came from different Americas. Their only common emotion was mutual disdain. The fundamental divide between the two antiwar cultures was that the vocal antiwar people focused on what the war was doing to Vietnam and the pragmatic opponents of war focused on what the war was doing to America. The vocals perceived the war to be wrong; the pragmatics perceived it to be pointless.[122]

When one examines public-opinion surveys charting the growing popular opposition to the Vietnam war from 1967 on, it is the rising pragmatic opposition that registered most of the numbers because they were at least ten times more numerous than were the vocals.[123] It was the pragmatic opponents of war—patriotic, law-abiding, God-fearing Middle Americans—who, along with the determined efforts of NLF and PAVN soldiers, eventually forced U.S. withdrawal from Vietnam and ensured American defeat in Southeast Asia. It was not the noisy protests of the comparatively few left-wing activist dissenters.[121] Pragmatics were not influenced by nor took their cues from the vocal antiwar movement whose ideology, style, tone, rhetoric, and tactics they resented and repudiated. Television coverage of the vocal antiwar movement, which highlighted and exaggerated all its features that angered and appalled pragmatics, may have strengthened their rejection of antiwar activists.

After Tet, television provided less hostile and more objective coverage of some antiwar activities, especially after Senator Eugene McCarthy, Democrat from Minnesota, entered the New Hampshire presidential primary in February 1968 as a peace candidate challenging President Lyndon Johnson's policy of gradual escalation of the war. In the eyes of television journalists, McCarthy's challenge to Johnson gave antiwar activities a legitimacy they had not enjoyed previously. Television news stories about McCarthy's primary bid highlighted the efforts of freshly shaven, short-haired youngsters, wearing coats and ties, trooping through the snow, knocking on the doors of New Hampshire voters, and courteously asking citizens to vote for McCarthy and for peace in Vietnam. These clean-cut young people were contrasted sharply and favorably with the uncouth rabble in the streets cheering Ho Chi Minh and cursing their own government.[125] Thereafter, television news tended to report objectively on the liberal elements within the antiwar movement who chose to work within the political system—those who supported the peace candidacies of presidential hopefuls McCarthy and later Robert Kennedy.

Radical antiwar protest declined following Lyndon Johnson's March 31 speech, which was widely interpreted by both hawks and doves as a dovish turn by the administration away from escalation and toward a negotiated settlement. Many young people found their political energies absorbed by the peace candidacies of McCarthy and Kennedy as the two liberal Democratic senators battled each other in a series of dramatic Democratic presidential primaries across the nation.[126]

Then organizers for the National Mobilization to End the War in Vietnam (MOBE) and the Youth International Party (Yippies) planned a series of demonstrations in Chicago to protest the war and to pump new life into the activist movements. It would be timed to coincide with the holding of the Democratic National Convention scheduled for late August 1968, which was expected to nominate Vice-President Hubert Humphrey, a longtime supporter of the administration's war policy and President Johnson's hand-chosen successor. Chicago Mayor Richard Daley, the official host of the convention, vowed that antiwar demonstrators would not disrupt his city or its convention. The stage was set for the most violent confrontation of the Vietnam era.

In the days preceding the convention, thousands of youthful antiwar activists filtered into Chicago, gathering mainly in Grant and Lincoln parks, far from the convention site, the downtown International Amphitheater. Mayor Daley mobilized his entire 12,000-man police force to contain the challenge. In addition, Mayor Daley persuaded Governor Samuel Shapiro to order 5,649 Illinois National Guardsmen to round-the-clock duty in Chicago, starting Friday, August

23, to head off a threat of "tumult, riot, or mob disorder."[127] Lest these forces prove insufficient, President Lyndon Johnson ordered 5,000 federal troops, specially trained for riot duty, flown to Chicago on August 26, the day the convention opened, to be standing by in case Daley's cops and the Illinois National Guard needed help.[128] The assembled police and soldiers outnumbered the protesters, whose numbers never exceeded 12,000.

Tension built between police and demonstrators during the days of the convention. There were skirmishes in the parks. Police used tear gas to break up a demonstration in Lincoln Park. Young people cursed and taunted the police. The Yippies staged a rally on behalf of a pig they had named Pigasus that they were running for president. The police and National Guard troops kept the protesters far from the convention site and nearby hotels where the delegates were staying and where the various candidates for president had their headquarters.

The convention, tightly controlled by Johnson supporters, turned back efforts by antiwar delegates to adopt a peace plank and ensured Humphrey's first-ballot nomination. Humphrey was nominated Wednesday evening, August 28. That night about 3,000 demonstrators managed to outmaneuver some of Daley's forces and marched down Michigan Avenue toward the Loop and the convention site. As they headed for the amphitheater, other police forces blocked their way.

Taunted by the words and acts of demonstrators, some of whom were probably undercover agents and *agents provocateurs*,[129] the police attacked in force, using their clubs and tear gas. Some demonstrators, seeing television cameras recording the action, chanted, "The whole world is watching, the whole world is watching."[130] What ensued during the next couple of hours was ugly and violent. A federal commission appointed to study the violence in Chicago later termed it "a police riot." The police attacked not only the protesters, but also observers, passersby, residents living in the area out for a nightly stroll, tourists, and media people.[131] Newspaper and television reporters and photographers were attacked and beaten by the enraged police. The television cameras recorded many scenes of police attacking and beating demonstrators. Hundreds of protesters were arrested, and hundreds more were injured. Scores of police also suffered injuries at the hands of protesters who fought back.[132]

Violence also penetrated the convention itself. A security officer punched CBS reporter Mike Wallace in the face. Wallace was trying to report on efforts by security personnel to remove a delegate who had refused to show his pass.[133] Senator Abraham Ribicoff of Connecticut took to the podium to denounce the use of "gestapo tactics in the streets of Chicago."[134]

Television coverage of the riot was vivid and, for once, sympathetic to the antiwar protesters. Reporters and anchors both criticized the violent police tactics. Viewers sympathetic to the demonstrators and the cause of peace were everlastingly horrified by the sickening, surrealistic sights and sounds of mayhem. Next day, the nation's media establishment angrily attacked both Mayor Daley and his violent police. Arthur Ochs Sulzberger of the *New York Times*, Katharine Graham of the *Washington Post* and *Newsweek*, Otis Chandler of the *Los*

Angeles Times, and Bailey Howard of the Chicago *Sun-Times* and *Daily News* joined the top executives of the three television networks and Hedley Donovan of *Time, Inc.,* to send a wire to Mayor Daley protesting that news reporters were singled out and beaten by police to prevent them from reporting "an important confrontation between police and demonstrators which the American public as a whole has a right to know about."[135]

But August 1968 was a time of increasing polarization, and viewers' reactions to the televised violence reflected that polarization. The vast majority of viewers identified with the police, whom they saw defending the Democratic convention and Chicago from an intolerable threat posed by a few thousand young people embracing radical politics and a countercultural lifestyle. All the networks were deluged by angry letters, telegrams, and phone calls. By an 8 to 1 margin, they condemned the demonstrators, the antiwar movement generally, and what they perceived as biased television coverage that favored the protesters. Mayor Daley got 75,000 letters from all over the country in the first two weeks following the convention, 90 percent of them praising his police. Public-opinion polls taken shortly after the violence showed a large majority of respondents were angered by the demonstrators and sympathetic to the police. Other polls showed a sharp increase in support for Richard Nixon, the Republican candidate, who had been nominated three weeks prior to the Chicago violence, and who was running on a platform promising to bring peace and restore order.[136]

Television journalists and network executives were surprised and frightened by the hostile audience response to their coverage of the Chicago riot. Walter Cronkite, after reflecting on his uncharacteristic professional lapse, apologized to Mayor Daley for his remarks. All the networks issued defensive, apologetic statements claiming their right to cover important news stories. In the aftermath of the hostile audience response, they also quietly changed their news coverages. Thereafter, they gave less live coverage to antiwar demonstrations and less coverage to combat in Vietnam.[137] The prime political achievements of the antiwar effort in Chicago were to help elect Richard Nixon, hurt the peace movement, and perhaps prolong the war, despite favorable television coverage that condemned police violence.

The largest and most successful antiwar demonstrations occurred in October and November of 1969 when organizers called for a series of "Moratoriums" across the nation. The Moratoriums were organized by antiwar liberals and involved sober, middle-class citizens; dramatically contrasting with the crazies and cops who had combined to generate a Walpurgis Night of violence in the streets of Chicago the previous year. Meetings, rallies, and marches were held. More than 100,000 people marched for peace in parades staged in Boston, New York, and San Francisco. An estimated 300,000 people gathered in Washington to "March Against Death."[138] These Moratoriums represented the greatest organized expression of pacifist sentiment in U.S. history; the Washington demonstration was the largest ever held in the nation's capital. It was the high-water mark of the antiwar movement.

But this massive outpouring of popular opposition to the Vietnam entanglement had no impact on President Nixon's war policy or public opinion. On November 3, 1969, Richard Nixon made an effective speech defending his Vietnamization policy. He firmly defended the American commitment in Vietnam, warning that a rapid pullout of American forces would result in a bloodbath in South Vietnam and a loss of confidence in American leadership around the world. He directly attacked the Moratorium organizers, accusing them of sabotaging U.S. foreign policy and aiding its enemies. He openly appealed for support from the American people for his war policy and concluded with a dramatic warning: "North Vietnam cannot humiliate the United States. Only Americans can do that."[139]

Vice-President Spiro Agnew launched a series of attacks on the news media for alleged biased coverage that harmed the Nixon presidency, hurt American foreign policy, damaged the war effort, and promoted both the antiwar movement and other dissident elements in society. Together, the efforts of both Agnew and Nixon isolated the antiwar movement, put its leaders on the defensive, and intimidated the television networks. Pro-Nixon rallies appeared in many cities. Public-opinion polls showed solid support for administration war policy.

For the duration of American involvement in the Vietnam war, sporadic antiwar activity usually received television coverage. Generally, television news stories about antiwar activity were framed to cover the activity itself as an issue, not what antiwar organizers had to say about the war. Antiwar protesters could be seen but not heard on the evening news. Framing also continued to be predominantly negative; negative statements about antiwar activity outnumbered positive statements by about a 2 to 1 margin.[140] Most domestic criticism of the war aired on television news came from past or present public officials, not from antiwar spokesmen. Always administration officials had greater access to television news to defend and explain their war policies, and they were thus able to maintain control of the news flow and public support for their policies during these final years of war:

> As a forum for political debate, television remained opened primarily to official Washington, despite the rise in political protest.[141]

VII   Television News: Reality and Myth

Did television lose the Vietnam war? Could American power have been used more effectively in Vietnam and have achieved more favorable political outcomes than the utter defeat experienced by Americans and the people that they tried for so long to help? Those who assert the case that television lost a war that America could have won have assumed that if it hadn't been for television coverage of the war, the public would have stayed firmly united behind the government's Vietnam policies. They believe that it would have become clear to Hanoi's leaders in time that Americans were determined to prevail, that we were determined to contain the threat posed by the NLF and we were equally determined to punish North Vietnam until it accepted a non-Communist South Vietnam. Such assumptions rest upon ignorance of Vietnamese history and culture. By 1965, the Vietnamese drive to expel foreign forces from their country was decades old. The historic identity of the Vietnamese people had been forged in a crucible of struggle to free themselves from foreign domination, whether at the hands of Chinese, French, Japanese, or Americans. Before Hanoi would have been induced to abandon its drive for control of the entire country, the United States would have had to destroy Vietnam and exterminate the Vietnamese people.

Would the outcome of the Vietnam war have been different had the news been censored? Or had television coverage remained supportive of the war effort and government policy for their duration? There is, of course, the example of Korea where public support fell off sharply for a war that was shorter and less costly than Vietnam. For most of its duration, Korea was an unpopular war. During that war, television news was in its infancy, censorship was tight, and journalists, most of them veteran correspondents who had covered World War II, faithfully supported the war effort. Why assume Vietnam would have been different?

Military critics of Vietnam policy have argued that America could have won the war had the United States escalated both ground combat and the air war at a more rapid pace in 1965–1966 before the North Vietnamese had time to build up its ground forces, air defenses, and gird the economy and population for full-scale war. But President Johnson and the other architects of America's Vietnam involvement did not chose to fight a limited war because of television coverage of the war, because of domestic opposition, or because of concerns about public opinion. Moreover, during the first years of the war, television coverage was favorable, there was little vocal opposition to the conflict, and both Congress and public opinion supported the war.

Johnson chose not to wage an all-out war because he defined American objectives in Vietnam as limited. The strategy of limited war was crafted to fit within a larger framework of global U.S. political and strategic interests. The United States had to retain the capability of projecting its power elsewhere in case of crises or perceived threats to its interests in the Middle East, Europe, or the Caribbean. In addition, Johnson and his domestic advisers retained important social welfare and civil rights priorities they did not wish to sacrifice on the altar of all-out war in Southeast Asia. Johnson also did not want a war large enough to require mobilization of reserves, the drafting of all our young men, tax increases, or wartime controls. He wanted a war sufficiently small in scale that it would have no discernible adverse impact on the home front.

War planners also feared that if U.S. forces appeared on the verge of defeating North Vietnam, this would provoke Chinese intervention. President Johnson had vivid memories of the Korean war. Just when it appeared that UN forces would win that war and liberate Korea from Communism in November 1950, hordes of Chinese troops poured across the Yalu river and drove General MacArthur's armies back down the Korean peninsula. A short, popular war quickly changed into a protracted, controversial war, and Korea cost President Harry Truman any prospect of relection in 1952. Johnson was determined to avoid any such disastrous reprise at any cost. Finally, Johnson and his advisers were confident that the limited war policy that they conceived and implemented in 1965–1967 could bring victory within a reasonable time at a reasonable cost. The fateful decisions that transformed a civil war in Southeast Asia into a large-scale American war lasting more than seven years did not incorporate concerns about television coverage and public opinion. In any case, more of the early criticism of the U.S. war effort came from hawks impatient with the self-imposed political restraints of the war managers in Washington than from doves or peace activists.

A major turning point in the Vietnam war came in the wake of the Communists' failed Tet-68 offensive. But a close examination of polling data at the time of Tet shows that Tet registered only a small impact on public opinion. Public opinion about the war after Tet showed little change from public opinion in November 1967, months before Tet. Among those who opposed Johnson's policy of gradual escalation that was challenged by Tet were hawks, who still outnumbered doves in the spring of 1968. The antiwar movement was inactive when Tet occurred and even among the public opposed to Johnson's war policy, antiwar activists were more hated than the war itself.

Television news coverage of the dramatic events of Tet had little measurable impact on public opinion no matter what the content of the news stories or how they were framed. But Tet did provoke a crisis among this country's political elite entrusted with responsibility for crafting and conducting foreign policy. In March 1968, a coterie of senior advisers told Johnson that his war policy was bankrupt—it was not winning the war, it was dividing the people and harming the national interest. They insisted that it must be changed. Johnson abandoned his policy of gradual escalation and announced the implementation of what in time would be called Vietnamization. But at the time he changed course, Johnson had no intention of abandoning American efforts to win a military victory and save South Vietnam. Johnson was shifting tactics, buying time, and searching for a politically viable policy.

Eventually, public opinion imposed limits on America's Vietnam policy. By 1969, public opinion had turned against the war, and popular support continued to erode until the end of American involvement; for about half its duration, Vietnam was an unpopular war. But it is important to understand that the factors turning most of those Americans who came to oppose the war against it had little to do either with television news coverage of the conflict or the vocal antiwar movement. Close examination of public-opinion polls shows that negative television coverage comes after negative public opinion has already registered. The rise of opposition among Washington officials and declining morale among combat soldiers in 1968–1969 combined to turn television coverage against the war. Evidence gleaned from polling data also suggests that the main reasons most Americans came to oppose the war were grounded in their perceptions that America was not winning, that the conflict was claiming the lives of too many American young men, that it was too expensive, that it was taking too long, and that the political elites in Washington in charge of the war were neither competent nor honest. Had the cathode ray tube not been invented nor had any vocal opposition to the war been voiced, both the course of public opinion and the course of the war would have been similar. America would have eventually been forced to withdraw its forces from Vietnam, and South Vietnam would have still fallen to the Communists.

Failure in Vietnam derived mainly from political failure, not from television coverage of the war. The crucial failure was a colossal error in geopolitical judgment; the United States tried to fight a limited war for a limited purpose that was not vital to its strategic interests. The key reason for the failed effort was that the United States committed far more of its wealth, manpower, and prestige than most policymakers and advisers had considered rational at the outset of the war in 1965. Before Tet, the war had already gone on longer than anticipated, cost more, and had generated growing opposition and worrisome social divisions. Tet-68, the fact that it could occur, that PAVN and NLF forces could stage a coordinated series of assaults against supposedly secure cities and towns all over Vietnam, catching both ARVN and U.S. forces by surprise, all of these factors, confirmed establishment suspicions that the stated goals of the Vietnam intervention could not be won at any reasonable price within the near future. Amidst an environment of official confusion and hesitation, rising popular opposition, a raging debate within the ranks of government, the Wise Men intervened to persuade Johnson to abandon his policy of gradual escalation.

Once America started down the Vietnamization road, it proved impossible for either Johnson or Nixon to reintroduce U.S. ground combat forces. Efforts to transform the South Vietnamese military into an effective fighting force capable of defending itself without U.S. advisers, or massive American logistic and air support, failed. After the withdrawal of all American forces early in 1973, the Thieu regime lived on borrowed time. South Vietnam lay at the mercy of the powerful men in Hanoi who waited until they were sure that the Americans would not intervene again in force to save their clients in Southeast Asia, to finish the political task that they had set for themselves 30 years earlier. When the end came with brutal suddenness on April 30, 1975, Americans averted their gaze and tried to console themselves with the thought that they had done all that they could reasonably have been expected to do to help the South Vietnamese.

The tragedy of television news coverage of the Vietnam war was not that it prevented America from winning a war; not that it provided the viewing public with brutal images of war that eventually turned viewers against it; not that television journalists, opposed to the war, imposed their biases on viewers. Rather, it is that television never presented the American viewing public with a coherent picture of men at war in Vietnam. It never placed the events of war in an intelligible context so that viewers could make sense of the war that they watched on television. Why was the South Vietnamese government so unpopular, inept, and corrupt? Why didn't the ARVN forces fight effectively? Why were NLF troops, with support from PAVN forces, able to control so much territory and so many people in the South? Why did American military strategies and tactics fail to defeat the PAVN and NLF forces? Why did television reporters and anchors tell us that we were winning in 1965–1967 and that we weren't winning after 1968?

One could watch every television newscast of the war and not be able to answer any of these important questions. Like the characters in Plato's cave, television news watchers saw only shadows and became prisoners of preconceived mental pictures that television lost the war when in fact it only carried the message that we lost the war. So television got blamed for causing heartbreak in Vietnam and a massive loss of faith in our government, our military, and ourselves. Symbolically, the believers in the myth that television lost the war are shooting the medium that brought us the bad news that it could never explain.

NOTES

1. Robert Elegant, "How to Lose A War: Reflections of a Foreign Correspondent," *Encounter* (August 1981), pp. 73–74.
2. William Westmoreland, *A Soldier Reports* (New York: Doubleday, 1976), pp. 556–558.
3. Quoted in the *New York Times* sometime in 1987. (He said it in 1984.)
4. Keyes Beech, "How to Lose A War: A Response from an 'Old Asia Hand,'" in Harrison E. Salisbury (ed.), *Vietnam Reconsidered* (New York: Harper & Row, 1984), p. 152.
5. James Reston, "End of the Tunnel," *New York Times* (April 30, 1975), p. 33.
6. Douglas Kinnard, *The War Managers* (Hanover, N.H.: University Press of New England, 1977), p. 89; Anthony A. Adams, "A Study of Veteran Viewpoints on TV Coverage of the Vietnam War," *Journalism Quarterly*, 54 (Summer 1977), pp. 251–252. Adams found that over 80 percent of the veterans he interviewed thought negative TV news coverage of events undermined public support for the war.

7. Peter Arnett, "Tet Coverage: A Debate Renewed," *Columbia Journalism Review*, 16:5 (Jan./Feb. 1978), pp. 44–48.
8. Morley Safer, "How to Lose a War—A Response from a Broadcaster," in Salisbury (ed.), *Vietnam Reconsidered*, pp. 158–163.
9. Charles Mohr, "Once Again—Did the Press Lose Vietnam?," *Columbia Journalism Review*, 22:4 (Nov./Dec. 1983), pp. 53–56.
10. Michael Arlen, *Living Room War* (New York: Viking, 1969), pp. 6–9.
11. Quoted in Clarence R. Wyatt, "At the Cannon's Mouth," *Journalism History*, 13:3–4 (Autumn-Winter 1986), p. 105. Wyatt has examined the Vietnam war coverage of the *New York Times* and five regional newspapers. He finds all were dependent on official sources for most of their news stories and that the government managed to control the flow of news for the duration of the war.
12. Lichty and Bailey have written several articles together and individually that have described television coverage of the Vietnam war and have challenged the belief that television coverage had much to do with turning public opinion against the war. Articles include George A. Bailey, "Television War: Trends in Network Coverage of Vietnam 1965–1970," *Journal of Broadcasting*, 20:2 (Spring 1976), pp. 147–157; George A. Bailey, "Interpretive Reporting of the Vietnam War by Network Anchormen, 1965–1970," *Journalism Quarterly*, 53 (Summer 1976), pp. 319–324; Lawrence W. Lichty and George A. Bailey, "Violence in Television News: A Case Study of Audience Response," *The Central States Speech Journal*, 23:4 (Winter 1972), pp. 225–

229; Lawrence Lichty, "Video Versus Print," *The Wilson Quarterly,* 6:5 (1982 Special Issue), pp. 49–56; Lawrence W. Lichty, "The War We Watched on Television," *American Film Institute Report,* 4:4 (Winter 1973), pp. 30–37; and Larry Lichty, "The Night at the End of the Tunnel," *Film Comment,* 11 (July-August 1975), pp. 32–35.

13. Oscar Patterson III, "An Analysis of Television Coverage of the Vietnam War," *Journal of Broadcasting,* 28:4 (Fall 1984), pp. 397–404.

14. John Mueller, "Trends in Popular Support for the Wars in Korea and Vietnam," *American Political Science Review,* 65 (June 1971); also John Mueller, *War, Presidents, and Public Opinion,* (New York: John Wiley, 1973), pp. 23–65.

15. Michael Mandelbaum, "Vietnam: The Television War," *Daedalus,* 111:4 (Fall 1982), pp. 157–169.

16. Daniel C. Hallin, "The Media, the War in Vietnam, and Political Support: A Critique of the Thesis of an Oppositional Media," *Journal of Politics,* 46 (February 1984), pp. 2–23; Hallin, "Myth of the Adversary Press," *The Quill* (November 1983), pp. 31–36; and Hallin, *The Uncensored War: The Media and Vietnam* (New York: Oxford University Press, 1986).

17. George Herring, *America's Longest War: The United States and Vietnam, 1950–1975,* 2nd ed. (New York: Knopf, 1986), p. 203.

18. Stanley Karnow, *Vietnam: A History* (New York: Viking, 1983), p. 488.

19. William M. Hammond, "The Press in Vietnam As Agent of Defeat: A Critical Examination," *Reviews in American History,* 17:2 (June 1989), pp. 312–323.

II

20. Michael Schudson, *Discovering the News* (New York: Basic Books, 1978), p. 181.

21. Godfrey Hodgson, *America in Our Time: From World War II to Nixon, What Happened and Why* (New York, Vintage Books, 1976), pp. 142–146.

22. ABC kept its 15-minute format until 1967.

23. Lichty, "Video Versus Print," p. 53. The Harris and Roper polls are cited in Hallin, *Uncensored War,* pp. 106–107.

24. The Robinson study is cited in Evans Witt, "Here, There, and Everywhere: Where Americans Get Their News," *Public Opinion Quarterly,* 6 (August/September 1983), pp. 46–47. See also Lichty, "Video Versus Print," pp. 49–55, who also uses the Simmons data to argue that during the Vietnam era, regardless of what pollsters found, most people got most of their news from newspapers and newsmagazines. Witt observes that it is impossible to determine precisely the sources from which people get their news in a multimedia society like ours. People get their news from many, often overlapping, sources. People read newspapers, newsmagazines, watch television news, and talk to people who tell them news.

25. Ibid.

26. Ibid., p. 52; Patterson, "An Analysis of Television Coverage," pp. 401–403.

27. Hallin, *Uncensored War,* p. 107.

28. Ibid., pp. 172–175.

29. Edward Jay Epstein, *News from Nowhere: Television and the News* (New York: Vintage, 1973), p. 201.

30. Ibid., pp. 201–202.

31. Ibid., pp. 205–232; Epstein's survey of television producers and editors is cited in Phillip Knightley, *The First Casualty* (New York: Harcourt, 1975), p. 412.

32. Ibid., pp. 215–217.

33. Hodgson, *America in Our Time,* Chap 4., "The Ideology of Liberal Consensus," pp. 67–98. J.F.

MacDonald, *Television and the Red Menace: The Video Road to Vietnam* (New York: Praeger, 1985) argues that television reinforced the anticommunist consensus ideology through a variety of programming—news, entertainment, and public affairs. He shows that the theme of "good" Americans vs. the "evil" Communists contributed to our going to war in Vietnam.

III

34. The data and many of the ideas expressed in this segment of my essay are taken from Mueller, *War, Presidents, and Public Opinion*, pp. 23–167; and Mueller, "Trends in Popular Support for the Wars in Korea and Vietnam," pp. 358–375.

35. There was limited television coverage of the Korean war. But television technology was primitive, cameras were not portable, and military censorship was enforced. Most households did not have television sets in 1950, and for those that did, there was very little television news to watch. For all practical purposes, it was an untelevised war.

36. Mueller, *War, Presidents, and Public Opinion*, pp. 33–38.

37. Ibid., pp. 38–39.

38. Ibid.

39. Ibid., pp. 40–41.

40. Ibid., p. 51.

41. Mueller, "Trends in Popular Support for the Wars in Korea and Vietnam," pp. 360–361.

42. The data for Vietnam are: mid-1965—65% support; mid-1966—53% support; mid-1967—47% support; mid-1968—40% support; mid-1969—33% support. These data show that the Vietnam war was more popular than the Korean war for three years.

43. Mueller, *War, Presidents, and Public Opinion*, p. 106.

44. Mueller, "Trends in Popular Support for the Wars in Korea and Vietnam," p. 363.

45. Ibid., p. 371.

46. Burton I. Kaufman, *The Korean War: Challenges in Crisis, Credibility, and Command* (New York: Knopf, 1986), p. 294.

47. *Time*, 60 (November 10, 1952), p. 19.

48. Kaufman, *The Korean War*, pp. 294–295.

49. Mueller, *War, Presidents, and Public Opinion*, pp. 108–109. Alonzo Hamby, "Public Opinion: Korea and Vietnam," *The Wilson Quarterly*, 2:3 (Summer 1978), pp. 137–142 confirmed Mueller's finding that, contrary to public impressions, the Korean war was at least as unpopular as the Vietnam war.

IV

50. See Patterson, "An Analysis of Television Coverage of the Vietnam War," pp. 397–404; Hallin, "The Media, the War in Vietnam, and Political Support," pp. 2–23; Daniel Hallin, *The Mass Media and the Crisis in American Politics*, Ph.D. dissertation, University of California, Berkeley, 1983; Hallin, *Uncensored War*; Bailey, "Television War: Trends in Network Coverage of Vietnam, 1965–1970," pp. 147–157, and Bailey, "Interpretive Reporting of the Vietnam War by Network Anchormen," pp. 319–324.

51. Peter Braestrup dedicated his study of the press coverage of Tet to the many journalists who were killed or missing in Vietnam.

52. Bailey, "Television War," pp. 153–155.

53. Hallin, *Uncensored War*, pp. 129–130; Patterson, "An Analysis of Television Coverage of the Vietnam War," pp. 400–403.

54. Patterson, "An Analysis of Television Coverage of the Vietnam War," pp. 401–402.

55. Hallin, *Uncensored War*, makes this point that television could not convey the intensity of combat; pp. 130–131.

56. There is an excellent Vietnam literature of accounts, memoirs, diaries, journals, and anthologies of interviews written by journalists who covered the war and the soldiers who fought it. Unlike television, they convey the experience of combat with powerful realism. See Michael Herr, *Dispatches* (New York: Avon Books, 1978); Philip Caputo, *A Rumor of War* (New York: Ballantine, 1977); and Mark Baker (ed.), *Nam* (New York: Berkeley Books, 1981).

57. Hallin, *Uncensored War*, p. 131.

58. Michael Arlen, "Television's War," in *Living Room War*, pp. 80–85; Adams, "A Study of Veteran Viewpoints on TV Coverage of the Vietnam War," pp. 249–250. Adams found that most combat veterans he interviewed said that television news did a poor job of providing the public with an accurate view of the war. They said that journalists often arrived after the fight was over, staged news stories, and provided incomplete coverage.

59. Hallin, *Uncensored War*, pp. 130–131.

60. Ibid., p. 107.

61. Ibid., p. 110.

62. Arlen, "The Bombs Below Go Pop-Pop-Pop," in *Living Room War*, pp. 45–50.

63. Hallin, *Uncensored War*, pp. 155–158.

64. Ibid.

65. *Newsweek*, LXX:2 (July 10, 1967), pp. 20–24.

66. Polls cited in Mueller, *War, Presidents, and Public Opinion*, pp. 41–66.

67. Lichty, "The War We Watched on Television," pp. 33–34; Joanmarie Kalter, "Exposing Media Myths: TV Doesn't Affect You as Much as You Think," *TV Guide*, 35:22 (May 30, 1987), pp. 3–4.

68. W. Russell Neuman, "Patterns of Recall Among Television News Viewers," *Public Opinion Quarterly*, 40:1 (Spring 1976), pp. 115–123.

69. Ibid., p. 116.

70. Dr. Frederick Wertham, "Is TV Hardening Us to the War in Vietnam?" *New York Times* (December 4, 1966); the *Newsweek* survey is cited in Knightley, *The First Casualty*, pp. 411–412.

V

71. Quoted in Herring, *America's Longest War*, p. 183.

72. Kathleen Turner, *Lyndon Johnson's Dual War: Vietnam and the Press* (Chicago: University of Chicago Press, 1985), pp. 182, 204–207, 216–217.

73. My principal sources for the Tet campaign are Don Oberdorfer, *Tet!* (New York: Doubleday, 1971) and Dave Richard Palmer, *Summons of the Trumpet: A History of the Vietnam War from a Military Man's Viewpoint* (New York: Ballantine, 1978), pp. 207–267.

74. Hallin, *Uncensored War*, pp. 161–163.

75. Ibid., pp. 188–189.

76. Hallin, *Uncensored War*, pp. 172–173.

77. George A. Bailey and Lawrence Lichty, "Rough Justice on a Saigon Street: A Gatekeeper Study of NBC's Tet Execution Film," *Journalism Quarterly*, 49 (Summer 1972), pp. 226–227, 238. There is also a famous still photograph which captures the moment General Loan squeezed the trigger and killed the VC. It was taken by AP photographer Eddie Adams, who won a Pulitzer Prize for it.

78. Lawrence W. Lichty and George A. Bailey, "Violence in Television News: A Case Study of Audience Response," *The Central States Speech Journal*, XXIII:4 (Winter 1972), pp. 225–229,

offer a detailed analysis of the audience response to the showing of the NBC film report of the murder.

79. See Peter Braestrup, *Big Story: How the American Press and Television Reported and Interpreted the Crisis of Tet 1968 in Vietnam and Washington*, 2 vols. (Boulder, Col.: Westview Press, 1977). A one-volume abridged edition was issued by Yale University Press, 1983. Braestrup has also addressed the matter of press coverage of Tet and the Vietnam war in other writings, including Braestrup, "Covering the Vietnam War," *Nieman Reports* 23 (December, 1969), pp. 8–13, and "The Press Corps in Vietnam," *Freedom at Issue*, 41 (1977), pp. 9–11.

80. From Braestrup's two-volume study. Several leading journalists who covered the Vietnam war have challenged both Braestrup's facts and his conclusions, including Peter Arnett and Charles Mohr. Mohr, a *New York Times* reporter who spent a total of four years in Vietnam, writes in *Columbia Journalism Review*, 22 (Nov./Dec. 1983), pp. 51–56, that most American journalists covering the war from Vietnam never thought that the Communists could win a military victory and never reported that they were.

81. See Peter Braestrup, "The Tet Offensive—Another Press Controversy: II," in Harrison Salisbury (ed.), *Vietnam Reconsidered* (New York: Harper & Row, 1984), pp. 167–168.

82. Ibid., p. 170.

83. Ibid., p. 171.

84. Peter Braestrup, "The Press and The Vietnam War," *Encounter* (April 1983), p. 92.

85. Quoted in Oberdorfer, *Tet!*, pp. 250–251.

86. See notes 50, 51. Mueller, *War, Presidents, and Public Opinion*, cites public-opinion poll, p. 90.

87. Ibid. Mueller cites a poll taken in late January 1968, on the eve of Tet, showing 56 percent of the population called themselves hawks; another poll cited, which was taken in early February while the Tet campaigns were raging, showed 61 percent of the population called themselves hawks and favored expanding the U.S. war effort, an increase of 5 percent, p. 107.

88. Ibid.

89. Ibid. The sharp rise in dovish sentiment following the March 31 speech may also reflect the fact that Johnson's abandonment of his policy of gradual escalation meant that doves could now support him.

90. See note 48.

91. Philip E. Converse and Howard Schuman, "'Silent Majorities' and the Vietnam War," *Scientific American*, 222:6 (June 1970), p. 22.

92. Ibid.

93. The unknown McCarthy got almost as many votes as the president. But it turned out that 60 percent of McCarthy's support was hawkish and later voted for George Wallace. There are two reasons for the hawk vote for a peace candidate: McCarthy was the only vehicle available for citizens who wanted to send Lyndon Johnson a message that they were unhappy with his war policy and ideological differences did not matter. Secondly, apparently a lot of New Hampshire voters misunderstood McCarthy's candidacy and mistakenly believed him to be a hawk.

94. Converse and Schuman, "'Silent Majorities' and the Vietnam War." The authors studied in depth a decade of polling on the Vietnam war. From a 1968 poll, they concluded that at the time of Tet, a majority of Americans had come to regard U.S. entry into the war to have been a mistake, but at the same time those calling for escalation, even if that meant invading North Vietnam, outnumbered doves by a 3 to 2 margin.

95. William L. Lunch and Peter W. Sperlich, "American Public Opinion and the Vietnam War," *Western Political Quarterly*, 32 (March 1979), pp. 25–28.

96. The "Wise Men," besides Acheson, included George Ball, McGeorge Bundy, Douglas Dillon, Cyrus Vance, Arthur Dean, John J. McCloy, General Omar Bradley, General Matthew Ridgway,

General Maxwell Taylor, Robert Murphy, Henry Cabot Lodge, Jr., Abe Fortas, and Arthur Goldberg.

97. Herbert Y. Schandler, *The Unmaking of a President: Lyndon Johnson and Vietnam* (Princeton, N.J.: Princeton University Press, 1977).

98. Clark Clifford, "A Vietnam Appraisal: The Personal History of One Man's View and How It Evolved," *Foreign Affairs* 47 (July 1969), pp. 601–622. The best account of Johnson's painful decision is in Schandler, *Unmaking of A President*, pp. 266–289; also see Herring, *America's Longest War*, p. 184.

99. Schandler, *Unmaking of a President*, pp. 300–302.

100. Herring, *America's Longest War*, 207–209.

101. Harry G. Summers, Jr., *On Strategy: A Critical Analysis of the Vietnam War* (New York: Dell, 1982).

102. I have used several sources to analyze Tet from the PAVN perspective. The two best English-language sources are William S. Turley, *The Second Indochina War: A Short Political and Military History, 1954–1975* (New York: New American Library, 1986) and William J. Duiker, *The Communist Road to Power* (Boulder, Col.: Westview Press, 1981). Duiker discusses Giap's grand strategy of attrition to interpret his Tet strategy and tactics within that frame on pp. 235–271.

103. Duiker, *Communist Road to Power*, pp. 263–269.

104. Ibid.

105. Ibid. See also Turley, *Second Indochina War*, pp. 114–117.

106. Duiker, *Communist Road to Power*, pp. 269–270.

107. Palmer, *Summons of the Trumpet*, pp. 265–267.

VI

108. Hallin, *Uncensored War*, p. 180.

109. Karnow, *Vietnam: A History*, p. 582.

110. Ibid.

111. During the early 1960s, young radicals began calling themselves "the movement." They were civil rights and peace activists working to bring about radical political, economic, and cultural change in this country. SDS borrowed the term "New Left" from young British radicals of the late-1950s. Its members adopted the name in order to differentiate their new breed of leftist politics from the Old Left, that is, Stalinists, Social Democrats, and their sectarian progeny. In the early 1960s, the New Left shared an allegiance to participatory democracy and a generally socialist concept of political economy.

112. Several studies of the various antiwar movements exist. The best include Thomas Powers, *Vietnam: The War at Home* (Boston: G.K. Hall, 1984), which covers the 1964–1968 period; Nancy Zaroulis and Gerald Sullivan, *Who Spoke Up? American Protest Against the War in Vietnam, 1963–1975* (Garden City, N.Y.: Doubleday, 1984) is comprehensive in scope; and Charles Debenedetti, *An American Ordeal: The Antiwar Movement of the Vietnam Era* (Syracuse, N.Y.: Syracuse University Press, 1990).

113. Todd Gitlin, *The Whole World Is Watching: Mass Media in the Making and Unmaking of the New Left* (Berkeley, University of California Press, 1980), p. 28.

114. Ibid., pp. 29–30.

115. Hallin, *Uncensored War*, p. 193.

116. Ibid., pp. 193–194.

117. Gitlin, *Whole World*, pp. 119–122.

118. Hallin, *Uncensored War*, p. 194.

119. Michael Mandelbaum, "Vietnam: The Television War," p. 165.

120. Howard Schuman, "Two Sources of Antiwar Sentiment in America," *American Journal of Sociology*, 78:3 (November 1972), pp. 519–535. The most frequent reasons pragmatic opponents of the war gave for their opposition were: The United States was not winning; American soldiers were being killed; U.S. resources were being wasted; and the war was a Vietnamese responsibility. Few raised any moral considerations about any aspect of the war or showed any concern about what the war might be doing to Vietnam and its people.

121. Ibid., p. 519. Schuman, developing in-depth analyses of public-opinion surveys, has located the two sources of antiwar sentiment among the general public and college campuses that I have labeled the "vocals" and the "pragmatics." Schuman, aware of their disjunction, writes, ". . . extreme dislike of war protesters was shown by many people who on other questionnaires indicated their opposition to the war" (p. 519).

122. Ibid., pp. 520–523, 528–532.

123. Philip E. Converse and Howard Schuman, " 'Silent Majorities' and the Vietnam War," *Scientific American*, 222:6 (June 1970), p. 24. The authors characterize the two antiwar cultures in these terms: "One current is made up of a tiny fraction of the population, but one that is highly educated, articulate, and visible. The other group tends to be less educated than the national average, and is much less politically visible, although it is far larger than the set of vocal critics—perhaps by a factor of 10 or more."

124. Schuman, "Two Sources of Antiwar Sentiment in America," p. 535.

125. Gitlin, *Whole World*, p. 216.

126. William L. O'Neill, *Coming Apart: An Informal History of America in the 1960s* (New York: Quadrangle/The New York Times Book Co., 1971), pp. 362–372.

127. *New York Times* (August 21, 1968), pp. 1, 32.

128. *New York Times*, (August 26, 1968), pp. 1, 25.

129. Gitlin, *Whole World*, p. 189, says that one demonstrator in six was an undercover agent. According to CBS television, at least 200 of those involved in the melee on Michigan Avenue were undercover agents. Jerry Rubin's bodyguard, dressed as a long-haired biker, was a Chicago policeman. Some of the most violence-prone demonstrators were evidently agents provocateurs.

130. Gitlin, *Whole World*, pp. 186–187.

131. *New York Times* (August 29, 1968), pp. 1, 23.

132. Ibid.

133. Ibid.

134. Ibid.

135. Hodgson, *America in Our Time*, p. 372.

136. Hodgson, *America in Our Time*, p. 373, and Michael J. Robinson, "Television and American Politics, 1956–1976," *The Public Interest*, 48 (Summer 1977), pp. 26–29, note that viewers blamed the rioters, not the police, and condemned the newscasters for biased coverage.

137. Epstein, *News from Nowhere*, pp. 16–18.

138. O'Neill, *Coming Apart*, p. 405.

139. Quoted in Herring, *America's Longest War*, p. 229.

140. Hallin, *Uncensored War*, p. 201; C. Richard Hofstetter and David W. Moore, "Watching T.V. News and Supporting the Military: A Surprising Impact of the News Media," *Armed Forces and Society*, 5:2 (1979), pp. 261–269. Hofstetter and Moore interviewed a standard opinion sample during the 1972 presidential campaign, at a time when television news coverage of the Vietnam war was mostly negative. But they found that people who regularly watched television news had a higher opinion of the military and favored maintaining a strong military than did people who did not watch television news regularly.

141. Ibid.

THE VIETNAMIZATION OF NICARAGUA

by Kevin O'Keefe

Kevin O'Keefe has written a timely analysis of the way government officials, their opponents, the media, and the general public have used (and misused) history when debating Central American foreign-policy issues, particularly Nicaragua, during the 1980s. Recent foreign-policy debates in this country have often been dominated—indeed, haunted by—the spectre of the disastrous American Indochina intervention. The language of contemporary U.S. foreign-policy discourse is replete with rhetorical phrases and analogies drawn from the Vietnam debacle. In deriving their arguments, both defenders and opponents of American intervention in Nicaragua during the Reagan years felt compelled to draw upon what they regarded as the lessons learned from Vietnam. Richard Nixon has termed this power of the memory and rhetoric of the Vietnam war to shape the debate over U.S. policy in Nicaragua the "Vietnam syndrome": the belief that the Vietnam debacle demonstrated the folly of American military intervention in any Third World country, an intervention that could only lead to another disastrous "Vietnam quagmire."

In their efforts to counteract what they regarded as its debilitating effects on the conduct of American foreign policy, a number of neo-conservative analyists have labored to eradicate the Vietnam syndrome. They have argued that Vietnam was a noble cause, an anti-Communist crusade that the United States could have and should have won. We only failed because we defeated ourselves. A loss of will was responsible for the American withdrawal from Vietnam and the subsequent fall of Saigon to the Communists. America must be prepared to undertake future interventions to protect its interests, and if we are resolute we can prevail.

President Ronald Reagan, a believer in the noble-cause thesis, made the restoration of American primacy in world affairs his number-one foreign policy goal. He was especially concerned about Central America, The United States's backyard.

The Marxist Sandinista regime in Managua quickly became a Reagan target. The president was determined to expunge both the Sandinistas and the Vietnam syndrome. With vivid memories of Vietnam dominating their thinking, Reagan officials evolved a policy based on low-intensity warfare (LIW), using proxies recruited from the ranks of expatriate Nicaraguans living in neighboring Honduras. These forces, called "Contras," would be the American surrogate in Nicaragua, a counterrevolutionary force that would depose the dreaded Sandinistas, win the "hearts and minds" of the people, and revitalize American foreign policy by ridding it of the Vietnam syndrome. LIW would avoid Vietnam-era "mistakes."

Washington's rationale for its intervention drew upon vintage Cold War ideology. Reagan applied the domino theory to Nicaragua. The Sandinistas were Communist agents, conduits through which flowed Cuban and Soviet domination. Nicaragua was a test of American will, of American credibility. If we cannot remove the Marxist menace from Nicaragua, it will engulf the countries of Central America, Mexico, and eventually the United States. Ronald Reagan called America "the last domino."

Reagan's opponents in the media, among the public, and in Congress responded by invoking the Vietnam analogy. They charged that once again, America, motivated by an obsessive anti-Communism, was trying to overthrow a revolutionary nationalist movement by military means. They expressed fears that the United States would inevitably become trapped in another Vietnam-like quagmire that the American public would never support.

Kevin O'Keefe's perceptive analysis shows how both sides in the Nicaragua debate were dominated by the ghost of Vietnam past and addicted to the use of simplistic, misleading, and false historical analogies. Both sides were guilty of careless and faulty historical reasoning, of superficiality and selective uses of the past. Both drew lessons from the Vietnam experience that best served their polemical purposes. They trafficked in faulty parallels and misplaced analogies. In their hands, the past was more often abused than used.

O'Keefe's study raises some challenging issues. What can Americans, particularly American officials with policy-making responsibilities, and their critics, learn from history? Specifically, what can they learn from the Vietnam experience? Apparently nothing, unless they study it objectively and systematically. Nothing unless they resist the temptation to use the past as a political and ideological resource to bolster or undermine current foreign-policy initiatives. O'Keefe believes that it is possible to learn from the past. He finds that the real lesson from Vietnam is not that it was a noble cause or a quagmire: The American disaster in Vietnam resulted from ignorance about the people there, not only those whom we were fighting but also those whom we tried so hard and so long to help.

I

At the very beginning of the Reagan administration, an ABC *World News Tonight* broadcast, focusing on the new president's efforts "to head off criticism that in

Central America he is headed down the same road which led to U.S. military involvement in Vietnam," aired on national television. The program included Senate Majority Leader Howard Baker, whose opinion was that the United States was not headed into another "quagmire."[1] This 1981 broadcast also cited a new "domino theory," one in which Cuba and Nicaragua would subvert El Salvador and then overrun Honduras and Guatemala. Eight years after this program, the *Boston Globe,* in the aftermath of a Central American summit meeting in Honduras, called upon President George Bush to "give peace a chance.... Why not choose the path Senator George Aiken suggested during the Vietnam War: declare victory and call it quits."[2]

During the intervening years public discussion of Central America and Nicaragua was continuously affected by the memory of Vietnam. Administration officials often seemed haunted by the earlier conflict. As the United States became more deeply involved in Nicaragua, public discourse resonated with references to "escalation," "dominoes," "enclaves," "credibility gaps," "hearts and minds," "hawks" and "doves." Later, as American involvement diminished, commentators added to the Vietnam comparisons by asking, "Is peace at hand?" and by describing fleeing refugees as "feet people." Throughout the decade, the Nicaraguan issue was inextricably linked to Vietnam as Americans voiced their concerns about the possibility of America being drawn into "another Vietnam."

The Vietnam experience which, in 1975 Secretary of State Henry Kissinger hoped would be "put behind us," affected the Nicaraguan controversy in several ways. First, Vietnam was crucial to the consensus reached by American policymakers after the Sandinista victory in Nicaragua. Second, the Vietnam experience was an important component of the Reagan administration's technique for subverting the revolutionary government in Managua. Third, the memory of Vietnam played a key role in the administration's public-relations campaign to sell its Nicaraguan policy to the American people. Finally, Vietnam was raised, most often in the form of the "Vietnam analogy," by those in opposition to the administration's policy.

II

The revolution that brought the Sandinistas to power in Nicaragua coincided with the years following the fall of Saigon. The Vietnam debacle persuaded many Americans that United States' interventions in Third World countries were often misguided. Critics became increasingly skeptical of official explanations for such foreign adventures. They refused to accept automatic assurances that our objectives abroad were noble and wise. By 1979 a large segment of the American public stood alert to oppose any policy that smacked of "another Vietnam." Such opposition to American interventionism was dubbed the "Vietnam syndrome."

At the same time, however, a significant body of conservative opinion held that the Vietnam War could have been won. "Ours was ... a noble cause," said one prominent politician, "but we defeated ourselves." Many Americans contended that domestic dissent, restricted military force, and, most importantly, a loss of will were responsible for America's defeat in Vietnam and the subsequent decline of American prestige. A number of national events in the late 1970s reflected this loss of American power and prestige. The OPEC boycott, the Panama Canal treaties, the Iranian hostage crisis, and the Soviet invasion of Afghanistan convinced many Americans that the United States appeared weak and in retreat before the rest of the world. America seemed to be losing sight of its historic destiny. By 1980 public-opinion analysts concluded that Americans considered themselves "bullied by OPEC, humiliated by the Ayatollah Khomeini, tricked by Castro, out-traded by Japan, and out-gunned by the Russians.... Fearing that America was losing control over its foreign affairs, voters were more than ready to exorcise the ghost of Vietnam and replace it with a new posture of American assertiveness."[3]

The candidacy of Ronald Reagan seemed to offer some promise in restoring the international preeminence enjoyed by the United States before its defeat in Vietnam. Reagan pledged to "make America great again" by supporting an activist, if not aggressive, foreign policy. A confident and strong leadership would replace the weakness and indecision of President Jimmy Carter. A massive military buildup would demonstrate our strength. We would "stand tall" once again. The post-Vietnam period of "self-doubt" would be ended.

For Reagan, the commitment to reassert American power abroad had a special urgency in relation to America's "backyard." In Nicaragua the FSLN, or Sandinistas, had seized power from the American-supported dictatorship of Anastasio Somoza. At first the Sandinistas enjoyed broad support, improving the health and education of Nicaraguans, but they soon lost the backing of moderate groups that had welcomed the revolution. Although most of the economy was left in private hands, the new government nationalized the banks, foreign trade, and some land (primarily holdings of the Somoza family). The Sandinistas received economic assistance from Western Europe, Canada, and Japan. Military as well as economic aid also found its way to the Sandinistas by way of Cuba, the Soviet Union, and Eastern Europe. Central America became the primary concern in 1980 of the Committee of Santa Fe, Reagan's policy team for the region. In its report, "A New Inter-American Policy for the Eighties," the committee spoke in stark terms: "Containment is not enough.... Survival demands a new U.S. foreign policy ... a counterprojection of American power."[4] Privately, administration members were more specific and candid about policy goals. Later, Edgar Chamorro, a former director of the FDN, or Contras, recalled that he was promised supplies and other assistance soon after the 1980 election. According to Chamorro, the explicit goal was to remove the revolutionary Sandinista government.[5]

By the time the new administration came to power in 1981, there was a policy consensus among Reagan's principal advisers on the primary goal of U.S. policy in Central America—to eliminate Sandinista domination of Nicaragua. For some this policy would help expunge the "Vietnam syndrome." For others it would give the United States a chance to "win one for a change," to avenge the defeat in 1975. In either case, Vietnam was central in the formulation of policy.

III

If such a consensus was reached about the desirability of subverting the Sandinistas, there was no immediate agreement on which techniques to employ in order to achieve this end. A heated debate erupted within the administration over the most effective means of countering the revolution in Nicaragua. Understandably, this debate was haunted by the specter of Vietnam as many of the crucial advisers had been personally involved as military or civilian leaders during the earlier conflict.

Reagan's first Secretary of State was Alexander Haig, an army officer who participated in formulation and execution of the Cambodian intervention. Likewise involved in Vietnam and Cambodia was Thomas O. Enders, the new Assistant Secretary for Inter-American Affairs. Another Vietnam hawk, John Negroponte, became ambassador to Honduras, a country that would become the base for the subsequent military operations of the Contras. Enders selected L. Craig Johnstone as his chief adviser on Central America. Johnstone, who worked on rural pacification from 1966 to 1970, was another Vietnam hawk, as was Raymond Burghardt, principal political adviser to Negroponte in Tegucigalpa, the capital of Honduras. A newspaper described the overlap of personnel from the Vietnam war to the Nicaraguan conflict with the following headline: "The Gang That Blew Vietnam Goes Latin."[6]

At the beginning of the Reagan administration, Alexander Haig called for "a determined show of American will and power" in Central America. For the new Secretary of State there were lessons to be learned from the defeat in Vietnam. "To start slow, to show hesitation," he warned the National Security Council, "was to Vietnamize the situation." Haig opposed what he called the "incrementalism" that characterized the early stages of the Vietnam war: "If it is easier to escalate step by small step, it is easier for an adversary to respond to each step with a response that is strong enough to compel yet another escalation on our part. That is the lesson of Vietnam."[7]

A State Department adviser, Robert McFarlane, was assigned by Haig to eventually prepare a report that proposed the use of force against Cuba and the establishment of a naval blockade against Cuba and Nicaragua. There was, however, strong opposition to this within the Reagan administration, especially from Vice-President George Bush and Defense Secretary Caspar Weinberger. In his memoirs, Haig noted the concern of these skeptics that such an exercise of military force would be politically dangerous: it might be considered "another Vietnam."[8]

As Alexander Haig's influence declined, the administration increasingly turned to another method, a more sophisticated and subtle one. This new technique drew upon the Vietnam experience, in particular the frustration of many military analysts following the "defeat" of American forces. This frustration was starkly conveyed in a widely quoted conversation between American Colonel Harry G. Summers and Colonel Tu of the North Vietnamese Army:

"You know you never defeated us on the battle field," said the American colonel. The North Vietnamese pondered this remark a moment. "That may be so," he replied, "but it is also irrelevant."[9]

The United States, many critics contended, had experienced a tactical victory but a strategic defeat in Vietnam. As a consequence, the nation would have to devise a winning strategy for waging counterrevolution in the Third World. Such a strategy would have to recognize the "lessons" of Vietnam, and to take into account the errors and miscalculations that led to failure there. Important among these mistakes was the strategy of attrition. Americans approached Vietnam as a conventional war and relied heavily on technology, fire power, and mobility. General William Westmoreland's "big unit war" failed to deal effectively with the revolutionary situation in Vietnam. Massive military force not only alienated the Vietnamese people, but exhausted the patience of the American electorate. Another error in Vietnam was the apparent American failure to achieve coordination and cooperation between U.S. civilian and military authorities. The American military leadership clung to traditional doctrine, especially the belief that military issues should be separate from political ones. A final mistake involved the South Vietnamese political situation. The United States never succeeded in presenting a legitimate political alternative to the revolutionary forces. The absence of a stable and popular government in South Vietnam gravely injured the American war effort. Despite attempts at "nation building," a viable political community in South Vietnam proved to be an illusion.

These lessons formed the basis of a new strategy for U.S. military involvement in the Third World. At the heart of this strategy, known as low-intensity warfare (LIW), was a different approach to national liberation movements, now considered as political rather than military undertakings. According to proponents, the ultimate aim of engagement must be the political defeat of the enemy. One such advocate of low-intensity warfare has described it as both revolutionary and counterrevolutionary: "It is total war at the grassroots level—one that uses all the weapons of total war, including political, economic and psychological warfare, with the military aspect being a distant fourth in many cases."[10]

Proponents of low-intensity warfare contended that the battlefield should not be viewed in terms of territory: "The only territory you want to hold is the six inches between the ears of the peasants."[11] Low-intensity conflict would embrace various forms of coercion and violence, including riots and strikes, economic pressure, the threat of war, the use of surrogate forces, and "where necessary, kidnapings and assassination of enemy elites." Victory would involve delegitimizing national liberation movements and transferring power to a counter-revolution.[12]

Low-intensity warfare became the preferred military instrument for achieving the Reagan administration's goals in Central America. A group of Nicaraguans were supported, supplied, and trained by the United States. Called Contras, they were expected to bring overwhelming pressure on Nicaraguan political, economic, and military institutions. They were to become a viable political alternative after the Sandinista regime was isolated and discredited. The employ-

ment of these native troops by the United States, combined with a careful program of covert and overt activities, would build grass-roots support for the counterrevolution and subvert the regime in Managua. According to its hopeful
advocates, LIW would ultimately lead to victory in Managua just as it could have
led to victory in Vietnam.

IV

A third area where Vietnam influenced the Nicaraguan controversy was in the
administration's rationale for its policies. During the Vietnam conflict, the American effort had been hindered by domestic opposition. The chorus of dissent had
risen noticeably when an early victory was not achieved. One of the most widely
accepted "lessons" of Vietnam was that the nation should not fight a war without
the assurance of broad popular support.

Low-intensity warfare, involving a "long haul, low cost" strategy, could
help reduce such domestic opposition. According to LIW strategists, there would
be fewer casualties, lower economic costs, and greater evidence of success. The
type of sustained media attention that characterized the Vietnam conflict could
be avoided. Although protracted, low-intensity warfare would provide "light at
the end of the tunnel."

The success of the administration's policy required a persuasive public-
relations campaign. Robert McFarlane, who later became Reagan's National Security Adviser, was convinced that the lesson of Vietnam was not that American
policy was unwise, but that it had not been properly presented to the American
people:

> I spent a couple of years in Vietnam, as did millions of others. Time that was
> wasted, basically. Among the several reasons for failure, I cite foremost the in-
> ability of the American people to define the solution and evoke popular support,
> and then of course to carry it through to a solution. It was this incompetence at
> communications basically which has led today to a climate in which no adminis-
> tration can expect to sustain a policy unless it can evoke popular support for
> it.[13]

To be successful in Nicaragua the administration had to sustain its policies by employing an effective public-relations effort. As part of its public-relations campaign, the administration returned to themes that recalled the rationale
for America's Vietnam involvement. Just as the civil war in Vietnam had been
magnified into a great-power struggle, the Central American situation was described in East-West terms. "We consider the problem in Central America basically to be Nicaragua, as supported by Cuba and The Soviet Union," announced
Secretary of State George Shultz.[14] Other administration officials referred to
"Marxist Nicaragua," "Communist Sandinistas," "Soviet-style election," a "forward base of operation," and a "Marxist enclave." Reagan strategists clearly concluded that the East-West theme would have wider appeal if the ideological com-

ponent were stressed. As the rhetoric rose in intensity, the administration seemed to engage in verbal overkill. Nicaragua was denounced as "a Communist totalitarian state," "a brutal, cruel regime," and "a totalitarian dungeon."

Other themes common to both Vietnam and Central America were incorporated into the public-relations campaign. For example, the administration often emphasized the notion of the credibility of an American commitment. President Reagan's concern about the reliability of the United States as an ally echoed Lyndon Johnson's declaration at the outset of the Vietnam war:

> Around the globe from Berlin to Thailand are people whose well-being rests in part in the belief that they can count on us if they are attacked. To leave Vietnam to its fate would shake the confidence of these people in the value of America's word.[15]

In Reagan's view, Nicaragua put America's determination and credibility to the test just as Vietnam had done two decades earlier. If we would not defend ourselves in Central America, the president stressed in his April 1983 address to Congress, "we cannot expect to prevail elsewhere. Our credibility would collapse, our alliances would crumble, and the safety of our homeland would be put in jeopardy."[16]

As in the earlier conflict, Americans were warned about "falling dominoes." The rationale for Vietnam included the idea that if the United States did not stand up to Communist aggression, one by one all of the countries of Southeast Asia would fall and Americans would end up fighting in California. The Vietnam domino did eventually fall, but other dominoes did not follow. According to the Reagan administration, Central American nations were standing in line ready to fall. Costa Rica, Honduras, Guatemala, and Mexico were countries in the region on what Alexander Haig called the Soviet Union's "hit-list." The president solemnly added: "We are the last domino."[17]

Reagan strategists were careful, however, not to overplay the similarities between Vietnam and Nicaragua. In fact, they often distinguished between the two situations, especially after the administration realized that the "Vietnam syndrome" was not in total remission. The crucial difference for the administration was geography: the remoteness of Vietnam and the proximity of Central America. According to the administration, this closeness gave the United States vital national interests that were not present in Southeast Asia. The references to geographic proximity had the added advantage of addressing the charge so familiar during the Vietnam era that America had once again assumed the role of universal policeman. The United States might intend to exercise a police power in the Caribbean or Central America, contended the administration, but this was very different from the Vietnam era pretense of being "policeman of the world." In presenting these arguments, the administration effectively employed a metaphor from World War II instead of Vietnam: the Caribbean-Central American area was America's "soft underbelly."

Nicaragua's proximity and small size also bolstered the contention of some officials that the armed forces of the United States could easily launch a successful invasion of the area. "We make a lot of cautionary comparisons about Vietnam and they are valid," said General Wallace Nutting, "but there's this big difference: Central America is winnable." Unlike Vietnam, the region is "our Afghanistan," General Nutting noted, "and when push comes to shove, the outcome is not in doubt."[18]

V

For those opposed to the administration's Nicaraguan policy, the memory of Vietnam was also of significant utility. Critics at home and abroad raised the "Vietnam analogy," derived "lessons" from the earlier conflict, and preyed upon fears of "another Vietnam." The Vietnam involvement, critics argued, was based on a foreign policy obsessively committed to opposing revolutionary change in the name of anti-Communism. Although the world had become less monolithic between the onset of the Cold War and the 1960s, American policymakers ignored this pluralism. The United States forced revolutionary movements into the arms of its enemies and supported counterrevolutionary forces, many of which betrayed American values.

Turning from Vietnam to Central America, the opposition noted yet another instance of obsessive anti-Communism that produced a strong antagonism toward national liberation movements. Although the revolutionary movement in Nicaragua was basically the product of local historical circumstances and was strongly nationalist in character, the Reagan administration considered the Sandinistas to be nothing less than agents of Soviet imperialism. Critics maintained that America should learn from the Vietnam experience and deal intelligently with nationalist revolutions.

The Vietnam analogy became an important component in the rhetoric of the Sandinistas themselves. Nicaraguan leaders linked Vietnam and Central America at every opportunity. They predicted another protracted military conflict should an American invasion of Nicaragua take place. Visitors in the waiting room of the Nicaraguan Ministry of Defense, for example, took note of a large poster with the caption in English: "No more Vietnams in Central America."[19]

The Nicaraguan Ambassador to the United States made an effort to intensify American public concern about what he called a regional "Vietnam" in Central America. Carlos Tunnerman seemed to spend more time at public relations than at the traditional art of diplomacy. He and other Sandinista officials spread fear that, in the event of an American invasion, a Vietnam-style war would engulf Nicaragua and, in the words of President Daniel Ortega, would spread "all over" Central America.[20]

Most American critics, while not fully endorsing the party line of the Sandinistas, tended to share their concern about an "escalation" of the Nicaraguan conflict. The *New York Times* declared that "old memories stir uneasily" at the news that the Reagan administration planned to send "advisers" to train the Nicaraguan opposition. The editors at the *Times* recalled the 1961 mission of General Maxwell Taylor to Saigon, after which President John Kennedy significantly increased the number of American advisers in Vietnam. Kennedy's confidential remark to an aide seemed relevant: "It's like taking a drink. The effect wears off, and you have to take another."[21]

While many critics shared some of the administration's premises, especially its concern about Communist influence in Central America, it was Reagan's emphasis on a military solution that provoked strong opposition. Theodore Sorensen, special counsel to President Kennedy during the early stages of the Vietnam involvement, argued that the surest way to "Vietnamize and ultimately Communize" Nicaragua and all of Central America is for the United States to continue applying nothing but "military muscle, especially CIA financing of contra guerrillas."[22] Other critics seemed to implicitly accept the domino idea but urged the president "to energetically try to befriend Nicaragua in an effort to prevent the domino theory from taking place."[23]

The administration's concern about Nicaragua's proximity and its implications for American security was also shared by some opponents: "Precisely because it is ... closer than Vietnam," one editor maintained, "America could quickly snuff out any real security threat." If the Nicaraguan leadership wanted to spread revolution, its prospects were considered to be very limited: "Like Vietnam, Nicaragua may be too heavily armed for its size, but it has had much more reason to fear invasion."[24]

The memory of Vietnam led some dissenters to predict that military intervention in Nicaragua would be followed by domestic turmoil, political unrest, and a loss of popular support. Tom Wicker of the *New York Times* warned that "the public would not long support such a war—which certainly would be a staple of evening television—anymore than it supported the war policy in Vietnam."[25] A few administration opponents began to encourage dissent by staging protest rallies and "teach-ins" on university campuses across the United States. These never approached the scale of anti-Vietnam demonstrations of the 1960s, although some of the organizers were veterans of the earlier antiwar movement. At a teach-in held at Wayne State University in Detroit, a speaker announced, "I feel the ghost of teach-ins past."[26]

The principal forum for the opposition to administration policy was the Congress. During the course of the Nicaraguan controversy, Congress seemed to be, in the words of Leslie Gelb, "wrestling with the ghost of Vietnam."[27] A recurring theme was congressional fear of another blank check for executive warmaking. During the 1986 debate on Contra aid, for example, Senator Patrick Leahy reminded "my fellow Senators and the American people of ... the lessons of the Vietnam war." He elaborated:

> Twenty-two years ago this month, the U.S. Senate approved by a vote of eighty-eight to two, the Gulf of Tonkin Resolution. This resolution put the United States in the middle of the Vietnam war. It was used to justify sending hundreds of thousands of United States troops to Vietnam during the next ten years. Several of the Senators who voted for it will vote this week on the President's request for United States aid to the contras in Nicaragua. They, and those of us who were not Senators then but who saw what was done in the name of Tonkin Gulf will

be asked to send military advisors and trainers into this insurgency.... Most important, we will be asked to vote on giving the contras a commitment that they will have the money and equipment to carry on a bloody war for years to come.... I will not cast that vote and send us down that road.[28]

When the Congress finally assented to Reagan's policy in the summer of 1986, congressional opponents called it "Gulf of Tonkin II." They predicted a repetition of the earlier conflict: "This could be a re-run of Vietnam. First, American money, then American advisors, then American control of the war, then American troops."[29]

VI

The application of the Vietnamese experience to the Nicaraguan controversey— the "Vietnamization" of Nicaragua—was pursued and developed by policymakers, their opponents, the media, and the general public. These groups professed to have "learned" from history and to be guided by the earlier American experience in Vietnam. For the most part, however, history was not a very good guide. Some might conclude with Hegel that "we learn from history that we do not learn from history."

History was used throughout the period but it was not employed very well. In fact, the Vietnam experience was often blatantly misused. First, historical precedents that were cited were, for the most part, selective. Second, historical analysis was superficial and often oversimplified. Third, historical reasoning was careless and faulty.

The problem of selection related to the existence of several "Vietnams" that made up the Vietnam experience. The first Vietnam began with the formation of the National Liberation Front in South Vietnam and the commitment of Hanoi to support the southern Communist insurgency. Americans after 1961 advised and supported a counterinsurgency program while the Central Intelligence Agency coordinated a variety of covert operations to thwart the Communists.

The second Vietnam was the big-unit war that began in 1965. The Americanization of the conflict in that year prevented a South Vietnamese defeat. General William Westmoreland developed the American war of attrition. Massive firepower, superior mobility, and a devastating bombing campaign were supposed to inflict irreplaceable losses of the enemy and force their leaders to the bargaining table.

The third Vietnam followed the Tet offensive and involved the withdrawal of most American forces as the war was turned over to the South Vietnamese. However, American advisers, logistics support, and bombing continued. An attempt was made to pacify the rural countryside and a ruthless campaign against the secret civilian enemy was conducted.

The fourth Vietnam followed the Paris Peace accords, which called for a cease-fire that never materialized. During this period American military aid was reduced and Congress limited the president's power to reenter the war with

American forces. After the North Vietnamese offensive in the spring of 1975, South Vietnam collapsed.

A fifth and final Vietnam may be called the "domestic" Vietnam and is associated principally with the years 1966 to 1972. This period was characterized by "the wound within"—political turmoil, social unrest, and domestic dissent unprecedented since the American Civil War.

When Americans on both sides of the Nicaraguan controversy referred to Vietnam, they selected the Vietnam that was most useful, the one that conveyed the right "lesson." For congressional and media critics, the second Vietnam became the basic point of reference when "another Vietnam" was predicted. The LIW strategists considered the first and third Vietnams to be most instructive. Critics of so-called congressional "obstruction" used the fourth Vietnam as their didactic instrument, while both sides of the controversy pointed toward the domestic, or fifth, Vietnam to illustrate their respective positions. Those opposed to America's Nicaraguan policy prognosticated a Vietnam-era upheaval should the administration "escalate" the conflict. On the other side, LIW advocates, drawing upon the same apprehension of a possible new domestic Vietnam, assured policymakers that low-intensity conflict would elicit the necessary public support.

Whichever Vietnam was selected, the relevant historical content was invariably presented and examined in a superficial and uncritical manner. Complex events in history were misread or oversimplified. Circumstances peculiar to Vietnam were ignored, while deep and critical analysis of events was rarely exhibited. On one side, those in the administration who considered the counterinsurgency of the first Vietnam as a model for a successful Nicaraguan policy did not examine very carefully the efficacy of the earlier counterinsurgency. John F. Kennedy's strategy of combining military tactics with political and economic measures failed to win the "hearts and minds" of the Vietnamese. Unable to thwart the Communist guerrillas with his own special forces, Kennedy sent yet more advisers to protect the "credibility" of the U.S. mission. Ultimately those advisers were joined by regular combat forces. The political warfare of the third Vietnam, while more successful than the classic counterinsurgency of the Kennedy period, was seriously hampered by the lack of legitimacy of the South Vietnamese regime. Examined closely, these strategies were not useful historical models for America's Central American policy.

On the other side, critics of Nicaraguan policy also misread the earlier experience. They emphasized the disastrous outcome of the third Vietnam, but failed to ask pertinent questions about these critical years: Was American air power used effectively? Could an unrestricted bombing campaign have forced the Communists to negotiate on our terms? Could Westmoreland's war of attrition have been won if American combat forces were allowed to attack the enemy sanctuaries in Cambodia, Laos, and across the 17th parallel? The definitive answers to these inquiries may never be known, but such questions should have been considered by those who attempted to graft the Vietnam experience upon the Nicaraguan reality.

The principal errors of historical reasoning during the Nicaraguan de-bate consisted of faulty parallels and misplaced analogies. American policymak-ers and journalists, concurring with historian E.H. Carr that "today's citizen has that pronounced need for and is peculiarly susceptible to analogies," applied a variety of analogies to the Nicaraguan situation. Alleged similarities ranged from the "freedom fighters" of eighteenth-century revolutionary America to the "sur-rogate rebels" in Cuba at the time of the Bay of Pigs. Vietnam provided by far the largest reservoir for analogy-makers.

Most of these Vietnam analogies were characterized by faulty historical reasoning. Vietnam and Nicaragua did, in fact, share some similarities, but they were different in many substantial respects. These differences were such that a third Vietnam in Central America would be a most unlikely outcome of Ameri-can intervention. The domestic Vietnam predicted by administration critics would likewise be unlikely. The war in Vietnam coincided with generational and racial crises in American society. Such crises were not significant in America of the 1980s.

The sophisticated and cautious drawing of parallels or analogies might have provided a helpful perspective on the Nicaraguan problem. However, most of those who used analogies ignored a central fact. The Vietnam experience was a unique one; it consisted of a particular set of events at a particular time, neither of which could be exactly repeated. There were no timeless and universal "lessons" to be drawn from the American experience in Vietnam. The slogan "No more Vietnams," used so polemically by both sides during the Nicaraguan debate, was confusing and misleading. One is reminded of Mark Twain's story of the cat who sat on a hot stove, and thereafter presumed that stoves were at all times and places hot.

Hegel notwithstanding, we can, in fact, learn from history. From the Viet-nam experience, it is possible to recognize and thereby learn the paramount importance of knowledge. The United States should never conduct foreign un-dertakings without some knowledge of the area's history and the culture of the people. The "gang that brought us Vietnam" was, for the most part, ignorant of the Vietnamese people and their history. Unaware of the centuries-old antago-nisms between Vietnam and China, for example, American officials contended that the North Vietnamese were puppets of the Communist Chinese. Likewise, knowledge of the relevant history of Nicaragua, especially the history of Ameri-can intervention in the area, remains indispensable for intelligent public dis-course and wise government policy.

NOTES

1. *ABC World New Tonight,* March 3, 1981.
2. *Boston Globe,* August 10, 1989, p. 16.
3. Daniel Yankelovich and Larry Doagen, "Assertive America," *Foreign Affairs* (New York: Council of Foreign Relations, 1981), p. 696.

4. Council for Inter-American Security, *The Committee of Santa Fe: A New Inter-American Policy for the Eighties* (Santa Fe, N. Mex.: Council for Inter-American Security, 1980), p. 2.

5. *New York Times*, March 18, 1985, p. 8.

6. Quoted in Roy Gutman, *Banana Diplomacy* (New York: Simon & Schuster, 1988), p. 93.

7. Alexander M. Haig, Jr., *Caveat: Realism, Reagan and Foreign Policy* (New York: Macmillan, 1984), p. 125.

8. Ibid., p. 127.

9. Harry G. Summers, Jr., *On Strategy* (New York: Dell, 1982), p. 21.

10. John D. Waghelstein, "Post-Vietnam Counterinsurgency Doctrine," *Military Review* (May 1985), p. 47.

11. Ibid., p. 48.

12. For the best discussion of low-intensity warfare as applied to Cenral America see the entire April/May 1984 issue of *The NACLA Report on the Americas*.

13. Robert McFarlane, quoted in Mark Hertsgaard, *On Bended Knee: The Press and the Reagan Presidency* (New York: Farrar, Straus & Giroux, 1988), p. 185.

14. *New York Times*, August 7, 1985, p. 12.

15. *New York Times*, April 8, 1965, p. 16.

16. *New York Times*, April 25, 1983, p. 6.

17. Quoted in Marvin E. Gettleman (ed.), *El Salvador: Central America in the Cold War* (New York: Grove Press, 1981), p. 297.

18. Quoted in Allan Nairn, "Endgame," *NACLA*, (May/June 1984), p. 44.

19. Quoted in Jiri Valenta and Esperanza Duran, *Conflict in Nicaragua: A Multidimensional Approach* (New York: Allen and Unwin, 1987), p. 275.

20. Quoted in Valenta and Duran, p. 274.

21. *New York Times*, August 23, 1983, p. 22.

22. Theodore Sorensen, "America's Choices in Nicaragua," *New York Times*, April 21, 1985, p. E21.

23. *New York Times*, February 19, 1982, p. 30.

24. *New York Times*, April 28, 1985, p. E22.

25. *New York Times*, August 15, 1986, p. A27.

26. Quoted in *Chronicle of Higher Education*, April 13, 1981, p. 5.

27. *New York Times*, March 29, 1986, p. 12.

28. *Congressional Record*, August 11, 1986, p. S11228.

29. *Guardian* (July 23, 1986), p. 6.

CHRONOLOGY OF U.S. INVOLVEMENT IN VIETNAM: 1942–1975

1942
U.S. pilots attached to the Flying Tigers fly combat missions in Vietnam against Japanese military installations.

1943–1945
The OSS funds Vietminh actions against the Japanese in Vietnam, and OSS operatives work with the Vietnamese to rescue downed U.S. flyers and go on espionage and sabotage missions with them.

September 1945
America supports the French efforts to reimpose colonialism in Vietnam.

May 8, 1950
The United States signs an agreement with France to provide the French Associated States of Vietnam with military assistance.

August 3, 1950
A U.S. Military Assistance Advisory Group (MAAG) of 35 men arrives in Vietnam to teach troops receiving U.S. weapons how to use them.

September 7, 1951
The Truman administration signs an agreement with Saigon to provide direct military aid to South Vietnam.

September 30, 1953
President Eisenhower approves $785 million for military aid for South Vietnam.

April 7, 1954
At a news conference, President Eisenhower, stressing the importance of defending Dien Bien Phu, enunciates the domino theory.

July 21, 1954
The American observer at Geneva, General Walter Bedell Smith, issues a unilateral declaration stating that the United States will refrain from the threat or the use of force to prevent implementation of the Geneva accords.

September 8, 1954
The Manila Treaty is concluded creating SEATO. A separate protocol extends the SEATO umbrella to include Laos, Cambodia, and "the free territory under the jurisdiction of the State of Vietnam" (South Vietnam).

October 24, 1954
President Eisenhower sends a letter to the new leader in southern Vietnam, Ngo Dinh Diem, pledging U.S. support and agreeing to send $100 million to build up Diem's military forces. Eisenhower begins the U.S. commitment to maintaining a non-Communist government in South Vietnam.

April 28, 1955
Under severe pressure from a coalition of political enemies, Diem's fledgling regime almost falls. He is saved by the actions of Air Force Colonel Edwin Landsdale, who is also a CIA operative.

October 26, 1955
Diem, after defeating Bao Dai in a rigged election, declares himself to be president of the Republic of South Vietnam. His government is instantly recognized by the United States.

July 20, 1956
The deadline for holding reunification elections in accordance with the Geneva accords passes. America supports Diem's refusal to hold elections.

May 8, 1957
Diem makes a triumphant visit to the United States. Eisenhower praises him lavishly and reaffirms American support for his government.

October 1957
Small-scale civil war begins in South Vietnam between Diem's forces and cadres of Vietminh, who have remained in South Vietnam after the partition at Geneva.

April 4, 1959
Eisenhower delivers a speech in which he links American vital national interests to the survival of a non-Communist state in South Vietnam.

December 20, 1960
The National Liberation Front (NLF) is formed. It is the Vietminh reborn. The Communist-controlled NLF takes charge of the growing insurgency against the Diem regime. Diem dubs the NLF the "Vietcong," meaning Vietnamese who are Communists.

January 6, 1961
Soviet Premier Nikita Khrushchev announces support for all "wars of national liberation" around the world. His speech influences the incoming Kennedy administration's decision to support counterinsurgency in Vietnam.

April 1961
The Kennedy administration confronts a crisis in Laos. Kennedy considers military intervention, then decides to seek a political solution.

May 1961
Kennedy approves sending Special Forces troops to South Vietnam. He also authorizes clandestine warfare against North Vietnam and a secret war in Laos.

June 1961
Kennedy and Khrushchev, meeting in Vienna, agree to support a neutral and independent Laos. Kennedy rejects neutrality for Vietnam.

November 1961
Special Forces troops are deployed to the central highlands in the vicinity of Pleiku to work with Montagnards, and they begin developing the Civilian Irregular Defense Groups (CIDG). See Glossary.

December 1961
The *New York Times* reports that some of the 3,200 U.S. advisers are operating in battle areas and are authorized to fire back if fired on.

January 1962
The Air Force launches Operation RANCH HAND, the aerial spraying of defoliating herbicides to deny cover to the Vietcong and to destroy their crops.

February 8, 1962
MACV is established in Saigon; its first commander is General Paul D. Harkins.
December 1962
There are now about 9,000 U.S. advisory and support personnel in South Vietnam; 109 Americans are killed or wounded in 1962.
January 2, 1963
At Ap Bac in the Mekong delta, the ARVN 7th Division, equipped with American weapons and accompanied by U.S. advisers, cannot defeat a lightly armed Vietcong battalion of 300 soldiers. The battle demonstrates that South Vietnamese government troops cannot match the tactics or the fighting spirit of the insurgents.
May 8, 1963
In Hue, 20,000 Buddhists celebrating the birthday of Gautama Siddhartha Buddha are fired on by government forces. This action begins a series of events that will bring down the Diem regime.
June 11, 1963
Thich Quang Duc, an elderly Buddhist monk, immolates himself at a busy Saigon intersection to protest Diem's suppression of the Buddhists.
August 21, 1963
Military forces loyal to Diem and to his brother, Nhu, attack Buddhist temples. President Kennedy denounces these actions. Meanwhile, a coup to overthrow Diem is being planned by dissident ARVN generals.
September 2, 1963
President Kennedy strongly reaffirms the American commitment to Vietnam. He also criticizes Diem's attacks on the Buddhists and calls for reform.
November 1, 1963
A coup, led by General Tran Van Don and General Duong Van Minh, with the foreknowledge and encouragement of American officials, overthrows the Diem regime. A military directorate, led by General Minh, succeeds Diem.
November 24, 1963
President Lyndon Johnson affirms American support of the new South Vietnamese government.
December 31, 1963
There are about 16,500 American soldiers in South Vietnam at year's end. Four hundred eighty-nine were killed or wounded during 1963.
January 2, 1964
President Johnson approves covert military operations against North Vietnam to be carried out by South Vietnamese and Asian mercenaries. Called OPLAN 34A, these operations include espionage, sabotage, psychological warfare, and intelligence gathering.
January 30, 1964
Minh's government is overthrown in a bloodless coup by General Nguyen Khanh.
March 8–12, 1964
Secretary of Defense Robert McNamara visits South Vietnam. He affirms that America will remain in South Vietnam for as long as it takes to win the war.
April 1964
North Vietnam decides to infiltrate units of the NVA into South Vietnam.
June 20, 1964
General Harkins is succeeded by General William C. Westmoreland as COMUSMACV. Three days later, Henry Cabot Lodge resigns as the U.S. ambassador to the GVN, and is replaced by General Maxwell Taylor.
July 1964
Both sides are engaged in covert warfare in violation of the 1954 Geneva accords. North Vietnam is using the Ho Chi Minh trail to infiltrate NVA troops south and to supply the Vietcong. America implements the OPLAN 34A operations. One OPLAN 34A operation uses U.S. destroyers to conduct surveillance missions off the North Vietnamese coast. These operations are called DESOTO Missions.

August 2, 1964

North Vietnamese patrol boats attack the U.S.S. *Maddox*, which was on a DESOTO Mission in waters near the North Vietnamese coast.

August 3, 1964

South Vietnamese PT boats carry out OPLAN 34A raids, attacking North Vietnamese radar installations in the same area.

August 4–5, 1964

Both U.S.S. *Maddox* and another destroyer, U.S.S. *Turner Joy*, which has joined the *Maddox*, report that they are under attack at sea. Carrier-based U.S. naval aircraft fly reprisal raids, ordered by President Johnson, against North Vietnamese targets.

August 7, 1964

At Johnson's request, Congress approves the Gulf of Tonkin resolution granting the president the power to "to take all necessary measures to repel any armed attack against the forces of the United States and to prevent further aggression . . . including the use of armed force. . . ." Johnson will later use this resolution as a postdated declaration of war.

October 1964

General Khanh resigns and is replaced by a civilian, Tran Van Huong.

December 31, 1964

About 23,000 Americans are now serving in South Vietnam. There is now a full-scale undeclared war raging in South Vietnam, and there is also fighting in Laos and Cambodia. There were 1,278 U.S. casualties during the year.

January 4, 1965

In his State of the Union address, President Johnson reaffirms the American commitment to South Vietnam. He states that American security is tied to peace in Southeast Asia.

January 27–28, 1965

Tran Van Huong is ousted and General Khanh returns to power.

February 7, 1965

The Vietcong attack a U.S. helicopter base and other installations near Pleiku in the Central Highlands. Eight Americans are killed and 126 wounded. President Johnson orders retaliatory air strikes on targets in North Vietnam.

February 13, 1965

Johnson orders a sustained bombing campaign against North Vietnam that has been long-planned by his advisers. Called Operation Rolling Thunder, it will continue, with occasional pauses, until October 31, 1968. The American air war against North Vietnam begins on March 2.

February 25, 1965

General Khanh is forced out by Air Marshal Nguyen Cao Ky.

March 8, 1965

The first U.S. combat troops arrive in Vietnam.

April 6, 1965

President Johnson authorizes U.S. forces to take the offensive in order to support ARVN forces.

June 19, 1965

Air Marshal Ky becomes premier of the eighth South Vietnamese government since Diem was overthrown.

June 28–30, 1965

U.S. forces undertake the first major American offensive against the Vietcong in War Zone D, 20 miles northeast of Saigon.

July 21–28, 1965

President Johnson makes a series of decisions that amount to committing the United States to a major war in Vietnam. Among the decisions he makes: draft calls will be raised to 35,000 per month, 50,000 additional troops will be sent to Vietnam with additional increases as the situation demands, and the air war against North Vietnam is expanded. Johnson also makes it clear that he wants these decisions implemented in low-key fashion so as not to excite or alarm either the Congress or the American people. These decisions began the seven-and-a-half-year U.S. war in Indochina.

August 7, 1965
The Chinese government warns the United States that it will send troops to fight in Vietnam if necessary.

October 23–November 20, 1965
In the largest battle of the war to date, the U.S. 1st Air Cavalry defeats NVA forces in the Ia Drang Valley, in a remote corner of Pleiku province.

December 31, 1965
This was a pivotal year of the war. America began a sustained air war against North Vietnam. It also committed large numbers of forces to ground combat operations in South Vietnam. At year's end, there are 184,000 U.S. troops in South Vietnam. U.S. casualties for the year: 1,369 KIA and 5,300 WIA. The year 1965 is Year One of the American war in Vietnam.

March 9, 1966
The U.S. Department of State issues a White Paper claiming that American intervention in Vietnam is legal under international law, the UN Charter, and the U.S. Constitution.

June 29, 1966
U.S. aircraft strike North Vietnamese petroleum storage facilities near Haiphong and Hanoi.

October 15–November 26, 1966
U.S. forces are involved in one of the biggest operations of the war in Tay Ninh province near the Cambodian border, 50 miles northwest of Saigon.

December 31, 1966
The Vietnam war has become the dominant event in world affairs. During the year the United States increased its forces in Vietnam from 184,000 to 385,000. The air war against North Vietnam has been expanded significantly; 5,008 Americans were killed and 30,093 wounded during the year.

January 8–26, 1967
American forces are involved in the largest offensive of the war. About 16,000 American troops participate in Operation Cedar Falls to disrupt Vietcong operations in the Iron Triangle region northeast of Saigon.

February 22–April 1, 1967
The largest Allied offensive of the war to date takes place, Operation Junction City, involving 34 U.S. battalions. Its goal is to smash the VC stronghold in War Zone C near the Cambodian border and ease pressure on Saigon.

March 10–11, 1967
U.S. aircraft bomb the Thainguyen steel works near Hanoi; they are the first bombing raids on a major industrial target.

May 14–16, 1967
A U.S. newspaper reports that Chinese Premier Chou En-lai threatened to send Chinese troops into North Vietnam if the United States invaded that country.

May 19–24, 1967
McNamara sends a memo to President Johnson arguing against widening the war and proposes curtailing the air war against North Vietnam. Responding to McNamara's dovish memo, the Joint Chiefs call for expanding the air war against North Vietnam and for sending 200,000 additional troops to South Vietnam.

July 7–12, 1967
A compromise is worked out between Johnson's dovish and hawkish advisers. McNamara recommends a troop increase of 55,000. The president accepts it.

July 30, 1967
A Gallup poll shows that 52 percent of Americans disapprove of Johnson's Vietnam War policy; 56 percent believe that America is in a stalemate.

October 16–21, 1967
Antiwar activists hold antidraft demonstrations throughout the United States. The largest occurs at the Army Induction Center in Oakland, California.

October 21–23, 1967
Fifty thousand people demonstrate against the Vietnam War in Washington, D.C.

October 25–30, 1967
The air war against North Vietnam intensifies. Sustained attacks are carried out on targets near Hanoi and Haiphong.

November 2, 1967
President Johnson meets privately with a group of distinguished elder statesmen. Dubbed the "Wise Men," they generally support his war policy.

November 3–22, 1967
One of the bloodiest and fiercest battles of the war between American and North Vietnamese troops occurs at Dak To in the Central Highlands.

November 22, 1967
President Johnson brings General Westmoreland home to rally support for the war. Westmoreland tells his audiences that the United States is winning the war.

November 30, 1967
Senator Eugene J. McCarthy announces that he will challenge President Johnson for the Democratic presidential nomination in 1968. He will run on a platform calling for a negotiated settlement of the Vietnam war.

December 31, 1967
At year's end, there are about 500,000 U.S. troops in Vietnam. For the year, the war cost taxpayers about $21 billion. Casualties: 9,353 KIA and 99,742 WIA.

January 20–April 14, 1968
One of the most famous battles of the war takes place at Khe Sanh, an American Marine base located just south of the DMZ. NVA forces besiege Khe Sanh. It is feared that Khe Sanh will become an American Dien Bien Phu. But U.S. airpower eventually breaks the siege, and the Communists are forced to withdraw.

January 30–February 10, 1968
On the first day of the Tet truce, Vietcong forces, supported by NVA troopers, launch the largest offensive of the war. Simultaneous attacks are mounted in South Vietnam's largest cities and many provincial capitals. The offensive is crushed by American and GVN forces. Tet is a decisive military victory for the Allies, but turns out to be a psychological and political disaster.

February 28, 1968
General Earle Wheeler, Chairman of the Joint Chiefs, tells President Johnson that General Westmoreland needs an additional 206,000 troops. A crucial point in the war has been reached. If Johnson does not send the troops, he will be conceding that the United States cannot win a military victory. But if he sends the troops, it will require a reserve call-up, and significantly raise the costs and casualties of war. Johnson delays a decision and asks Secretary of Defense Clark Clifford to conduct a thorough reappraisal of U.S. Vietnam policy.

March 12, 1968
Senator Eugene McCarthy, in the New Hampshire primary, makes a strong showing in a hawkish state. Four days later, Senator Robert Kennedy announces that he too will seek the Democratic nomination and run on an antiwar platform.

March 16, 1968
In what will become the most notorious atrocity committed by American soldiers during the Vietnam War, two platoons of American GIs slaughter hundreds of unarmed villagers in the hamlet of My Lai-4.

March 25–26, 1968
Johnson reconvenes the "Wise Men." Most advise against any more troop increases and recommend that the United States seek a negotiated peace in Vietnam.

March 31, 1968
Johnson announces a unilateral halt to all U.S. bombing north of the 20th parallel and that he will seek to get negotiations started with North Vietnam. He also stuns the nation with an announcement that he will not seek reelection.

April 22, 1968
Clark Clifford announces that the GVN is going to take responsibility for more and more of the

fighting. This is the first announcement of a policy that under President Nixon will come to be called "Vietnamization."

May 3, 1968
America and North Vietnam agree to begin formal negotiations in Paris on May 10.

June 10, 1968
General Creighton W. Abrams succeeds General Westmoreland as COMUSMACV.

August 5-8, 1968
The Republican National Convention, meeting in Miami, nominates Richard M. Nixon for president. The Republican platform calls for an honorable negotiated peace in Vietnam and for the progressive "de-Americanization" of the war.

August 26-29, 1968
The Democratic National Convention meets in Chicago. Democrats adopt a platform endorsing the administration's war policy and nominate Vice-President Hubert H. Humphrey for president. On the evening of August 28, there is a full-scale riot in the streets between Chicago police and antiwar radicals.

October 31, 1968
In a televised address to the nation, President Johnson announces a complete bombing halt over North Vietnam.

November 5, 1968
Richard Nixon is elected president of the United States.

December 31, 1968
The major turning point of America's involvement in the Vietnam war occurred in 1968. After Tet, Lyndon Johnson had to abandon his policy of measured escalation in search of military victory and replace it with an early version of Vietnamization, looking to a negotiated settlement. Richard Nixon was elected president, and the general sense at the time was that he had a plan for bringing the war to an early end. The year 1968 is the largest and costliest of the American war—14,314 KIA and 150,000 WIA. Cost is about $30 billion.

January 25, 1969
The first plenary session of the four-member Paris peace talks takes place among the Americans, the North Vietnamese, the South Vietnamese, and the National Liberation Front.

March 18, 1969
President Nixon orders the secret bombing of Communist base camps and supply depots in Cambodia.

May 10-20, 1969
The battle for Hamburger Hill takes place near the A Shau valley. In ten days of intense fighting and heavy casualties, Allied forces take the hill. The hill is abandoned soon thereafter.

June 8, 1969
President Nixon announces that 25,000 U.S. troops will be withdrawn by the end of August and that they will be replaced by South Vietnamese forces. The gradual phase-out of the American war in Vietnam has begun.

June 10, 1969
The NLF announces the formation of a Provisional Revolutionary Government (PRG) to rule in South Vietnam. It amounts to a formal challenge to the Thieu regime for political control of South Vietnam.

August 4, 1969
Secret negotiations began in Paris between U.S. special envoy Henry Kissinger and North Vietnam's Xuan Thuy.

August 17-26, 1969
During a major battle between U.S. and NVA forces in the Queson valley about 30 miles south of Danang, the first combat refusal by U.S. troops takes place.

September 23, 1969
Eight antiwar leaders go on trial in Chicago for their part in organizing the antiwar demonstrations in Chicago at the time of the Democratic National Convention in August 1968.

October 15, 1969
The largest antiwar demonstrations in American history take place at many sites across the country.

November 3, 1969
President Nixon makes his most successful speech in defense of his Vietnam war policies. Congress and public opinion overwhelmingly support Vietnamization as he successfully blunts the efforts of the antiwar movement.

November 15, 1969
More than 250,000 people come to Washington, D.C., to protest the Vietnam war. It is the largest single antiwar demonstration to date.

December 31, 1969
At year's end, there are 479,000 U.S. troops in Vietnam. GVN forces have increased and now number over 900,000. Fighting continued during the year on a large-scale. American KIAs totaled 9,414 for the year. The U.S. forces are beginning to show signs of declining morale, discipline, and fighting spirit.

February 19–20, 1970
All defendants in the Chicago trial are convicted of conspiracy to incite rioting and receive maximum sentences of five years in prison and $5,000 fines. All will be acquitted on appeal.

March 18, 1970
In a bloodless coup in Cambodia, pro-Western General Lon Nol ousts Prince Norodom Sihanouk as head of state.

April 11, 1970
Polls show that only 48 percent of Americans support Vietnamization, down from 70 percent in November 1969.

April 20, 1970
President Nixon promises to withdraw 150,000 more U.S. troops over the next year if Vietnamization continues to make progress.

May 1, 1970
American forces totaling about 30,000 invade the Fishhook region of Cambodia. The Cambodian incursion is the last major offensive of the Indochina war involving U.S. ground combat forces.

May 4, 1970
Ohio National Guardsmen fire into a group of student demonstrators on the campus of Kent State University, killing 4 and wounding 11.

May 6, 1970
More than a hundred colleges and universities across the nation shut down because of student protests and rioting in response to the Cambodian invasion and the killings at Kent State.

May 8–20, 1970
In New York City, construction workers attack antiwar demonstrators on Wall Street. An estimated 80,000 young people, mostly college students, demonstrate peacefully in the nation's capital. They protest the "Kent State Massacre" and call for the immediate withdrawal of all U.S. troops from Indochina. In New York City, more than 100,000 workers march in support of Nixon's war policies.

June 24, 1970
The Senate, by a vote of 81–10, repeals the Gulf of Tonkin resolution. President Nixon states that the legal basis for the American war in Vietnam is not the Gulf of Tonkin resolution, but the constitutional authority of the president as commander-in-chief to protect the lives of U.S. military forces in Vietnam.

August 19, 1970
America signs a pact with Cambodia to provide Lon Nol's government with military aid.

November 9, 1970
The Supreme Court refuses to hear a case brought by the state of Massachusetts challenging the constitutionality of the Vietnam war.

November 11, 1970
On this day, for the first time in more than five years, no American soldier is killed in Vietnam.

December 31, 1970
The U.S. war in Vietnam is winding down. At year's end there are about 335,000 U.S. troops in South Vietnam. U.S. KIAs for the year number 4,221. But the war has spread to Cambodia and no progress is reported at the Paris peace talks.

January 1, 1971
Congress forbids the use of U.S. ground troops in either Laos or Cambodia.

March 6–24, 1971
ARVN forces invade Laos to interdict enemy supply routes down the Ho Chi Minh trail. Communist counterattacks drive the invaders out of Laos and inflict heavy casualties. It is a major defeat for the GVN.

April 19–23, 1971
Vietnam Veterans Against the War stage a demonstration in Washington, D.C. It ends with veterans throwing combat ribbons and medals at the Capitol steps.

April 20, 1971
The Pentagon reports that fragging incidents are increasing. There were 96 incidents in 1969 and 209 in 1970.

June 13, 1971
The *New York Times* begins publication of the leaked portions of the 47-volume Pentagon analysis of the U.S. involvement in Vietnam through 1967. These are the so-called *Pentagon Papers*.

July 1, 1971
The 26th Amendment to the Constitution, granting the vote to 18- to 21-year-olds, is ratified.

July 15, 1971
In a surprise announcement, President Nixon tells the American people that he will be visiting China before May 1972.

December 31, 1971
The American role in Vietnam is ending; 156,800 U.S. troops remain in the country. There were 1,380 KIAs during 1971. As the Americans withdraw, the Communists intensify their attacks in Laos, Cambodia, and parts of South Vietnam. U.S. morale continues to deteriorate. Vietnamization is not working and the Paris peace talks remained stalled.

February 21–27, 1972
President Nixon makes his historic visit to China. The North Vietnamese fear that China and the United States will make a deal behind their backs, Taiwan for peace in Vietnam.

March 30–April 8, 1972
A major NVA offensive begins as Communist forces attack South Vietnamese towns and bases just south of the DMZ. The Communists open a second front with a drive into Binh Long province about 70 miles north of Saigon. Communist forces open a third front with drives into the Central Highlands. The fighting in South Vietnam between GVN and Communist forces is the most intense of the entire war.

April 10, 1972
America responds with air attacks. B-52s strike targets in North Vietnam for the first time since November 1967. B-52s and tactical bombers also strike targets in South Vietnam. America is waging an air war over all of Vietnam.

May 8, 1972
Nixon announces that he has ordered the mining of all North Vietnamese ports.

May 20, 1972
The summit conference between President Nixon and Leonid Brezhnev takes place on schedule in Moscow. Both sides are unwilling to risk détente over the Vietnam War. Nixon's Soviet visit is the first ever by a U.S. president.

June 28, 1972
President Nixon announces that no more draftees will be sent to Vietnam unless they volunteer.

August 11, 1972
The last U.S. combat unit is withdrawn from South Vietnam. There are now 44,000 American servicemen in South Vietnam.

August 16, 1972
U.S. aircraft fly a record 370 sorties against North Vietnam. Most American aircraft fly from carriers in the Gulf of Tonkin or from bases in Thailand.

September 15, 1972
ARVN forces recapture Quang Tri City. The fighting destroys most of the city, which formerly had a population of 300,000. Most of these people now reside in squalid refugee camps.

October 8–11, 1972
Lengthy secret meetings in Paris between Henry Kissinger and Le Duc Tho produce a tentative settlement of the war. The substance of the agreement is a cease-fire, to be followed by both sides working out a political settlement.

October 22, 1972
President Thieu rejects the proposed settlement.

November 7, 1972
Richard Nixon is reelected president in a landslide victory. He promises that he will achieve "peace with honor" in Vietnam.

November 11, 1972
The U.S. Army turns over its giant headquarters base at Long Binh to the South Vietnamese, symbolizing the end of the direct American participation in the war after more than seven years.

December 14, 1972
The U.S. breaks off peace talks with the North Vietnamese, which have been going on since Nixon's reelection.

December 18–31, 1972
President Nixon announces the resumption of the bombing and mining of North Vietnam. The most concentrated air offensive of the war begins, mostly aimed at targets in the vicinity of Hanoi and Haiphong.

December 28, 1972
Hanoi announces that it is willing to resume negotiations if the United States will stop bombing above the 20th Parallel. The bombing ends on December 31.

December 31, 1972
At year's end there are about 24,000 U.S. troops remaining in South Vietnam. For the year, 312 Americans were killed in action.

January 8–18, 1973
Henry Kissinger and Le Duc Tho resume negotiations in Paris, and they reach an agreement that is similar to the one that had been rejected by General Thieu.

January 19–26, 1973
There is heavy fighting in South Vietnam between GVN and Communist forces as both sides try to gain as much territory as they can before the cease-fire.

January 23, 1973
Nixon announces that the Paris accords will go into effect at 7:00 P.M. EST, January 27, 1973. He says that "peace with honor" has been achieved.

January 27, 1973
The draft ends. For the first time since 1949, America has no conscription.

February 12–27, 1973
American POWs begin to come home.

February 21, 1973
A cease-fire formally ends the 20-year war in Laos.

March 29, 1973
The last U.S. troops leave South Vietnam. Only a DAO (Defense Attache Office) contingent and Marine embassy guards remain. About 8,500 U.S. civilian officials stay on.

June 4–August 15, 1973
The Senate blocks all funds for any U.S. military activities in Indochina. The House concurs. The Nixon administration works out a compromise agreement with the Congress to permit continued U.S. bombing in Cambodia until August 15. The cessation marks the end of 12 years of American military action in Indochina.

November 7, 1973

Congress enacts the War Powers Act over President Nixon's veto. It requires the president to report to Congress within 48 hours after committing American forces to combat on foreign soil. It also limits to 60 days the time that the president can commit soldiers to foreign combat without congressional approval.

December 31, 1973

The war in Vietnam continues without U.S. involvement. Most of the provisions of the Paris agreements are not observed by either side. During the year, 13,788 RVNAF and 45,057 Communist troops were killed.

August 5, 1974

Congress makes sharp cuts in the amount of military aid going to the South Vietnamese government.

December 31, 1974

During 1974, 80,000 people, both civilians and soldiers, were killed in Vietnam. This is the highest total for any year of the wars that began in 1945.

January 6, 1975

NVA forces overrun Phuoc Long province. When the Americans do not react, Hanoi concludes that America will not reintroduce its military forces to save the GVN.

January 28, 1975

President Gerald Ford requests an additional $722 million in military aid for South Vietnam. Congress refuses his request.

March 1975

NVA forces launch an offensive in the Central Highlands. In a desperate effort to save the southern half of his country, General Thieu orders his forces to abandon their Highlands positions.

March 24, 1975

Hanoi launches its Ho Chi Minh Campaign to "liberate" South Vietnam before the rains begin.

April 8–21, 1975

The last major battle of the Vietnam war is fought at Xuan Loc, about 30 miles from Saigon. After hard fighting, the Communists win.

April 16, 1975

The Cambodian government surrenders to the Khmer Rouge, who promptly occupy the capital city of Phnom Penh.

April 23, 1975

President Ford pronounces the Vietnam war "finished as far as America is concerned."

April 29–30, 1975

The last Americans and eligible South Vietnamese are evacuated from Saigon.

April 30, 1975

The Communists conquer Saigon. The Vietnam war ends in victory for the VC/NVA forces. The long American effort to create a non-Communist state in southern Vietnam fails.

Major Sources for the Chronology

BOWMAN, JOHN (general ed.), *The World Almanac of the Vietnam War* (New York: Bison Books, 1985).

DAVIDSON, PHILLIP B., *Vietnam at War: The History 1946–1975* (Novato, Calif.: Presidio, 1988).

GRAVEL, MIKE (ed.), *The Pentagon Papers: The Defense Department History of U.S. Decision Making in Vietnam*, 4 vols. (Boston: Beacon Press, 1971).

SUMMERS, HARRY G., JR., *The Vietnam War Almanac* (New York: Facts on File, 1985).

GLOSSARY

AK-47: A Russian and Chinese assault rifle used extensively by the Vietcong and by PAVN forces.

Annam: Central section of Vietnam, a French protectorate from 1883 to 1954.

APC: Armored Personnel Carrier.

ARVN: Army of the Republic of Vietnam. The regular South Vietnamese national forces.

A Teams: Twelve-man Special Forces units.

Attrition warfare: A strategy with the objective of destroying enemy personnel and materiel faster than they can be replenished until the enemy's ability to wage war is exhausted.

Binh Xuyen: A criminal army led by Bay Vien, a.k.a., Le Van Vien, who controlled portions of Saigon in 1954/1955.

Can Lao: The Can Lao Nhan Vi Cach Mang Dang, or Personalist Labor Revolutionary Party. Ngo Dinh Nhu's secret political party and police force.

Cao Dai: A religious sect formed in 1925 in southern Vietnam.

Charlie: GI slang for the Vietcong, a short version of Victor Charlie, from the U.S. military phonetic alphabet for VC.

Chinook: CH-47 transport helicopter.

CIA: Central Intelligence Agency.

CIDG: Civilian Irregular Defense Groups, teams devised by CIA operatives that combined defense functions with social and economic development programs designed to win the allegiance of the Montagnards.

CINCPAC: Commander-in-Chief, United States Pacific Command.

Cobra: Bell AH-1G fast-attack helicopter, armed with machine guns, grenade launchers, and rockets.

Cochin China: The southern section of Vietnam, a French colony from 1863 to 1954.

COMUSMACV: Commander, United States Military Assistance Command, Vietnam.

CONUS: Military acronym for the Continental United States.

CORDS: Civil Operations and Revolutionary Development Support.

Corps: Two divisions assigned to defend a military region.

COSVN: Central Office, South Vietnam, the headquarters controlling all Vietcong political and military operations in southern Vietnam.

Counterinsurgency: The guiding doctrine of U.S. military forces in Vietnam during the early 1960s; its fundamental purpose was to win the allegiance of the people, not to destroy the enemy's armed forces. Inspiration for the phrase "winning hearts and minds."

CTZ: Corps Tactical Zone.

DAO: Defense Attache Office, an agency that was part of the U.S. mission sent to South Vietnam following the January 1973 accords that ended the American war. It was a replacement for MACV; DAO administered the U.S. military assistance program to the GVN, 1973–1975.

DEROS: Date eligible for return from overseas. The date a soldier's tour of duty in Vietnam ended, usually one year after arriving in the country.

Dien Bien Phu: Site in northwestern Vietnam next to the Laotian border where the French suffered a major defeat that led to the end of their presence in Vietnam.

DMZ: Demilitarized Zone.

DOD: Department of Defense.

DRV: Democratic Republic of Vietnam (North Vietnam), created by Ho Chi Minh Sept. 2, 1945.

EAGLE PULL: Code-name of the U.S. evacuation of Phnom Penh in April 1975.

FAC: Forward Air Controller; a forward spotter who coordinated air strikes, usually airborne.

FMFPAC: Fleet Marine Force, Pacific Command.

Fragging: The murder of a commissioned or noncommissioned officer by an enlisted man of lower rank, usually with a fragmentation grenade.

Free-fire zones: Territory considered completely under enemy control. South Vietnamese officials authorized the use of unlimited firepower in such zones.

FREQUENT WIND: Code-name of the U.S. evacuation of Saigon in April 1975.

FSB: Fire support base, a protected forward artillery base.

Green Berets: Famed nickname of soldiers serving in the U.S. Army Special Forces trained for counterinsurgency operations. The name derived from the green berets worn by these elite troops.

Grunt: The most frequent nickname given Army and Marine ground combat forces.

GVN: The Government of Vietnam (South Vietnam).

Hoa Hao: A religious sect formed in 1939 in southern Vietnam by Huynh Phu So.

Huey: Nickname given the UH-1 series helicopter.

ICC: International Control Commission, created by the Geneva accords (1954) to supervise implementation of the agreements.

ICCS: International Commission of Control and Supervision; agency responsible for administering the January 1973 Paris agreement.

JCS: Joint Chiefs of Staff.

JGS: Joint General Staff, the South Vietnamese equivalent of the U.S. Joint Chiefs.

JMC: Joint Military Commission, consisting of members from North Vietnam, South Vietnam, the PRG, and the United States, responsible for implementing the military provisions of the Paris agreements.

JMT: Joint Military Team, consisting of members from North Vietnam, South Vietnam, the PRG, and the United States, responsible for accounting for all prisoners of war and MIAs.

Kampuchea: The name given Cambodia in 1975 by the victorious Khmer Rouge.

Khmer Rouge: Members of the Pracheachon, a left-wing revolutionary movement that came to power in Cambodia in April 1975.

KIA: Killed in action.

Lao Dong: The Vietnamese Worker's Party, the North Vietnamese Communist party founded in 1951. The ruling party of North Vietnam until 1975; thereafter it ruled the entire country.

LINEBACKER I: Code-name for U.S. bombing of North Vietnam resumed in April 1972 in response to the Nguyen Hue offensive.

LINEBACKER II: Code-name for the U.S. bombing of North Vietnam during December 1972, the Christmas Bombing.

LST: Landing Ship Tank; a large, shallow-draft cargo-hauling and landing craft.

LZ: Landing Zone, for helicopters.

MAAG: Military Assistance Advisory Group, the forerunner of MACV, 1955 to 1964.

MACV: Military Assistance Command, Vietnam, formed in 1962, lasted until 1973.

Main Force: Regular army forces of the North Vietnamese and Vietcong.

Medevac: Helicopters with the mission of transporting wounded soldiers quickly from the battlefield to forward hospitals.

MENU: Code-name for the secret B-52 bombing missions in Cambodia.

MIA: Missing in Action.

Montagnards (mountain dwellers): Indigenous tribal populations of Vietnam who generally inhabitant hilly and mountainous terrain.

MR: Military Region, formerly a CTZ, Corps Tactical Zone.

Napalm: A jellied incendiary weapon used by the French and the Americans during the Indochina wars. It could be dropped from aircraft in cannisters or fired from flamethrowers. Used as both a defoliant and antipersonnel weapon.

NCO: Noncommissioned Officer.

NLF: The National Liberation Front, formed December 20, 1960.

NSAM: National Security Action Memorandum.

NSC: National Security Council.

NVA: North Vietnamese Army.

NVN: North Vietnam or North Vietnamese.

OB: Order of Battle, a comprehensive arrangement and disposition of military units deployed in battle.

OCS: Officers' Candidate School.

Operation VULTURE: A planned U.S. operation to relieve the siege at Dien Bien Phu in April 1954. It was never implemented.

OPLAN: Operations Plan.

OSS: Office of Strategic Services; a World War II intelligence organization, forerunner of the CIA.

PACAF: United States Pacific Air Force.

PACFLT: United States Pacific Fleet.

Pacification: South Vietnamese and U.S. programs designed to win the allegiance of the South Vietnamese people and to eliminate Vietcong influence.

Pathet Lao: Laotian Communist insurgents who came to power in 1974/1975.

PAVN: People's Army of Vietnam; the North Vietnamese army.

Pentagon Papers: Secret Department of Defense studies of U.S. involvement in Vietnam, 1945–1967. The papers were stolen by Daniel Ellsberg and Anthony Russo in 1971 and given to the *New York Times*, which published them that same year.

PF: Popular Forces.

PHOENIX: A joint U.S./South Vietnamese program to detect and to neutralize the Vietcong infrastructure.

PLA: People's Liberation Army of South Vietnam, the military arm of the Vietcong.

PLAF: People's Liberation Armed Forces of South Vietnam; a.k.a., the PLA.

Politburo: The executive committee of the Lao Dong; members were responsible for making all government policies.

POW: Prisoner of war.

PRG: Provisional Revolutionary Government, formed by the NLF in 1969.

PRP: People's Revolutionary Party; the Communist party apparatus that controlled the National Liberation Front, founded in 1962.

PTSD: Post-Traumatic Stress Disorder.

RD: Revolutionary Development Cadres, teams of South Vietnamese pacification workers trained to carry out various missions.

RF: Regional Forces.

ROTC: Reserve Officer Training Corps.

RVN: Republic of Vietnam (South Vietnam).

RVNAF: Republic of Vietnam Armed Forces; all South Vietnamese military forces including ARVN, Regional Forces, and Popular Forces.

SA-2: Medium-range Communist surface-to-air missile, effective up to 60,000 feet, speed about Mach 2.5.

SAC: Strategic Air Command.

SAM: Surface-to-air missile.

SANE: Committee for a Sane Nuclear Policy, an organization opposed to the nuclear arms race, active in the late 1950s and early 1960s.

SDS: Students for a Democratic Society, the largest radical student organization in the country during the 1960s; led antiwar activities on many college campuses.

SEATO: Southeast Asia Treaty Organization.

17th parallel: Temporary dividing line separating northern and southern Vietnam, created by Geneva accords (1954), pending unification elections scheduled for July 1956, which were never held.

Sortie: An operational flight by one aircraft.

Special Forces: U.S. Army personnel trained to carry out counterinsurgency operations, often covert and unconventional. They also trained Montagnards and South Vietnamese Special Forces.

Strategic Hamlets: A South Vietnamese program begun in 1962 that concentrated rural populations into fortified villages to gain their allegiance and to both separate and protect them from Vietcong guerrillas.

SVN: South Vietnam.

Tet: The Vietnamese lunar New Year and their most important holiday.

Third Countries: U.S. Allies that furnished military forces for the Vietnam War: South Korea, Thailand, the Philippines, Australia, and New Zealand.

Tonkin: The northern section of Vietnam, a French protectorate from 1883 to 1954.

USAID: United States Agency for International Development.

VC: Vietcong, a derogatory contraction meaning a Vietnamese who is a Communist.

VCI: Vietcong infrastructure; the political leaders of the Vietcong, also responsible for logistic support of the military forces.

Vietminh: A coalition political party formed by Ho Chi Minh in 1941 and dominated by Vietnamese Communist leaders; it came to power in Hanoi September 2, 1945.

Vietnamization: The word was coined by Secretary of Defense Melvin Laird to describe Nixon's policy, inherited from Lyndon Johnson, of withdrawing U.S. forces from Vietnam and transferring their responsibilities to the RVN forces.

VNAF: Vietnamese Air Force (the South Vietnamese Air Force).

WIA: Wounded in action.

FURTHER READINGS

There is a vast and growing literature on the American Indochina intervention that culminated in the U.S. Vietnam War. America in Vietnam has quickly become a major field of study within recent U.S. diplomatic and military history. Many former civilian and military officials, journalists, and scholars have made, and continue to make, major contributions to our understanding of the greatest foreign-policy disaster in American history. The following selections constitute a sampling of the best and most accessible books that you may wish to consult for further reading. A short list of film and television treatments of the war is also appended.

The best bibliographic reference through 1983 is Milton Leitenberg and Richard Dean Burns, *The Vietnam Conflict* (Santa Barbara, Calif.: ABC-Clio Press, 1983).

For accounts of the French Indochina war that served as prelude for the American debacle and of the early phases of the U.S. involvement in Vietnam, see the writings of Bernard Fall, a prolific bilingual French scholar-journalist. See especially his *Vietnam Witness, 1953–1966* (New York: Praeger, 1966).

A unique and indispensable primary source for understanding the making of American Vietnam policy from the Truman administration through 1967 is the *Pentagon Papers,* a vast compilation of official documents put together by Defense Department analysts at the request of Secretary of State Robert S. McNamara. There are three editions of the *Pentagon Papers:* a 12-volume official U.S. government edition; a five-volume edition edited by Senator Mike Gravel, and a one-volume condensed version edited by Neil Sheehan and others, which reproduces the documents and analysis originally published by the *New York Times* in 1971. Students will find the one-volume *Times* edition the most accessible and easiest to use version of the *Pentagon Papers*.

Several studies of the Vietnam war have been based on the documents found in the *Pentagon Papers*. The two best include Leslie Gelb and Richard K. Betts, *The Irony of Vietnam: The System Worked* (Washington, D.C.: Brookings Institution, 1977), and Herbert Y. Schandler, *Lyndon Johnson and Vietnam: The Unmaking of a President* (Princeton, N.J.: Princeton University Press, 1977).

The best general historical accounts of the long American involvement in Indochina include George Donelson Moss, *Vietnam: An American Ordeal* (Englewood Cliffs, N.J.: Prentice Hall, 1990); Stanley Karnow, *Vietnam: A History* (New York: Viking, 1983); and George C. Herring, *America's Longest War: The United States and Vietnam 1950–1975*, 2nd ed. (New York: Knopf, 1986). Moss's account is the most recent study. It combines diplomatic, military, and political history to provide the fullest account of how and why the United States got involved for so long in the affairs of Indochina, and why America fought, and lost, a major war in Vietnam.

The best military history has been written by Phillip B. Davidson, *Vietnam At War: The History 1946–1975* (Novato, Calif.: Presidio, 1988). A critical study of the U.S. air war is James Clay Thompson, *Rolling Thunder: Understanding Policy and Program Failure* (Chapel Hill: University of North Carolina Press, 1980). Harry G. Summers, Jr., *On Strategy: A Critical Analysis of the Vietnam War* (New York: Dell, 1982) is a critique of U.S. strategy in Vietnam. James William Gibson, *The Perfect War* (New York: Vintage Books, 1986) argues that the American defeat in Vietnam flowed from an American conception of war, which he calls "technowar."

Three fine studies of America's Vietnam intervention are Frances Fitzgerald, *Fire in the Lake: The Vietnamese and the Americans in Vietnam* (New York: Random House, 1972); George McT. Kahin, *Intervention: How America Became Involved in Vietnam* (New York: Knopf, 1986); and Loren Baritz, *Backfire: A History of How American Culture Led Us Into Vietnam and Made Us Fight the Way We Did* (New York: Ballantine, 1985).

An important study of the Vietnamese revolution is William J. Duiker, *The Communist Road to Power* (Boulder, Col.: Westview Press, 1981). Douglas Pike, *Vietcong: The Organization and Technique of the National Liberation Front of South Vietnam* (Cambridge, Mass.: MIT Press, 1966) is an informed account of the National Liberation Front. Douglas S. Blaufarb, *The Counterinsurgency Era* (New York: The Free Press, 1977) is the best general account of American and South Vietnamese pacification efforts.

The *Pentagon Papers* tell the story of the American involvement in Vietnam up to 1968. For the Nixon years, 1969–1974, in addition to the general accounts mentioned above, readers should consult Henry Kissinger, *The White House Years* (Boston: Little, Brown, 1979). Kissinger's book is a lengthy, tendentious, well-informed, and entirely readable diplomatic history. Two other good books about the latter phases of American involvement include Frank Snepp, *A Decent Interval* (New York: Random House, 1977) and Arnold Isaacs, *Neither Peace Nor Honor* (Baltimore: Johns Hopkins University Press, 1984).

The best account of the antiwar movement is Charles DeBenedetti, *An American Ordeal: The Antiwar Movement of the Vietnam Era* (Syracuse, N.Y.: Syracuse University Press, 1980). A recent study that makes a good case for Vietnam dissent influencing the war policies of the Johnson and Nixon administrations is Mel Small, *Johnson, Nixon, and the Doves* (New Brunswick, N.J.: Rutgers University Press, 1988). Lawrence M. Baskir and William A. Strauss, *Chance and Circumstance: The Draft, the War, and the Vietnam Generation* (New York: Vintage Books, 1978), is a uniquely valuable study of the conflict between the Vietnam-era draft and the generation of young men who had to make choices: choices to accept, evade, or resist the draft.

The best Vietnam war biography is Neil Sheehan, *A Bright Shining Lie: John Paul Vann and America in Vietnam* (New York: Random House, 1989). A sensitive study of Vietnam veterans and their problems is Robert J. Lifton, *Home from the War: Vietnam Veterans: Neither Victims Nor Executioners* (New York: Simon & Schuster, 1973).

The histories of African Americans and American women in Vietnam have yet to be written. The best available works are collections of oral histories. See Wallace Terry (ed.), *Bloods: An Oral History of the Vietnam War By Black Veterans* (New York: Ballantine, 1985) and Kathryn Marshall (ed.), *In the Combat Zone* (New York: Penguin, 1987). Marshall's anthology is a collection of vivid personal accounts of women who served in the Vietnam war.

For studies of the media coverage of Vietnam, history's first televised war, see Peter Braestrup, *Big Story*, 2 vols. (Boulder, Col.: Westview Press, 1977) and Daniel C. Hallin, *The Uncensored War: The Media and Vietnam* (New York: Oxford University Press, 1986). Hallin persuasively exposes the notion that television coverage of the war contributed to the American defeat in Vietnam for the myth that it is.

A rich literary harvest of novels and novelistic memoirs has come out of the American Vietnam experience. One of the finest novels is Tim O'Brien, *Going After Cacciato* (New York: Dell, 1978). O'Brien has also written a powerful memoir, *If I Die in a Combat Zone* (New York: Dell, 1973). The finest journalistic account of American men at war in Vietnam is Michael Herr, *Dispatches* (New York: Avon, 1977). John Hellmann, *American Myth and the Legacy of Vietnam* (New York: Columbia University Press, 1986) is an original study of Vietnam war literature and films.

Because the Vietnam war turned out so badly for us and for the people that we tried to help, there has been a proliferation of studies concerned with the lessons and legacies of America's Indochina intervention. Two good collections of essays on the lessons and legacies of the war are Anthony Lake (ed.), *The Legacy of Vietnam* (New York: Council on Foreign Relations, 1976) and Harrison Salisbury (ed.), *Vietnam Reconsidered: Lessons from a War* (New York: Harper & Row, 1983).

Also available are various cinematic and television treatments of the war. The finest American documentary film remains Peter Davis's controversial and biased *Hearts and Minds.* The best of many fiction films about the war is the flawed *Apocalypse Now.* The finest television documentary of the Vietnam war is *Vietnam: A Television History,* a 13-part series first aired on PBS in 1983/1984. It tries hard to make an even-handed presentation.